What people said about the previc

Sharpe as a Blade is a rare book that p(...itle grabs. You must take a look or miss a tt ...ack cover you're hooked. It is a warts and ...an individual growing up in mean streets that weep poverty, lack of local necessities, an urban tale of decay, of how a young lad surmounts it by his allegiance to 'the game'. Anyone resident in our good old island knows to what that simple phrase 'the game' refers – FOOTBALL. Yes! Come on!

Ronnie, with his mates, is part of a growing legion of fans who travel countrywide by coach, rail or by simply using 'the rule of thumb' in order to be there, cheer their team; urban gangs who came of age wearing the scarf, who touted banners proclaiming their everlasting pride (win or lose) in the players. Atmosphere swells, created throughout the period of drugs, sex and rock 'n' roll. He's talking 60s and 70s, years in which the music of the times drives its solid beat as a foot will (hopefully!) slam a ball into the net. This is a must read. Learn and digest. The magic of the game and of the time, as written here and will appeal to all.

Derek M. Fox, Author, Screenwriter, Lecturer.

Ronnie Sharpe, lifelong Sheffield United fan, Dronfield scrapman and semi-retired football hooligan has just written the X-rated first volume of his life story, *Sharpe as a Blade*.   Nick Hornby has nothing on him; Ronnie's book is footballs answer to the Fred Pass phenomenon with added sex and violence.

Once a Shoreham Bootboy, his book has a photograph of his police charge sheet after being caught with a knuckleduster at United's away game at Chelsea in 1967- he's not lost his love for the Blades but he has of the game. On match days he visits the United pubs with his mates, sinks a pint and often something stronger, then follows the score on teletext. "The games lost all the buzz. It's all about money isn't it? Modern day football as passed me by," mourns Ronnie. He writes, "We chat about the old days when we stood under rusty corrugated tin sheds or on open rain-swept, crumbling terraces. When the grounds had some style, some soul, some history and some individuality. Every ground was different and had its own unique feel, smell and atmosphere unlike the safe, sanitised, Americanised stadia of today."

Born in 1951 and brought up in a back to back terrace on Cammell's Row, Dronfield, Ronnie charts every rough and tumble and fumble. He loses his cherry after being third in line to an energetic girl in a barn and has a bizarre three in a bed experience with a female circus lion tamer in Blackpool.

His previous writing experience was penning his name on charge sheets. Ronnie was never shy of putting the boot in and had his collar felt several times, but he has a tale to tell and he tells it very well.

Martin Dawes, The Sheffield Star.

Sharpe As A Blade is a brilliant book that paints some wonderful images. I found it really fascinating and humorous, some of the stories made me laugh out loud. I urge people who grew up in that era and those too young to remember, who want to get an insight into what it was like back in the 1960s to buy the book.

Gareth Evans, Radio Sheffield.

"This book is a load of fucking crap."
Diana Pigg, chairperson of the Sheffield Wednesday gay and lesbian Supporters Association (Dronfield branch)

Sharpe as a Blade

To John

All the Best

Ronnie Sharpe

V·T·B

Publisher's Note

Don't read this book if you are of a nervous disposition or if your middle-class sensibilities are easily offended. Don't read this book if you'd rather stay in your cosy little curtain-twitching, suburban bubble where everyone is nice and respectable and you'd rather not be made to think about the real state of the nation. Don't read this book if you'd rather pretend that inequality and poverty of background and education has no effect on criminality, or if you believe there is no such thing as society, or if you believe you have no responsibility for the determinants of crime, or that criminality and poverty are biological traits.

I have published *Sharpe as a Blade* because it will entertain and amuse, but also because it is gives insights into life in the 50s, 60s and 70s that you won't find in the media at the time. It tells of the rise of youth and gang culture from the inside, not through a middle-class lens. It helps explain football violence, why it happened and how society failed to understand it and was incapable of dealing with it − why Thatcher and the likes of Eric Morecambe's calls to price the hooligans out of the game was a form of class war.

Please note: none of the language has been sanitised − the text contains words that are offensive and discriminatory, words which were more current during the period described, but unacceptable nonetheless. I took the decision that censorship would diminish the reader's understanding of how these things arise and of how much progress has been made over the last fifty years or so.

Sharpe as a Blade

Ronnie Sharpe

1889 books

Sharpe as a Blade

Copyright © Ronnie Sharpe 2021

The moral rights of the author have been asserted.

Cover © 1889books

www.1889books

ISBN: 978-1-9163622-6-0

Born in Dronfield in 1951, Ronnie Sharpe was educated at Dronfield infants, Dronfield County Primary and Gladys Buxton Secondary Modern schools.

He then went to Cambridge... but Sheffield United were relegated there that day and he was arrested for throwing lumps of concrete at Harry Haslam and Danny Bergara.

Bibberdy-bobberdy-boo.

This is for my friends and family.

This is Shoreham Street and I'm never gonna leave it
And I'm always gonna stay here, if I live to be ninety-nine
Cos all the people I meet, seem to come from that street
And I can't get away, because it calling me
Come on home, (hear it calling me) come on home.

PART ONE
The 50s and 60s

Foreword

The fortnightly Saturday scenario once again unfolds. I stand on the platform of Dronfield train station alongside Dicky, Bruiser, Sheep and Ryan O'Brian the Lion of Zion. We kick our heels hanging around for the one o' clock train into Sheffield, destination Bramall Lane.

My mind drifts back some forty-odd years to when, as a ten-year old lad I stood in the same spot waiting for the old steam locomotive to ferry us into town. The train fare, way back then – one shilling return, the same price as the admission into the football ground. How times have changed.

Ten minutes later, after dodging the ticket inspector like a bunch of school kids we land at Sheffield Midland station. Depending on the calibre of the opposition, various numbers of the South Yorkshire constabulary clad in fluorescent banana jackets stand inside and outside the station making their presence known.

We head for the Penny Black pub in Pond St. Already inside are Stocksy and his son China, China's mates Biff, Andy and Davy, Clink, Gav, and maybe a couple of others make up the motley crew. Stocksy eyes up friends and strangers alike with distaste.

I've known Bob since the early 70s, an old Darnall soul boy, the classic football hoodlum, skinhead haircut, goatee beard, loud, nasty, evil and brash. Back then as of now, always neatly dressed, always on the front line and always full of bottle. His front would often drop us in it, but he would never leave anyone in the shit if it came on top. Stocksy has always found it impossible to swerve trouble.

After a pint or two we move off to the Howard Hotel. The Howard, an old black and white gabled watering hole stands opposite the train station and is the designated pub for away fans. It's usually scarfers and normals, but sometimes there might be a few lads inside.

It's time to put on a show: have a bit of fun, show a bit of front. A squad of police encircle the front entrance, so the ten/twelve of us, all virtually sober and drug-free sneak in through the back door. Stocksy and Dicky are pushing fifty, Clink and me have seen the Big Five-O, come and go; we really should know better. Well, it's only a laugh, int it?

Derby County are the visitors today and there's about a hundred or so Derby fans inside. Stocksy, as ever, is wearing some form of Blades regalia, be it hat, shirt, badge – he likes the opposition to know who he is.

Derby songs fill the air, we're the only one's not singing and it's not long before we're sussed. Someone notices the printed Blades badge on Stocksy's T-shirt. Heads turn, nod to each other and glance in our direction. Young *Stone Island*-clad Derby lads push their way to the front.

1

"Run from the Wednesday, United run from the Wednesday," is directed straight at us.

China, small, stocky, built like a pit-bull gives the Derby lads a wry smile.

"Run from the Wednesday, eh? Well were not fucking running from you, are we?" This has a marked effect on the Derby boys, a two-yard gap appears in front of us.

I remove my blue, tinted glasses in anticipation; everything is blurred, so I put them back on again. What the hell am I doing? Both my knees are on the way out, Stocksy's got platinum rods holding his back together and Clink's so crippled with vibration white finger, he can barely lift his pint... at least that's what he told the compensation panel. What the fuck are we doing? A few braver Derby lads push their way to the front. We look them straight in the eyes.

"Come on then, who's fucking first?" Before they can respond the coppers are in and we're ushered out of the front door. Stocksy protests to one of the coppers.

"We come in here every home game for a quiet drink and never cause any trouble; it's them Derby cunts."

"Yeah, yeah," the constable says, "but you know you shouldn't be in here and you don't want to get nicked, do you? C'mon, on your way."

Outside we laugh at our audacity; I really must stop doing this shit. It's nearly come on top a few times.

When Portsmouth's 6.57 crew were in the pub they thought we were spotters for the BBC[1], but after a few minutes uneasiness we ended up having a chat and a drink with them.

Another time, thirty or so Stoke boys were stopped from getting out by the police after being invited by Stocksy to "Come for a walk."

Swansea's boys did attack, well one did, but after booting Clink on the shin, he disappeared into the crowd before the coppers came in and chucked us out.

Fifty yards up the road we notice police riot vans outside The Globe pub. We know there's more Derby fans inside and think about pulling the same stunt; fuck it, we wouldn't even get through the door, so we head off to The Lord Nelson. Fanny's, as the Nelson is known, is a Blade stronghold and stands on a back street just off Arundel gate about a five-minute walk from the ground.

I greet some of the old Heeley Green mob, Herman, Jimmy Milligan and Mick Scanlan. Friendships built and cemented on the concrete steps of The Shoreham forty years ago can never be broken. Even though the Heeley lads have long since retired from the hustle-bustle, hurly-burly, fun and games, shenanigans, whatever you want to call the times everybody loved; we're all still Bladesmen through and through. With a gleam in our eyes we sit and chat about the olden days like seasoned war veterans. Herman has two or three of his grandchildren running under his feet.

"These are only half of the little fuckers," he tells me. Another swift drink and it's off to the Cricks.

2.30 p.m. the Cricketers Arms on Bramall Lane is packed solid. We force

---

[1] Blades Business Crew – the Sheffield United Hooligan firm

our way through the mass to try to get served. Iron bar Jack as always props up the counter in the opposite tap room. Jack earned his nickname many, many moons ago for smashing a Wednesdayite to within an inch of his life with... well, we don't really want to go into that now do we?

I shout out my usual greeting: "What's score today Jack?"

"3-1 to Blades, Ron. Doc Pace hat-trick, two wi' his hand and one wi' his nose."

At either side of him stand, Shred sporting a Frank Gallagher wig and Derek Goodison. Neither has missed a Blades game home or away since 1889.

The juvenile section of the Blades Business Crew saunter into the pub. These young bucks stroll up to the far end of the boozer and gaze through the window onto Bramall Lane. They scan the road looking for signs of any opposition boys who might be entering the away end turnstiles. Not that anything is likely to happen. Police surround the Cricks, perched on their high horses, squashed inside riot vans: dressed, and with a licence to kill. They twirl extendable steel batons like drum majorettes, waiting and hoping something will kickoff. Police dog handlers with snarling shit-machines straining on the end of their leashes show no discrimination. Young children walking to the match holding their dad's hand, as well as likely looking lads are treated to a flash of German shepherd teeth.

Innocent or not, fans in designer gear that leave, or even pass, the boozer have video cameras pushed in their faces. Like the Met at the miner's strike, officers on foot stand in groups, laughing and chatting, counting their overtime pay in their heads. They're the boys these days. Back in the 70s at least the coppers earned their wages. Jason King look-alikes sporting Mexican moustachios, pork chop chads[2] and hair hanging well below their helmets were given the run around by thousands of marauding yobs, up and down the country week in week out.

As kickoff approaches the Cricks' crowd thins out a little, making visible small groups of the older, logo-ed up BBC lads, chatting and checking out each other's clobber. Some of these lads are in their late thirties early forties. No longer active, their photos sit in police files. Put one foot wrong, step out of line once and they're fucked. They know the scene is all but dead. The South Yorkshire Police, and the powers that be, took it upon themselves to rid the streets of Sheffield from the menace of the notorious Blades Business Crew. By the use of civil banning orders, they took out the Field Marshals, Generals, Captains, Sergeants, foot-soldiers and even a few of the catering corps. The police really deserve a pat on the back for finally getting the situation under control. It's only taken them forty years.

"You going in today Ron?" somebody shouts.

"Like fuck," I shout back. "Not unless I get a freebie." Some of lads I'm sat with wouldn't go in if they were paid. The hundred-mile-an-hour, win-at-all-costs, modern-day game played with a beach ball has passed me by. I never, ever thought I'd lose the buzz of attending the games. It must be like losing your sex-

---

[2] sideburns

drive: no one thinks it's ever going to happen though. Just substitute Viagra for cocaine. The buzz of having the crack with the lads, both pre-and post-match remains as strong as ever.

Ten past three, and about half a dozen of us take up the back seats under the clock. A few more absentees join us. Stocksy insults each one in turn. They've heard it all before and take no notice as we settle down for the afternoon session.

Pints of dry apples (cider) are ordered, someone rolls a spliff, lads wander in and out. More elderly boys walk over and shake hands. A gathering of crazy Granddads with fading tattoos, thinning hair and missing teeth, trying to relive their youth; holed up in the last chance saloon for one final throw of the dice. 40 years ago, we looked like rock stars, today we look like a mob of Winston Churchill's.

Clink's a true Blades character, the life and soul, larger even, a Grant Mitchell look-alike, bulky, broad shouldered, tanned shaven head and trademark leather jacket glued to his back. He's been out since opening time knocking back buckets of tarmac (Guinness) and dry apples. Hyper now, after necking a mixture of narcotics, he trawls the pub chatting in his unique back-to-front lingo to anybody willing or unwilling to listen.

"Just got back from Reef as in Tenna, brought back ten thousand duties, as in free, not going through the stiles, as in turn are we lads? Oi, Rifles (as he calls me), Lee Van Cleef, (Dicky) come and have a chat to these crew as in business lads."

Strangers are baffled, even lads who know him are baffled.

"Put Sharpy's CD on," Stocksy screams at one of the bar staff. "And turn the fucker up."

A barmaid, fearing Stocksy's wrath, scuttles over in a flash and slips the disc into the player. The CDs of old Blades songs I'd put together a couple of years back hangs around my neck like a millstone – still if they make folk happy and make me a few bob, who cares eh! The CDs play non-stop for the next two or three hours.

"You're gonna get your fuckin' heads kicked in," blasts out from the sound system and transports us back in time, "Shoreham boys we are here oh-oh, Shoreham's here, Shoreham's there, Shoreham's every fucking where."

Clink grabs the whole boozer's attention by climbing onto a table and squatting down. He shits on the bastards below as he flies over Hillsborough with the wings of a sparrow and the arse of a dirty black crow. The zac as in pro must be kicking in.

The scores from the game filter in. We're the Ceefax Blades. We cheer United goals, and goals that go against are greeted with: "They're shit anyway."

At half time a few more lads come in from the game, they don't go back; it's a better atmosphere inside the Cricks.

At the end of the game the serious marijuana smokers arrive. Ibbo, Wasp, Little Chippie, Big Cog, Mark, Joby, Neil, and me old mate from the 60s: Wafer.

Wafe's not been to the game. He swears blind he'll never set foot inside the Lane again until standing is brought back, and the floodlight pylons are re-built.

Not much chance of that, pal. A constant stream of joints are built and passed round.

The old daddies of the gang: Dreads (now minus his locks) and three fingers Raymondo arrive; these two fucker's have laid me low in a cloudy mist many times. Little Irish, the in-house comedian, mingles amongst the crowd cracking everybody up. Abby, Rammy, Nobby and Mo, breeze in. No, it's not the four stooges, it's the Wybourn Muslims, always whizzing along nicely. They pass the bag of base around, pinkies are licked and dipped into the cellophane.

"Cheers lads, nice one."

Even after a defeat, by six o'clock the place is buzzing.

I try to abstain from the barrage of joints heading in my direction; I'm heading down the path to whitey-land and need to slam the breaks on.

"No, no, I'm all right for a bit, honest."

"Come on fuckinell, what's up with ya? Don't start getting paranoid."

I drop half of the E, bought earlier. For the price of a pint it gives me a psychological boost even before it starts working.

"Come and have a line of class A, mate, this'll sort you out," one of the lad's whispers in my ear. "Keep it to yourself though, I can't give every fucker one."

The legend, Reginald Basking Shark, A.K.A. Bent-Nose Mitchell, along with his sons and two brothers enter the arena. Picture if you dare that famous 70s Bradford pugilist and punch bag, Richard Dunn, add a dash of Jack Palance, a drizzle of Michael York, a sprinkling of Eric Pollard, and you've got Reg.

Smoke twenty-seven joints; take nine trips and a kilo of mescaline to enter the strange world that only exists inside Reg's head. I exchange insults with Tony, his older brother. Tone's the same age as me. We call each other, old, ugly, wrinkly cunts and then have a kiss and a cuddle to show there's no hard feelings.

We chat about the old days, when we stood under rusty corrugated tin sheds or open rain-swept crumbling terracing. When the grounds had some style, some soul, some history and some individuality. Unlike the safe, sanitised, Americanised, shite stadia of today, with row upon row of plastic seats in the club's colours.

The only way to tell one from another is by the team's name or initials spelt out in white lettering. The new purpose-built stadiums are even worse, often stuck in the middle of nowhere surrounded by nothing, devoid of any beauty or atmosphere. The promised land of the Premiership, they can stick it. Stavros Kowaslanovicoski wearing number 37 means fuck all to me. Swedish, Portuguese, Italian and French managers have, or should have no place in the English game. Entrepreneurs and billionaires interested, only in money and winning, now run the game that once belonged to the working classes, because no fucker else wanted it. Greedy, cheating, diving players seem almost saint-like compared to the parasite agents that represent them. Fuck 'em all.

Stocksy reckons anyone who's not singing is an away fan or an undercover copper.

"Whose them cunts?" he shouts, jumping to his feet and pointing to a group of lads stood at the bar. "I've not seen them before, let's have 'em."

"It's okay, Bob," somebody, says. "I know them."

"Who the fuck are you?" Bob replies. "You'll get a slap an' all if you don't fuck off."

The ganja posse move off to the Earl of Arundel, another marijuana-friendly dump a few hundred yards up the road, leaving one or two tangled up casualties in their wake.

Clink never relents for a second, he's up and down the pub singing, laughing, dancing and now offering to take on all-comers in arm wrestling contests.

By seven o'clock things are starting to calm down a bit, so it's either a trip to the Sportsman or to the pubs on London road. We decide on the Sportsman and walk the 50 yards or so along a cobbled back street, where back in the good old days we fought running battles with the police and away mobs.

The Sportsman is still pretty full. More old boys shake hands and say hello. We find seats and Stocksy goes into his familiar routine, yelling out to no one in particular, but to anyone in earshot.

"Oi, ya fucking bastards, this boozer used to be two rooms not one. Sharpy and the other long haired cunts in one room listening to shite rock music and us soul-boys in the other, we were the fucking boys."

"Yeah, Bob," I answer. "You used to be into that fat bastard, Barry White back in the 70s dint ya?"

"Better than them dirty bastards you were into," he shouts back.

Stocksy and the Manor Park boys are ready for the off. Clinks going back to Darnall (or Bosnia as he calls it). Bruiser – big, quiet, ex Para – has hardly spoke a word all day. He sits, watches, listens and observes. Bruiser phones a cab and ten minutes later we're on our way back to Dronny.

The taxi ride home is a blur. By 8.30 we're in our local, The Dog. I take the other half of the E. The 60s-70s disco in full swing is made all the more pleasurable by the amount of drugs I've taken. I know all the songs, all the words, and can't help doing a little shuffle and jig as I make my 50th visit to the bogs. I catch a glimpse of my missus, out with her mates.

"Hope you've been behaving your self today, Ronald?" she shouts. "Course I have, duck. You know me."

I dance back from the toilet and someone shouts: "Fuckin hell, Sharpy aren't you ever gonna grow up?"

"What for, I'm having a fucking good time. Do ya fancy a game of dominoes? Anyway, shut the fuck up and listen to this record, it's the best song I've ever heard in my life." Somebody else asks Dicky, now manic and as drunk as a monkey, if he's been to the game.

"I've been in the vicinity," he replies.

So what's it gonna be then, eh? I ask myself. Saturday morning car wash? Spot of shopping with the missus at Meadowhall in the afternoon? (oh, how she'd love that). Do a bit of unpaid charity work? Water the geraniums? Settle down to watch those lovable cheeky, young plastic Geordie rogues, Ant and Dec, the Terry Wogan twins. Maybe have half an hour with one of the multi-talented Osbourne family and their whooping, planted audience… and then: Who Wants to be a fucking Millionaire?

Hard choice… one more season, just one more, swear to god, our kid, swear to god, and then I really must stop doing this shit.

Dronny lads on Dronfield station in the 1920s en-route to Birmingham to sort out the Peaky Blinders.

Chapter 1

Highway 61 revisited

Dronfield, a town of some twenty-odd thousand lost souls and more than twenty licensed premises, lies in a valley on the banks of the stream Drone on the North-East Derbyshire/ South Yorkshire border. The steel city of Sheffield stands six miles to the north, the historic market town of Chesterfield, famous for its crooked spire, Teddy Boys in the 60s, flower-power in the 70s and tank top jumpers in the 80s, is the same distance to the south.

In the year 1883 the Wilson Cammell steel works, world famous for the manufacture of high quality Bessemer steel railway lines, upped sticks and moved its entire workforce of six hundred men and their families to the town of Workington in Cumbria. Dronfield went from boom town to ghost town as shops and businesses associated with the company went bust. The Silkstone Colliery, which provided coal for the steel plant was one of the biggest casualties. Some three hundred terraced houses, specially built for the steelworkers were left empty. Many remained unoccupied for years after. Some were even used to house livestock (pigs, goats and chickens) and some were sold for the handsome sum of £7 per property.

Buckingham Terrace, known locally as Cammell's Row, was once owned by the company. It consisted of forty-four, back-to-back, one-up, one-down, crumbling, bed bug and rat-infested dwellings. It was sited on land adjacent to the A61 Sheffield to Chesterfield trunk road.

"excellent dwellings...constructed for the labouring classes." House and Shop on Cammell's Row.

From The Times August 23rd, 1920:

As the clock struck midnight on the 19th day of August, in the front bedroom of number 37 Buckingham Terrace Dronfield, Sara Ann Pendleton slit her husband James's throat. After writing a suicide note Sara Pendleton turned the razor on herself.

When James Pendleton failed to turn up for work at the Grasscroft colliery after two days, his employer, Mr R Jackson, caused an enquiry to be made, and it was this that bought the tragedy to light. The house was locked from the inside, and as no reply could be got the police were sent for. Admittance was gained through the cellar by acting

Police Sergeant Albert Buttle and Dr H.B. Fletcher was immediately sent for.

The man was undressed and in bed, and his wife, fully clothed was lying across his body. Both had terrible wounds to their throats, which must have proved fatal in a few moments. A razor, covered in blood, was found lying open on the bed where it had apparently fallen from the woman's hand as she collapsed on her husband's body.

Dr Fletcher told the inquest, there was a lot of blood on the pillow and bedclothes. The woman's body was lying partly on the man. They were both dead. The wound in the man's neck was six inches long and deep. The woman was not undressed, she had a very deep wound right across her throat, and from the large clots of blood on the floor it looked as if she had been standing up and then fallen on the bed afterwards.

The suicide note read; 'He tried to kill me at 11a.m, so I killed him at 12 tonight. I have been my own detective. She need not come under my front window any more asking for money, where I have seen her many times. Tell my sister Anna, hell is too good for her and hers. Goodbye all enemies.'

A verdict was returned that the woman murdered her husband and then committed felo de se.

That same year, my Grandfather William Sharpe, his wife Alice and their five children lived with relatives in a small cottage in Chesterfield Road, Dronfield.

37 Buckingham Terrace, due to the stigma of the murder stood empty for many months, no one would move in, but the overcrowded conditions at Chesterfield Road, forced my Granddad to rent 'The Death House,' as number 37 was now known.

DRONFIELD PETTY SESSIONS.

DRUNK AND REFUSING TO QUIT.—William Sharpe, collier, Dronfield Woodhouse, for the above offence at the Blue Stoops, was fined 10s. and costs, and for assaulting Police-constable Clifford at the time 25s. and costs, or in default seven days in each case.

Granddad Bill, the newspaper cutting is from 1892. My Mum used to tell me 'He were a bugger thi Granddad, Ron. He once got arrested for knocking a Bobbies helmet off.' I thought she was joking.

I was born there on the 12th of April 1951, the youngest of five children. My sister, Anne, died aged eight months, two years before I was born. I lived with my mother, Annie, her brother, Uncle Chris, my grandma, Alice, my two brothers Terry (21 years my senior), Tony (14 years my senior) and my sister Joan who was exactly 12 years to the day older than me.

Cammell's Row back yard in 1951 with me, aged a few months in my sister Joan's arms. You can just make out the steel works in the background with overhead crane and piles of bombs underneath.

Mum was unmarried and suffered the eternal shame of having five illegitimate kids with different fathers, a truly terrible sin back in the dark days of the 1930s and even up to the 1950s when I was born. I was the last straw. Our Terry, who headed the family, had had enough of Mum's wicked ways and we were shipped out to a home for unmarried mothers in Bakewell, Derbyshire, where I was put up for adoption.

All was going to plan, the paperwork signed and a very posh couple (Mam told me years later) came to collect me. My mother changed her mind at the last minute and took me back home to face the consequences. It was agreed Mum would go out to work and Gran would look after me. I found out fifty years later that I was six months old before our Terry even looked at me.

The Row (or Cammell's Hump as it was sometimes known) was split into four yards. A dividing wall separated each one, access being gained from the front by the use of a gennel. The back-yard view just past the outside closets looked out over the Sheffield to London Midland railway line. I grew up to the sound of trains. Freight and goods trains carrying hundreds of tons of iron and steel rumbled and rattled past on their journeys to unknown destinations. Coal trains, passenger trains and trains carrying livestock steamed and whistled only a few yards from my back door step.

I also grew up to stories of Sara Pendleton's ghost, who my brother, Tony, had seen many times floating around the double bed I shared with him, my Uncle Chris and ten thousand bed bugs. Our Terry slept in a single bed in the same front bedroom. At the age of about four I'd been moved from the back bedroom I shared with Gran, Mum and my sister. Gran said I'd started 'Noticing things.'

"She was there again last night Ron," Tony would tell me. "Stood at the bottom of the bed – Mrs Pendleton – you could see straight through her, did ya see her? She had a razor in her hand with all this blood dripping off it."

"Mam, Mam, he's doing it again, our Tony, he's scaring me, tell him Mam, tell him."

"Ya big bleeding bully, ya nowt else, leave him alone ya rotten bleeder," Mam would shout at him. Our Tony took no notice and when Mum wasn't around he'd whisper in my ear, "Mrs Pendleton gonna get thi." The rotten bastard.

Most of the houses had now been knocked through, making them two-up two-down. A kitchen and parlour made up the lower floor; there were two bedrooms on the upper floor and an attic, which could be used as a spare bedroom. Our attic was full of old tea chests, cardboard boxes, junk and dust. Leant up against the back wall, stood a massive gilt-framed oil painting of a majestic stag with a mountain in the background. The beast had a strange look in its eyes, like it knew something that I didn't. I didn't like being in the attic on my own and after a quick peep, I would shoot back down the stairs in case Mrs Pendleton's ghost was lurking up there.

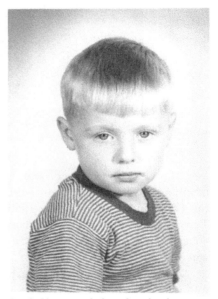

The front parlour was furnished, but we used it only for special occasions, and there weren't many of them. A cast iron fireplace and grate stood on the facing wall, but I never saw it lit. The stone kitchen sink had just one cold water tap. Water had

Little Sharpy aged about five; the photo must have been taken after the Friday night weekly tin bath dip; I don't remember being clean at any other time.

to be heated up in a copper at the side of a Yorkshire range stove, fuelled by coal. All the cooking was done on the range; the washing, boiled up in the copper and the excess water squeezed out by the compressed rubber rollers of a large iron mangle that stood outside the back door. With a lot of help from me Mam, a flat iron heated on the gas ring did the ironing.

Before our house was wired up to electricity in the mid-50s, gas mantles hanging from the ceilings lit the rooms. A rolled-up sheet of newspaper, stuck in the fire, ignited the mantles into life, with a loud "Boooom."

At the top of the coal cellar steps, a pantry with a cold shelf kept perishable food cool in the summer months. In the winter the ice on the inside of the windows kept everything cool, especially us. Every Friday evening, I bathed (as did all the family) in a grey tin bath parked in front of the fire.

Not all of the families had a TV We were all thrilled when our Terry picked up a second hand one from somewhere. It sat on the sideboard in the corner of the kitchen and took ages to warm up. When it did, the twelve-inch screen flickered and rolled, and it buzzed like a swarm of bees. There were no arguments about which channel to watch, as only the BBC station was available. By the late 50s some of the homes that had the ITV channel were usually full of kids who called in to see the Popeye cartoons and the new-fangled adverts, which were fascinating.

The close proximity of the houses kept us all together. There was always activity, someone going up or coming down the gennel, men arriving home from or setting off to work, women gossiping as they hung out the washing, donkey-stoned the front doorsteps or made trips to the dustbin to empty the ashes.

Little lads made aeroplane noises as they weaved in and out of the flapping bed sheets and terry towelling nappies on washday. Legions of infant soldiers invaded each other's back yards, fighting running battles with stick swords and dustbin lid shields. Teenagers sat laughing and chatting on the dividing walls, and groups of young girls chanting nonsense rhymes, jumped and skipped over lengths of old clothesline.

Toddlers, with snot candles hung from their noses, wandered aimlessly, munching doorsteps of bread and jam, and future England football internationals banged rubber balls against the slime-green painted shithouse doors. We lived from day to day and from hand to mouth. Kids were sent round to the neighbours to borrow all kind of things.

"Me Mam sez, can she lend a cup of sugar, a fag, a drop of milk, a pinch of salt, a cup of tea, an egg, a shovel of coal, a penny for the gas meter? Just until pay day, like." Some kids got more than they bargained for on cadging missions, especially the girls. They soon learnt to steer clear of the Smith's, as old man Smith's stang always seemed to accidentally flop out and stand to attention.

Even though our Tony worked down the pit and got coal on the cheap, there never seemed to be enough. Sometimes only a bit of slack or coal dust could be scraped up from the corner of the cellar. Women and kids walked up and down the train tracks filling buckets with bits of coal that had fallen from the trains. My sister was once prosecuted and had to attend court for trespassing on British Rail property when she was caught by a railway Bobby.

I had no idea we were poor, maybe we weren't poor, because all the family, except Gran, went off to work every day and there was always snap on the table. It could just have been the unsanitary condition of our surroundings.

A giant witch's cauldron of Gran's rabbit broth simmering on the stove. Me Mam's, red-hot fat cakes (pieces of spare pastry left over from the pies) straight from the oven.

Every Saturday dinnertime after he'd finished work, our Terry brought home a large newspaper parcel of greasy fish and chips from Hetty's chip hole on Dronny bottom.

On Sunday it was the full mashings roast dinner. My favourite breakfast, thick chunks of uncut crusty bread dipped in Cirio tomatoes cooked in slimy bacon fat. Calories weren't invented back then. I always felt full, safe, happy and secure. The sound of laughter and the smell of cooking filled the house and the back yards.

The back yards flooded after heavy rain. The drains, clogged up with sludge and dead rats, couldn't cope. Kids splashed around in a six-inch-deep pool of black stagnant water until one of the grown-ups had the courage to wade to the middle of the yard and poke out the blockage with a stick

Cammell's Row was a close-knit community with many large families of five, six, seven kids. The Smiths in the second yard had ten. Our next-door neighbours the Cardwells had five lads; Steve, the eldest was my age, the rest went down in order with only a year or eighteen months separating them. The Cardwell's house hadn't been knocked through, so the five lads, their mum and dad, Uncle Colin, Auntie Joyce, their son John, and a scary, slit-eyed English bull terrier called Judy, shared the two room house.

We laughed, cried, played, fought and threw bricks at each other for most of our childhood. The back doors were rarely locked at night. Nobody had much money, but no one would ever dream of stealing from each other as we were all in the same boat.

Me, Mick Cardwell, Uncle Chris, Steve Cardwell and Jeff Cardwell at the front on Henry's Bank late 50s

A hundred yards over the railway tracks, the site where the Wilson Cammell works once stood, was now occupied by the English Steel smelting factory. Thousands of bomb and shell cases of various shapes and sizes left over from World War II waited their turn to be melted down and littered the surrounding banking.

Sundays always felt quiet, Sundays went at a slow and easy pace; Sundays felt twice as long as the other days, but in a nice way. The roar from the traffic on the road outside our front door sounded less fierce without all the big lorries, and the overhead crane at the steelworks lay dormant and silent until it groaned back into action on Monday morning.

At ten minutes to twelve every Sunday morning the men from the Row and surrounding streets dressed in their best suits gathered outside the Masons Arms pub. If the bolts on the front doors weren't released at exactly midday, the blokes banged on the pub doors and windows, swearing and demanding entry. The Masons Arms stood in the shadow of a thirty-foot high coal slag heap. That and a couple of air-shafts – the last resting place for the dead cats and dogs of the area – was all that remained of the long forgotten Fallswood Colliery.

We'd gather at the top of the black mountain waiting in turn to slide down the steep slopes. We rode chariots of corrugated tin sheets, pieces of old oilcloth and wrecked car doors. Fingers caught under the tin sheets were sliced open. Heads were cut, knees and elbows grazed as we hit the bottom of the tip at break-neck speed. We received or gave out no sympathy when anyone got hurt.

"What's up wi' thi? Stop being a bleedin' mardy arse."

I had an idyllic childhood; the whole area around Cammell's Row was an adventure playground. On summer evenings we'd sit on the steps outside the boozer, where dads (or uncle in my case) brought out packets of Castle crisps with the little blue paper twist of salt inside and a bottle of lemonade, orange squash or ginger beer. We took empties back to the off-sales, where we gazed through the serving hatch, and clouds of Park Drive and Woodbine smoke, at the flat-capped men lounging by the bar in the tap room. I prayed for the day when I would be old enough to join them. The smell of Stones best bitter almost knocked me backwards.

Dronfield, far from being a poverty-stricken town was in fact quite an affluent place with many larger private houses than the back-to-backs. We were on the bottom rung of the ladder. A number of medium-sized steel works and iron foundries dotted the town; plus many small tool factories, manufacturing edge tools, spanners, hammers, knives and chisels. The Spear and Jackson works, known as the 'Tilt,' which made shovels, spades and other garden tools, was also housed in the town and a fair number of men worked in the North East Derbyshire coalfields.

A lot of my family were miners. My grandfather (who died before I was born) worked down the pit for most of his life, my brother, Tony, along with many relatives, uncles and cousins also did. My Uncle Chris (only twenty-one years old at the time) was buried in a fall down the mine in 1922; it took his mates hours to dig him out. A broken back had him bedridden for a full year. He carried the legacy of a hunch-back for the rest of his life.

My earliest memories, are of my Unk, eating big lumps of tripe swimming in vinegar, and telling me crazy stuff,

"What's a funklenut Ron?" he'd ask me.

"Don't know Unk," I'd say

"It's the same as a barkleberry."

"What's a barkleberry, Unk?

"It's a clinker."

"What's a clinker, Unk?

"It's a little brown man on a swing when you forget to wipe your bum."

He told me about the Coal Aston dockyards where ocean liners sailed in from the West Indies to unload their cargoes of coconuts and bananas – Coal Aston's a small village about half a mile from Dronfield, ninety miles from the nearest coast. I really thought the ocean was just over the hill.

"Don't you ever go over them train lines," he told me when I was about three.

"Nan Nutter the goblin lives over there, and he eats little kids for his dinner." I was terrified of Nan Nutter for years and I always kept an eye out for him when I played near the train tracks.

The Cardwell's bogeyman was a black caped phantom named 'Red Eye.' He only had one eye in the middle of his forehead and it was red. Just like Nan Nutter, Red Eye lived on a diet of little kids. Huddled together in the Cardwell Kitchen on dark winter nights, Uncle Colin scared us shitless with Red Eye tales.

"Red Eye's comin, he's on roof, he's in attic now, he'll get thee first Sharpy."

Aunty Joyce would join in with the sound effects, "Oooooooo, he's comin downstairs."

I reckon if Judy the bull terrier had started howling, it would have finished me off.

"I've got to go home now," I'd say. "Can you watch me to our house, Mrs Cardwell? Mi Mam sez I've not to go home on mi own."

Our back door was two yards away.

Over the railway bridge on Chesterfield Road, just past old Man Haig's small holding where he kept loads of fowls in an old rickety lopsided chicken hut, stood the sewerage. It was surrounded by an 8-foot-high wire mesh fence topped with barbed wire. At weekends, when the sewerage men weren't working, we entered through a hole in the bottom of the fence. There were stacks of stuff to do in the sewerage, there was like this giant roundabout on a bed of stones with all these pipes and water dripping out and we'd jump on and ride around and around for ages. The best bit though was the enormous concrete shit tanks where all the shit went. One of big kids told me the shit tanks were miles deep and if you tippled in, you were a gonner. We'd get big rocks and boulders, roll them up the bank, drop them over the edge and watch the evil smelling shite splash right up into the air.

In the Little Wood at the side of the sewerage, raw sewage flowed into the river from a broken shit pipe. Egged on and taught by the older kids we fished rubber johnnies out of the river with sticks. The spunk bags, as they called them were filled with water, hung in the branches of trees and pelted with stones.

I rolled in late for my tea one day and my sister asked me where I'd been

"I've been down Little Wood wi' our David gerrin spunk bags outa river," I answered.

My cousin, David Raynor, was five years older than me. Our Dave knew everything, our Dave told me loads of great stuff.

"Ya mucky little bugger," our Joan said. "You'll bloody catch summat, and where did you get that word from?"

"What word?" I said.

"Spunk bags," our Joan said, trying her best not to smile.

"Our David told it me," I said.

"Right, we'll go and see our bleedin David," Joan said, dragging me up the gennel and down to the bottom yard where my Auntie Alice lived. Our Joan burst into Auntie Alice's house and shouted, "Our David been teaching our Ronnie swear words again."

"What ya been saying to him this time?" my auntie Alice said.

"I've not telled him owt," our David said.

"You lying little bleeder," our Joan said. "You've been telling him about spunk bags."

"I've not telled him about spunk bags," our David said.

"What have you telled our Ronnie about spunk bags for, ya little bleeder," my Auntie Alice shouted, clipping our David around the ear hole. Our Joan gave me a scutch for listening to our David. Our David gave me a look that said: next time he saw me on my own I'd be getting another one.

Our heroes were all cowboys, the Lone Ranger, Roy Rogers, Kit Carson and Buffalo Bill. Bejewelled rhinestone-studded holsters, housing silver six-shooters with fake plastic bone handles hung from our gun belts; firing rolls of caps that cracked and gave out little puffs of smoke and whiffs of sulphur. Tribes of Arapaho, Comanche, Navaho and Sioux (led by Big Chief Shitting Bull) our sworn enemies. Davy Crockett, King of the Wild Frontier was the main man.

"Born on a mountaintop in Tennessee, kilt him a b'ar when he was only three." Crockett didn't fuck about; imagine that, killing a bear at three years old! When I wore my fringed Crockett buckskins (my Christmas box for 1957) with the long-tailed Coonskin cap falling over my eyes, I feared no man or beast – except for Nan Nutter and Red Eye.

Geronimo and his band of bloodthirsty renegade Apache braves, who had a camp in the wooded area at the far end of the iron slag tip were no match for the Cammell's Row 7th Cavalry and their chief Indian scout: me.

Platoons of imaginary German troops were put to flight as we dived into trenches lobbing stone hand grenades ("angry nades," I called 'em) after pulling out the pins with our teeth. We whistled as they sailed through the air and made exploding noises as they landed. Wooden Bren guns hammered together with rusty nails finished off the Nazi invaders. We marched home as black as the fire-back, singing, "Rule Britannia, two tanners make a bob, Hitler never-never-never washed his knob."

The Germans (according to my Uncle Chris) had tried to bomb Cammell's

Row during the war, the reason he said: "All the best fighting men lived here." Ten thousand bombs had all missed the target and landed on the banks of the English Steel, the proof was there for all to see.

One Saturday summer evening a couple of the big lads, busting with excitement ran into the top yard shouting, "Submarine on English Steel, come on everybody, we've seen it, submarine on English."

Word soon spread around the four yards as lads climbed on the closet roofs shouting, "Submarine on English." Just before dusk and with the light fading, dozens of youngsters, teenagers and even some of the grown-ups pelted across the train lines and scrambled up the banking onto the site. And there it was, looming big and black and leaning slightly to one side, not a full submarine, but half of one. No matter; we swarmed aboard, whooping and swinging on the railings. Some of the big lads went right inside searching for periscopes and torpedoes. The grown-ups stood back shouting, "Be careful, come down, it might bloody tipple ovver, Bobbies'll be here in a minute." We were too excited to take any notice and stayed until it went dark.

Early Sunday morning we were back and played on the Sub all day. Our David reckoned it must be a German Sub, what with it being blown in half like. By the next weekend the Sub was gone, dismantled and melted down into who knows what.

Gary 'Cuttsie' Cutts, and four of the Cardwell brothers, Jeff 'Mc Duff', Mick 'Moose Mulligan', Steve 'Brontosaurus' and Phil 'Nupper' in the top back yard of Cammell's, late 1950s

We never ever got bored, there was always something to do, always loads of games to play: British Bulldog, Hide-and-seek, Tiggy, Tiggy off-ground, Snobs and Kick-can. We did the spuds to see who was "on," standing in a line with fists clenched and held out in front of us. "One potato, two potato, three potato four, five potato, six potato, seven potato more."

We played moppties (marbles) in the back yards and up and down the terraced streets. I had a huge peg bag containing hundreds, but the Jack (the brightest coloured and best of the bunch) I always kept in my pocket. Nobody ever wanted to lose his Jack.

Cratches (trolleys) were knocked together using old pram wheels and bits of wood. The steering mechanism consisted of a length of clothes line tied to the front axle. The carts could also be steered using our feet. Daredevils though we were, no one had the bottle to ride from the top of Hallows Rise, the steepest hill in town. Brakes were non-existent, our shoe heels or the causey edge slowed us down, brick walls, trees and thorn bushes stopped us dead in our tracks.

Fag cards (cigarette cards) were carried round in bundles wrapped in elastic bands.

We played games of covers or fars. With a deft flick of the wrist and the wind behind us we could skim them half a mile at least. The cig cards were like our own form of money, we could trade them for all kinds of stuff, especially the ones needed to make up a full set.

The same with comics: piles of *Beanos*, *Beezers* and *Hotspurs* were swapped for *Victors*, *Eagles* and *Dandys*. Until I was way into my teens I spent hours reading comics, lost in a wondrous world of colour, fantasy and adventure. Giggling at the antics of the Bash Street Kids, particularly Plug, whose face could stop a bus, Little Plum, your Red Indian chum who said "Um." The strength and appetite of Desperate Dan, who lifted up buildings with one hand and devoured giant cow pies with horns stuck in the crust. Dan lived in the Wild West town of Cactusville – a cross between Dodge City and Attercliffe with back-to-back terraced houses built on the prairie. The Wolf of Kabul with his sidekick Chung, knocked the shit out of Afghan tribesmen. The Wolf used a battered old cricket bat he called Clicki-ba.

The dodges of Roger the Dodger, the mischief of Dennis the Menace and the guts of Alf Tupper, 'The Tough of the Track,' who could deliver two ton of coal by hand, do a full shift at the welder's yard, scoff a bob's worth of chips and two fish, and still win a ten-mile race, barefooted, all in the same day.

We laughed in the face of danger, climbing the steel spiral walkway on the massive gas tank at the gas works at the bottom end of the Row on Mill Lane. Some sections of the steps, bolted onto the tank were loose and almost hanging off. The rails swayed and creaked; they could have broken free at any time. At forty-foot high it would have been certain death if we fell.

A barbed wire fence surrounded the scrap yard on Mill Lane. We climbed over and stole four-foot long stainless steel rods. The ends of the spears were sharpened to a point on an old foot operated grindstone stuck in some bushes on the ghitty on Callywhite Lane.

We threw stones at the bombs on the banks of the steel works hoping to explode them. We threw stones at everything, including each other – strange how the stones never seemed to hit us on the arm, body or leg, they always landed on our heads.

Occasional passing cars or buses copped for it. Trains were easy targets; they couldn't stop to chase us. We put all kinds of stuff on the train lines; from halfpennies – which we hoped would squash into full pennies, to large rocks, pram chassis, lumps of iron and logs of wood. Without even a thought about derailment, we sat a couple of yards away on the banking and cheered as the train wheels smashed them to smithereens.

We were connoisseurs in the art of catapultry, and with a nice round pebble or an iron punching we could hit a rat up the arse from twenty paces. The rats came out at night. Every bed on the row had a piss pot or the old Jerry from Poland under it, in case we got took short, but crapping in the po, was a no-no. We had to cross the back yard, carrying a candle in pitch darkness to the closet, where layers of flaking whitewash flapped from the cobwebbed walls and ceiling. Sheets of *The Daily Herald* newspaper cut into squares hung invitingly on a nail, hammered to the back of the bog door. The rats scuttled around the dustbins foraging for scraps of food. They sent a shiver down my spine. I was (and still am) petrified of them. A large tribe of the bastards took up residence under the floorboards of a cupboard under our kitchen sink. We could hear them moving around and the stink turned my stomach.

Roy Maisfield was part of a large rough and tumble family who lived in the bottom yard. Roy, a Teddy Boy and expert poacher could always be relied on for a rabbit or two, and fresh fowls were sometimes available when he'd had paid a visit to old man Haig's chicken hut.

For the price of a couple of pints off our Terry, Roy emptied two ferrets from a filthy sack into the cupboard under the sink. A couple of minutes later, after a few bumps and squeals, the ferrets appeared with their faces covered in blood.

I still see Roy to this day, holding court at the Sunday dinnertime sessions in the Bridge Inn. He even partakes in the odd blast of weed. After a smoke he shouts, "My missus can fucking get ready tonight, this stuff gizz me the horn." He then treats the whole pub to a rendering of My Brother Silveste; everybody joins in the chorus. Roy's 70 now and is what anybody with any spirit should aspire to be, when they reach his age. He still walks tall, takes no shit from no one, and unlike many of his generation who went through hard times, shows no signs of bitterness. We always reminisce about the old days. He grabs my mates and tells them, "Little Sharpy, when he were a babby, used to follow me all over, till I tied him to a tree and set fire to him, I had to piss on him to put him out, he dint fucking follow me again, did tha Ron?" Everybody's in stitches.

"We had fuck all on Row, dint we Ron?" he shouts out. "We lived on fuckin rabbit stew. Nobody had a vacuum cleaner, cos no fucker had a carpet, and there were always three or four rats sat waiting under kitchen table at snap time in case we dropped a few crumbs.

"There's not many of us old Cammell's Row lads left Ron", he tells me. He then tells the whole boozer, "Me and young Sharpy... fucking Cammell's Row lads, nobody fucks with us, if they do, (he holds up a fist as big as a ham shank). Enid-fuckin-Blyton: end of the story, Roy-fuckin-Orbison: It's over." I love the man.

(Postscript) Roy woke up dead on Sunday 14 January 2007, it was one of the few Sunday dinnertimes sessions he had ever missed. The day before, he had been in The Bridge doing his usual stuff. Flirting with the barmaid, buying rounds of drinks, singing songs and crushing fingers with his handshakes. I thought he was indestructible; the 'big strong man' and the last of the Mohicans, he'll be sadly missed by all.

Roy's older brother Johnny, a seasoned criminal had contacts (it was rumoured) with the London criminal underworld and he'd once done a seven stretch in Dartmoor. Johnny – a sharp dresser, lovable rogue, Robin Hood-type character held the respect of everyone.

"He's always well-mannered and polite," me Mam said of Johnny, "and he always buys me a drink if he sees me in the pub."

The greatest thrill of my young life came late one Sunday night when I awoke to the sound of torch-carrying policemen running past my bedroom and up our attic stairs.

"They're after Johnny Maisfield," my Uncle Chris told me. "He's busted out of prison." Everybody went out to the back yards, watching the coppers going in and out of the houses. The women, dressed in their nightgowns stood tutting and ooooing, shouting: "It's not bleedin on, gerrin us out of bed at this time of night." All the kids ran around wild and the men pointed upwards as coppers helmets appeared through the skylight attic windows and torchlight flashed across the roof tops.

Not long after the police left, Johnny appeared from behind Frank Turner's chimney-stack and received a cheer from the crowd.

We'd go on nesting expeditions, following the big kids to far away woods and forests. Just like a grizzly bear, if I needed a crap, I shat in the woods. I weren't no animal though and always wiped my arse on a dock leaf to keep the funklenuts at bay. We tramped miles over the fields, searching every bush and hedgerow, occasionally stopping to climb and wreck haystacks. We explored old broken-down barns and farm outbuildings looking for swallows, swifts and house martin's nests. We waded through swamps, through jungles of wild rhubarb, peashooter plants with exploding seed pods and sticky bud trees that grew on the river-banks. Sticky bud fights were okay until the buds got stuck in our hair, then our mums had to cut them out with a pair of scissors. We drank the clear water from a spring that ran into the Red Ochre pond. An early morning eerie mist rose from the Green Cheese pond where we waded out to steal moorhen's eggs from nests built in the clumps of reeds. Great Crested newts with beautiful orange markings on their under bellies swam past, waving side to side like miniature prehistoric monsters. We learnt how to scrawm up trees, crawl along thin, bendy branches to the nests, dodging dive-bombing, kamikaze mistle thrushes. The eggs were carried in our mouths, as both hands were needed to climb back down, then punctured at each end with the spike of a hawthorn twig and carefully blown out to prevent them from going bad. Most of the Row gang had a bird's egg collection. The eggs were kept in cut down cardboard boxes, labelled and laid out on a bed of cotton wool. We were taught how to tickle rainbow trout that swam around shaded pools in the streams that ran into Barlow Dam. Crayfish were boiled alive in tin cans full of river water, hung over an open fire. The older lads would cloth off and swim bare-Bob across the lake. The younger ones paddled and splashed around the edges of the dam.

We came back home at dusk, knackered and starving, covered in muck, mud and midge bites. A mug of 'Pobs' (hot milk with bread dipped in it), then off to the magical world of Rupert the Bear and his mates, read by my mum, and I was out for count. I didn't have a clue what seven eighths multiplied by three quarters were in the maths lessons at school (still don't). I think it had something to do with 1066, but I knew everything about nature. The names and the habitats of all the different wild birds, the colours and markings of their eggs and even the names of the trees they nested in.

Our football pitch was a patch of waste ground at the side of the Row, called Henry's Bank. Goalposts were chalked on the gable end of the last house of the top yard. A couple of coats, jumpers or piles of white dog shit made the others. Cricket stumps were also chalked onto the gable end. Even Fiery Fred Truman wouldn't have knocked the bails off them fuckers. Dads and older brothers taught us the dribbling skills of Stanley Mathews and how to trap a ball like Jimmy Hagan. The games lasted until dusk and then we carried on in the street, hammering the ball against a wall under the dull glow of a gas lamp. We used any kind of balls we could find, usually tennis or rubber.

Pete Goldthorpe was the envy of us all when his Dad bought him a size four case ball for Christmas. When it went under the wheels of a passing lorry a few weeks later we were all heartbroken. Football was my passion, me Mam reckoned I were football daft.

At the far end of Henry's Bank, what we were told was a bomb crater, but probably wasn't, stood the 'Big Hole.' 'The Big Oil,' as we called it, was just a dip in the ground, maybe three or four feet deep, surrounded by trees and bushes. It was like a private hiding place/ den, where our mums and dads couldn't see us.

So we're all in the Big Oil one day and this lass turns up. She weren't off Cammell's, she came in the school holidays to visit her auntie who lived in second yard. She's stood at the top looking down at us for ages. She had a posh frock on and she kept lifting it up a bit, so you could nearly see her knickers.

Piggy Bacon shouted up, "What's ya name?"

"Suzie Clegg," this lass said.

"Suzie Clegg, boiled egg," Bobby Marriott sang out. Bobby Marriott were crackers, he were always making rhymes up and saying daft stuff to make us laugh. Bobby was the smallest out of our lot, and I think he tried to make the big kids laugh so they wouldn't belt him as much. Suzie Clegg pretended she hadn't heard Bobby Marriott. She kept doing this little dance, she were just sort of swaying side to side and twirling her frock higher and higher, and then she said, "What ya playing?" I can't remember what we were playing, but Piggy said, "Lasses can't play."

"Not bothered," Suzie said, "but I know a right good game and you lot aren't even big enough to play it."

"What is it then?" Piggy said.

"Not tellin ya," Suzie said. "You're only little kids and I'm at the big school after the holidays."

So Piggy says, "You can play with us then, if you tell us this game." By now Suzie's moved down and she's in the Big Oil with us.

"It's a secret game," Suzie said. "My Uncle taught it me, and he's a bloke, and he said I hadn't to tell my mum and dad or anybody else, and if I did, the Bobbies would come and put me in a home, so if I tell you, you've got to promise not to tell your mums and dads or anybody else, or the Bobbies'll come and put you in the homes."

"I haven't got a Dad," I said. "Well don't tell ya Mum," Suzie said.

"I waint," I said.

Anyway, Suzie Clegg's telling us about this new game.

"It's called tickle tails," Suzie said.

"How do you play it then?" Piggy said.

"You've got to get your tails out first," Suzie said.

I knew where my tail was, but I always called it mi sparra. So we all got our tails out and Suzie pulled her knickers down a bit and got her tail out. Trouble was though, Suzie dint have a tail, there were nowt there.

"What do you do now?" Piggy said.

"You have to tickle my tail with your tail and say, 'Tickle Tails, Tickle Tails.'" Suzie said.

I dint know how we were gonna tickle Suzie's tail, cos she dint have one. Anyway, Suzie made us all tickle, where her tail should have been, with our tails.

When we'd all done it, Suzie lay down, took her knickers right off, and made us take turns to get on top of her. She said we had to go up and down and push right hard and say, 'Tickle Tails'.

"You're not doing it right," Suzie kept saying.

The next day we're all down the Big Oil and Suzie Clegg comes again. We played tickle tails again until we heard some big kids shouting on Henry's Bank. Suzie pulled her pants up and said she was going playing with them.

Suzie came a few more times and we always had to play tickle tails with her. We started paying tickle tails on our own, it was a lot better than playing it with Suzie.

One day, me and Turnip were playing it behind the big brown armchair in our kitchen. Mam must have heard us whispering and giggling cos she pulled the armchair out.

"What ya doing ya mucky little buggers?" Mam shouted.

"Were only playing tickle tails, Mam. Suzie Clegg made us do it down Big Oil," I said.

"I'll bloody tickle tail Suzie Clegg when I get hold of her, the little chuffin madam, I've a good mind to slap both your bleedin arses," Mam said.

"You get yourself home, Terry Turner." Mam said to Turnip, "And don't think I won't be telling your mother when I see her lad, cos I bloody well will.

Just you wait and see if I don't."

With no dad around to keep us all in line, our Terry laid down the law. Terry made sure everybody pulled their weight and handed out their board money on payday. He told me when to go to bed, when to get up and he told me off when I got naughty. Terry worked as an electrician at Prestwich's iron foundry and he always seemed to be dressed in navy blue overalls, except at the weekends, when he dolled himself up in one of a number of suits he owned. His wardrobe also contained a fine selection of flash ties and silk shirts. A treasure chest of tiepins and gold-coloured cuff links sat on his dressing table.

Big Band swing music was our Terry's thing. He listened to Benny Goodman and Duke Ellington records and travelled miles to see the Ted Heath band and the Victor Sylvester orchestra.

My brother Terry. 1950s

When I reached the age of six, Terry started taking me to football games both at Bramall Lane and Hillsborough. I would love to say I went to the Lane first, but I honestly can't remember. The Hillsborough games were always midweek night matches; we never went on Saturdays. Some were England under twenty-three games or England B internationals. One or two though were league matches. We travelled in Terry's white Morris Minor car. Night matches at both grounds were magic. The floodlights, visible from miles away seemed to suck in the crowds as they flocked through the streets heading towards the beacon.

At Hillsborough they were always groups of scruffy young kids hanging around the streets offering to look after cars for a few pennies. Terry told me as soon as they had enough money for the entrance fee they went into the ground. He always gave them money anyway; he was like that our Terry.

We usually went in the seats, applauding good moves and goals from both teams. We stood on the Kop one night, where an old bloke dressed in a long overcoat and flat cap stood directly behind me shouted in a broad Sheffield accent right in my ear, "Gerrartarfuckinrooad!" (roughly translated into English it meant, "move out of the way.") I shifted to one side closer to my brother.

"Nay lad," the bloke said, "am not talking to thee; it's that daft bastard on t' pitch." I was somewhat relieved, our Terry doubled up with laughter.

The first game I remember at the Lane was Jimmy Hagan's testimonial in March 1958, just before my seventh birthday. Hagan was our Terry's hero,

"Best player I've ever seen," he told me. I don't recall much of the game, only the freezing cold weather and the snow-bound pitch. We stood on the John Street terrace and Terry kept lifting me up, so I could see. I couldn't wait for the match to finish so I could get back to the car for a warm.

There was a marked difference in our Terry's behaviour at United matches. He shouted and cheered them on all through the game. He picked me up in the air when they scored, shouted abuse at the opposing team and the referee when a decision went against the Blades. It pissed him off for a while if United lost. So that's how I must have become a 'Unitedite', you had to one or the other. The visits to Hillsborough got less and less and then stopped altogether.

Terry loved all kinds of sports and he loved a bet on the horses. As well as the football games, he took me to boxing matches, the dogs and horse racing meetings at Doncaster, Pontefract and Nottingham. It's a wonder the gambling bug never bit me. My Uncle Chris worked as an illegal bookies' runner in the 20s and 30s and had a bet most days. My mum had an account at the local bookies until the day she died.

Our Tony (nicknamed Luke by his mates) never took me anywhere. He did his own thing and always had a kind of faraway look in his eyes, like he was not of this world. Apart from scaring the shit out of me with tales of Mrs Pendleton's ghost, my lasting memory of him is when he sent off for the Charles Atlas body-building course, whose ads appeared on the back page of American comic books. Charlie reckoned he could turn seven stone weaklings into men and stop bullies kicking sand in their faces on Mablethorpe beach. To the great amusement of the rest of my family, Tony exercised in front of the open bedroom window every night and drank a mixture of six raw eggs, herbs and milk every morning before he went to work. After a month or so Charles Atlas sent him his money back.

The characters on the Row and neighbouring streets kept life interesting. The Lockets, who had too many kids to count, lived opposite us. They kept a strange pet in the form of a donkey. Nowt wrong with that I suppose, but the beast was part of the family. Like a giant dog it lived in the front room and slept by the side of the fire. Mam told me that, as a nipper, my sister Joan, along with the one of the daughters, her best mate Lucy and the rest of the Lockett tribe, rode around the house on the donkey's back. When she came home, Gran would shout, "Thaz been on that bleeding donkey again; I can smell thee from here."

The Barlow's could have done with Lockett's donkey. The two kids, Kenneth and Deirdre pulled a large handcart filled with bundles of firewood for sale around the streets in all weathers. If that wasn't bad enough, their dad, a bastard of a man, armed with a whip, oversaw the whole proceedings, often stopping and thrashing them for no reason.

In later life they both ended up with serious mental problems. As adults they had completely lost it. Deirdre walked the streets pulling an empty shopping trolley, twitching and suffering fits. Ken was around until the mid-70s. He could often be seen, dressed in rags, hanging on street corners or outside one of the pubs. He usually had a penny or a halfpenny and would ask passers-by to, "Make this up to the price of a pint."

We were rotten bastards in our teens and every now and again we took him in the boozer purely for entertainment and got him so drunk he could hardly walk. He was finally found frozen to death in a hedge bottom on Mill Lane.

The Marriotts, another massive family who'd moved to the town from Sheffield, lived in Badger Row, a line of terraces (still standing today) fifty yards down the street. A full-sized snooker table filled their front room. It was needed to seat the whole family who squeezed round it at mealtimes. The eldest lad, Bill, made the local newspaper when it was reported he ate a full loaf with every meal. The Sheffield Star showed a photo of Bill with a big smile on his face, sat at the snooker table with his daily bread: three loaves of Mothers Pride stacked up in front of him.

Badger Row, the next street down from Cammell's, these were 'pit houses' built for the pit workers who worked at the Fallswood colliery across the street.

Sally, a year my senior, and the only girl in the Marriott clan, taught me, the rest of the Row gang and even some of her brothers, many, many things we daren't tell our mothers. It all started one night after the gang had been out scrumping. Three of the Marriott brothers were with us. We were sprawled out in the slag tip wood when Sally showed up. In return for an apple each, Sally took her knickers off, and let us to do whatever we liked. I reckon Sal, must have had tickle tail lessons off Suzie Clegg. We prodded, probed and poked around her parcel, until Danny, one of her brothers (who was about thirteen and a lot older than the rest of us) shouted, "Get outa way." Shoving us aside he whipped out an enormous stonker and dived on top of her. He went up and down for a few seconds and left a pool of gooey stuff on her belly. I wondered what it was and thought he'd pissed on her.

We often called round for Sal with our jumpers stacked up with apples or a hand full of guzgogs (gooseberries). Many a happy hour was spent in the backfields, the Little Wood or any other secluded spot exploring Sally's slice. Piggy Bacon once dropped a note through her letterbox saying: Dear Sally, are you coming out, cos we want to fuck you. Her mother found the note, went mad and showed it to all our parents. We were all interrogated, but nobody owned up.

The rag and bone man, Fat Freddy Ashmoor regularly mosied into town on his horse and cart. It was a great occasion. Fat Fred sported a bushy black beard, wore a battered trilby hat and a flashy waistcoat. His 'Tatting' hollers, "Any old rags" (I thought he shouted, "Johnny oh rags") or "Ray-aaaaaaags, old iron." It was sung rather than shouted. On seeing him approach we scattered like ants down the gennels, searching the sculleries for bits of old cloth. We followed Fat Freddy round the streets; he was like the pied piper. We mocked his cries, patted the horse and jumped on the back of his cart. He seemed oblivious to us all. The rags he collected were exchanged for wooden clothes pegs or balloons. For scrap metal he handed out disintegrating goldfish that fell to pieces and vanished after a couple of days. I think Fat Freddy died a millionaire.

The older kids told us that lads from the neighbouring villages, who came into town to visit the Electra Palace cinema (or Dronny bug-hut as we called it) were too scared to walk past Cammell's Row. They gave it a wide birth and went over the fields instead, but there was always a pile of stones at the top of the four gennels just in case any of them dared to venture back that way. The Palace, a decrepit building with peeling, white-painted walls, stood in the centre of town. Portcullis style railings at the top of the steps guarded the front entrance. Inside, the small foyer housed the admission desk and refreshment counter. The films were usually in black and white and months or years out of date, the admission, 9d downstairs and 1 shilling and 3d in the balcony. We only needed three pop or beer bottles with 3d refund on each and we were in. A couple more empties bought us a knickerbocker-glory ice cream, a tub or a Lyons Maid lolly from the usherette who stood at the front during the interval.

The cowboy films had our pulses racing. We were transported to a world of bandits, trail blazing cowpunchers, desperados and quick-on-the-draw lonesome drifters dressed in black. Covered wagons headed way out west, over plains and through canyons to Tombstone and Dodge City where whooping gunslingers downed slugs of red-eye in one swig, pinged green hangers into a spittoon and shot holes in the saloon ceiling.

We stared in wide-eyed amazement and anticipation as the cavalry or the sheriff and his posse of deputies rode in at the last minute to save the day. We whistled and cheered as the Red Indians scattered for their lives across the prairie. At the end of the film we stood and sang the national anthem: "God save our gracious cat, feed it on bread and fat, God save our cat."

We galloped back to Cammell's Row clicking the roof of our mouths with our tongues and slapping our buttocks. "Last one back's a sissy."

On Saturdays there were two shows at the flicks. The afternoon one (the first house) showed U films the young 'uns could get in to see. It finished about seven and we'd sit on the railings outside, eyeing up the Teddy Boys and their birds, queuing to watch an over eighteen x-rated film. I found out from my older mates, the Teds and their birds always sat on the back row and played a game called finger pie, whatever that was.

Our Tony was a bit of a Ted, but my cousin Kenny Raynor was a real Ted: he had all the gear. I'd been down at my Aunty Alice's at weekends and seen him dolled up ready to hit town. I'd seen him slip on an ice-blue drape jacket over a crisp, white shirt and slim tie. I'd watched him run a comb through his curly blond hair, watched him flick it into a quiff, get it just right, perfect and then smile as he stepped back from the mirror, Fonzie style. Our Kenny was a face and he knew it. Me mam reckoned our Kenny were: 'Too bloody good-looking for his own good and he had kids all over the place.'

Gran died on a Sunday; I was six years old. She hadn't been down from her bedroom for a few days. My Aunty Florrie and Uncle Fred came up on the bus from Sheepbridge with our Bobbie and our Graham and our Jean. Aunty Alice and our Kenny and our David and our Margaret and our June, all came up from the bottom yard. My other Uncle Fred and Aunty Violet, who lived in the posh houses up Hallows Rise, came down with our Gloria and our Freda.

Uncle Fred's house had a front and back garden – and a real bathroom. Uncle Fred sometimes let our Joan go up for a bath on Friday when she'd finished work at Robinson's factory. If Aunty Violet saw Mam in the street she'd shout, "Bring our Ronnie up for a bath Annie, anytime, anytime you like."

"Bleedin show off, with her bloody bathroom," Mam used to say.

Everybody stood around Gran's bed staring at her. Gran was laid on her back, dead still, with her eyes closed and her mouth wide open; Gran dint have any teeth at all. Somebody said, "She's not got long to go," and our Tony said, "I don't think she'll last the night by the look of her." Everybody looked at our Tony right funny. I got fed up, so I went out in the back yard and booted a ball against our closet door.

Mrs Simpson came out and shouted, "How's ya Gran doing, Ron?"

"She's not got long to go, Mrs Simpson; I don't think she'll last the night by the look of her," I answered. Mrs Simpson shook her head, but she was smiling when she did it.

Mam once told me Mrs Simpson helped young lasses out when they got in trouble. I wonder if she had a word with the Bobbies and told them they hadn't done owt?

I went back in and then everybody came down and started roaring and saying, "She's gone, she's gone." And cos everybody was roaring, I started roaring an' all. Mum told me I wouldn't be seeing Gran any more, cos she'd gone up to heaven to live with our Ann and Jesus.

A few days later these big black cars came and parked outside our house. I think it was on Thursday, but I dint have to go to school. All the neighbours came out and stood outside their front doors and at the top of the gennels with their arms folded. We got in the cars and went to the graveyard on Cemetery Road. There was a wooden box in one of the cars; you could see it through the car window. We went in this building in the graveyard, it was like a church and we sang some hymns, like assembly at school. Then some men carried the box out and put it into a deep hole in the ground; Gran was in the wooden box. I thought she was supposed to going up to Heaven.

We got back in the cars and went back to our house. Mam, our Joan and my Aunty Alice had been in the front room all morning doing stuff. We went in and it smelled right strong of polish. The table from our kitchen had been moved to the front room and it had the lace tablecloth that we used at Christmas on it. There were all these potted meat and ham sandwiches cut in triangles, piled up on big plates. There was some angel cake and some chocolate biscuits, and the big, copper tea urn that Gran kept on the stone shelf at the top of the cellar steps was on the sideboard under the front room window. All the neighbours and some people I'd never seen before kept coming in the front room. We were having a party, it was great.

Sister Joan, looking like a Hollywood movie star. 1950s

Rock 'n' Roll fever hit Dronny when Elvis Presley's *Jailhouse Rock* was screened in the late 1950s. A large queue of excited, jabbering teenagers and younger lads and lasses formed outside the bug-hut. The manager, Mr Lawson, with a stern look on his face and his arms folded, stood at the top of the steps eyeing us all up.

"Can we sing, Mister Lawson?" I shouted.

"You can sing," he answered, "but I don't want no messing about."

When the film got going we went crazy. We danced in the aisles, stamped our feet, stood on the seats and threw lolly sticks and drink cartons into the air. The old woman and her torch, Evelyn Nicolson, nicknamed 'Flash', employed to keep law and order and throw out noisy kids, worked overtime trying to quell the mini riot. It stopped only when Mr Lawson, who doubled as the projectionist, stood at the front and threatened to turn the film off.

The steam and the irresistible smell from Arthur's chippie wafted across the street to the bug hut. A tanner bought us a bag of, crispy on the outside, soft in the middle, dark brown chips. Snow-white cod, covered in thick, crunchy batter that nearly broke our teeth cost a bob, and emerald green, sloppy peas were 4d a dollop. Scraps of fish bits floated in a pool of non-brewed condiment in the bottom of the paper chip bag.

Like hundreds of other regional cinemas, the bug hut closed down in the early 60s, but remained standing for many years after.

My Sister Joan often took me to the big posh picture houses in Sheffield, like the Odeon and the Gaumont. These cinemas were like real palaces, with thick bouncy carpets in the corridors and the aisles. The enormous screens were flanked by fake marble pillars. As the lights dimmed, red velvet curtains opened, as if by magic. My hairs stood on end as the MGM lion roared in the intro or when the muscleman in skimpy trunks whacked a giant gong. The spectacular film in glorious Technicolor was about to start.

The derelict bug hut, late 60s

At the age of eight my dream of playing football for England, Sheffield United, or even Dronfield bucket-bangers, were dealt a literally crippling blow. Walking home from school one day with a couple of mates we decided to do a bit of apple scrumping. I climbed up a wall, then onto the roof of a garden shed where I leant over to pluck the apples. I lost my grip and slid down the shed roof. I tried to grab the top of the wall to break my fall, but a coping stone (about one-foot square) came down with me. I hit the ground and tried to get up to run away. My right foot didn't move. I looked down and saw my foot almost hanging off. The stone had landed on it. Panic set in as I saw the green coloured tendons slither out like thick spaghetti. Only then did I feel the pain. I screamed out in agony and shock.

"I'm gonna die, I'm gonna die! Oh let me die! God let me die!" It must have flashed through my mind in a split second my footie days were over. Shit, I was only eight, I was never gonna play football again and I was going to die.

My mates scattered, screaming and crying. I must have passed out. One of my mates ran to a house to raise the alarm. A man came out, carried me inside and called the ambulance.

I remember briefly coming round in the ambulance, but I think they gave me a shot to put me out again. I again revived in the hospital as they wheeled me to the operating theatre. I tried to fight the nurses as they pushed a gas mask over my face. I'd lost a lot of blood and needed a four-pint blood transfusion.

The doctors managed to save my foot even though most of the bones in it were broken. They took skin from my arse and from the top of my legs and grafted it onto my foot. As I waited to go into theatre for one of the skin graft operations, the bloke in the next bed said: "What they do is put you on a conveyor belt with a bacon slicer on the end. It takes a slice off your arse and if it doesn't fit, they give it you, with some tomatoes and eggs for your breakfast next morning." Nice bloke eh!

I had a terrible time in hospital, as the minutes, hours, days and weeks dragged along. Most of my family came to visit every night. I cried like a baby when visiting time finished, pretending my foot was hurting. The hospital food was horrible; I couldn't eat it (it was probably okay, just me being a mardy little bleeder). I spent most of the time reading, eating sweets and getting fat.

After six, long, long weeks, five operations and a week convalescence at the Ashgate Hospital, I was finally released. At eight years old, a week seems a hell of a long time, so two months sempt like an eternity. I spent some time on crutches and then used a walking stick. I had physiotherapy sessions and had to spend ten minutes, three times a day wiggling my toes, within a year I was back playing football again. My balance was never the same again, but I did learn to use my left foot a bit more. I made the junior school football team and even had a trial for North East Derbyshire boys.

The most exciting night of the year came around on November the 5th, Guy Fawkes Night. Bonny Neet we called it. Forget Christmas or birthdays, Bonny Neet was *the* neet. From the beginning of October, we rushed home from school every day to start building. Entire weekends were spent searching for firewood. Brushwood, logs, dead branches, live branches, wounded branches, wooden crates, fence posts, mattresses, broken chairs, car seats, car tyres and anything else remotely combustible were dragged through the streets to the bonfire sites on Henry's Bank or to the top of the iron slag tip that backed on to Cemetery Road.

In the weeks leading up to the big night, every penny I could lay my hands on, I spent on fireworks: firecrackers Uncle Chris called them. I collected bottles to take back to the off-sales, ran errands, and even went without spuss to build up my stash. A biscuit tin on a shelf at the top of the cellar steps gradually filled up with jumping Jacks, Roman candles, spinning wheels, air bombs, penny cannons, two penny cannons, threepenny cannons, four penny cannons and tanner cannons that could blow your hand off.

The bangers were the best, but I also bought some of the 'Fizzy 'uns' as we called them. They all did the same thing, shooting out loads of sparks about three feet into the air for a minute or so and that was it, but they all had marvellous names like Silver Star Fountains, Golden Showers and Cascading Flashing Moonbeams. Then there were the Volcanoes, Erupting Volcanoes, Bubbling Volcanoes and Cascading Erupting Vesuvius Volcanoes. Names like Screaming Demon, Gushing Erupting Cascading Volcanoes of Death and Blazing Exploding Mountains of Terror were enough to scare the shit out of any young toddler. The colours on the cardboard outer packaging of the fireworks attracted me to the fizzy 'uns. Fiery oranges, yellows and reds with contrasting blues and purples. The loose gunpowder gathered at the bottom of the biscuit tin gave off a strong, fusty sort of metal smell.

Even when I was skint I went into shops just to gaze in awe – or maybe try to swipe the fireworks stacked up on the counter. Selection boxes of Standard, Brock and Lion, costing 5, 10, and 15 bob were displayed on the back shelves. We called round to mates' houses to check out and admire each other's stashes.

The bonfires were everywhere. Travelling to Sheffield or Chesterfield on the top deck of the bus I could see a bonfire every few hundred yards. Any patch of wasteland or cleared slum site had a bonny on it. They came in all shapes and sizes. Some were huge mountains of rubbish, some were just cardboard boxes and paper, others neatly erected with a centre pole in the middle and branches stacked around, looked like Tepee's on a Red Indian reservation.

When the big night finally arrived and the afternoon light began to fade we went round the houses collecting newspapers to get the fire started. Everybody came out, scores of people gathered around the fire as it crackled into life.

No firework safety code existed, we expected to get burnt or injured, it was all part of the fun. If the fireworks said on them, 'Not to be held' we held them. Some said, 'can be held at arm's length' what did they think we were gonna do, hold them under our chins? We chucked bangers and shot molten Roman candle balls at each other. The brave kids let bangers go off in their hands (not the tanner cannons though). The trick was to lightly hold the banger between the first finger and thumb so when it exploded it didn't hurt too much. Tanner rockets launched from milk bottles gave off a 'whoosh' and a few sparks and then vanished into the darkness. Today's rockets, more reminiscent of nuclear missiles and costing as much as a decent second-hand car, give us a glimpse of what World War Three might be like. Groups of mothers with babies in prams did little dances as Jumping Jacks were dropped at their feet. All we got was: "Oooh you little buggers." Unsupervised kids waving sparklers and sucking chunks of bonfire toffee skipped close to the fire. If a chabbie fell in, he just ran to his Mother with his clothes ablaze to be extinguished with a bottle of Tizer.

"Try and be a bit more careful Johnny that coat cost 17/11."

It always seemed to be foggy on Bonny Neet; maybe it was the smoke from a million bonfires from every part of the country all-merging together. When the fires died down we lobbed a few spuds in the ashes. We gave 'em ten minutes then poked them out with sticks. We juggled the balls of charcoal from hand to hand until they cooled down before biting into them. The first centimetre or so was cooked, the middle, still slimy, cold and raw.

As the night wore on, the mums the dads and all the grown-ups went home and left us to it, they knew it was our night and our time. Late into the night we sat around the embers with black hands, lips and teeth, each armed with a stick. The occasional explosions in the distance got fewer and fewer and then stopped altogether. The silence that told us it was all over for another year was sad, yet beautiful. Thousands of young kids all across the land must have felt the same. Next morning at school, half the boys rolled in, swathed in bandages. Oh, how I loved Bonny Neet.

As the 1950s ended, we found out Cammell's Row was to be demolished. We were to be re-housed, in brand spanking new, semi-detached council houses with front and back gardens, running hot water and best of all... a bathroom. A new age dawned, and as the bulldozers revved their engines, the Swinging 60s began.

With a certain twinge of sadness all the Cammell's Row gang turned out to say goodbye when the demolition men laid the old Hump to rest. A massive steel ball on the end of a crane soon reduced it to a pile of rubble. Rumour had it, a workman found a box containing one hundred gold sovereigns hidden in a cranny in old man Bingham's cellar. We hunted around the dust and the ruins for the next couple of days trying to find some more.

View from Cammell's Row in the late 50s. The Masons Arms pub sign, the air raid shelter in the Mason's car park. The Castrol advertising hoarding where we climbed and stoned buses, a couple of young 'uns ready to slide down the pit tip, and the gas works on Mill Lane in the distance

Chapter 2

The times they are a-changin

March the 12th 1960: I should have been at Bramall Lane watching the quarter final FA Cup tie between United and Wednesday, but no, I was dragged off to some cold, old church somewhere or other dressed in a new light-blue suit (with short trousers) and a white carnation pinned to my lapel to watch our Tony get married. I'm certain if me and our Terry had been there to cheer them on, the Blades would have beaten Wednesday and gone on to win the Cup (Wednesday won the game 0-2).

In the summer of 1960 we flitted to 132 Stonelow Road on the Holmesdale estate. The keys were handed over a couple of months before we moved in. We would regularly walk up to the estate as it began to take shape, to check out the new house. The road was still bumpy and unsurfaced; building materials, piles of sand, breeze blocks, dumper trucks and curb stones were strewn all around. Scaffolding surrounded the half-built maisonettes on one side of the street. The house smelt of new wood, paint and plastered walls; it all seemed so fresh and clean. All of the Row residents (although not everyone admitted it) had to move what few belongings they took to the Promised Land, in green painted, council fumigation (stoving)

Brother Tony, marrying a wedding cake

wagons. Our Joan was engaged at the time and made the whole family promise not to tell her fiancé 'The Bug Wagon' moved us.

All the families were kept together; it was just a different, newer version of the old row. We had new lino in the kitchen, a new gas cooker, new beds, and a latest model TV with the ITV channel. The every-night bath I'd promised myself lasted about two days before it was back to the once a week Friday night dip.

The Holmesdale estate was built on land where years before the Parsley Hall rhubarb farm once stood. Acres of ground surrounding the estate still housed the derelict packing sheds and rhubarb still grew as far as the eye could see. We ate it raw, dipped in sugar and had 'Roobub' fights throwing sticks of the stuff at each other. Every Sunday me Mam made a couple of rhubarb pies for tea. In the mid-60s the land was redeveloped into playing fields, but to this day they're still known as the rhubarb fields.

It took a while to get used to the silence at the new house. For the first few weeks I found it hard to sleep. I missed the lullaby of trains slowly clanking through the night and the noise from heavy traffic on the A61 which had stood only two yards from the front doorsteps.

Terry and Joan both got married that year, leaving just Mum, Uncle Chris and me in the new house. My Unk got stuck into the garden straight away. I helped him dig over the front and lay a new lawn. We planted all kinds of vegetables in the back. Unk loved it.

It was around this time when I started to take a real interest in music. I'd grown familiar with Rock 'n' Roll and Skiffle music by listening to our Tony and Joan's 78s. I learnt how to work the gramophone and change the needle after a couple of plays. The needles came in brightly coloured little tin boxes of 100 or 200.

Radio Luxembourg – 208 metres on the medium wave – was the only radio station playing pop music and I tuned in on an old, crackling Bush wireless set as big as a suitcase.

The three-minute 45 single arrived, *Shakin All Over* by Johnny Kidd and the Pirates sent shivers down my backbone. I didn't really know what a Dream Lover was, but I wanted one to come my way. The Red Indian war drums intro to the Shadows' *Apache*, conjured up visions of tomahawks, smoke-signals, Geronimo and his band of braves. The bloke the Shadows backed, had the audacity to attempt to de-throne the King, but just as it was either United or Wednesday, it was Elvis or Cliff, no half measures. So for me, it's Elvis and the Blades. My mate Turnip chose Cliff and Wednesday, poor fucker.

Our Terry still took me to the Lane on occasions, but I'd started to go regularly with a group of older Dronny lads. Toffee Sharpe, Mick McDermott, Crep Keeble, Brownie, Curly Havenhand, Sid Gilbert, Ansh, me and a few others, always boarded the one o'clock train into Sheffield for every Saturday home game. Mick McDermott usually carried a pack of cards and we spent the 15-minute journey playing 3-card brag or pontoon with a bob limit.

After a tanner's worth of chips from the chippie at the bottom of Howard Street we took a steady walk up Shoreham Street to the ground. We sometimes hung around the players' entrance on John Street, hoping to get autographs.

We always stood on the Kop, usually right at the back directly behind the goal. We climbed up and wedged ourselves in between the steel girders that held up the corrugated iron Kop roof. Sometimes we wandered down to the front and leant over the white railings, close enough to smell the embrocation on the players as they warmed up in front of the Kop goal.

The football was easy, unhurried, five forwards attacked, five defenders defended. The halfback passed to the inside forward, who passed to the winger; the winger beat the fullback and crossed to the centre forward who rose like a rocket, hung in mid-air for a few seconds before thundering an unstoppable header into the back of the net. He then shook hands and received a pat on the back from the players nearby and that was it. No, somersaults or back flips, if I'd wanted to see acrobats I'd have gone to the circus. The forwards were expected to score, the wingers were expected to run rings around the fullbacks; it was all about goals. The best footballers were the attackers, greedy for the ball not the money. Fullbacks rarely crossed the halfway line, but on occasions would nip over to blast a thirty-yard screamer into the top corner.

United fielded the same eleven just about every week, Hodgkinson, Coldwell, Shaw, Richardson, Joe Shaw, Summers, Allchurch, Russell, (sometimes Kettleborough) Pace, Hodgson, Simpson.

Derek 'Doc' Pace was my first hero. A small battling, goal machine, centre forward who looked about 50 years old. Most of his goals came from Jack-Knife headers, but some were credited to his large nose. A great trick of Doc's, when on the blind side of the ref, was to rise for a header and punch the ball into the net. The standing joke amongst Blade fans at the time: "Doc Pace hat-trick today, two wi his hand and one wi his nose."

Hodgy, the goalkeeper was (according to the song) better than Yashin. He stood only four-foot two inches tall. A bit short for a goalie you might think, but he was as agile as a young chimpanzee and could leap miles into the air and catch the ball just under the crossbar in one hand. There was only one goalkeeper better than Hodgy in the whole land – Ron Springett, but, alas, the fucker played for Wednesday and was the regular England keeper.

None of the players ever got injured, cos they wore shin pads thicker than the Holy Bible, and nobody got dropped, sent off or booked. If a player did manage to get his leg broke, the trainer ran on and rubbed a bit of butter on it. Within seconds he was back on his feet running around as if nothing had happened. Managers were never sacked; the only way they lost their jobs was if they dropped dead. Many Wednesday managers dropped dead and nobody was any the wiser. If a player got transferred, that was it, no speculation in the newspapers, no shock moves, why is every transfer these days, according to the press, a 'shock'?

Amidst old men in long overcoats and flat caps, young boys looking like war evacuees dressed in short trousers, gabardine rain macs, school caps, or balaclavas. I stood every other week swinging my red and white rattle, watching the dramas on the pitch unfold.

Sometimes we won, sometimes we lost, it was no big deal, no after-match analysis; I just looked forward to the next game. I watched footballers, not super-fit prima donna athletes, but they could, and did, wade their way through six inches of thick mud like it wasn't there and skim an orange ball over a foot of compact snow, no bother.

We usually took the bus to the night matches. The six-mile journey took us along the A61, though Norton and then into Woodseats. As the bus turned the corner just past Woodseats quarry and ran down the hill towards Meersbrook, my heart skipped a beat as the floodlights came into view. I could see the Lane illuminated a mile or so away in the distance. Today's view sees the twin towers of the Lowfield Mosque dominating the skyline.

The night matches were special; magic even, close to a spiritual experience. The artificial glow seemed ten times brighter than daylight and made The Lane appear almost serene. On winter nights the rain and sleet swirled sideways in the glare of the floodlights towering 100 feet above the stadium. When the game started, the dull lights under the Kop roof faded. Gazing out from the darkness the ball flashed across the sacred mud. Directly opposite the corner flag the Shoreham end curved round to the right. Sometimes we stood on the bend behind the white wall. From this vantage point, not only could we see the whole pitch, it also gave a raised, sideways view of the Kop crowd. Every split-second dozens of matches and cig lighters ignited, sparking up cigarettes, cigars and pipes.

As the Blades attacked, the volume of noise slowly increased, reaching a crescendo as the ball hit the back of the net, then thousands of hands and rattles shot into the air. At half time, we queued for lukewarm meat and tater pies and heated our hands on steaming hot cardboard cups of Bovril. I loved the night games.

On Easter Monday 1961, I travelled with the Dronny lads to my first away game. I was nine years old, the Blades, pushing for promotion from the old Second Division played Rotherham United at Millmoor. We all made banners to take to the game, mine: half of a white bed sheet frayed at the ends with UP THE BLADES written in my mother's best red lipstick. We caught a packed train from Sheffield Midland station for the ten-minute journey past the huge steel factories and rolling mills in the east end of the city which merged into Rotherham. All I remember about the game is United winning 2-1, with Len Allchurch scoring the winner in the last minute. At the final whistle we danced in celebration on the edge of the pitch. The train journey back was even worse; with hundreds of fans crammed into a small train I could hardly breathe.

In August '61 a few of us planned to make the trip to Nottingham Forest. The Blades had been promoted and were now playing in the First Division. On the morning of the game, the lads I was going with went into Sheffield, as one of them was buying a new white, lightweight rain mac (all the rage at the time). We'd found out the train times and arranged to meet up on the train to Nottingham that I thought stopped at Dronfield on the way from Sheffield. Bursting with excitement I boarded the train and walked up and down the corridors searching for my mates. The train pulled out of the station. Again, I walked up and down looking in all the compartments, but they were nowhere to be seen. I didn't know what to do. I was ten years old and on a train to Nottingham on my own. Deciding there was nothing I could do I convinced myself the lads would turn up somewhere or other.

Quite a few Blades were on the train and I noticed a gathering around one of the compartments where a lad of about sixteen was holding court. I managed to push my way to the front. He came out with a string of jokes, everyone around was laughing. I clearly remember one of the jokes: "I was shagging this bird last night," he said. "And she shouted out, more rope, more rope, I gave her another inch and she shouted again, more rope, I didn't have any more, so I shoved my bollocks in, more rope she shouted again, but less of the knots."

The jokes carried on all the way to Nottingham helping my dilemma for a while. I decided I would follow Joker and the rest of the crowd up to the ground. We all left the train and I walked a few paces behind them. I reached the ticket barrier and started searching my pockets for the ticket. It wasn't there. "Oh, fuckin hell." Panic set in, I searched and searched and after a few minutes of digging deep I found it in corner of my back pocket. I let out a few sobs of relief and went through. I'd lost Joker and the others, so I just followed the crowd and by asking directions arrived at the City Ground. I went in the first turnstile. I came to on the side terrace, with the Trent End to my right, still convinced I'd find my mates somewhere around.

The ground started to fill up. I moved further and further towards the back, so I could see the pitch. When the game started I was right at the back of the terrace but couldn't see a thing.

At the end of the match, again by asking directions, I made my way back to the station, checking my pockets every couple of minutes to make sure I still had the ticket. To my relief my mates stood on the platform waiting for the train back. They told me they'd caught the train we'd arranged, but it didn't stop at Dronfield. Jack Foster, the lad with the new mac looked a bit pissed off. Some Nottingham lads stood behind him in the ground and burnt holes in his brand-new coat with their cigs.

My first brush with the law came at the age of ten.

I'd just started smoking – again urged on and taught by the older kids, and I thought it was so clever to sit in Dronny park shelter puffing away on a Woodbine or a Park Drive dog end. All my family (except my sister) smoked; everybody on the telly and in the movies smoked. Huge roadside advertising hoardings showed cool, handsome chaps dressed in evening suits or tweed jackets and beautiful model-type, red lipped women with pointed tits, all happily puffing away. Full-page adverts in newspapers and magazines proclaimed: 'Tobacco is good, very good, if you don't smoke then you're a cunt.' The teachers at school smoked. Doctors, brain surgeons and nurses smoked. Everybody smoked, so no wonder I started smoking. All the lads would ask and tell each other how many cigs they each had.

"Got any fags?"

"Yeah, got two and a flip," a flip being a fag that had been smoked halfway down, then flipped or docked. If it had been flipped twice it was known as a little flip. On Sundays my Unk wore his best suit when he went to the boozer for the dinner-time session. The small side pocket of his jacket was always full of Parky flips. I would root them out (along with a tanner or a threepenny bit) while he was asleep. When asked if I'd got any fags on a Sunday I'd answer, "Yeah, I've got eight flips."

"Thaz been in thi uncle's flip pocket again then, Ron!"

Older lads who had plenty of fags would save us their dog-ends, but you had to bags it first. If someone bagged before you and you smoked it, a scrap was on the cards.

So, this Sunday afternoon we're at Dronny park and in walks Malcolm Robinson, who was in my class at school. He whipped out a full 20 packet of cigs. Now this was unheard of amongst the young smoking fraternity. Nobody ever had a twenty pack. If two or three lads sometimes clubbed together there might be a ten-packet knocking around, but it was usually a five or a three Domino packet. The Dominoes came in a paper carton and cost 6d. Malc was weird kid and a bit of a loner. His pear-shaped head was covered in snow-white, tight-knitted curls, he went by the nickname of – Curly Pear. He'd been an accomplished burglar since the age of one and was forever helping the police with their inquiries. Anyone who didn't know Curly could be fooled into thinking the lad was a swot, as he entered the school gates with his satchel bulging at the seams, but instead of maths, English and geometry books, the bag contained pounds of scrumped apples or piles of spice swiped from the corner shop. Curly told us there were plenty more cigs where they came from.

Two or three of us followed him to the works canteen of Sullivan's steel factory just down the road from the park. We climbed through an open window Pear had earlier prised open with his penknife and went behind the snack bar counter. He opened a cabinet packed with many different brands of cigarettes. Pear told us to take just one packet each then nobody would ever know – very wise, but then again, he was a ten-year-old hardened criminal. We took a packet each and a couple of chocolate bars from the shelves and climbed back out. We went back to the park, losing Pear on the way.

Half an hour later, along with a few more mates we went back and cleared out the lot. The cigs were hidden in various places, but word soon got around.

Pear was arrested and split on us all. When the coppers came knocking we in turn unashamedly grassed each other up.

The police decided not to prosecute, as most of the cigs were recovered. It was left to the school headmaster to dish out our punishment and old man Taylor certainly knew how to lay the stick on.

"Which hand do you write with Sharpe?"

"Right sir."

"Left hand out then, boy. Come on lad, hold it up."

Curly Pear, had an older brother 'Sugar' Roy Robinson. He had the same, snow-white, tight-knitted curls as his brother. One of the older Dronny lads told me a great story about when Sugar and a couple more Dronny lads went down Woodseats in Sheffield looking for women. They pulled a couple of birds, and the night after went to meet them again. This time a gang of Woodseats lads were waiting. One of them pulled out an iron bar and whacked Sugar on the head. Sugar never flinched, he just rubbed his head and said: "Giowa, av had trouble wi mi head before."

The great inventions of the 20th century paled into insignificance with the coming of the Rizla machine. One day in the park a few of us mooched around without a cig between us. One of the older lads arrived and announced: "I've got a machine that makes fags."

"Fuuuuck ooooff, ya havin us on," one of the lads said. There were different ways of telling mates to "Fuck off." A long drawn out "Fuuuuck ooooff" said with a smile was okay, a nasty quick "Fuck off" said with aggression, meant you had to be able to back it up. Nobody ever called a mate "cunt" unless they could beat them (or thought they could beat them) in a scrap.

"Right," he said, "go down to the shelter and get me some doggers and I'll show ya." (There was always some dog ends, under and around the benches in the park shelter).

We scuttled down and came back with handfuls of mucky flat flips. Some people just stood on the dog ends to put them out, but other sadistic bastards screwed them into the ground making them completely useless. He took a small device about three inches long out of his pocket and opened the rollers under a red rubber tube. He then broke open the doggers, poured in the tobacco, evened it out, closed the tube and rolled it round a few times. Taking out a packet of Rizla papers, he carefully slipped one in the tube, gently rolling it down with both thumbs until only the sticky bit was visible. He licked the sticky bit, rolled it round a few times, opened it up and out popped a fag, a bit thinner maybe, but as good as any Parky or Woody I'd ever seen. We gazed open-mouthed in amazement. We were in the presence of a magician.

The lad told us the Rizla machines cost nine pence and could be bought from any tobacconist. There were tobacconist shops in most of the towns and villages. They were usually the smallest shop in town and sold everything a smoker could possibly wish for, but little else, except for some strange reason: walking sticks. Pipes, pouches of pipe tobacco, pipe cleaners, cigars, cig lighters, cig cases (some of the flash kids owned lighters and cases) and hundreds of different varieties of cigarettes including exotic brands, such as Passion Cloud and Black Russian. Cocktail cigs came in fancy boxes and were all different pastel colours with gold tips.

A couple of us bought Rizla machines and we roamed the streets picking up doggers from the pavements. These were known as 'Gutter brand'. After a few weeks the novelty wore off and we were back to buying the five packets or nicking them from our parents.

Not only did we nick cigs off our mums and dads, we also nicked matches. Swan Vesta were the best: a dozen or so could easily be robbed from the box without anybody being any the wiser. There were plenty of places to strike the matches: walls, pavements, with our finger nails, between our teeth, on the heels of our shoes, but the favoured place was the metal zip on our jeans. All my jeans had a pink zip, with minute burns all around where tiny bits of sulphur had burst into flames on the cloth. I always kept my matches in the back pocket of my jeans, until during a game of footie in the park, while performing a sliding tackle the matches rubbed together and ignited, burning a hole in my jeans and scorching my arse.

In January 1962, Terry took a couple of mates and me in his car to Bury for a 3rd round FA Cup match.

Inside the ground we met a couple of Dronny lads who'd travelled by train. They told us a group of Blades on the train threatened them and nicked their scarves (first case of taxing?) After a 0-0 draw and a 2-2 draw at the Lane, the 2nd replay was played at Hillsborough. Hoisting my new cardboard 'Bertie Blade' on the end of a stick, I watched Doc Pace net two goals to put us in the next round.

Terry took me to Peterborough for the 4th round tie. The Blades again did the business, winning 3-1. Before the game we saw Jimmy Hagan, Peterborough's manager at the time. Terry had a good chat to him and it made his day. Hagan gave me a pat on the head, and his autograph. Great stuff.

After another 3-1 home win against Norwich in round 5 we were drawn to play Burnley at the Lane in the quarter final.

It was a great time to be a Blade; Doc Pace, be it with foot, head, hand, or nose, scored every week. Along with a load of schoolmates in a crowd of 57,000, I stood on the Kop side of the cricket pavilion to see Burnley win the game 1-0. We were only a few yards away from a perimeter fence that collapsed, injuring many people. Everybody reckoned the Ray Pointer goal that won the game had hit him on the head. Years later I saw a British Pathé newsreel film of the match, and it turned out to be a clever, glancing header that Doc Pace would have been proud of.

SHEFFIELD UNITED   *Bertie Blade mascot*

The early 60s lazy summers we spent in Dronny Park, which always sempt to be permanently bathed in sun. We played football, cricket, or just hung around for hours and hours doing absolutely nothing. Sometimes the footie games were tight; after a couple of hours or so, the scores could reach thirty-five – all. Lesser players as a rule kept the score, adding a couple on or taking them off. Next goal winner usually decided it. We rowed and fought over whether the ball had gone over the bar or over the post (coat). The bar we defended was four-foot high – the one we attacked about twelve. If the games were too one-sided, a couple of the better players swapped teams to even it up.

Sunday's Pick of the Pops broadcast on the BBC Light Programme was the highlight of the week. The first hour played all the new releases and then came the eagerly awaited top twenty. We sprawled out in the shade under trees, cigs in hands, taking in the sounds from a small hissing transistor radio. Sometimes, girls who would let you have a bit turned up; they were taken up to the wooded area at the top of the park.

The whole universe centred on Dronny Park. The tarmac playground surrounded by spiked railings was a death trap. The bobby's helmet, a large roundabout, didn't only spin round at two hundred miles an hour it also bounced in and out. A thin steel framework all the way around it allowed us to climb up the sides and even to the top where it narrowed out to a point. It could easily hold twenty young kids who swung and hung upside down from the bars, like troops of baboons. Kids often fell off or were hit if they stood too near. As many as ten lads would spin it round then dive on as it gathered speed, get the timing wrong and we were scraped along the asphalt.

The main culprit though was 'The Plank'. A twelve-foot long plank of wood hanging horizontally from two steel bars attached to a metal framework. Four passengers could sit on the structure, holding on to steel handles bolted to the plank. Two lads, one stood at each end, swayed backwards and forwards to work the plank up. Whoever designed the device must have been a madman, or a sadist, probably both. It swung backwards and forwards gradually getting higher and higher. At full height the lads who worked it up could stamp their foot on the back end of the plank to smash it onto the metal frame. I've seen terrified young lads and toddlers, even the older lads screaming, crying and begging for mercy as their heads got closer and closer to the bar. It was a fine art and we could work it and time it to take it within a few inches of someone's head, or, if they were crouched over, make their backs touch the bar. Of course, there were accidents: heads were cut open and backs cracked. I saw one lad ride past on his pushbike, the plank hit him at the side of his head and we all thought he was a gonner.

The Plank was a rites-of-passage vehicle. It wasn't enough just to learn to work it up. Anybody worth their salt, could and would, with the plank at its full height and in full swing, leap from one end, land on their stomach on the framework, forward roll over and land on their feet in one movement. It took some bottle to do it the first time, but after a while we could do it in our sleep.

During the six weeks school holidays there were so many kids in the paddling pool they were lucky to get their feet wet. Groups of lads with bleeding knees queued for the slide; buffed up by a thousand raggy arses, it got so fast, unsuspecting belly flopping toddlers shot off the end and kissed the tarmac.

"Bummer Albert's here, run." Albert Taylor, the friendly neighbourhood paedophile, hung outside the park bogs offering young lads (he wasn't interested in girls) a threepenny bit or a tanner to go in the toilets to look at his stang. Always smartly dressed he wore a collar and tie, white rain mac and a trilby hat. To us, he looked about sixty years old, but was probably only in his forties. The older kids warned the young 'uns to keep away from him. If he approached us we either told him to fuck off or threw bricks at him. The park keeper,

Cheyenne, stood about four foot tall. Cheyenne was cruelly nicknamed after Cheyenne Bodie from the TV series *Wagon Train* played by Clint Walker, a seven-foot giant. If Cheyenne saw Albert in the park he'd threaten to kill him and chase him off. Sometimes the police were called, but Albert always protested his innocence. He was around for years, but strange as it may seem today, he was somewhat tolerated; no one ever beat him up or tried to run him out of town. Dirty old men were just part of life back then. Even to this day the old Dronny lads call anyone of the bum bandit persuasion 'Albert.'

September 1962, after failing the eleven plus exam, I moved, along with the rest of the factory fodder to the Gladys Buxton secondary modern school, togged out in my new school uniform purchased from Chesterfield Co-op with a clothing grant. Low-income and one-parent families on National Assistance were awarded the grant every year to help with the cost of school clothing. There was only enough money for a cheap, shitty, navy blue blazer, grey flannels, a couple of white nylon shirts and a light grey v-necked jumper. I soon ditched the blazer after scrounging an old black one from a mate. I got a pair of black trousers from a jumble sale and lobbed the grey jumper and kaks.

All the first and second-year boys had to wear school caps, (the girls wore straw boaters or bonnet things). Every pupil had to wear the black, yellow and light blue school tie. We only ever wore the caps when entering or leaving the school gates, but woe-betide anybody who was spotted by a teacher walking home bare-headed.

The brand new school opened in 1960 to cater for the kids from the council estates on the east side of town. The kids who lived on the west side of the valley went to the Gosforth secondary modern. The dividing line being the A 61 main road that ran through the town centre.

The eleven-plus passers (the Grammar Dogs) were schooled at the Henry Fanshaw grammar school on Dronny Bottom. They swanned around in flash red and blue blazers with a coat of arms on the breast pocket and the Latin school motto 'Cleverus Cuntus' embroided underneath.

All the best-looking birds went to Henry Fanshaw's; the lads though were all ugly fuckers, so it evened itself out.

A lot of the older lads I knocked about with were already at Gladys Buxton, so I was excused the trauma of the big step up. Listening to the stories from the older kids, I knew which teachers to avoid and to be wary of. I also knew about the ones who were reasonable, so certain liberties could be taken. We were still screamed at, slapped, belittled, pushed around and generally bullied by our new tutors. Not that we didn't deserve it; heinous crimes such as laughing, or farting were more than frowned upon.

Polly Perkins, the maths teacher and deputy headmaster, was a larger version of Adolf Hitler. A swarthy dark-haired, military-type bastard with a little tash, whose very presence screamed out order and authority. Even the other teachers feared him, never mind the pupils. On the day I started school, Polly wore a dark grey suit, light blue shirt and a maroon coloured tie. He wore the same attire, four years later the day I left.

If he approached us in the corridor or walked into the school yard everyone fell silent. The maths room, his domain, had a strange, deathly, unnatural feeling about it. No one fucked about, laughed or even spoke unless spoken to, during a maths lesson. The class comedians suddenly lost their sense of humour for forty-five minutes and the farters squeezed in the cheeks of their arses. Young kids who brought messages to his room stood quaking in their boots as they waited for his reply.

He'd slipper us for slightest reason. A dropped book or even a scraped chair could bring on his wrath. Polly really put his heart and soul into laying on the slipper.

It was rumoured he was a die-hard Blades fan and had been seen on occasions at the Lane. No one ever had the balls to ask him. I can just imagine him stood on the Kop, chilled out, red and white scarf tied round his head, shouting: "Come on, you fuckin red and white wizards."

Most of the teachers had nicknames, but all were called Old Man or Old Lass whatever their second names were. We all reckoned the teachers were shagging each other. We used to write shit in the back of our jotters (which were never checked) things like, 'Old Man Shaw, fucks Old Lass Davenport' then cross out fucks, after it got a laugh and write loves instead.

As a fully paid up member of the smoker's club, I had my fair share of thrashings. The morning, afternoon and dinnertime breaks meant that we had three chances a day of getting caught. We would alternate the smoking locations on a weekly or even a daily basis, but we were caught many times. When three or four of us were nabbed together, getting caught smoking was no big deal. We would walk down the corridor to the headmaster's office or Polly's room if we were sent to him, nervously giggling and nudging each other.

Getting caught on your own was a different matter. I had been made to stay in during the first break for some kind of bad behaviour and missed my morning nicotine fix. I nipped off to the bog for a few drags during the next lesson; the teacher followed me, caught me and sent me down to receive my punishment. I shuffled along, dragging my heels trying to put off the inevitable. I knocked on the headmaster's door and heard the shout, just one word: "Come."

In I walked, and a beaming Old Man Eyre called out "Ronald... what can I do for you"?

So, Ronald is it, not Sharpe or boy, strange I thought. Across from the headmaster, an elderly lady, wearing a giant hat and a multi-coloured flowing frock lounged in a comfy chair.

"I've been smoking sir," I answered.

"Oooooh," the lady said. "You'll never grow, you know, if you smoke," she was right as well: I never did reach the dizzy heights of over five foot six.

"Excuse me for one moment," the head said as he led me out of the room. He closed the door behind us and bounced me off the opposite wall. He grabbed my lapels and held my face half an inch from his own, hissing out like a snake: "Do you know who that lady is?"

Fuck knows I thought, is she the Queen Mother?

43

"I'll tell you who she is shall I, its Mrs Gladys Buxton."

Shit, I thought, so this is she, the one and only, Gladys, who our fine school had been named after.

"Get back to your lesson," he screamed. "I'll deal with you later." I slunk off and when Old Gladys had been whisked off in a chauffeur driven limo, I was dragged from my classroom, told that I had shown the headmaster up, brought shame on the good name of the school and given a damn good beating. The size twelve slipper had replaced the cane used by the Headmaster of the junior school. I couldn't make my mind up, which was worse, stinging fingers or a stinging arse.

Hector the protector of the woodwork room, a Mr Edward Hector Kyme used a leather strap. Hector, a nasty, ancient, bald fucker taught woodwork, metalwork and gardening. Gardening, now that really was an education. Twenty lads stood in a row with crippling wood and steel clogs on our feet, armed with spades and forks. We were taught how to hold the tools, press them in to the ground with our feet, turn over the soil, break it up and arrange it into neat rows – and that was the extent of a gardening lesson. Any messing about would see Hector freak out and hit us on any part of the body with the strap: arse, hand, back of the neck, head, anywhere. Another trick of his was to hit us over the head with any piece of shit we had made in the woodwork lesson that wasn't to his liking.

I was only really interested in the games lessons, where we played football or cricket during the summer months. I represented the school at both sports at all levels. I was shit at running though (the 100 yards, the 220, the mile). Running around at football was necessary, that's what you had to do to get the ball. Running round a track in circles seemed pointless and a complete waste of time. I was even worse at the cross-country runs. The runs were about three of four miles around the woods at the back of the school. The sports teacher came with us a couple of occasions, but most times we were sent on our own. About half a dozen of us would run out of the school gates and straight into our house, just around the corner where we supped tea, smoked and played snooker for an hour or so. We'd watch through the front room window for the first lads coming back, give it ten minutes then nip out, just in front of the fat kids at the rear, who huffed and puffed their way up the hill back on to the school field.

When the annual school cross-country race took place, we were fucked. Markers were positioned at various points along the route and our names were ticked off as we passed. The smokers would have a cig and match rolled up in the bottom of their shorts and stop for a few quick drags on the way round. Even some of the fatties made it back to school before we did.

We had decent football sides all through school; cricket though was a different matter. In my last year at the school the under 15s played a home game against the Abbeydale Grange School from Sheffield. We had played them at football a few months earlier and beaten them 4-0 and even though we weren't all that good at cricket we were confident of doing okay.

We just managed to scrape eleven players together for the game including a couple of fatties to make up the numbers. Abbeydale arrived and walked into the changing room. We all fell silent.

I thought the West Indies tourists had turned up. Most of the team were big, black and bad.

"Bleedin hell," one of our lads whispered to me. "They're all blackies."

"I know," I whispered back. "I'm not bleedin blind."

The blackies changed into immaculate cricket whites and studded cricket boots. None of us had any of the gear, but most managed to root out a white shirt. The rest of the kit consisted of jeans and either skimpy plimsolls or Cuban heel boots.

In the warm-up the Sheffield lads swung professional looking bats, doing mock forward and backwards defensive strokes. They wore proper cricket caps and snow white pads. We had two bats to choose from: a massive one I could barely lift and the other was about as big as a rounder's bat and a fast ball would knock it clean out of your hands. The pads we wore were more of a grey colour than white, with broken straps and the tops hanging off.

Abbeydale batted first. I fancied myself as a bit of a fast bowler. After a couple of overs from the two opening bowlers (one was me) the score reached about 50 for none. Shining up the ball on my bollocks hadn't worked, but it had given me a semi. As a punishment I was banished by our teacher/coach, who doubled as one of the umpires, to the long-on boundary. A couple of 6s had already sailed miles over my head when a Garfield Sobers type hooked another in my direction. The ball whistled towards me like a guided missile. I heard shouts from the teacher and my team mates: "Catch it Sharpe, catch it."

Like fuck I thought, it'll have me hands off. I crouched down, legs bent like a frog, hands cupped above my head, teeth gritted, and eyes shut tight. I heard it whizz past me and thanked God it hadn't snapped my fingers.

"What's up wi thi Sharpy, why dint tha catch it?" one of my team mates shouted.

"Why dunt tha come and stand here and catch it thissen," I shouted back.

Abbeydale amassed a huge total and had to declare, as we couldn't get any of them out and the sun was going down.

As I walked out to bat at number five the score was 0 for 4. I chose the large bat, reasoning it would cover more of the stumps than the smaller one. After a hundred-yard run up Wesley Hall thundered down the wicket towards me. I didn't even see the ball as it flashed past me, the wicket keeper and then the slips. 4 byes. Yes, we were on the scoreboard and flying. 4 for 4. The next ball shattered my stumps. A few more byes and lucky snicks took our total to a respectable 20-odd all out.

The Abbeydale lads were all very sporting and considerate in their annihilation. As we clapped them from the field they shook our hands, saying "Hard luck," and "Well played." It was standard practice to give the opposing team three cheers at the end of whatever sport we played. Our captain would shout: "Three cheers for (whatever name of the school we were playing), Hip-hip." If we'd won it was a rousing "Haraaaay." If we lost we mumbled "Ray."

"Three cheers for Abbeydale Grange... Hip-Hip"... "Ray"... "Hip-hip,"...

"Ray." "Hip-Hip"… (barely audible) "Ay."

I didn't give a shit about the other lessons; I knew where I was heading. We got no encouragement or help from the teachers because they didn't give a shit either; they just moved us along the conveyor belt, year after year until they were finally rid of us.

I'd been pretty average all the way through school, never rising to the A group, but never falling to the C. I was a B lad, like most of my mates. The B lads were the elite. A, lads were looked down on and clipped for being too clever, but nobody wanted to be in the C group and be classed as thick. In our final year they changed the way we were categorised. Those staying on to take the A levels were in the class 4X. The O level students were 4Y and the levers, 4Z. 4Z eh! It doesn't get much lower than that.

School memories are many and varied: some just brief flashbacks, fondly remembered. Other bad recollections stick inside your head and never ever leave you. From an early age, infant school, in fact, I was always aware class discrimination existed. I knew who were rich, poor, working class, and middle class. I knew none of the lads from Cammell's Row would be playing the sultan or the captain of the ship at the Christmas pantomime. We'd be seen in the school photo, stood on the back row dressed as eunuchs or able seamen.

The education system in the 50s and 60s left much to be desired. I accepted the slipper the cane, the straps and the slaps, because most of the time I deserved them. What I couldn't accept was the humiliation of being dragged to the front of the classroom, ridiculed, told I was a scruffy, useless good-for-nothing who was going nowhere fast.

"Get out, smarten yourselfs up, you're a disgrace."

The rest of class laughed out loud at my shame and embarrassment, egging the teachers on to be even crueller. This happened to some of my mates as well, but never to the posh kids or the swots.

Another form of shame the teachers inflicted on some of us was the issue of free school meals. Every morning they took the register, shouting out the names of all the pupils to which we answered, "Here."

Then came the dinner register where those who stayed for school meals paid the teacher. After this came the names of the two or three of us who were awarded free meals. The teachers knew we were in the class because they'd just taken the register, so why did they have to shout our names out for free meals every morning? The free dinners and the school uniforms were the only awards I ever received during my ten years of schooling.

The one thing that really brought home the class divide to me was the school trips. Not the Manchester airport, Belle View Zoo, Great Yorkshire Show, Liverpool Docks trips, which were all affordable, fantastic, riotous occasions. We brought in our pennies, threepenny bits, tanners, bobs, every week until the fee was paid.

The elite school trips were something else. The first one came about when I was in the second year of senior school. The chosen few were to be taken on an, 'educational' skiing holiday to Austria, Switzerland or some snowy place somewhere or other. Educational? what were they going to do, learn how to fuckin yodel? All this done on a first come first served basis. Nothing to do with merit or ability but everything to do with money. The price of the trip... well, it could have been £20, £50, £100 who knows? But what I did know was that it ruled me out and it ruled out about 95% of the other kids in the school.

The next trip came when I was in my final year. Now this one took the biscuit. Again billed as an educational trip, this was (can you believe it) a Mediterranean cruise, taking in the French Riviera, Spain, Morocco, Turkey, Timbuktu and other various sun-drenched destinations. Not many kids at that time had been much further than Bridlington, let alone to any foreign shores. Roughly the same fifteen-twenty kids who had been skiing and maybe the same three or four teachers who accompanied them, again signed up for the jolly. A lad in my class, who couldn't even spell his own name, was suddenly acknowledged by the teachers for the simple reason, his parents were loaded, and he'd paid the full amount for the trip in one go. Every morning the teachers gave us the countdown: "Only 16 days to go before the Mediterranean cruise sets sail."

We were expected to be excited.

Then the day finally arrived, to a fanfare of trumpets, off they went on an air-conditioned coach bound for Southampton to board a luxury liner and sail off somewhere behind the sun.

We were given progress reports and shown maps of where they would be on certain days. Then it was over, at last, or so we thought. After they were applauded back into the morning assembly I sighed a mighty sigh of relief. But no, it wasn't over, far from it. There was still another crock of shit to ram down our throats. We had to sit through hundreds of slides of the trip at a special screening that all the school was made to attend. We had to smile, we had to pretend.

The most significant thing I ever learned at school, was that the system stank, one rule for the rich and one for the rest: money doesn't talk, it swears. I don't blame or begrudge any of the kids who went, or any of the parents who paid for them to go. I blame the education board, the administration or whoever allowed such terrible shit to happen. I blame the useless headmaster and the spineless teachers, for making the kids with the money feel even more special and for making me, feel worthless.

Harry Hall's travelling funfair came to the town every summer. It was always a special, magical occasion. The fair pitched on wasteland next to William Lee's iron foundry. In mid-July in the late 1950s early 60s as soon as the home-time school bell rang, we sprinted to the site to watch lorries and trailers stacked high with the carnival drive up Callywhite Lane. Tied on twenty-foot lengths of clothesline to the backs of caravans, scabby, wild fairground mongrels growled and snarled if we went too near. Their owners were even more fearsome. Every day we gathered and watched in awe as all the main rides took shape. The Waltzer, the Dodgems and Noah's Ark.

The sideshows were erected around the perimeter. Stalls sold cowboy hats and silver plastic guns, Red Indian feathered headdresses, wooden bows with fluffy handles and arrows with red rubber suckers on the end. At the rifle range, sharp shooters shot lead pellets from chained up air rifles with twisted sights; aiming to knock down tiny metal targets shaped like little men. Hit 'em on the head and down they went. Six wins for a carnival glass bowl, four wins for a cuddly toy, and two wins for a goldfish. Goldfish (so it's said) have a memory span of six seconds; well these little fuckers had a life span of about the same. Handed over in cellophane bags the fish were on their last fins and even if they made the journey home, they would be stone dead by the next morning.

In the early 60s we congregated outside the fairground entrance at 6 o'clock on the first Friday evening of the week long stint; half a crown or five bob burning holes in our pockets. My Uncle Chris always gave me five bob on the first Friday. Friday was payday. All the adults got paid on Friday. At a tanner a go, I had enough dosh for ten rides.

The fairground livened up on warm, late Saturday evenings. By then we were skint, all our money spent in the first hour. We watched Gene Vincent style ton-up kids and Teddy boys posing on the steps of the Waltzer. Drunken men in their best suits, who'd staggered up from the Midland and the Swan pubs tried to win coconuts to impress their pals and girlfriends. Jackets off, and white shirtsleeves rolled up high, they threw wooden balls that smacked and echoed against a dented steel back plate if the target was missed. Loose nettings draped around the sides of the stall stopped the balls from ricocheting back. The nearest coconuts must have been glued to their stands, because even a direct hit couldn't budge them. When one of the nuts at the back wobbled off its bed of sawdust and dropped to the ground, we all cheered. The chucker received backslaps and handshakes from mates and onlookers. The stallholders stood expressionless through the whole proceedings; they'd seen it all before.

The smell of hot dogs, fried onions, candyfloss and toffee apples blended with the aroma of industrial diesel, powering huge humming generators on the backs of lorries. I could hear the buzz of the fairground as well as feel it. Brand new pop songs hammered out and we were off, this was it. We raced in and headed straight for the Waltzer.

All of us coming of age, we'd started noticing the girls. Strange sexual stirrings both aroused and confused us. Afraid to chat up girls for fear of rejection, I admired the lads with the courage to ask a lass to accompany them on the dodgems.

With our gobs full of Beechnut chewing gum, we slouched casually on the wooden railing circling the Waltzer. Loose fitting, red and black or blue and black striped shirts, skin-tight Jet brand black jeans with turn-ups and green stitching on the seams was the latest style. Two inches of comb stuck out of the zipped back pocket gave the outfit its finishing touch. Our hair styled in post Teddy boy, greasy, brilliantine quiffs, we tapped long, pointed winkle picker shoes to the beat of the music.

After weeks and weeks of waiting, my first pair of winks finally arrived, courtesy of the catalogue. I kept taking them out of the box, unwrapping the thin

48

transparent paper (later to be used as luxury bog roll), sticking my nose inside the shoes to smell the brand new leather, trying them on, then putting them back in the box, trying them on again, then lifting the mirror off the front room wall and placing it on the floor for a close up look. They were almost too good to wear. I had to put cotton wool in the end of the right shoe, as my mangled foot was about two inches shorter than my left one.

The latest music blasted out from large speakers suspended from the roofs of the rides. Del Shannon's *Runaway* with its wailing organ solo could have been written especially for the Waltzer. Groups of teens and pre-teens stood around the boards stamping their feet in unison to the lead break in Joe Brown and the Bruvvers *Picture of You*.

The Red Indian war drums intro to Chris Montez's *Let's Dance*, 'Hey baby won't you take a chance.' Screaming youngsters scrambled and fought to squeeze inside the brightly painted high backed cars, safety rails raised and held out by our feet in a show of bravery.

"Gizza spin mister."

If we got lucky the blokes who worked the Waltzer would spin us; this was usually reserved for the girls though. Sometimes three or four lads worked on one car full of hysterical girls for the whole duration of the three-minute ride, while we bobbled along leaning one way and then the other trying to make the car spin on its own. When we did get a good spin, the gravitational force pulled our heads back in a mixture of terror and ecstasy. Some kids couldn't take it, some leaned forward and spewed.

We were all scared of the fair blokes; they were nasty, rough, scruffy-looking, gypsy-type lads, covered in tattoos. I couldn't help admiring their skills, though, as they skipped and danced along the rolling boards dodging the spinning cars. If one slipped down or got clipped by a car we had to stifle our laughter in case they saw us and took their vengeance out on us. The girls though, went all giggly and weak at the knees after a few spins on the Waltzer or some pole gymnastics on the back of a dodgem car. We watched in envy as the girls were led by the hand into their caravans or nearby bushes.

The older lads told us the fair lads never fought one on one. If you had a scrap with one of them, all the rest would join in. I suppose they had to stick together and look out for each other, turning up in a new town every week, and moving in on the local talent meant jealous boyfriends and husbands.

The women who worked the fair were just as bad. Hard-faced, sharp-tongued fuckers, with a couple of half-dressed, bare-footed, hot-dog ketchup-faced chabbies clung to their skirts. If they caught us cheating on the Roll a Penny stall we were in deep shit. We hung around the slots hoping to find an odd penny stuck up the chute or better still, hoping someone would win the jackpot on the tanner machine and treat us all to a ride. Why anyone risked putting a tanner – the price of a ride on the Waltzer, in a slot machine was beyond me. Anybody older than the age of five who was spotted on one of the babby rides were verbally destroyed for the rest of their lives.

When dusk fell, the lights flashed and sparkled. The music grew louder, and the rides seemed twice as fast. I left the fairground in a daze, buzzing and drunk on the whole experience; I couldn't wait to get back the next day. It sempt like the end of the world when the fair packed up and moved on to the next town.

We watched the last lorries pull out and then searched every inch of the flattened grass for lost money.

Shoreham end 1962

Boxing Day 1963, and this time I made sure my mates were around as I boarded the train to Nottingham for the game with Forest. Football fans were now starting to travel in larger numbers to away games on the trains. Quite a few of the older Dronny lads, some as old as fifteen and sixteen, came along and headed straight for a boozer when we left the station. The younger ones amongst us hung outside the pub freezing to death. Mick McDermott came out and gave me a sip of his beer, I wanted to like it, but it tasted like shit. How could anybody enjoy this stuff? I pretended it was all right and tried not to grimace. After a couple of pints, the older lot came out and we walked up to the ground.

We went into the open end behind the goal and stood with a group of fellow Uniteditites; mostly young lads numbering maybe a couple of hundred or so. The Blades went 3-0 down after about ten minutes but came back to draw 3-3 with our new hero, Mick Jones, scoring in the last minute. When the equaliser went in, I swayed, surged and hugged complete strangers; it was marvellous. At the end of the game we invaded the pitch, but soon scampered off again when a copper scutched Piggy Bacon round the ear hole.

As I moved into 1964 and reached the tender age of thirteen, the most important things in my life were, in no particular order, Sheffield United, clothes and the Rolling Stones. From the moment I saw the Stones on *Thank Your Lucky Stars*, I was hooked. Their long-haired, rebellious image was so fascinating to a pubescent lad on the lookout for fun. I'm gonna be a Rock 'n' Roll star, a Rollin Stone, I'm gonna be Brian Jones, I told myself. I had a head start, blond hair just like my hero; I just needed to grow it.

Long hair, now there's a thing. So, I'm thirteen years old and my hair's just covering half of my ears, but even that was considered outrageous. The older age group couldn't quite grasp it. Elderly ladies who I passed in the street turned their heads and tutted, some screamed in horror, others fainted. Grown men huffed and puffed, mumbling, "I've never seen anything like it. Bloody disgusting."

Building site workers shouted hilarious comments like, "Is it a boy or a girl? Tha can't tell em apart these days."

"Gizza a kiss love."

"Where's ya handbag darling?"

"Narthen Ringo, sing us one," then they fell about laughing.

I thought, Ringo's a fuckin drummer, ya stupid old cunt, but I just flobbed on the floor and went along my merry way.

Some folk had scientific theories on the subject. Someone, who no doubt had a university degree in hair maintenance and management, told me that being a boy (or was *it* a girl!) and by growing my hair, it would become weak and by the time I got to twenty-one, it would all have fallen out. Wow-ee, pretty scary, by the time I reached twenty-one I would be an old man and wouldn't give a fuck. The surprising thing though, it was tolerated at school. Only half a dozen lads at the most in the whole school had long hair. A lot of my mates would have loved to have grown their hair but were forbidden by overzealous parents still stuck in the 1940s.

Already a full-grown man by the time I was born, our Terry came from a different generation. He had different values and morals, different tastes in music and different heroes. He'd never been able to handle what Mum had done and who could really blame him? It must have been bad enough being illegitimate as a youngster in the 1930s, but then he had to suffer the shame of Mum having four more kids. I never once saw him show any love or affection towards me Mam, because he could never quite bring himself to forgive her. Mum, in spite of this would never hear a bad word said about him (or indeed any of her kids).

As a nipper I had a few digs aimed at me about not having a dad: "Tha ant even gorra Fatha Sharpy," but I tried not to let it upset me. As I got older it became less and less important until it didn't really matter at all. Some of my mates were scared to death of their dads. They had to be in at certain times, wear what they were told to wear, and do what they were told to do. It was still a male dominated society; women fetched the coal in, washed the dishes and emptied the piss pot. Men went out to work, expected their tea on the table when they got in, went out and got pissed, clipped the kids, abused and sometimes even battered the missus. I didn't have to put up with any of that shit.

I could twist my Mum around my little finger. My Uncle Chris (who'd never married or had kids) gave me all the good things a father would give a son. A kind, humorous and gentle bloke, who made me laugh, told me crazy stories, jokes and tall tales. He bought me clothes, presents and gave me money. Never once did he scold me or tell me off. I was spoilt rotten. The one thing I lacked was discipline; I thought I could do anything I wanted.

Terry couldn't understand the long hair; he threatened to kill me if I didn't get it cut. He was only doing what he thought was right though. It wasn't just the hair; I'd been in trouble with the police a few times and was turning into a little shit. Terry got to hear about this and tried to keep me in line. I avoided him for weeks, keeping out of the house when I knew he was visiting my mother or my uncle. If I saw his car outside I would wait for hours hid behind a wall at the end of the street until he left.

He made it his mission to get me and when he finally did, he pinned me against the wall and threatened me with all kinds of shit, saying he'd have me sent to the homes. I reluctantly agreed to see the barber, just to keep the peace as my mum was crying and in a right state. I hated him for months after, but even though I was scared shitless of him I promised myself he'd never make me do it again and he never did.

My first guitar was a little Spanish number with a sunburst finish, white plastic scratch plate, tortoiseshell plectrum and a length of multi coloured rope for a strap. Even though I knew my Uncle Chris had bought it, I'll never forget the thrill of opening up the box on Christmas morning, smelling the new polished wood and hearing the strings twang for the first time. It cost my Unk ten guineas out of the catalogue and must have took him months to it pay off. About six months later I'd learned the first eight notes of the Shadows *Apache*.

Every Wednesday night we flocked to Coal Aston village hall to watch a local group, Ian and the Drumbeats. The Drumbeats were our band, they belonged to us, we knew all their first names and felt honoured if they said hello to us. They wore silver suits and played all the Shadows numbers. They even had the Shadows walk off to a tee, crossing their front legs over and walking backwards as they reached the edge of the stage.

The Drumbeats

They also performed old rock 'n' roll classics, plus some of the latest pop hits. During Jerry Lee Lewis's classic *Whole Lotta Shakin* the three guitarists did a little choreographed dance, kicking their right legs in the air in the "Shake baby shake" bit. The highlight of the evening – the Coasters *I'm A Hog For You Baby* – when the lead guitarist, dressed in a loincloth and covered in fake blood, leapt around the stage like a mad man.

The older girls jived together on the dance floor. We ran around the hall pushing each other, like little kids at a wedding reception, only brave enough to do little five second twists. As much as I sat and watched I just couldn't get my head round the guitar. It never entered my head to buy a tutor book; I didn't know they even existed.

Tallymen were a strange breed of chaps who went from door to door carrying around suitcases full of clothes and wares, which could be paid off on a weekly basis. Even when money was still owed, other stuff could be acquired simply by upping the payments by a few bob. For some strange reason whenever my mother was skint, and the tallyman was due, she'd put on her best frock and half a yard of lipstick. I was sent out to play with orders not to return for at least half an hour.

One of our regular tallymen was a bloke in his early 20s called Jimmy, who came round every Wednesday. Wednesday was also the day my sister Joan came for her weekly visit to my mums. Jimmy always stayed for a cup of tea and constantly flirted with my sister. One day he saw my guitar gathering dust in the corner. He picked it up, tuned it and started to play. It was amazing, he played Buddy Holly's *Peggy Sue* all the way through. I was in the presence of a genius. He asked me if I could play and I stumbled through my eight-note *Apache* repertoire.

"Don't you know any chords?" he asked.

"What's chords?" I answered.

"Look I'll show you. This one's A major. Try it."

He held my first three fingers on the strings of the second fret.

"Just use your fingertips, bend your fingers, like this."

He went on to show me the chords of D and E major. I made sure I was in the house every Wednesday teatime. If I was going to be a Rolling Stone I was going to have to learn to play the guitar.

After a month or so, even though my fingertips were on fire I'd mastered the three chords of *Peggy Sue*, but I was completely baffled when the tune changed for just four bars on the "Pretty, pretty, pretty, pretty" bit to an F chord. I could hear the change, but didn't know what to do about it, fuck it, I thought, just keep playing A.

On Summer Saturday mornings a gang of us often took the train into Sheffield to visit the Rag and Tag market. I loved the old market at the bottom of Dixon Lane. It sold everything and anything: pots and pans, fruit and veg, old books, clothes and American super-hero and horror comics. We could pick up a latest style shirt for 14/6d or 17/11d. The shirts came in cardboard packaging with a see-through cellophane front to show the style. You couldn't beat the thrill of opening the packet, removing dozens of tiny pins and smelling the fresh cotton. The shirts were worn still creased, just to show everybody they were brand new. Rogue pins always seemed to turn up, usually found stuck in the back of our necks.

A pair of Jet jeans cost around ten bob. Winkle pickers or chisel-toed shoes could be bought for a couple of quid. Afterwards we nipped into Woolies café for a plate of chips. Then into a tobacconist shop to buy a six-inch long 'Joy-Stick' cigarette to smoke on the journey home.

In the winter of late 62 – early 63 all of Great Britain froze up solid for a couple of months. Not many folk had a car, but everybody had a shovel. We dug our way out of the house through six-foot high snowdrifts, but the trains and the buses ran as normal and everybody made it to work and to school. Every night after school or during the holidays we sledged down the steep hills surrounding the town. I thought the cold spell would never end.

From 1960 to 1963 there'd been a void; a sort of lost, in-between teenage group with no true identity and no real music of their own. Kids only a few years older than me were stuck in the middle. They'd been just a little bit too young to be Teds and a bit too old or not brave enough to grow their hair or to progress into the new movement of the mods who were now beginning to evolve.

Eighteen, nineteen and twenty-year-olds were thinking about becoming men, finishing their apprenticeships, getting married and turning into their dads. These lads were old before their time, dressed in the safety of white Bri-nylon shirts, sensible, black or dark grey two-piece suits and ties. The girls still dressed like their mothers.

By 1964, instead of shopping at Woolies, C & A and Marks and Sparks, kids were now using the new boutiques springing up in every major city and specialising in ready-to-wear clothing for the new youth market.

A generation gap was already forming. Rock 'n' roll in its original form was now old hat; Buddy Holley and Eddie Cochran were dead, and Elvis had sold his soul to Hollywood, churning out movie after movie: so bad they were actually good.

The Southern Californian surf sound of Jan and Dean and the Beach Boys swept through America in the early sixties. Bronzed Adonises and bikini-clad babes partied all through the summer, but in England, riding a six-inch-high, grey river Humber wave on an ironing board at the picturesque beaches of Cleethorpes didn't quite hold the same mystique. "Wipe out," my arse.

America had always led the way, but now it's music had become stale and boring. Phil Spectre's mass reverb Wall of Sound featuring American girl groups, the Crystals and the Ronnettes were the best the States had to offer.

Britain still had Cliff and the Shadows and a few cardigan-clad crooners, churning out gooey shit. There was nothing wrong with the Shadows instrumentals, but even if everybody wanted to play the guitar like Hank Marvin, nobody wanted to look like him. The same could be said of Roy Orbison. The Big O could reach notes angels only dream of, but he didn't have the look or charisma of a pop star. A new era was dawning: the British Beat boom was about to explode onto the scene and take the whole world by storm.

The Beatles emerged and changed everything. Beatlemania, but more importantly long hair arrived. The girls at school screamed and squealed when their records were played at the dance club, held once a week, and every rainy or snowy dinnertime in the school hall. The one-penny admission fee went towards the purchase of new records; we also took along our own records, played by a teacher or one of the prefects on an old wooden-sided record player.

I couldn't help but love the Beatles, but that would soon change when their greatest rivals burst on to the scene a few months later. Cliff and the Shadows still dominated the charts in early 63, but by the summer the Mersey Sound had taken over. The Beatles, Gerry and the Pacemakers, Billy J Kramer and the Dakotas and the Searchers all made number one in the charts. Liverpool was *the* place; the heart of the British Beat boom. All its citizens were (according to the telly and the press) good-looking, tough, quirky and cool, exhibiting their legendary Scouse wit and humour. Somebody should have had a word with Jimmy Tarbuck and let him in on the secret.

At our house, the tallyman was hammered again for a black corduroy collarless Beatle jacket with silver buttons. It cost me Mam the ridiculous sum of six quid, she paid it off at half a dollar a week.

Every child of the 60s (so it's said) remembers where they were and what they were doing the day John F Kennedy was assassinated. Well I don't remember the exact place, but I was huddled around a transistor radio in a shop doorway or on a street corner when the news broke. Then, for what reason I've never been able to fathom, Radio Luxembourg started playing classical music as a mark of respect. So, Lee Harvey Oswald, the CIA, the gunman on the grassy knoll or whichever cunt wasted the Pres, thanks a lot for depriving a bunch of twelve-year old kids their daily fix of Rock 'n' Roll.

Not only could we hear all the new groups on Luxembourg and the pirate radio stations, we could now see them on the TV. *Thank Your Lucky Stars* went out every week and showed all the latest pop sensations. It was on that very show I first saw a new group whose music and image would have a lasting effect on the rest of my life.

Blades in Leeds, 1961

Chapter 3

Like a rollin' stone

The first prize in a raffle held at a dance in the village hall just happened to be The Stones brand new debut album (or LP as they were called then) simply entitled: *The Rolling Stones*. One of my older mates, Stu Freeman, who already had shoulder length hair, looked like a rock star and was by far the coolest kid on the planet, calmly announced: "I'm having the fucker."

Stu was a great lad, always smiling and always having time for myself and the other younger kids who hung around him hoping some of his magic would rub off onto us. He told one his mates to get a pass out, go outside and wait by the toilet window. He walked onto the stage, stuffed the record under his coat, went to the bog and passed it out of the window to his mate; he then went outside himself and hid the record in some bushes collecting it at the end of the gig. Fucking hell, I thought, he's done it. Whoever won the raffle must have been really pissed off.

Stu knew I was into the Stones and a couple of months later he asked me if I wanted to buy the record for fifteen bob, which was half of what it would have cost new. I had to do three days spud picking at five bob a day to raise the cash.

America, inaccessible America, the land of freeways, highways, boulevards, skyscrapers and Cadillac's, lay ten million miles away across the Atlantic Ocean. The only possible way to get there was through music. America, home of Rock 'n' Roll, Mississippi Delta Blues, Sunset Strip and Surf City (where there were two cute honeys for every guy and all you had to do was just wink your eye) Everything American was classy, cool and romantic. Who was to know America would go on to eat up the rest of the world and then shit on it?

The Stones hard-driving, raw rhythm and blues transported me to a new world. I had no idea at the time, most of the tracks on the album were covers. I took a California trip from Chicago to L.A., courtesy of Bobby Troup's *Route 66*. Exotic sounding place names drifted by as I cruised through the plains and prairies of the United States of America, where Red Indians and wild buffalo once roamed. I motored west, from St Louis to Missouri, Oklahoma City was oh-so-pretty, then on to Amarillo, Gallup New Mexico, Flagstaff (I thought it was backsup) Arizona, all the way to San Bernardino. *Mona*'s wobbling, vibrato Bo Diddley guitar sound, Jagger's maracas and a pounding, thumping, pulsating backbeat had me drooling with delight. *Oh Carol*, a hundred mile an hour Chuck Berry rocker with Keith Richards matching, if not bettering Chuck's trademark lead guitar riff. "Oh Carol, don't let her steal your heart away, I've gotta learn to dance if it takes me all night and day." Bill Wyman's perfect ascending baseline and Brian Jones dazzling slide guitar in Slim Harpo's *I'm A King Bee*. "I'm a King Bee baby, want you to be my Queen, together we can make honey, the world has never seen, Weeelll, buzz awhile, sting it baby," and Marvin Gaye's soulful,

56

upbeat boogie-woogie *Can I Get A Witness*. Steady as fuck Charlie Watts, the human drum machine kept it all ticking along perfectly. No flash fills and fancy rolls from Charlie.

Every track was pure, pure joy. I played the record constantly; full blast on my blue and beige Dansette record player. Once again it was either the Stones or the Beatles (Turnip chose the Beatles). The Dansette was bought from the catalogue, where else! It had a unique smell I can't really describe, especially when it was brand new. As soon as I opened the lid and the turntable spun, this sort of electrical, plastic aroma kinda added to the excitement as the record crackled into life. The metal spindle in the centre of the turntable held a stack of ten 45s, trouble was I only had one, borrowed from a mate. The Chuck Berry EP (extended play) on the red and yellow Pye International label, had four tracks, *Johnny B Goode*, *Oh Baby Doll*, *School Day* and *Back in the USA*.

The first record I ever bought in early 64, costing six shilling and eight pence was the Stones cover version of Buddy Holly's *Not Fade Away*, done in a speeded-up Bo Diddley style. "I'm gonna tell ya how it's gonna be, Wednesday one United three."

The Stones were on the blue Decca label, the Kinks on pink Pye, the Who on black Brunswick, the Beatles, black Parlophone. I don't know why, but it was important to know that shit at the time.

A few years ago, in a conversation about music, one of my daughters asked "What were them black round things called, what you used to play music on Dad?

"Do you mean records?" I said.

"Yeah that were it: records – ancient."

Bleeding kids eh!

Twenty years later a maroon coloured mark three Jaguar pulled up outside a shop on a lonely road in Sheerness Kent. Our band, Like Ice Like Fire were heading to a recording studio on the Isle of Sheppey to cut our first record. The Jag, which used nearly as much oil as petrol on the journey down south, had been bought by our manager as a kind of status symbol to show the world he now looked after the interests of a rock band. The money for the car came from the proceeds of a kilo of finest quality Afghanistan Black, stolen at knifepoint from three students who were dealing gange from a house at Havelock Square in Sheffield.

I walked into the shop leaving the other band members in the car.

"Twenty Embassy number one please love," I said to the woman behind the counter.

"I recognize that accent," she said. "Sheffield is it?"

"Yeah it is," I said.

"I used to go out with a lad from Sheffield, well it wasn't actually Sheffield, it was a place just outside called Dronfield."

Fucking hell, I nearly said. "I'm from Dronfield."

"Are you? Do you know Stuart Freeman?"

Fuck me, I nearly said again.

"Yeah I know Stu, not seen him for years though."

Our manager kept blasting the hooter trying to get me out of the shop. The woman told me she'd met Stu in Sheffield when she was a student there in the 60s.

Small, small world as they say.

Top of the Pops first hit the T.V. screen in 1964. It was must watch television. No matter where we were, or what we were doing, we'd rush home to catch the show. Few teenagers could be seen on the streets at 7.30 on Thursday evenings. We sat glued to the box, waiting in anticipation to see our favourite pop stars, or maybe discover a new one. Had the Stones moved up the chart? Was there a new number one? Checking out the latest gear, not only what the bands wore, but also the young kids in the audience who pushed each other to pose and dance in front of the cameras.

A lot of the young groups looked genuinely overwhelmed, star-struck even, to be appearing on such a high-status show. Not surprising really, as maybe only six months or a year earlier they might well have been working in some factory or office. To be thrust into the limelight, miming in front of millions of viewers must have been a scary shock to the system. What an amazing buzz it must have been for them. I told myself, 'One day I'm gonna be on that show.'

One of my older mates borrowed my record player for the night for a relative's party. In exchange he said he'd buy me a record. He bought the player back along with the promised disc by a new group called Them. The song, an old revamped Big Joe Williams blues number entitled *Baby Please Don't Go.*

Straight in came the guitar riff, with the two-note bass line in the key of E major thumping in the background. Drums and Hammond organ came in together, wailing blues harmonica and then Van Morrison's roaring magnificent vocal.

"Baby please don't go, baby please don't go, baby please don't go down to New Orleans you know I love you so, baby please don't go."

What a song, this was by far the best thing I'd ever heard; I played it a hundred times before turning it over to give the flip side a spin.

Whaaaaat, fuck me, how could it be? Impossible, but this was even better. The lyrics not sung, but spoken, growled even, the perfect rock song.

"G-L-O-R-I-A, Gloria, Glo-or-ria, I'm gonna shout it all night, I'm gonna shout it every day, yeah-yeah-yeah-yeah-yeah-yeah." A simple three-chord riff, again in the key of E major blew my head off. Two of the greatest songs ever on one seven-inch lump of vinyl.

What a discovery.

The *New Musical Express*, as well as Charles Buchan's *Football Monthly* was now added to Mum's paper bill. I had to keep up with everything that was happening on the pop scene.

·It was around this time when I first started using Provident cheques. These were clothing vouchers for £5 and sometimes even £10. They were accepted at certain (but not many) clothing and shoe shops in the Sheffield area. A fiver in

64/65 could get me well kitted out. The interest on them, maybe 25/50% I can't remember exactly. Mam paid it off on a weekly basis just like most of the other new stuff we ever bought. I used these up until the early the 70s.

Masons Arms pub early 1950s

During the six weeks school holidays in the summer of 65 I rarely rose from my pit before noon.

Our next-door neighbour's son, who was a few years older than me had married a nineteen-year-old girl from Nottingham and the couple moved in to live with his parents. The girl was slim and not bad looking, but to a young lad just turned fourteen, she seemed kinda old. She often popped round for a cup of tea and a gossip with me Mam when the rest of her family were out working. She openly flirted with me in front of my mother and was forever dropping little hints about what she would like to do with me, all a bit scary and puzzling really. She started coming up to my bedroom at the ungodly hour of 11o'clock in the morning, armed with a cup of tea in the pretence of getting me out of bed. She would sit on the edge of my bed, twirl her finger around my locks and say things like, "Look at you, all that gorgeous blond hair, you look just like an angel, I feel like getting into bed and making love to you." Well back then, making love was something that the film stars said at the pictures.

"Oh my darling, I want to make love to you."

I thought it was just snogging, holding hands and shit like they did at the flicks. I laid there with a stupid grin on my face thinking, I wish she'd fuck off and let me get back to sleep. This happened quite a few times. She'd make suggestions and always talked about 'making love' and, "we should make love together." I just thought she was teasing me.

It just so happened that at the time I really was madly in love with a girl called Angie. I walked Angie home most weekday nights. She lived across the road from where the old Cammell's Row had once stood, just up from the Masons pub. It was a complicated love story and the thought of sex never even entered my head... well hardly ever. I was happy enough just to be near her. Angie was a good mate and a group of us hung out together most nights. We were into the same pop groups, the same kind of music, and we really got on well together, she even came to the Lane with me a few times. I phoned her up quite often and sometimes we chatted for hours. Phone calls were free at the time. All you needed to do was to take the phone off the hook, and tap out the number on the bar where the phone rested. If the number was 2, two taps, three taps for 3, seven taps for the number 7 and so on.

A mate of mine, Grunter (so called because as a nipper he had poured a can of petrol over a pig at Smithy's farm and set it on fire) openly admitted he wanted to go out with Angie. Through fear of rejection I just couldn't bring myself to reveal my true feelings. If she'd have said no to me, it would have been the end of the world. I spent the whole journey from Dronny Park with my arm around her shoulder, asking her to go out with Grunt. I was mixed up and confused. Ange was a grammar school girl who lived in a private house with a telephone, I was a Cammell's Row boy.

"Go on, go out with Grunt," I'd say. If she'd have said yes, I think I would have dropped dead... she always said no. I hoped and prayed that one day she'd say, "I don't want to go out with him, I want to go out with you." But alas and alack – it never happened.

One night I was leant up against the garages on the Ghitty at the back of the Masons Arms getting as close as I could to Angie. Grunt stood a few yards further down with the rest of the gang, kicking stones. My lips were about an inch from hers and I was dying to kiss her, as I spouted the usual shit for a good ten minutes.

"Go on, go out with him, he really likes you."

My next-door neighbour's son, along with his wife was returning from visiting his grandma who lived on the same street as Angie, as they passed he laughed.

"What you up to Ron? Wait till I see ya Mother."

His wife just gave me a wicked smile and a wink. *Shit*, I thought.

A few days later Mam sent me next door to borrow some milk. The girl was alone in the house. I stood fidgeting in the kitchen looking at my feet and said, "Me Mam sez can she borrow a drop of milk?"

"I saw you the other night with that girl," she said. "What were you doing?"

"Nowt," I said

"You were doing something; I saw you. Is she your girlfriend?"

"Yeah," I lied.

"What have you been up to with her then? Have you had the bottom bit yet, or just the top?

"Just the top," I lied again.

"How big were her tits?" she said.

Oh shit, I thought.

"Don't know," I said. She undid the buttons of her blouse and opened it out revealing a black bra underneath. Oh fuckin hell, I thought, what's happening.

"Are her tits bigger than mine?"

"Don't know," I said, looking at the floor.

"Well you better have a feel and tell me."

I didn't know what to do. I was crapping myself.

"Come on," she said, "I'm not going to bite you, have a feel."

I moved forward, grabbed her left tit and held my hand there like Dustin Hoffman with Mrs Robinson.

"Well? Are they bigger than mine or smaller?"

"About the same... an – an – and can I have that milk cos me Mam's dying for a cuppa and I've got to go." I grabbed the milk and shot out of the house.

I kept out of her way as much as I could for the next few weeks. If she came round to our house I went straight out. I told my Mum not to let her come up to my bedroom any more and to say I'd gone out.

The couple eventually moved away from the area. It must have been five or six years before I saw her again on a visit back.

Right I thought, as I undressed her with my eyes, I'm ready for you now darling. She looked at me like I was a piece of shit and sneered, "Bleedin ell... you've changed." Maybe the forbidden fruit had got a bit too ripe, or perhaps it had all been just a joke?

Football violence really started to take off 1965. Why 1965? I don't know.

From the beginning of the decade I'd been to many of United's home games and a few away games and apart from the odd argument, I'd never seen any trouble at all. Liverpool and Everton fans had been smashing up trains since the late 50s, but trouble inside the grounds was rare.

In 1964 I stood on the Kop at the Lane, by the side of a large group of Manchester United supporters, other groups of Mancs (or wherever they were from) stood in other parts of the Kop happily chanting and cheering on their team. They didn't want to hit me or anybody else and as far as I could see nobody wanted to hit them or chase them out of the ground.

How come, about one year later, Man Utd and the Merseyside teams in particular would to try an invade every football ground in the land and how come fans of the home were ready to fight them? Who told them? Nobody (or very few) even had a house phone back then, let alone a mobile.

Did it really happen so quickly? I think it did. Overnight, so to speak. Was it the scrapping of national service, where lads from all parts of the country bonded and got on so well together for two years out of their young lives? Was it the lack of wars? There hadn't been one for years. If we'd been born forty years earlier would we have bounced up the Normandy beaches on D-Day? Yeah, course we would. It was obviously territorial, and it all began to happen in 1965.

A group of young lads started to congregate behind the goal at the front of the Kop. We moved down from the back and at first stood just to the left of this new mob. As we got a bit braver, we stood amongst them joining in with the songs and the chants. Every set of fans were doing the 'Brazil clap' first done by

Brazilian fans during the 1962 world Cup. So for us it was, "yoo-ni-ted." clap-clap-clap, with the emphasis on the "yoo." As the years went by it gradually changed to "yaa." which sounded harder and more aggressive.

Their seaside battles put behind them, mods and rockers stood side by side on the Kop in the common cause that was Sheffield United F.C.

My regular companions at the games were Tiny and Ansh. Tiny moved to Dronny from Pitsmoor in Sheffield when he was about ten years old and we'd been mates ever since. He lived in the posh houses on the next street. Both lads were a year older than me. Quite a few of the young lads in the mob (including myself) were now wearing green army combat jackets. These were decorated with biro or felt tipped pen, with the words Blades or Sheffield United written on the back. We were usually in the ground at around 2 p.m. for the Saturday games.

A group of older lads all dressed in smartly tailored, sharp Italian suits, tab collared shirts with gold cuff links and slim Windsor knotted ties appeared just after kickoff when the pubs shut. These boys were all in their late teens-early twenties and were mostly from the Pitsmoor area where Tiny once lived.

Suits had always been a sign of manhood, just as twenty-one years old was. If you were twenty-one, it was time to wear a suit, you were a man and in my inexperienced eyes, old and fucked, but when the mod culture arrived things began to change, now smart suits were hip, smart suits were cool. We were starting to get to know some of the lads in the mob including the 'Suities' as we called them. Everyone looked up to Melvin Harrison, the King of the Kop. Mel was a good-looking, smartly dressed kid, brimming with confidence. Tiny's first name was also Mel; the Suities called him Tiny, so as not to confuse him with big Mel.

Willie Ward, a Heeley Green lad vied with Mel Harrison for the title of King of the Kop. Willie would bellow out in a high-pitched voice: "Zigga-zagga-zigga-zagga," his minions would respond with, "U-NI-TED." Others in the suit mob were Snowy (Mel's younger brother) Ted Devine, Lob, a big lad with a lazy eye from the Arbourthorne estate, Walesy and a few others.

Walesy's claim to fame – so the story goes, is after a game against Leeds at the Lane, he lay in wait for Jack Charlton outside the players' entrance. Giraffe neck had riled him during the game. Walesy sneaked up behind Big Jack and booted him up the arse. He then ran like a whippet up John Street with Charlton in hot pursuit, to the great amusement of the rest of the lads.

Away fans were starting to appear at the Lane although not in large numbers; any who ventured on to the Kop and tried it on (so I was told) were dealt with by the Suities and the older mods and rockers. I was surprised to see the Leeds United fans wearing white scarves with small blue and yellow bands on them. I imagined their scarves would be all white, the same as their kit. Leeds brought a large following to the Lane, but they all seemed to be old women who looked like my mother.

The first time I was involved in any sort of violence at the Lane, came at a night match in September 1965. Some suited-up Liverpool fans who were at least twenty-five years old came to the front and started pushing us about. One of them kicked me up the arse and scared me half to death. What made it ten times worse, Angie was with me. I was relieved when they moved round to the Lane end for the second half.

Later on in the season Everton came for a Saturday fixture. On arriving at the ground at the usual time we found our spot taken over by a group of a hundred or so Everton fans. A lot of them carried banners and flags and looked really impressive.

Just like their Merseyside brothers, they were a lot older than us and just as bad with their bullying tactics. They started pushing us around and threatening us, so we moved to the left-hand side to get out of the way.

I couldn't help staring at them; I hoped none of them would catch my eye and ask what I was looking at. A leather-jacketed Blade stood near the Evertonians was pushed by a much older Suitie. I was shocked to see him pull a knife from his back pocket and lunge at the Everton fan. He was overpowered in seconds when about six Everton piled into him; they took his knife and threw him to the floor. They rolled him over, so he was face down, then one of them sat on top of him and slashed his coat open with his own knife.

Nobody went to help; we stood transfixed to the spot. The lad got up and slunk off towards the John Street side. He could easily have been stabbed to death. This was the cue for the Everton mob to start hitting any Blade in the vicinity. We ran and jumped in all directions and ended up at the back of the Kop well out of the way. We eventually moved further down and stood on a raised bit, just above the walkway that ran horizontally all the way across the Shoreham end.

The Everton mob stood directly below us only a few yards away.

The ground started to fill up, and fifteen minutes before kickoff, more and more Blades gathered where we were stood. It was the nearest we could get to our own spot. We told all the newcomers about the knife incident. In between listening with fascination to the Everton songs and chants I was picking up snippets of conversation from the lads around me.

"Wait till Mel and Willie get in; they'll not be so fucking clever then."

Right on cue just after the kickoff the Suities arrived. What was going to happen? There must have been fights before, because everybody talked about how good the Suities were, but I'd never seen them in action.

"What the fuck are ya doing stood here?" Melvin shouted at us all. I was more scared of him than the Everton lot. He slipped his jacket off (as did three or four of the others) they carefully folded them and passed them to lesser mortals. Sleeves were rolled up and neckties loosened. Followed by a small group of rockers (who left their jackets on) they marched into the Everton mob.

Fucking hell, I thought, this is it. It didn't last long, the Blades waded in and the Everton ranks split, on seeing this, more Blades ran down. Some of the Scousers leapt the fence behind the goal to escape the fighting, some tried to fight back, but they were no match for the Blades boys.

Half a dozen policemen came in to try and restore order. More and more Blades (who ten minutes earlier had been shitting themselves) joined the throng; it now looked safe, so the rest of us chabs swung under the crush barriers to reclaim our place.

The Everton fans didn't run away, they just moved to one side and carried on singing and chanting as if nothing had happened.

We were back in our own spot though. I'd never seen anything like it before; I was shaking with excitement.

One thing I picked up on as I got to know more and more of the Sheffield lads was their loathing of Sheffield Wednesday. Years and years of rivalry, turned into hatred, and had been passed down through the generations from grandfathers to fathers and from fathers to sons. It wasn't as simple as that though; families could be split, with three brothers supporting the Blades and one the Owls. I've heard Blades say, all the rest of their family are 'Fuckin Wednesdayites.' Very strange indeed.

"Fucking Wednesday bastards," could be heard when their scores were put up on the old Cricket pavilion scoreboard, or "I hate them blue and white cunts." They called Hillsborough the Shithouse.

In Dronfield it was probably an even split (although nearly all the lads at my school were Blades). There was little if any animosity between the two groups, but plenty of banter. It was a Sheffield thing at first, but as we got more and more involved in the new scene, the more we got to hate Wednesday.

In between the Liverpool and Everton games I travelled, along with Tiny and Ansh to Northampton. We went on one of six red and silver coloured, aptly named S.U.T. (Sheffield United Tours) charabancs that left from Pond Street bus station. Tiny always called the coaches charras, he still does. It amused me the Wednesdayites travelled to away games on the S.U.T. coaches. If they'd been called Sheffield Wednesday Tours, I wouldn't have gone anywhere near them.

We found ourselves on the same bus as the suit crew. I felt honoured to be around these lads. Tiny had travelled with them before; they knew him and even spoke to Ansh and me as well. We arrived at Northampton and followed a few paces behind the suits as they went in search of a boozer. I noticed Ted Devine had a rip in the back of his trousers and I could see his arse. This set me off laughing and I pointed out the tear to Tiny, which set him off as well. Ted obviously knew about the rip as he kept pulling his coat down trying to cover it up. He turned round to us, shot us a nasty look and shouted, "What you little bastards laughing at?" Our faces dropped; he knew we'd seen his arse and I expected a clip. The other lads twigged on and gave Ted some real grief. They kept lifting his coat up and poking his arse with their fingers through the rip. I thought he was going to explode and was scared he'd blame me for discovering it.

Outside the ground a couple more supporter's club buses pulled up, and we all queued to go on the covered end, Northampton's Kop. We joined a group of Blades stood at the side of the Northampton mob, who sang songs and chanted about the Cobblers. A bit of pushing, shoving and threats were exchanged between the two groups, but nothing serious, until a Cobbler stood next to us blew his bugle once too often in Tiny's ear.

"Why don't ya stick that fucking bugle up your arse," Tiny shouted. The

Northampton lad responded by smashing Tiny on the side of the head with the trumpet. This caused a bit of a scuffle, but the lad disappeared into the Northampton ranks.

An old former flour mill on Leadmill Road Sheffield, housed The Esquire club. (It's now the site of Leadmill nightclub).

The three-story building with a small doorway at street level, led up a steep narrow staircase to the first floor. Past the admission desk to the right was the TV room, where a television that nobody watched sat flickering in the corner. This area could also be used as an early form of chill-out room away from the roar of the music, where punters dossed down for a while at all-nighters, or watched courting couples snogging and groping in the corners.

The toilets, on the same floor, had strange, foreign, toilety type names stuck on the door, one was lavabobo and we used this name for the bogs for years after.

The Esquire coffee bar

"Just nipping to the lavabobo for a shit."

Another narrow flight of stairs led to the dance floor. At the far end, a stage, made – so the rumour went, from the tops of two grand pianos with the legs sawn off. In the centre of the stage, a graffiti-covered wooden pole held up the ceiling.

Yet another narrow staircase led to the snack bar on the upper floor. A rectangular hole in the floor surrounded by three-foot high wooden balcony railings gave punters a bird's eye view onto the dance floor and the stage.

The walls and ceilings were decorated with fishing nets, ancient blunderbusses, steel-rimmed wagon wheels, tribal masks, a large stuffed crocodile and other paraphernalia. A skeleton wearing at a top hat and a pair of wellies hung from the roof, the seats and the tables were different sized barrels.

The Esquire, what a place: smoke-filled, dark, damp and dangerous, tremendous, pounding, roaring beat music, a fourteen-year-old boy's dream come true. There were no dress or age restrictions and no alcohol, just coke and other fizzy drinks.

The Esquire was in direct competition with Pete Stringfellow's (whatever happened to him?) Mojo club. The Mojo stood in the mainly black, Pitsmoor area of the city. The clientele there were pure mod; whereas the punters of the Esquire were a mixture of mods, beatniks and young lads and lasses from all walks of life.

The DJ at the Esquire always slagged off the Mojo and vice-versa. We all joined the membership scheme, for cheaper admission and proudly wore our Esquire pin badges.

So now, it was, Elvis, the Stones, the Blades and the Esquire for me. Turnip, my Wednesday/Cliff/Beatles mate, had given up on life by now.

Tiny was well into the soul music and the mod scene, but he used both clubs; I was more into the beat groups. I only went to the Mojo once (with Tiny) to see Wilson Pickett at an all-nighter. We queued for ages along with hundreds of others, but the club was packed, and we couldn't get in. We sat outside for an hour or so, then headed off to Pilgrim Street where Tiny's auntie lived. We planned to knock her up and stay the night.

An oldish West Indian guy dressed in a baggy zoot suit, trilby hat and the loudest tie I'd ever seen, wobbled from side to side outside a blues party on Minna Road. He had been thrown out and stood shouting threats in a marvellous Jamaican accent at the building.

"Bastard house, shithouse, ya not a house, ya a fucking shithouse."

He staggered up the path then fell backwards disappearing over a wall. He reappeared minus his hat and shouted, "Bastard, fucking shithouse," again. Tiny and me were laughing so much; we had to hold each other up.

All the up-and-coming beat groups played the Esquire, the Kinks, Small Faces, the Who, the Pretty Things and the Animals. Rod Stewart, Long John Baldry, Georgie Fame, Eric Clapton, plus American rhythm and blues legends including, Howling Wolf, Memphis Slim, Sonny Boy Williamson, Muddy Waters, John Lee Hooker, Sister Rosetta Tharpe and Screaming Jay Hawkins.

There were also regular appearances from local Sheffield acts, Frankenstein and the Monsters, Dave Berry and the Cruisers, Joe (the Blade) Cocker and the Frank White Band.

New Year's Eve 1965, the Pretty Things (whose singer, Phil May, had the longest hair of all the new bands) headlined the all-nighter. We went to the first session which finished at 11 o'clock and then back outside to join the queue for the nighter, starting just before 12 o'clock.

I was a midnight to six man. In the queue I got chatting to a young mod girl from Barnsley, who looked about thirteen. She told me she was sixteen (I told her I was sixteen as well). It was her first visit to the club.

"I've been here loads of times, I'm a member," I told her, and with a horn that nearly burst through my hipster's zip, I promised to show her around the club.

Pass-outs, in the form of a piece of wallpaper ripped off a full roll were

66

available at the pay-in counter. After an hour or so, hand in hand, we took our pieces of woodchip and went for a walk around the deserted back streets. Although I'd been close on several occasions I still hadn't lost my cherry. We stopped, snogged, groped, fumbled, and mauled each other at the back of a derelict house for a good ten minutes, but I was too scared to actually do it. This happened on two more occasions during the night. I'd had the horn on for so long, I got guts ache. I left the girl for a while and found my mates.

"Did ya fuck her Ron?" Tiny said.

"No, I feel reight badly, I've got guts ache," I said.

"I know what's up with you, Ron," Wuss said. "She gave ya a blow back, dint she?"

"What's a blow back?" I said,

"Well," Wuss said. "When you're ready to shoot your load, she puts her thumb over your Jap's eye, and it shoots back down and nearly blows your bollocks off." Everybody cracked up.

The dance floor heaved with sweaty bodies as the Pretty Things took to the stage. I swayed and surged forward trying to reach the front. It's like the Shoreham end I thought, but with music and birds. Sweet smelling older girls gave me New Year kisses. What could be better than this?

We left the club at six o'clock in the morning and were on too much of a high to go home, so Ansh, Tiny and me decided to hitchhike somewhere. We managed to thumb a lift to Mansfield, where we walked round the town for half an hour or so. We thumbed it back, grabbed a few hours kip, then off to the Lane to see United play Northampton.

"Watch out for that bugle boy," I said to Tiny.

'The weekend starts here.' Home from school to a roaring coal fire, with the damper down to heat the water for the Friday teatime weekly bath. Hair, sleek and shiny, courtesy of a sachet of Silverkrin egg and lemon shampoo. Best mod togs washed, ironed and laid out on the bed. A yellow, black and white button-down collar, a pale blue pointed tab collar, or my favourite-ever shirt – a Black Watch tartan tab collar, bought from the Rag and Tag that hung to perfection. Checked Rupert Bear hipsters that itched like fuck, due to me not wearing undercrackers. The kaks were held up with a thick leather, brass buckled belt (stolen from the boy scout cupboard in the church hall), a high-collared, small-check jacket, and for the finishing touch, Cherry Blossomed, black Cuban-heeled Chelsea boots with blue satin lining.

Ten bob, scrounged from my Uncle Chris's brown paper wage packet. Switch on the TV to hear Manfred Mann's *5-4-3-2-1* introduce Ready Steady Go hosted by the gorgeous Kathy McGowan. Ooh Kathy, every red-blooded teenage boy's fantasy and dream. The bus into town, the Esquire… magic.

This became the weekend routine in late 65 early 66. On Saturdays we sometimes stayed in town after the Blades home games and went straight in the club when it opened at 7 o'clock. It closed at 11 o'clock and most nights we stopped even trying to get the last bus home; we didn't want the night to end. We walked around town shouting insults and laughing at ancient, thirty-year-old

Suities, too drunk and too old to chase us, until midnight: then the streets were all but deserted. We walked or hitched-hiked the six miles back home, completely sober and drug free, but nevertheless flying.

The highlight of my Esquire days came in February 1966 when the Who played the club. Along with the Stones and the Kinks, the Who were my favourite group of the era. The tickets cost 7/6d and the place was packed to capacity. The bands back line stack of speakers almost touched the ceiling and the noise was incredible.

It seems weird that I can't remember any of the songs, but I do remember Keith Moon bouncing his sticks off the bass drum, propelling them into the audience. The girls jumped up trying to catch them and fought each other to scoop them up as souvenirs.

The Esquire

Lowedges – a large sprawling council estate in south Sheffield stands just over the border from Dronfield. Like many of the inner-city estates of today, it's now run-down and plagued with crime and drug problems. Some bad feeling still continues between the two districts, just as it did back in the 60s. Lads ventured into each other's territory on the lookout for girls and trouble.

I'd been on the estate a few times with the older lads, where we hung on street corners, around the shopping precinct or outside the Magpie pub, checking out the local talent.

The older lads I went with were all streetwise, and were friendly with a few of the Lowedges boys, but there was always an air of danger about the place, and trouble could at start anytime.

A girl from our school who was ripe for the picking, started hanging around the streets of Dronny at night-time, flirting and dropping hints to the young bucks of the area, that she was maybe… available.

Some Lowedges boys came over one night and started chatting up the girl and a group of her mates. A few Dronny lads took exception to this and after an argument the two mobs arranged a meet. Word went around school that the Lowedges mob were coming. About thirty fourteen/fifteen-year-olds met outside the Coach and Horses pub on the Dronfield side of the border.

Kek Keeble worked weekends at Smithy's farm directly across the road from the boozer. Kek took us in the farmyard, where we grabbed lumps of wood, iron bars and other rusty farm tools. We sat on the wall outside the farm swinging our weapons in mock battles to psyche each other up.

Four lads emerged from the darkness at the bottom of the hill, all openly carrying knifes. We jumped off the wall and moved towards them. This could easily have been a scouting party with more on the way.

"Hold it," one of the Lowedges lads said. "There's only four of us: nobody else would come, but I'll fight the best one among you, one on one, as long as nobody else joins in."

I had to admire his bottle. Kek took up the challenge. I knew he would. We walked off to a disused quarry a couple of hundred yards down the road.

The girl and her mates turned up; they stood giggling and fidgeting a few yards away. The two lads squared up, the rest of us stood in a semi-circle shouting, "Come on Kek, kill him, batter the cunt."

It didn't last long. Kek fired off half a dozen swift punches, knocking one of the lad's front teeth clean out. Some of our boys got the taste for blood and wanted to pummel the other three, but Kek said, "Leave em, it was a fair fight, that's enough."

Nobody argued with Kek. The Lowedges lads picked up their mate and were allowed to leave. About twenty of us went back to the farm; Kek grabbed the girl and led her into the barn.

The rest formed a disorderly queue outside, nudging, pushing and hitting each other. After five minutes Kek came out and shouted, "Next."

We fought in the doorway to get in. I was third in line and stumbled around in the darkness, whispering, "Where are ya?"

I heard a voice say, "I'm over here."

I found her spread-eagled on some bales of hay. To the mooing of half a dozen Guernsey's, the sweet aroma of rotting straw, fanny juice and cow-shit I became a man. Trumpets blew, and angels sang. Two minutes later I was back out breathing fresh air again. Seventeen boys did the business that night, (or at least said they did). Not quite Annabel Chong, but there you go.

We'd started meeting the Chesterfield lads, Sinny, Dave Parton, Podge, Dec Fields, Alan and Little Terry at most of the home games and travelled back with them on the Chesterfield bus which stopped at Dronny on the way through. The way the Chezzy lads spoke made me smile; they called Chesterfield, 'Tairn', called each other 'Serry' and 'Mi Duck' and the coppers: 'Bobbies.'

Ansh and me arranged to thumb it to Leicester on Saturday March the 19th 1966. Parton, a couple of years older than me and who was quite a lad, said he'd join us. One of the Chezzy lads told us (it just sort of just cropped up in conversation) Parton had the biggest stang in Chesterfield and all the surrounding towns and hamlets. Whenever he was out and about in town, a posse of birds always surrounded him. I don't know if the stang story is true, but he did go on to marry a famous American Country and Western singer with big blond hair and giant buzzoms.

Parton gave us his address and we called at his house at Stonegravels early

Saturday morning. He invited us into his bedroom to show us his souvenirs and scalps. Blade pictures, banners and flags covered the walls. He had about twenty different scarves he'd nicked from fans up and down the land.

"What shall I take today," he mused. "Shall I take one of my banners? All my scalps? No fuck it, I'll take my gun."

What! I thought. He opened a draw and took out a small revolver. Fucking hell what's going on.

"It's all right he said, it's only a starting pistol, but you wanna hear the fucking noise it makes."

He grabbed a handful of cartridges, slipped the gun in his pocket and we were off. We had trouble getting lifts, but finally got one to Derby arriving there around one o'clock. Time was getting on, so we decided to catch the train from Derby to Leicester, which wasn't too far away and only cost a few bob. We walked into the station and hung around the platform waiting for our train.

A train rolled in and the roar and noise coming from it meant only one thing... a football special. Heads hung out of the windows, bottles flew through the air and smashed on to the platform. The doors opened, and scores of Man City fans poured out. They walked past us singing and chanting. A group stopped in front of us, one of them shouted.

"Are you fucking United?"

"Yeah," I replied,

"Yeah, Sheffield United," Parton said. "We're on our way to Leicester."

"Oh, that's all right then," the City fan said. "I thought you were Man Utd."

We arrived at Filbert Street about half two and joined a group of about thirty Blades stood outside Leicester's Kop. We entered the Kop at the left-hand corner and could see the Leicester mob stood behind the goal. They saw us and walked over towards us. Parton moved to the front, pulled the pistol from his pocket and held it out at arm's length slightly above his head.

Seeing this, the Leicester fans stopped dead in their tracks. We carried on walking towards them and as we got closer Parton fired a shot that echoed under the double-decker stand above us. The whole mob backed off. The Blades with us were just as shocked. They'd no idea they had a mad gunman in their ranks. We moved forward and occupied the spot behind the goal where the Leicester fans had stood. A couple of coppers stood pitch side made no move to come into the crowd. They must have heard the shot, the whole ground must have heard it, but maybe they thought better of tackling some lunatic with a gun. More Blades arrived and joined us. The Leicester mob returned in dribs and drabs and took up a position just to our right. By kickoff both mobs were stood side-by-side singing songs and chanting.

I got talking to a Leicester fan called Greg. A good-looking, stocky lad with long blond hair, he wore a leather rocker jacket and a long blue and white scarf. We hit it off straight away and chatted about everything and anything, but mostly about music and football. He stayed with us all the game and when we left we promised to look out for each other when our teams met.

My old adversary, the 'good looking' Leicester City fan Greg Chapman in 1969, with not one, but two.. yes two Man City scalps hung from his belt

There was no trouble after the match. We hitched it back in good time and spent the night in Chesterfield with the Chezzy boys.

Three weeks after my fifteenth birthday, the final game of the 65-66 season took us to Chelsea. Tiny, Ansh and me had planned for weeks to hitchhike down to London on the Friday night before the match. We talked about it constantly. My mates at school – maybe a little bit envious – said I was crazy for even attempting such a stunt.

With rain bouncing around our feet we sent off thumbing around 9 o'clock in the evening. I'd borrowed my Uncle Chris's pack-a-mac (a lightweight plastic waterproof over-garment that could be folded up and kept inside your pocket). I wore Tiny's red and white knitted scarf, which wrapped around my neck about ten times and still nearly touched the floor. It must have taken his mother two years, using the wool from a flock of sheep to knit it.

With just under £1 (nineteen shilling and eleven pence, halfpenny) in my pocket I felt rather flush. I also took along about a dozen football programmes to sell on, hoping to make a few bob.

As a hobby, my mother drank gallons of tea and gossiped with the neighbours. I often found her, when she was needed to cook my dinner, or iron me a shirt, at an old lady's house at the end of our street. I called round one day dying of hunger. I was hoping to drag Mam back home to boil me an egg and cut my bread into soldiers.

I got talking to the lady's son about football: John Thornilow, a die-hard Unitedite, and me hit it off straight away. He asked if I collected football programmes, "Yeah, I've got loads," I said. I had about fifty.

"Come and have a look at my collection," he said, leading me through to his bedroom in the ground floor flat. He opened a large cupboard, a wardrobe and two chests of draws packed with thousands of programmes, my mouth fell open. 1940s and 50s Cup finals, semi-finals and internationals from the same era. Just about every team in the four divisions (fifty times over), non-league and hundreds of old, and up to date, Blades programmes. He also had every copy of Charles Buchan's football monthly, which started publication in the early 50s. I was amazed; I sat on the floor flicking through them with a massive grin on my face. For weeks after, I pestered my mum to call back, so I could have a look at the programmes.

Months later Mum told me to, "Go round to Mrs. Thornilow's, their John

71

wants to see you." I had no idea what he wanted but shot round straight away.

"Look Ron," he said. "I know how much you like the programmes, I'm getting married soon and I can't take them with me when I move out, so I want you to have them. I know you'll appreciate them and look after them... you can have the lot."

He must be joking I thought. I realised he wasn't as we packed them into bags and cardboard boxes and ferried them on to our house. I was in seventh heaven for weeks after.

We trudged down Chesterfield Road in the warm, late spring rain, buzzing with excitement. Not a care in the world, our heads full of the latest pop songs as we headed off on the great adventure. The first lift took us to Chesterfield town centre; we walked along Derby road heading for the M1 motorway, which back then only reached as far north as Derby.

A car pulled up and we ran over to it. A youngish girl about eighteen years old opened the door. "Where you going, lads?"

"London," we all said at once.

"Well, we're not going that far, but we can drop you near Derby if that's okay," said the bloke who was driving.

"Yeah that's fab," we answered. The mini-skirted girl leaned over the seat to talk to us.

"What you going to London for lads, not running away from home are you?"

"No were going to Chelsea to watch Sheffield United."

"Sheffield United," the bloke said smiling. "Who are they?"

"Best team in the world that's all," I answered. The girl's skirt hitched up shorter and as her legs slightly parted I caught a glimpse of her knickers. She chattered away for the rest of the journey while we giggled, fidgeted and nudged each other, we couldn't take our eyes of her crotch.

We were dropped off a few miles from Derby; the couple wished us good luck and waved to us as they drove away smiling.

"Fuckin hell, did ya see that bird's fanny, she was showing it us," Tiny said. "Ansh's got horn on, look."

"I haven't," Ansh said,

"I fucking have," I said.

We stood there laughing in the pissing rain; we were on our way to London to see the best team in the world, and a gorgeous bird had just given three soaked to the skin, snotty nosed little kids a flash and the thrill of their lives, could it get any better than this?

We walked a couple of miles until we reached the slip road leading onto the M1. After a while a lorry screeched to a halt about 50 yards down the slip road. We sprinted to the lorry and reached it as the door swung open.

"Where ya going lads?" the driver said.

Again, we all shouted "London," as we climbed up into the cab.

"Well I can take you about 50 miles down to the next service station (or were they called transport cafés at the time?). Wait until the lorry drivers come in, ask who's going to London, and you should be okay," he told us.

He dropped us off and we managed to get another lift to the last service station before London, we were nearly there. I noticed a group of about a dozen lads dressed in combat jackets wearing blue and white scarves, they were older than us (late teens maybe).

I walked over to them, bold as brass and said, "Who do your lot support then?"

One of them smiled and said to me in a mock northern accent, "Sheffield United, we're thumbing it to Chelsea to watch the Blades."

I said, "We're Millwall mate, were going to Walsall watch the Lions."

All the rest of them were laughing. Millwall, I thought. Who are they? Never heard of 'em. These lads were sound, and we chatted a while, one of them even bought me a cup of tea. We must have looked as young to them as they looked old to us. They told us to watch ourselves at Chelsea and to be careful.

We asked around the tables if anyone was going to London and a couple of suited-up, darkish-skinned, middle-aged blokes said they were going in ten minutes or so and would give us a lift. We jumped in the back of the car and a strange smell hit me. It smelt like a dead Cammell's Row rat. The others noticed it too and we screwed up our faces for the next twenty miles or so. The blokes told us they were Greek Cypriots, maybe they were gangsters or something and had a dead body hid in the boot.

Dawn broke as we jumped from the car, we thanked the driver and as it drove away we held our nose's shouting

"Fucking hell, what a stink, what the fuck was it?" But we'd made it, we were in London, we had no idea which part, but we were here.

I'd been to London twice before, but I'd never really seen the place. In 1960 I went to Wembley Stadium in my brother's car along with three of his mates to watch England play Spain. I had to be on my best behaviour as one of Terry's mates was the local copper, P.C. Rowbotham. I'd risen at four o'clock in the morning to set off at five. I hadn't slept a wink all night.

The Spanish side included two of the greatest Real Madrid players of the era, Di Stephano and Ghento. England had Ron Springett in goal and "Who's-been-a-bribing Peter Swan" at centre half, which pleased Terry's other two mates who were Wednesdayites. We sat in the stand bang opposite the halfway line all wearing black and white England rosettes. England won the game 4-2. It was an unforgettable experience.

The second time was a world Cup qualifier in 1961, this time against Portugal. One of my mates, Toffee Sharpe (no relation) came with us. Terry paid for the whole day: match tickets, programmes, meals and sweets for both of us; he was generous to a fault our Terry. England won the game 2-0. Portugal included a brilliant up and coming young player named Eusebio.

There's something eerie and scary about walking around the deserted streets of a strange town or city at first light; but this was London, this was special. London awoke as we reached the centre. I was overwhelmed by the vastness of it all; some of the Streets were half a mile wide.

We met two Man City fans about our age, who like us, had thumbed it down the night before to see City play at Leyton Orient. I sold them a couple of programmes and we arranged to meet up after the match in Trafalgar Square.

We went in search of the legendary Carnaby Street, but we couldn't find it, so we spent an hour or so in the National History Museum, marvelling at the giant dinosaur skeleton.

Then we strolled up the Mall to Buckingham Palace where I seriously thought about going for a paddle in the fountain outside, as the floor was covered in coins.

The tube stations were something else, with fantastic names like Seven Sisters, Marble Arch, Piccadilly Circus, Angel, Cockfosters and Elephant and Castle. I was amazed when the first never ending escalator came into view. We rode down to the centre of the earth, rode back up, and then down again, twice. The Underground gave off a marvellous mechanical, oily, fusty kind of smell. The trains thundered in and out and the wind whistled down the tunnels.

About one o'clock we headed to Stamford Bridge and hung about outside the ground waiting for the turnstiles to open. We went in and stood behind one of the goals. It was mostly open terracing with a covered bit at the back. The rain had cleared up and the sun shone as we leaned on a crush barrier taking in the sights and the smells of this strange new stadium. A speedway track encircled the pitch making it seem a long way from the terracing.

I can see us stood there now; I can picture the scene exactly, and I remember how good I felt. We'd hitch-hiked 170 miles through the night to see our team; we'd made it, it's a sensation I'll never forget.

All three of us wore red and white scarves. Small groups of young Chelsea fans clad in blue and white eyed us up, we had no idea we were on… the Shed.

We stood there a while longer, still getting stares from the Chelsea lads who were moving a bit closer, when we noticed patches of red and white appearing on the other end of the ground. As with most of the grounds back then you could walk from one end to the other. We decided to go round. We left to a few shouts of, "Fuck off!" We took no notice and walked behind a stand on our right, to the other end.

Three coaches of Blades arrived, and we told everyone who was willing to listen and even those who weren't, how we'd thumbed it down the night before. Some lads who'd travelled on one of the S.U.T. coaches, told us there were some spare seats on their bus that was leaving St Pancras at midnight and they would sneak us on. Relieved we had a lift back, we settled down to watch the game. One of the older Dronny lads, Terry Jones, who was in the Army at the time turned up and, just before kickoff, the Suities and the Chezzy lads strolled in.

At half time, with United kicking towards the Shed, we walked, along with most of the other Blades back under the stand and gathered behind the goal at the front. We had no intention of 'taking their Kop' so to speak, and if United hadn't been kicking that way we would have stayed on the other end.

As soon as we arrived, coins, tin cans and other missiles started raining down on us. Chelsea lads moved down from the back and pushed into us; one of them caught my eye and shouted: "Who's your facking barber?"

Before I could answer "Vidal Sassoon," Terry grabbed him by the throat and pushed him back. The Suities and a couple of big rockers pushed their way up to the back, and, followed by the rest of us, got in behind the Chelsea mob who were stood under the covered bit.

Again it wasn't an attempt to take the end, if they hadn't started chucking things at us we would have probably stayed where we were.

The Chelsea fans tried to get their place back, but they couldn't move us. Mel Harrison slipped off his coat and backed by the other suits and the rockers he offered to fight anybody. One of the older lads hoisted me up on his shoulders; I held my scarf out and shouted, "Fuck off ya Chelsea bastards." I really didn't give a shit; I wasn't in the least bit scared. Why? I don't know. I was young and naive; I've been in far less tricky situations since and nearly crapped myself.

A lad I'd never seen before appeared at the side of us and started swinging out at the Chelsea fans. He told us he was a Sunderland fan working in London; he'd seen the trouble and he'd come to fight for the Northern team.

We stayed until the end of the game singing and chanting, we left the ground with the Suities and walked back to the Tube with no trouble at all. Nobody seemed really bothered about what happened on the Shed, it was no big deal and not much was said about it, we were having a great day and the night was still to come. Six months later we would return to the Bridge and the outcome would be so, so different.

We spent the night in the west end and around Trafalgar Square, which swarmed with Man City fans celebrating promotion back to the First Division Then it was back to Pancras for the midnight coach. The driver sussed us out and tried to get some money out of us. We said we were skint and after some threats from the other lads aboard he let us stay on the bus. We were dropped off in Dronfield about five o'clock Sunday morning. It had been about forty-five hours since I last had a kip. I slept like a rat for most of day and couldn't wait to get to school the next morning to tell my mates the tale.

Ever since that day, Stamford Bridge (the old Stamford Bridge that is) as always held a place in my heart. Maybe it was the adventure of the all-night journey, the brilliant day we had exploring London, and our first real taste of football violence.

What a bastard. Wednesday made it to the 66 FA Cup final and I was jealous as fuck. The one thing I wanted more than anything else in the world was to see the Blades at Wembley. What could be better than to march along Wembley Way, up to the twin towers, sing *Abide with Me* and then watch the Blades skipper lift the trophy? FA Cup-ties were always magic occasions, even the early rounds. The attendance rose by thousands. Cup replays played under floodlights on dark winter nights had a special, breath-taking atmosphere that couldn't be beaten. The whole crowd sang the Yorkshire anthem *Ilkley Moor Baht 'at* as the Blades ran out. "Weer as tha bin sin I saw thee."

The FA Cup final and the European Cup final were the only live games shown on TV so all the football fans tuned in to see them. The BBC also showed all the build-up to the final, and 'How they got there' with the goals from the early rounds. I watched the game at home wearing my red and white scarf and Blades rosette.

When Wednesday went two up I nearly died, but Everton came back with two goals from – I'll never forget his name – Mike Trebilcock – the man with three stangs. Then 'Shovel face' Gerry Young, the Wednesday left half, let the ball slip under his foot for Derek Temple to run through and win the game for Everton 3-2. When the third goal went in I danced out of the house, then up and down the street, whooping and screaming, waving my scarf round my head.

A civic reception was laid on for Wednesday. An estimated 100,000 Wednesdayites crawled out from under stones and emerged from forgotten dusty cupboards. They flooded the city centre and massed outside the town hall to welcome the team home. The Heeley Green mob also turned up carrying a large Blades banner. Slightly outnumbered, the Heeley lads had their banner pulled down, but not without giving a good account of themselves.

As stated earlier there wasn't much hostility between the Dronny Blades and Owls, but this was starting to change. A group of celebrating Dronny Wednesdayites, returning from the semi-final at Villa Park boarded the last bus from Sheffield. We were on the bus coming home from town and some of the older Blades amongst us took exception to the singing Owls.

What started out as a bit of fun soon turned nasty as the playful slaps being dished out by the Blades turned into full-blooded punches, leaving the Wednesdayites cowering under the seats.

As well as the trips to the Esquire, we started attending the Saturday all-nighters at the Victoria ballroom in Chesterfield. The Vic was a massive dance hall, housed on the top floor in a Tudor style building on Knifesmithgate in the centre of town.

On the way to my first visit to the club, half a dozen of us stretched out on the top deck of the number 12 Chesterfield bus. We took up a seat each and engaged in a spot of ruthless teenage banter. Paddy O'Brien's two-sizes-too-big and four-years-out-of-fashion, battered winkle-pickers dangled over one of the seats.

"Nar-then Pad," one of the lads shouted. "I bet your big 'un's had to stay in tonight hasn't he?"

"I don't know," Paddy answered. "Why?"

"Well you've only got one pair of shoes between ya and you've got the fuckers on."

The nighters were again 12 till 6 in the morning with no alcohol on sale. Some of the older lads had been before and told me how easy the Chesterfield birds were. To the latest pop sounds the girls filled the dance floor performing the Frug, the Shake, the Watutsy and the Boogaloo. Older tarts still did the Twist, the Jive and the Locomotion.

Hardly any blokes, and certainly none of the Dronny lads ever danced, as it was considered puffy. The lads walked in circles round and round, trying to pluck up courage to talk to the lasses. I got talking to this bird, and now being a man of world, my usual strategy was to say hello and go straight for the tit. It saved messing about and you knew where you stood if the girls didn't object, but remembering what my mates had said about the Chezzy birds being easy, after a few seconds or so I stuck my hand up her mini-skirt. She gave me a slap that made my cheek burn and stormed off.

We also used the Vic on Mondays for the 7 till 11 Soul nights.

Hodgy, a small seventeen-year-old, red haired, Dronny fireball with a permanent grin, was as hard as a mongoose. His idea of fun was to walk round Dronny (or Chesterfield) swigging a bottle of whisky, looking for people to fight. When we arrived in Chesterfield for the Vic nights, he'd nip off on his own to a pub somewhere, to buy a few Black Bombers (Dexedrine pills). I think he paid about half a crown each for them. None of the rest of us had ever seen, or even heard of the Dexys. Hodgy was very secretive about the whole thing and wouldn't even tell us which boozer he went to, to pick up the gear.

The first time we went to the club I could feel the tension. Groups of mods eyed us up and gave us the stares. A group came over and stood close to the five or six of us.

"Who's these cunts?" one of them said, loud enough for us to hear.

"Get ready," Hodgy said. We didn't have to, as he calmly stepped forward, and to the strains of Lee Dorsey's *Working in the Coalmine*, with one swift punch, put one of the lads straight on to his arse. The rest of the Chezzy lads picked up their mate and moved off.

One shouted," You're fuckin dead."

Every eye in the club was on us, but no one came over. Our Chezzy Blade mates arrived and said they would try and sort it out. They knew the lads who'd tried it on and calmed things down a bit. Mario, the main Chesterfield lad of the time, came from a large, rough family of Italian descent. We had Gig Ellis aboard, the 'cock' of Dronny. Gig and Mario knew of, and had mutual respect for, each other. They met and spoke for the first time and got to know each other. Mario and his crew even came down to the Esquire one night, in a joint venture with the Dronny mob after we had some trouble with a group of Sheffield lads in the club.

Later on, Hodgy and me pulled two birds. Mine looked at least twenty-one years old. This little cracker left nothing to the imagination. She wore a white see-through blouse with a black bra underneath and a six-inch mini-skirt. She had a foot high, circa 1960 beehive hairstyle and eyelashes like a camel. We left and went down an alley at the back of the club. Marge Simpson leaned back against the wall and hitched her skirt and girdle up over her hips saying, "Come on, hurry up I haven't got all night, I'm on early shift at Robbo's in morning." (Every bird in Chezzy worked at Robinson's jam-rag factory.)

"Yeah," I replied undoing my zip. "I've got to be up early mi sen for school."

"School," she said. "Fuckin' school, what ya talking about, you're still at school?"

"Yeah," I said. "but I leave next week."

"Fuck off," she shouted pulling her skirt back down.

She stormed off and grabbed her mate who stood a few yards further down with Hodgy, saying, "Come on, they're both at fuckin school."

"I'm not at fuckin school," Hodgy said. "I left ages ago."

The other girl pulled away from Hodgy. The last we heard from the two trollops was the scraping and echo of stiletto heels as they wobbled across the cobbles and disappeared out of the alley.

Hodgy cracked up saying, "Still at fuckin school, I can't believe ya said you were still at school. Fuck me, you do me in Ron."

We stood and rocked with laughter, Hodgy, whizzing off his head, kept shouting, "I'm still at fuckin school," at passers-by.

We'd missed the last bus and had to walk the six miles back home. I dossed on Hodgy's settee and he rose at the crack of dawn and went off to the farm where he worked. I went back to sleep and was late for fuckin school.

Blackpool, the finest place on God's wide earth.

My first ever week's holiday started there on Saturday the 23rd of July 1966. Five mates: Ansh, Kek Keeble, Rocket, Andy Ellis, Steve Buckley and me, spent seven brilliant days in a boarding house for around a fiver, full board.

The maroon coloured tower surprised me; I expected it to be black.

The hotel was on a road, bang opposite the Central Pier. The rooms were basic and clean, the food, out of this world. The only downside... it was Scottish week and the town was overrun by Jocks. We had to be careful, especially at night when gangs of growling, drunken Caledonians prowled the streets, remembering Bannockburn while looking for Englishmen to fight. To be fair though, we got on well with a group of Glasgow lads, all around our age, who were staying in the boarding house next door. Most of the other guests in our hotel were Scottish families, who, again were all okay. On arriving at our digs the landlady told us there had been a mix up with the rooms. Four of us she said, could have one room; the other two would have to share with another guest. Kek and me volunteered.

"You'll be okay, he's about your age," the landlady told us. We dragged our cases up two flights of stairs to the attic room on the top floor. A bloke lay stretched out on a single bed on one side of the room, a made-up double bed stood at the other.

"Hey-up," the bloke, shouted. "I'm Brian from Rotherham." Brian rose from the bed. He was massive, standing well over six feet tall and weighing about sixteen stone. His hair cropped in the early 60s crew-cut style. About our age, like fuck I thought. He told us he was twenty-three years old, and to a bunch of fifteen and sixteen-year-olds, that meant an old man. For some reason, that I can't remember we nicknamed him Icky.

The other lads came up from their room and Icky had us all laughing straight away. None of the room doors had locks; we just had a key for the front entrance. We all decided to head off to the beach for a game of football; Icky said he'd join us. On the way, he sneaked up behind girls and squeezed their arses. When the girls turned round he would clip one of us round the ear saying, "Sorry about that love, it's my lads, I can't do a thing with 'em, the little bastards." Then to us: "If you don't bleeding behave yer-sens I'm sending you home." We couldn't believe him; he was a complete madman.

A bikini-clad girl, laid sunbathing on the beach had the football dropped on her tits by Icky. He apologised, blamed me and gave me a scutch. During the football game he wouldn't pass to anybody, and he barged, and kicked us all over.

Like the kids we were, we got up to all kinds of childish tricks and pranks. We hid each other's clothes and toothbrushes, pissed on the soap, filled shoes with sand and put itching powder in each other's beds. Icky was worse than all of us put together. Some days he came out with us to the Pleasure Beach, where we spent the day riding the Big Dipper. I always stopped and had five minutes with the laughing clown outside the Fun House. The clown creased me up, the other lads had to drag me away, or I'd have stayed there all day.

When we walked and up and down the Golden Mile, Icky stopped complete strangers in their tracks to tell them a load of bollocks. He was one of the funniest blokes I have ever met, and he kept us amused all week. At night time though he always went off on his own; dolled up in a brown tonic suit, he trawled the boozers and the night-clubs.

On Wednesday, Gig Ellis, Locky and Pedro Fern, drove over in Locky's little, red, ex-post office van to spend the day with us. They planned to stay the night, sleep in the back of the van and drive back the next day. We decided to smuggle them into the digs: Gig in our room, Locky and Pedro in the other. We let Icky in on it; we knew he wouldn't say anything.

Blackpool. July 1966. The boys in Blackpool, from left to right, Rocket with Ansh on shoulders looking like a Ramone. Andy Ellis, me stood at the front, Gig Ellis, and Steve Buckley with Kek Keeble on his shoulders.

After our evening meal we went to our room to get changed. Icky had nipped out to the shops for something. His suit hung on a hanger on the wardrobe door. In a flash of inspiration, I grabbed the suit, climbed out of the window on to the fire escape and hung the suit from the guttering. It was drizzling outside, but all of a sudden the heavens opened, and the rain bounced down. Five minutes later Icky returned and shouted, "Weers mi fuckin suit?"

We told him the others had nicked it and he stormed down to their room to confront them. I nipped back out of the window, fetched the suit back in and hung it on the wardrobe. He came back up and saw it dripping onto the floor. With a big smile on his face he looked at Kek and me saying, "You little bastards, I'll get ya back for this."

After a night at the Pleasure Beach we returned to the digs and sneaked the lads in with no trouble. We jumped into bed with Gig squeezed in the middle.

Icky was still out doing the town.

After ten minutes or so we heard female voices outside the door. We thought for a moment the landlady had sussed us. Gig slid down the bed hiding under the covers. The door slowly opened, two women walked into the room, one of them flicked on the light. These fuckers were old, really old, well into their thirties at least. One had bleached blond hair with black roots; she looked a bit like Myra Hindley with a sprinkling of Yootha Joyce. The other was small and fat with bushy brown hair, brown coat and skirt to match.

"Hello," Myra/Yootha said "We're lion tamers from Bertram Mills's circus, we've got the sack and we've nowhere to stay."

As she spoke the other one shouted, "A bed, oh, a bed, I haven't slept in a bed for days, we're lion tamers from Bertram Mills circus you see, and we've got the sack."

We lay open mouthed in amazement. Before we could react, the fat brown one stripped off down to her underskirt and dived into Icky's bed. Fucking hell I thought, what's going on? Gig's head peeped out from under the covers.

"Hold on a minute," I said. "You can't sleep there, its somebody's bed."

"You don't understand," Myra said. "We're lion tamers from Bertram Mills's circus and we've nowhere to stay."

"Yes," fat brown said. "Lion tamers from Bertram Mills's circus, we've got the sack you see."

"Yeah but that's somebody's bed and he'll be back soon."

"But we're lion tamers from Bertram Mills circus."

I was starting to get a little bit scared.

Myra took off her coat; underneath she wore a tight fitting, sleeveless, knee length, white dress covered in printed roses. Even though this boiler was ancient I couldn't help but notice her curves. We really didn't know what to do, the fact that we'd smuggled Gig into the room made matters worse. We kept saying, "You can't stay here," but all we got was, "We're lion tamers."

I was thinking what the fuck is Icky gonna say when he comes back? Myra switched off the light, walked over to our bed and lay horizontally across us, on top of the covers with her head resting on my chest.

"We really must get some sleep," she said. "We're lion tamers from Bertram Mills circus you see."

If I'd have known at the time what tripping was, I would have sworn somebody had spiked my drink and I was having one. All three of us were worried about the dodgy situation, but that didn't stop us having the giggles. We eventually calmed down and my eyes adjusted to the darkness. What happened next... well I hang my head in shame and may the lord have mercy on my soul. I accidentally brushed my hand against Myra's breast. She didn't react, so I did it again but held it there a few seconds. Again she didn't move, so I gave it a couple of squeezes. I thought if she rears up and starts going mad, I'll just pretend it's an accident.

What really worried me though, was Kek and Gig catching me with my hand on a pensioner's pap. I would have died of embarrassment and never gone out again. Saying that, knowing Kek he'd probably got his hand up her skirt. I got a bit braver and slipped my hand under the old Platex, fondling her bare tit. It felt pretty firm, just like a normal young bird's tit.

Please... please don't let the lads see me I thought.

I heard a noise outside the door and whipped my hand out sharpish. Icky walked in and turned on the light. He stood looking from one bed to the other.

"What the fuck is she doing in my bed? You've gone too far this time you little bastards," he shouted.

"It's not us Brian, honest, there're lion tamers from Bertram Mills circus, and they just walked in."

"Yes," Myra said. "We're lion tamers from Bertram Mills circus and these lads said we could stay."

"No we dint. Straight up, Brian, they just walked in."

Fat brown chipped in with, "Lion tamers."

"Fucking lion tamers," Icky shouted. "What the fuck are you on about?"

Myra and fat brown went through the lion tamers sketch finishing each other's sentences.

"We're lion tamers." Myra said. "From Bertram Mills circus."

"Well I'm not missing a night's kip for no fucker, lion tamers or whatever ya fucking are," Icky said, as he clothed off down to his crackers, switched off the light and jumped into bed with fat brown.

Myra was still laid across us. In the darkness I could hear Icky and fat brown whispering. The whispers got louder. I thought I was going to explode when Icky murmured, "You haven't got any hairs on ya fanny."

"No," fat brown whispered back, "I shave, it gets a bit sweaty down there." Our bed rocked as the three of us, faces stuck in the pillows tried to stifle our laughter. The bed didn't rock half as much as Icky's though, as he did the business in good style. Fat brown, moaned, squealed and cried out in ecstasy. I thought I was going to die. The ride carried on for ages. Myra, still laid across us, never made a sound.

I can't believe that through all this, I fell asleep, I really did, it seems impossible, but that's what happened.

I awoke next morning, and the lion tamers had gone. Gig had also gone. I woke Kek up saying, "Fucking hell, did that really happen last night?"

Icky lay alone snoring like a pig. The other lads came into the room. Ansh told me what had happened while I was asleep. Icky, Ansh said, had stormed into their room, putting the fear of death into the two smuggled lads. He filled the sink up with water and as he dropped his stang and bollocks in and began washing them, he shouted," Right you little bastards, you can get them two fucking women out of my room now."

Ansh and rest didn't know what he was talking about.

"Look," Icky said. "A joke's a joke, I know you've set me up, but I want the fuckers out."

The lads pleaded their innocence, but he dragged them out of their beds and marched them up to our room. They must have been shocked to see Myra, sprawled across us, (if she still was) and Fat Brown in Icky's bed. Icky dragged both the ladies, (still insisting they were lion tamers) up and with the help of the lads pushed them down the stairs and out of the front door. Gig, Locky and Pedro thought they had better leave as well and went and spent the rest of the night in the van. I had slept through all this commotion.

So what really happened that night? I pondered it over and over, and years later I realised, Icky had done us good style. It was impossible the lion tamers could have just stumbled into our room by chance. How could they have got into the boarding house in the first place without the front door key? Icky must have met them in a pub or a nightclub and devised the dastardly plan, just to do our heads in. He most likely gave them his key, and told them which room we were in. Where the lion tamers sketch came from, I really can't imagine. When he'd had his fun and got his rocks off, he'd probably got fed up and wanted the ladies out, but how did they all manage to keep a straight face through the whole escapade. So, it's congratulations to Icky. Well done lad, you fuckin crazy diamond.

On the way home on the coach we listened to a live game on the radio.

It was some World Cup final between England and West Germany. The England selectors had pissed me off by not picking Mick Jones, who in my opinion was not only the best player in England; he was the best player in the world. I didn't give a shit if England won or not, Sheffield United were my team, fuck everybody else.

By the late summer of 66, England were football world champions, school was finally out forever and thus began my lifetime battle against the evils of employment.

I'd decided against becoming a barrister, surgeon, scientist or lone round the world yachtsman and opted to try my hand at being one of the labouring classes.

Welcome to the machine. Fifty years of collar for a gold watch and a shackle for a chain, 'tote that barge, lift that bale,' oh lordy! Etch it on my tombstone, 'Here lieth a hard-working man.'

The shouts, screams and threats from the teachers at school were over, but foremen, gaffers, chargehands, works' managers and supervisors took over where the bastards had left off.

"Get a move on, hurry up, you're not doing that right, are you stupid or what?"

They could stick their jobs and their rules up their arses. Was I not a free spirit? A Rolling Stone? Part of the new generation? Course I was.

My fathers and forefathers (rightly or wrongly) took pride from their chosen trades and labours. Well jolly good for them, but I hated it. Rising in the mornings at seven o'clock and trudging off to the factory in blazing sunshine. Clocking on at eight o'clock – two minutes past eight and I was 'quartered', meaning fifteen minutes wages were docked from my pay. The looks the gaffer gave me when I turned in late, gave me the feeling he'd loved to have seen me hung and drawn as well.

My first stint of labour started on Monday the 29th of August 1966 at a small Dronfield steel factory called Hand Tools. Ansh and couple more mates worked there, along with the first lesbian I'd ever seen. Robbo, a seventeen-year-old Lowedges lass, dressed, looked, walked, talked and fought just like a bloke. She wore her hair short and quiffed at the front. Robbo was sound, a good laugh and one of the lads... so to speak. Anyone who didn't know her would never have guessed she was a girl.

The wages at Hand Tools were £3 a week, half of which went for board and lodgings. I lasted three long weeks. Why did I stick it so long? I skived, fucked about, slept and hid in the bogs trying to make the days go faster.

The thought of standing at a stinking, oily milling machine or stacking lengths of steel for eight hours a day filled me with horror. All I looked forward to was the morning and afternoon snap breaks, dinnertime and the five o'clock hooter announcing work was over.

All the factory's and foundries knocked off at five o'clock. With a canvas snap bag and enamel mashing can, slung over my shoulder, I joined scores of black-faced zombies plodding through the streets back home.

For the next few years I drifted from job to job, a few weeks here, a couple of months somewhere else. I became an expert in the fine art of malingering. It was off to visit my understanding Doc, where I used my busted foot as an excuse for many weeks, months even, on the panel.

Jobs were ten a penny: walk out one day, start another the next. What about a career in mining? The still thriving North Derbyshire coalfields lay on my doorstep, but a bag of diamonds a week wouldn't have got me down the pit. Jobs for life they told us. Yeah right, Maggie and McGregor loomed on a distant horizon sharpening their knives. Hundreds of steel factories in Sheffield and the surrounding districts had jobs aplenty, for now.

The habit of watching the Blades had to be funded (although it didn't cost much if I hitch-hiked to the games, as the entrance fee was next to nowt). I also needed cash to keep up with the latest fashions, fads and trends, but the trusty club-book always came to my rescue if things got desperate. It was off to the youth employment bureau in Chesterfield every Friday to collect my weekly dole money of around £1.

A couple of mates who'd stayed on to take their O levels, wagged school every Friday morning and joined me on shop-lifting expeditions around the town.

The 66-67 season, that would see me travel to fifteen away games, and every home match started off with a friendly at 4th Division Stockport County. What a season: a season of excitement and discovery – every away game with the early morning (or night before) start, was like setting off on holiday. Towns and cities I would never have dreamt of visiting, if it wasn't for the football, were out there waiting to be explored. I even started studying a map of England to check out our destinations.

Ansh, Tiny and me set off hitching over the Derbyshire moors on the Saturday morning (I had no trouble getting out of bed when there was a match to go to). We walked miles and miles, as there was hardly any traffic. I'd made a banner out of a white bed sheet with SHEFFIELD UNITED THE KINGS painted in red letters. I'd also made a cardboard top hat about a foot high painted in red and white stripes.

A car pulled up and we ran towards it, we all got in, all except my banner, which was fastened to two eight-foot-long bamboo poles. After a few minutes trying to force the banner in, the driver got fed up, drove off and left us.

"You're gonna have to leave the banner here Ron, or we're never gonna get a lift," Tiny said.

"Fuck that," I said, "It took me ages to make, I'm not leaving it."

A while later another car pulled up, and after a struggle we managed to get the banner in with half of it stuck through the front seat side window. Not only was it easy to thumb lifts, the drivers were always friendly and helpful. The driver went out of way to drop us off on the outskirts of Stockport, where we caught a bus into town.

We went into a café to get a bit of snap, and it was no wonder from my appearance, and Tiny's mod gear, that we received some nasty looks from a group of local rockers. We left pretty sharpish, glancing behind and made our way up to the ground.

It was around one o' clock, and we joined a group of twenty young Blades sat in the sunshine outside the turnstiles. We went in when the gates opened and sat on open terracing behind the goal. At halftime with the Blades kicking towards the covered end, we walked, with banner held up along the Pop side terrace, where a group of Stockport fans were gathered at the far end.

A couple of lads in the Stockport mob held up a large Manchester United banner. We were spat at and shoved as we walked through onto the covered end. One lad came from behind and knocked the top hat off my head. I smiled nervously as I bent down, picked it up and placed it back on my head. We gathered behind the goal and more Stockport lads came behind us. We walked off to what we thought would be the safety of the other terrace to our left but were followed by the Stockport lads. They again got behind us and started banging into us. Maybe because of my top hat and banner I was targeted more than the others.

A gap appeared behind us, as two Blade blokes who were in their mid-twenties (Derek Goodison and a monster known as The Bear) started slapping the Stockport lads, no punches were thrown, just scutches.

"Fuckin leave them alone," Derek said, "There only kids."

A leather jacketed lad who stood head and shoulders above me said to Derek, "I'm only sixteen, there're the same age as us." Another swift clip from Derek and he was off. We stayed close to the old blokes for the rest of the game, found out they were going back by train; so we walked back to the station with them and jumped the train home.

The obvious dangers linked with watching my team were becoming clear, but the buzz, the excitement and the out-and-out fun of it all far outweighed the thought of any shit I might get into.

The first league game of the new season took us to Burnley. I'd heard stories from the older lads about the fighting at the previous season's games both at Turf Moor and the Lane, but we were all looking forward to the trip and the match. We travelled by train from the now long-gone Victoria station. Loads of Blades lined the platform waiting for the train. We changed at Manchester and arriving in Burnley, saw groups of lads wearing combat jackets and clad in the claret and blue Burnley colours standing on street corners and in shop doorways across from the station.

We split from the main mass and went in search of a chippy. Some more Burnley fans came out of an alleyway and let fly a volley of eggs at us. The older Dronny boys ran at them and chased them off. We bumped into another set of Blades covered in yolk who'd copped for it from the egg chuckers. Up at the ground we again came under fire. This was mad, did they do this every week? Gig Ellis ran towards a group of Burnley and launched a bottle that smashed on a wall above their heads.

We entered the Kop about 2 o'clock and joined a couple of hundred Blades stood at the side of the Burnley mob numbering about the same. There were some nasty looking rockers in the Burnley ranks; I kept well back. Bricks, bottles and other missiles rained across between the two mobs, but there was no hand to hand fighting. This went on for a good ten minutes with half a dozen coppers trying to restore order.

The Burnley ranks swelled and with no Blades suities or rockers to protect us (they were probably still in the pub) my arse started twitching. Some Blades drifted off towards a large covered side terrace to our left. I was relieved when one of our group said we should join them. We walked off leaving twenty or so braver lads to face the onslaught. A few minutes later they were on their way out.

We all gathered on the open end behind the goal, and as kickoff approached I saw fighting erupt from the Kop. I was surprised to see three of the Dronny lads: Johnny Hall, Bezz and Beetroot, who'd travelled on a later train, climb over the fence behind the Kop-end goal waving a Blades flag. They walked straight across the pitch, did a little dance in the centre circle and joined us on the open end.

The suities, whose arrival at the Kop end had sparked off the latest fight, came round to the open end going crazy and scaring the shit out of the rest of us. "What the fuck are you doing on here? You should be on the fucking Kop." Mel Harrison shouted.

After a 4-0 drubbing we walked back to the station without a hint of trouble, it seemed that the fighting was for now confined to the terraces; that would soon change.

When we changed trains at Manchester, the Dronny and Chesterfield lads decided to stay and have a mosie round for a while. We weren't doing anything in particular, just walking the streets and having a laugh. We somehow copped for this gorgeous bird, who was maybe eighteen-nineteen. I can't even imagine why she tagged onto us. She just walked up to us, told us in pidgin English she came from Sweden; she was lost and was looking for a place called the International Club. Even though we all wanted to, none of us really had the bottle to move in on her, we probably thought she was out of our league, so as little kids do, we started taking the piss. When she told us her name (I can't remember what it was) I said, "My name's Stang." And pointing to Gig Ellis, I said, "and his name's Slice."

"Hello Stang, hello Slice," she said. Everybody started sniggering.

"Stang and slice go very well together," I said.

"Yes Stang and Slice," she said.

"Shove a stang up a slice, yes?" I said.

She looked a bit confused.

"Fuck a slice with a big fat stang," I said. All the lads were creased up now and I could hardly talk for laughing.

"You stang?" she said pointing at me. "You slice?" she said to Gig.

"Yes stang and slice very nice, and fuck very nice yes?" I said.

"Fuck, who fuck?" she said.

"He fuck," I said, pointing to Ansh.

"Hello fuck," she said. By now we were in bits. She stayed with us for a good half hour listening to the shit, before she just walked off and disappeared into the night. Maybe she was a Manc bird and it was her who was taking the piss, I hope so.

Back in Sheffield, the night was still not over, as the Chezzy lads knew of an all-night party in town. We caught the train to Chezz, and on board, we had a good chat and laugh with a gang of Millwall fans returning from Rotherham. There was no friction, we were all on the same wavelength, just high on the world. Groups of young lads returning from watching their team away from home, had some kinda connection.

At the following Saturday's home game against Nottingham Forest all the talk centred on the events at Burnley. Hats off to the bright spark who came up with the idea, as word spread around the Kop, that for the derby match against Wednesday at Hillsborough in a month's time everybody would be taking eggs. For the next few weeks a new song, rang around the Shoreham:

> "Don't forget yer eggs
> Don't forget yer eggs
> Eee-hi-addio don't forget yer eggs."

I was starting to meet and get friendly with more and more young lads at every game. The Heeley Green mob: Herman, (Brian Sellers) looked like Peter Noone from the pop band Herman's Hermits. Jimmy Milligan, Mick Scanlan,

86

Steve Bagley (Mouse), Urky, John and Babby Green, Pete and 'Squeak' O'Brian and Billy Robbo. The Groom mob from Gleadless: Stan Lake, Ro, Dave Lindsey, Drabs and Boiler. The Hackenthorpe boys: Woody, Bob Pixley and Witey. John Bramall (Jagger) his brother, Pete, Joe Speed, Phil Stevenson, Black Arthur, Phil Conners and 'Wandering' Walt Lightowler. The Killamarsh rockers. Haggis and Alfie, mods from the Herdings area. Lads from the east end of Sheffield (Attercliffe and Darnall) included Wafer and the superbly named Faggot. Wafe's rocker mate, Sam Shirt from Hillsborough. The Pitsmoor, Burngreave and the Chesterfield boys. Plus the Dronny crew: Ansh, Tiny, Johnny Hall, Beetroot, Lou, Ding and Les Bell, Bezz, Rocket, Evvo, Fruitbat, Wuss, Fordy, Rodge Vernon, Terry Jones, Piggy Bacon, and Gig and Andy Ellis.

It felt great to be on first name terms with so many new mates, our scarves and club colours identified us with our football team and with each other. The same thing was happening at every ground up and down the country as more and more boys gathered together to support their heroes, check out the latest terrace fashions and just like the American street gangs, try to defend their 'little bit of turf.'

Twenty, fifty, a hundred, two hundred, four hundred, the numbers didn't matter. Compressed together, we swayed, sung and chanted as one. When a goal went in we surged forward revelling in the noise, the colour and the chaos. Sometimes ending up on the floor or squashed against a crush barrier, but it didn't matter, euphoric, we hugged each other waving our scarves, whooping and screaming, "Yeeeeeesssss!"

The main reason we were all there though was our love for the game. All the Dronny lads who attended the games were good footballers, same with the Heeley lads who came up to Dronfield a few times for a game in the park; lads who were crap at footie, and the fat kids, could be found at Hillsborough.

At half time at the Forest game, a gang of parka-clad Blade mods attacked the visiting fans by the old cricket pavilion as they walked towards the Kop. The Forest fans retreated back to the Lane end.

Only two coaches made the trip to Fulham on the following Saturday.

Tiny, Ansh and me (along with a few of the older rockers) boarded one of them. The Blades had lost the first four games of the season, but we didn't give a shit if they won, lost or drew as long as we were there to see them. We all assembled on Fulham's Kop half an hour before kickoff, none of the Fulham fans bothered us. With United kicking towards the open end in the first half we walked along an open terrace, where over a wall to our right we could see the river Thames in all its glory flowing past the stadium.

At half time we walked back to the Kop end and stood directly behind the goal about half way up the terracing. A group of mods gathered behind us and started throwing coins and tin cans at us. Despite the name, tin cans, the weapons (because that's what they were) were made of plate steel and an empty one weighed about the same as a full one would today. If one hit you, you knew about it. The Blade rockers were having none of it and one of them picked up a can, walked up to the biggest mod and smashed it into his face. As blood

87

streamed down his nose he screamed, "My face, my face, look what you done to my facking face."

That put a stop to it straightaway, the mods moved off and left us alone. It wasn't a mod-rocker thing though, it was a football thing and just like at the Chelsea game, we would have been happy to stand there and watch the match, but it seemed that wherever we went, fans from the home team didn't like us stood in their territory.

Again, there was no trouble after the match. We had a brilliant night in the west end, where we called in a café and got chatting to the girl working behind the counter. It turned out the bird came from Sheffield and she gave us free snap. We met a couple of Liverpool birds who'd been to West Ham to watch their team. I had a tonguey snog and grope with one of them before catching our bus back home at midnight from St Pancras.

The next away game's Stoke City. 200-300 Blades caught the train from Victoria station, changing at Manchester. Loads of the lads now carried banners and flags, as was the trend. We marched out of the station looking pretty impressive with banners and flags flapping in the wind.

At the ground, we queued outside the Boothen End turnstiles (Stoke's Kop) where a squad of coppers told us: no banners or flags were allowed in the ground, as the poles could be used as weapons. The banners were confiscated, the police said we could collect them after the match.

We entered the Boothen end and stood to the left of the Stoke mob. I was close enough to hear their accents, they sounded a bit like Scousers.

I wore a brand new, sandy coloured army surplus, bush jacket (a new football trend) bought the day before from Yeoman's army stores, priced seven shillings and sixpence. I hadn't had time to decorate

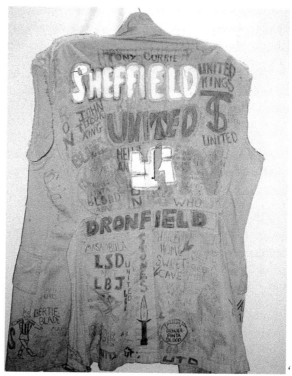

The bush jacket' essential terrace clobber in the mid-60s.

it with the SHEFFIELD UNITED, SHOREHAM STREET slogans that most of the young Blades had felt tipped on the backs of theirs.

To the tune of The Beatles Yellow Submarine, "We all live at the back of the Boothen end" rang out from the Stoke ranks.

"We all shit at the back of the Boothen end," we retorted. Bottles and coins flew back and forth. I stood with Heeley Green lads and some young Stoke lads about our age came behind us, we stared at each other and a few, "Fuck off's", but no punches were exchanged. The fighting (usually one on one) was done by the older lads.

More Blades arrived from the coaches and gathered on the open end. We could have done with some reinforcements as we were well outnumbered by this time. The Stoke ranks swelled, and banners and flags were raised from them. It seemed *they* were allowed to take them in the ground.

The main Stoke man, the King of the Kop, looked to be in his twenties and, strange as it may seem, wore Father Christmas robes. He pushed his way to the front, alongside a big lad with deep red, shoulder length hair. With their leaders at the front the Stoke mob moved towards us. The cavalry arrived in the shape of the suities who pushed their way through to face Santa and his mate. Willie Ward let out a piecing: "Zigga-zagga-zigga-zagga."

"Yoo-ni-ted," we bellowed back.

"Zigga-zagga-zigga-zagga," Santa responded.

"Stoke-ci-tee," echoed back from the Stoke troops. The coppers were now in the crowd trying to keep the two sets of fans apart. Lads from both sides were frog-marched down the terracing and thrown out of the ground. The pushing, shoving and threats continued all through the game.

I saw no trouble outside the stadium, the lads whose banners were taken, had them returned and we walked back to the station with no trouble. As we waited on the platform some Stoke fans arrived and a lad threw a Ben Shaw bottle at them. Ben Shaw pop bottles were the daddies of all bottles. Twice as big as a normal pop bottle with sixpence refund on them instead of the usual threepence, you hadn't been hit with a bottle unless it was a Ben Shaw.

I'd been to four away games already this season and there'd been trouble at all of them, it seemed to be getting worse every week. This was the shape of things to come, and although I didn't know it, it was happening all over the country. Fucking marvellous: I didn't realise being scared could be so exciting and so much fun, just like a big dipper ride. Could it get much better? It certainly could: next Saturday it's the eagerly awaited 'Egg day' where we would march through the barren wastelands of Hillsborough to hopefully do battle with our arch enemies, Sheffield Wednesday.

On the morning of Saturday September 24th, 1966, four fifteen-year-old Dronny Blades sneaked into Hopkinson's smallholding.

Johnny Hall, knew the layout well, he worked there doing odd jobs at the weekends. Scores of chickens roamed free around the sheds and outbuildings, laying eggs in makeshift nests, under bushes and in the corners of broken-down huts. The further away from the main house the rottener the eggs were likely to be. After filling a bag each, the lads made their way to the bus stop, to meet up with a couple of hundred or so fellow Blades who were gathering in Pond Street bus station at midday.

Willie Marples, a classmate from school, on his way to the match, clad in his Wednesday gear passed the lads on Dronny bottom. Beetroot let fly a rotten egg which splatted on Willies back. Johnny Hall reckoned an old bloke walking past with his dog, fainted from the stench and the dog dropped dead.

Willie and Beetroot slugged it out, one on one for a few minutes. Beetroot ended the scrap by whipping off his belt and smacking Willie round the lughole with the buckle end. The ill feeling had started already.

Beetroot (so called, because the one and only time he ever got told off by a teacher, he went as red as one) was a quiet, studious, intelligent lad who always did well at school. He always had a top pocket full of pens and would lend you one, no bother. Beetie however turned into a very naughty boy – a kind of Mr Hyde type creature whenever he went to a football game. I once saw him, after a testimonial game against Wednesday at the Lane, drag a Wednesdayite off a bus in Pond Street, beat him half to death with a walking stick then laugh his head off when he'd finished.

I'd left a note out for Mam's milkman (half a dozen eggs please) and arrived in town for the midday meet. Loads of Blades were already there, many carrying boxes of eggs.

We set off on the two-mile trek with our banners, flags and eggs, picking up small groups of lads as we walked through town. There wasn't a copper in sight. We showed off our eggs, like they were some kind of new thing that nobody had ever seen before. Some had the little lion stamp, there was large 'uns, small 'uns, free-range, and jumbo.

"Look at them fuckers for eggs then."

As we reached the bottom of Penistone Road a mob of Pitsmoor lads carrying a large banner joined us. Any Wednesdayites we saw en route had the odd egg chucked at them. On reaching the ground about one thirty, we queued outside the Penistone road end (Wednesday's Kop). We paid the one shilling or it might have been two shillings admission at the boy's entrance. Inside, a group of Blades said, the coppers were at the back of the Kop searching everyone for eggs.

I hid my eggs in some bushes and walked past two coppers (yes, two) trying to pat down dozens of youths as they entered the Kop.

"Got any eggs?" The copper asked me, patting my bush jacket; a couple of cartons lay at his feet.

"No," I said,

"Go on then," he said.

At least ten lads walked past as he did this. I waited a few minutes, walked back out and collected my eggs. Passing the same copper again I said, "You've searched me once."

"Yeah, go on," he said. The ground was all but deserted, except for us; we stood at the back of the Kop behind the goal waiting for the Wednesdayites to arrive. The plan was, at ten minutes to three, with our arms held up and to the chant of, "Sheff United, hallelujah" the mass throw would take place. By two o'clock, fifty or so Wednesdayites gathered at the front. This proved too

90

tempting for some trigger-happy Blades, and a few dozen eggs landed on the Owls.

By two thirty the ground started filling up, more Wednesdayites, more Unitedites and more eggs entered the stadium. At ten to three, with forty thousand in the ground, and the mass of Blades singing and swaying, hundreds of hands raised into the air, and the chant went up, "Sheff United – hallelujah – hallelujah."

What a sight, nowhere to run, nowhere to hide, its 'raining eggs, hallelujah.' A huge roar greeted the teams as they took to the pitch. Wednesday's banners were covered in yellow slime. "Scrambled eggs, scrambled eggs," we chanted. Our ammunition now used up, we turned to coins and other missiles. Stones were collected from the banking at the back of the Kop and chucked at the Wednesdayites. One of the young Dronny lads (who later went on to join the police force) was lobbed out by his later-to-be colleagues. The game ended in a 2-2 draw, but the Blades scored what we all thought was a late winning goal, only for it to be disallowed for offside.

We marched back down Penistone road towards town, chanting "We were robbed," but still laughing at any egg-stained Wednesday fans we saw.

The following Monday's edition of the *Sheffield Morning Telegraph* reported the trouble. It told of the many ejections from the ground, of youths throwing sharpened steel washers and carrying flick-knifes… but no mention of any eggs!

I was skint, so I had to miss the next away trip to Southampton. Tiny and Rocket did it though. After hitching all through Friday night they arrived on the south coast to find only two coaches had made the long trip, but, worst of all, they couldn't get a lift back on either of them and had to hitch home, arriving back late Sunday afternoon, Tiny swore he'd never hitch it anywhere again.

For the next game at Aston Villa, half a dozen of us caught the train from Dronny station, about the same number boarded at Chesterfield joining twenty or so Sheffield boys already on the train. We arrived at Birmingham New Street around dinnertime. We walked round the city centre and did a bit of shop lifting: useless items like books and pencil cases from Woolies, which we threw away outside. We walked up to Villa Park and hung around the ground wondering what to do, when a fleet of a dozen S.U.T. coaches pulled up. Blades swarmed off the buses and headed for the turnstiles.

We went into the massive half-covered banking of the Holte End. Only the North bank at Wolves, where I'd stood in a Cup match in early 66 matched it for size. We stood about halfway up, just under cover, directly behind the goal. The Villa mob stood just behind us, and the usual pushing, shoving and missile throwing went on between the two groups. We sang our songs, Villa sang theirs, each trying to out-do the other. Villa did a variation of the Zigger-Zagger chant: "Villa-Villa-Villa-Villa-hoy-hoy-hoy."

The different songs and chants fascinated me, there were new songs every week, most to the tunes of the latest pop songs. We stole songs from other fans, changing the words to fit to our players or team; other fans stole songs from us.

After a 0-0 draw, around twenty of us left the ground and set off on the long walk back to the station. The main mass of Blades went in the opposite direction to the coaches.

Scarf nicking was the in-thing, usually done by grabbing a much younger, or smaller boys scarf (often from behind) then running off and getting lost in the crowd. I only ever stole scarves off lads who were twice as big as me, honest… Bri Thurman and me whipped a couple of scarves off these six-foot-six Villa fans, but we lost the rest of the lads and had to walk the rest of the way to the station on our own. Both of us wore bush jackets with Sheffield United felt-tipped on the back. I got chatting to a young, good looking, dark haired Villa girl about my age. She said she'd show us the way back to the station and I thought: I'm well in here.

We arrived at New Street and found our platform just as the train was pulling out. I made a half-hearted attempt to catch it. The next train wasn't due for an hour or so. I left Bri sat on a luggage trolley and went and found a quiet corner for a fumble with the Villa girl. I returned ten minutes later and the three of us sat chatting, when a group of about twenty Villa fans walked onto the platform. They must have thought we were Villa at first until they noticed our jackets. They surrounded us and were just about to attack, when the Villa bird jumped to her feet, pulled a penknife from her back pocket and shouted: "Anybody touch him, and I'll fucking cut you up."

"They've nicked Villa scarves, " one of the lads said.

"I don't give a fuck," the girl replied waving the blade in the air. Fuck me: a knife-wielding bird was protecting me. I thought about handing the scarf back to defuse the situation, when Blades started to appear on the platform. I recognised some of Hackenthorpe mods. More Blades arrived, and the Villa lads moved off. They didn't run, they just stood about twenty yards away staring at us. Our train turned up and I said goodbye to the Villa girl, promising to meet her when the teams played at the Lane. I did go looking for her on the Lane end when we played Villa, but she wasn't there.

"Harry Roberts is our friend – he kills coppers." The song rang out at every football ground in the land. Harry Roberts, a London gangster gunned down two policemen before going on the run. The newspapers and TV news bulletins were full of the story; everybody in the country knew about Harry Roberts.

While Roberts was on the run, Beetroot and Grunter were out at Castleton in deepest Derbyshire on a trout-poaching mission. They were caught by the gamekeeper and dragged to the village police station.

"Name?" the copper shouted at Beetroot,

"Brian Crookes," Beetie replied.

"Your name?" the copper said to Grunt.

"Harry Roberts," Grunt replied.

"You little bastard," the copper said smacking Grunt around the ear hole, "Now what's your name?"

"Harry Roberts," Grunt said again, another smack to the head had Grunt reeling.

"But it's my name," Grunt said. "I can't help it, it's my name." After a few more slaps, both the lads finally convinced the copper that Harry Roberts was indeed Grunt's real name. A case of wrong time, wrong place, right name. Maybe Grunt should have given the coppers a false one.

Blackpool brought just one coach of supporters to the game at the Lane in early November. They stood behind the goal on the Lane end, so a few of us went round to have a look. They were mostly old men and women with just a few young lads about our age.

The Blades left winger Gill Reece was carried off with a broken leg and this incensed a big Scottish bloke from Dronny. He walked up from the front and sparked out a Blackpool fan out with one punch. This Scottish geezer really was a huge ugly monster and a lot older than us lot, probably in his late twenties. I'd seen him on the bus a few times on his way to and from the games. When he saw us lot in our Blades colours he sometimes growled out a few words, the only one I understood was "United."

After the game we made our way to the Blackpool coach, parked down a side street near St Mary's church. Half a dozen or so of the young Blackpool lads sat on the back seat; the rest of the bus contained the old men and women. We stuck our fingers up and shouted insults at each other for a while. Johnny Hall and me jumped on the coach and made our way up to the back. We asked the Blackpool lads if they fancied getting off, but they were having none of it.

Feeling dead cocky we swaggered down the bus, jumped off and banged on the sides as we walked away laughing and showing off. I never thought for one moment that little episode would soon come back to haunt me.

It was back to the capital and Chelsea in mid-November, just six months after we'd ventured onto the Shed. I was the youngest of eight Dronny and four Chesterfield lads who caught the midnight train from Sheffield Midland station. I could always get half-fare on the buses and trains. At the ticket counter, I said to the bloke.

"Half to London, return please."

"How old are you?" the bloke said.

"Thirteen, " I answered.

"Date of birth?"

"Twelfth of April 1953."

"Go on then, but tha shunt be out at this time, if tha's only thirteen," he said.

Sinny, a scrawny, dark haired Chezzy lad aged about nineteen was the oldest of our little crew. Although roughly the same age as the suit boys he was nothing like them. He dressed in the same way as us and knew, as we all did, that something was starting to happen. A new culture based around football that was fun, exciting and dangerous. He talked constantly about the gangs we were likely to encounter and what might happen if we did. He wanted to find out everything there was to know about the new scene, he relished every single second of it. No matter where we travelled, we had no idea what or who, could be lurking around the next corner. We were stepping into the unknown, that was part of the fun and the buzz of it all.

The bush jackets were left at home, not through fear, though: we were off for a weekend's fun in the big city and all wore our best togs for the occasion. Most of us wore red and white woolly scarves. Dave Parton brought along his old dented brass bugle. The fucker kept sneaking up behind us and blasting our earholes from six inches. The bugle also made a handy weapon.

The thrill of rattling down south all through the night and the anticipation of the day to come was overwhelming. We got talking to a Man Utd fan on the train. He came from Halifax and was heading down to Southampton. He bragged Man Utd were the best-supported team in the land, and fans travelled from all parts of England to watch them. Thousands went to every away game he said. Every football fan in the land knew about Man Utd so I had no reason to doubt him. We told him we were going to Chelsea.

"You want to watch it there," he said. "The last time Man Utd played 'em, we had 10,000 on the Shed end, but they still kept having a go at us." He looked amazed when we told him about the hundred or so Blades who'd been on there six months earlier, he clearly didn't believe us.

"How many are you taking today?" he asked.

"A couple of hundred maybe," we replied.

"Fuck me," he said. "You'll get fucking slaughtered."

We hung from the open doors, with the wind blowing our hair back as the train shunted into St Pancras at around four in the morning. The Man U fan nearly shit his pants when Parton's bugle blasted him as we left the train. We sat around the station, chatting, laughing and messing about; there was nothing else to do at that time of the morning. A couple of us went for a walk and stole a full crate of milk from outside a shop, which we bought back for the others to share.

The Beach Boys *Good Vibrations* crackled out from a transistor radio behind the counter as we entered a greasy café to pass a bit more time. We spent an hour or so having a laugh with the locals, while swigging steaming hot, weak southern tea. The waiter was quite obviously a puff-boy and did nothing to hide it. He flittered around the tables doing little twists and twirls, calling the customers 'Darling' and 'Sweetheart' in a marvellous camp voice. I cracked everybody up by shouting out one of me Mam's old sayings, "He walks like he's got a threepenny bit stuck up his arse."

When the streets were aired, and the tube stations opened we headed off to Buckingham Palace to visit the Queen. We walked up the Mall, singing, climbing on walls and swinging from trees. Nearing the Palace, Parton let out a series of ear-splitting blasts from his bugle, it sounded like a dying elephant. Two policemen came strolling over to us; one of them beckoned Parton over, and pointing to a mansion across the street he calmly said,

"Come here, son. Do you know who lives there?"

"No," Parton replied. The coppers voice grew gradually louder.

"Well, I'll tell you who lives there shall I. The Queen Mother – and she likes a lie-in on Saturday mornings, so if some scruffy bastard starts blowing a trumpet and wakes her up, it's me who gets the blame. So if you blow it one more time I'll ram it straight up your arse, understand?" By this time the copper was bawling his head off.

"Yes, sir. Sorry officer," Parton replied, the rest of us doubled up with laughter.

It was good enough just being in London, just walking around the streets. Tremendous buildings, statues and monuments everywhere. There was an air of magic and a promise of adventure about the place. I could smell London, taste it. I felt part of it. I loved it.

Trafalgar Square seemed enormous, we climbed the lions, gazed up miles at Lord Nelson and scattered ten thousand pigeons. We spent the rest of the morning shouting at passers-by, ogling dolly birds in kinky boots and squeezing mini-skirted bums. We met and got chatting to a group of 'Newcastleites.' Unitedites, Wednesdayites: I didn't know at the time it was a Sheffield thing. I thought 'ites' was the name for all football fans and called them Chelseites, Arsenalites, Portsmouthites even Accrington Stanlyites.

The Newcastle lads carried a black and white banner: felt-tipped in one corner the words, CHARLIE HURLEY, CURLY BASTARD. I asked what it meant. Charlie Hurley they told me played for Sunderland; he had curly hair and they hated the bastard. Fair enough, it seemed hatred between local rivals was nationwide.

We had a chat to some Norwich fans decked out in yellow and green and I swapped my Blades pin badge for one of theirs. All the different accents and club colours fascinated me. Fans from other clubs always got on, we were all in London having a good time, so no one wanted to fight or hurt each other. Fans we met from the London clubs were always friendly, chatty and helpful. With the hooligan scene in its infancy, London was still a quite safe place, away from the football stadiums. Fans had not yet started to bear grudges that in the near future would turn the capital into a battlefield when rival supporters crossed paths in the train stations or on the Underground.

Reading the morning paper, we learnt United had signed what they described as a speedy left winger from Norwich City, a certain Billy Punton as a replacement for the injured Gil Reece and he'd be making his debut today. We arrived at Stamford Bridge about 2.30 and went into the open corner bit of the Shed. Seeing a small group of Blades camped under a weird looking little stand on stilts at the corner of the open end, we walked under the main stand to join them. Only two coaches made the trip plus about twenty or so who travelled on the morning train.

As always, two lads carrying a huge silk banner were there. This banner was top class, the top half red, the bottom half white with SHEFFIELD UNITED in hand stitched black letters emblazoned across it. There'd always been a few flags and banners dotted around the grounds, but now more and more were starting to appear. "We took three hundred yesterday and we had ten banners." If I missed an away game the first questions I asked the lads who'd been, "How many Unitedites went? And "How many banners did we have?" The trouble with taking them to away games, was unlike scarves, you couldn't hide six yard of cloth and two eight-foot poles up your jumper. Just like the wars of centuries past, one of the new trends at the games was 'the taking of the colours' then ripping them to shreds in front of their owners.

The lads told us some Chelsea boys and been round earlier and tried to steal the banner. They said they'd be waiting after the match. Parton told the Blade lads to stick with us and that he'd carry the banner out at the end of the game.

The teams came out and we couldn't believe it when we saw Punton.

"Fuck me," Tiny said. "He's sixty-years old."

"Who's that?" somebody else shouted: "Yul Brynner."

Bald Bill turned out a good performance, though: setting up the equalising goal for Alan Birchenall in a 1-1 draw. We weren't to know it then, but a couple of months later Punton would turn out to be a Blade legend, remembered for ever, for one magic moment that would repay his £5,000 transfer fee ten times over.

The game ended and the twelve of us, plus the two lads with the banner made our way out. Parton handed his bugle to one of our lads and now carried the banner. As we hit the darkened streets, groups of Chelsea mods stood on both sides of the road. Another group headed straight towards us. I pushed my scarf under my jacket and could hear my heart thumping.

Parton – who bearing in mind was only seventeen years old – didn't wait for them to reach us. He charged into them swinging the banner round his head. A tall ginger haired Chelsea lad wearing a parka came from the side and landed a punch to Parton's head. He wobbled but managed to stay on his feet. Other Chelsea lads tried to grab the banner, but he wouldn't let go. We pushed our way through avoiding kicks and punches. Suddenly we were through them, we didn't run, and we weren't chased, it just stopped as quickly as it started.

Parton's eye was already closing as we walked into Fulham Broadway tube station; other groups of Chelsea fans stared at us, but no one said anything. With a big smile on his face Parton handed back the banner to the two lads. We caught the Tube and made our way up to the West End.

Soho – now that was something else. A compact collection of sex shops, rip-off strip joints, flashing neon signs and sleazy peep shows. The roasted ducks displayed in the windows of the Chinatown restaurants with their heads and long necks still attached, looked rather pissed off as they hung and waited their turn to be next on the menu. We cruised the narrow streets, trying to take it all in: fucking paradise – I wished I could stay forever.

We called into a café for a cup of tea. I noticed a piece of string with a small lump of cardboard on the end hanging out of my cup. I went back to the counter and said to the girl who'd served me, "What the fuck's that?"

"It's a tea-bag", she said. "Leave it in the cup to brew for a minute or two."

I went back to our table, lifted the bag out and swat it into the saucer in disgust.

"What about that," I said. "It's a fucking tea-bag, I've not seen one of them fuckers before." Everybody cracked up. Strange place, this London.

"Who do you support then lads, Liverpool, Man Utd?" A doorman shouted as we approached a strip club called the Red Mill.

"Sheffield United us, mate."

"Ah steel men are ya? Well get yourself in here boys, these girls are all smashers, show you everything, and I mean everything, I can do you a special price, ten bob each, that's if you're all eighteen? You're eighteen aren't ya, mate?" he said looking at me.

"Yeah, I'm eighteen," I said.

"Course ya are son, come on, in ya go."

Giggling and nudging each other, thinking we were right good, we paid our ten bobs and entered the Red Mill.

It was a small dingy hovel, dimly lit, with a raised stage at the front, about six rows of cinema type seats and standing room at the back. The place was packed, and we squeezed in at the back of the room.

We whistled, booed, cheered and shouted obscenities as the strippers came on, one by one, from behind a filthy curtain. Some were okay, some were old dogs. As punters from the front left their seats, others moved from the back to take them. Parton, now sporting a beaut of a shiner somehow managed to get himself on the front row, bang in front of the stage. One of the strippers noticed Parton's eye, and pretending to pluck a hair from her fanny, she leaned over to him and said, "That looks sore darling, put this on it; it'll sooth it." Parton reached out, took the imaginary pube between his finger and thumb, held it up, and shouted, "I'm saving this fucker, as anybody got a matchbox?" The place erupted in laughter.

On the midnight train home, we swore revenge on the Chelsea bastards if they ever came to the Lane, little knowing we would be back there in less than four months.

The Chesterfield mods main haunt was a place called the Scene club in the town centre. According to the Chezzy Blades, the Scene club crew were a rough set of lads who came from different areas of the town.

On Monday evenings we hung out at the church hall youth club, mostly to escape the weather. The youth club, ran by the local vicar didn't attract many teenagers, maybe a dozen or so lads and half a dozen lasses. There was a three-quarter-size snooker table in an upstairs room, table tennis in the main hall, a record player on the stage and that was about it.

The door of the upstairs snooker room burst open. About ten lads all around our age and dressed in the latest mod togs walked in. Half a dozen of us stood around the snooker table. I knew they were Chezzy lads as soon as I heard their accents. One of them shouted, "We're the Scene boys, and thiz twenty more dairnstairs." One lad pushed through us and scattered the balls round the table. Some of the others grabbed the balls and threw them round the room. I had no idea what this lot were doing in Dronny or how they'd found the youth club.

The church hall, at the top end of town was well away from any of the bus routes. We made a swift exit and as we walked through the main hall, the other twenty or so Scene boys, some a bit older, seventeen-eighteen maybe, were kicking over chairs and playing footie with the table tennis ball. A couple of lads were trying to calm the rest down, but they were having none of it. We crossed the road and sat on a wall wondering what to do. Two of our lads went for a scout round looking for reinforcements.

We could see the Chezzy lot through the upstairs window, still shouting and fucking about.

Our two lads returned with a few more mates. We now had around a dozen lads but were still outnumbered. The Blue Stoops pub stood about fifty yards up the road from the church hall. A couple of our lads went up to see if any of the older Dronny boys were inside. They came back with Billy Murphy and another half a dozen from the pub. The Murphy's, a large Irish family were my top yard neighbours from Cammell's Row and now lived next door but one to us on Stonelow. Billy, along with his older brother Jimmy, had already spent time in borstal. He was later jailed for life for stabbing a bloke to death. A complete madman at the best of times, Billy was even worse when he'd had a few pints.

The older lads said we should wait outside, as there was only one exit. Billy, who'd lived in Dronny for most of his life, but still spoke in a broad Irish accent, as did all of the Murphy clan, said: "Let's get insoide an batter duh cunts." We decided to wait.

The Chezzy mods had calmed down a bit by now and peered out from the windows into the darkness with their hands cupped around their eyes, watching us tapping sticks and lumps of wood against the wall. As soon the mods left the hall I knew they'd lost it. They huddled close together in silence as they walked out onto Church Street. We ran towards them as they scattered past the Green Dragon pub. They ran through the entrance to the church and into the graveyard. Panic set in as they scrambled over gravestones and through bushes. A couple were caught and clipped, but most escaped. We marched back into our club feeling well pleased with ourselves. It was only then that the vicar told us that one of the Chezzy lads was a DJ who wanted to put a disco on at the club. Maybe if they hadn't come mob-handed and started showing off the trouble could have been avoided.

It would be another four or five years before a mob from Chesterfield (this time in the guise of skinheads) would turn up in Dronny again. The skins were chased to the bus stop at the bottom of Green Lane and the bus was bricked as it drove off.

Chesterfield, the Lowedges, Batemoor and the Jordanthorpe estates in Sheffield, all found out nobody could come into Dronny and take the piss.

The week before Christmas Burnley came to the Lane and after the events at Turf Moor we all expected trouble.

Stuffed down the back of my jeans, a compressed rubber mallet stolen from, Butler's iron foundry where I worked as an apprentice moulder. I only took it for show; I had no intention of hitting anybody. I also took my new banner: a twelve-foot by six Union Jack, stolen from a cupboard inside the church hall youth club. My Mother had cut out and sewn on by hand, the words SHEFFIELD UNITED in white cloth letters across the centre. Although not on a par with the silk banner Parton saved at Chelsea, it was still one of the best on the Shoreham.

I don't remember if the Burnley fans were on the Kop (they probably were) but they were there outside the ground. Fights erupted as we made our way down John Street towards the coaches, parked on the side road near St Mary's. About ten coaches stood in a row and we joined a group of Blades dragging a banner from a small mob of Burnley fans. We ripped the banner to shreds, and I saved a piece to tie on my Union Jack as a scalp. Some of the Burnley fans tried to fight back, but most were scrambling to get onto the coaches. Ansh grabbed my mallet and whacked the coach windows, it just bounced off. We walked away chanting and showing off, nicking scarves off Burnley stragglers as they passed us. We walked on to Bramall Lane and made our way towards the Moor.

The Moor was, and still is, one of the main shopping areas in Sheffield. It runs from roughly the bottom end of Bramall Lane to the Peace Gardens in the centre of town. (The Peace Gardens were named after the notorious Sheffield criminal and cop killer, Charlie Peace who in the year 1879 was hung by the neck on that very spot until he was dead.) It was a ritual after every home game to walk from the ground, up the Moor into town.

There were maybe a 100-200 young lads. We were out for a bit of fun and vandalism, the terrifying Shoreham Street hooligans were on the march. A Blade villain looted a plum from a fruit shop and threw it up the road. A left footed shoe was robbed from Timpson's outside footwear display and chucked into a flowerbed. Innocent passers-by were pushed and jostled, and Saturday afternoon shoppers ran for cover in fear of their lives.

Another route we took back into town was along Eyre Lane, a long narrow alleyway running from the back of Arundel Gate to Howard Street near to the Midland station.

Little mesters workshops and small steel factories were housed on both sides of the street. A few windows would be put through (most of them were broken anyway) just for the hell of it.

An article appeared in the *Sheffield Star* entitled, 'Blades on Bomb Alley'. It told of the mob of Blades fans who, after every home game marched along the back-wack smashing windows and causing trouble. The police it said were determined to put a stop to it and punish those responsible.

Boxing Day 1966, Man Utd at home, and nearly 43,000, maybe half from Manchester, are packed in the Lane. Ansh, Andy Ellis and me, came in near the cricket pavilion and it took us a good ten minutes to squeeze our way into the Kop.

The Blades mobs stood in their usual place at the front. The Manchester hordes stretched across the full length of the back of the Kop and on both sides of the Blades at the front. I gazed in awe into the Man Utd ranks. Scores of banners and flags made a magnificent sight; I'd never seen anything like it. It hit me at that moment, why any young impressionable lad, could, and indeed would, be seduced by the phenomenon that was Manchester United.

It was breath-taking; what must it be like to be part of a mob like that? And have the added bonus of watching Georgie Best every Saturday. So many marvellous new songs echoed round the Shoreham. I tried to store them in my head for future use. Before the air crash, they were just another team, now everybody knew about Man Utd. The whole country had a soft spot for the Busby Babes. I don't suppose anyone needed any credentials to be a Man Utd fan, no initiation ceremony, just turn up wearing red and white and learn a few of their songs and you were in. It was easy, too easy. Anybody could be a Man Utd fan. Fuck em, I was still a Blade: just.

The crowd swayed and surged forward. Young kids at the front, jumped the fence. Manchester fans pushed into us. A Blade with a small flag on the end of a four-foot long lump of timber smashed anyone who came near him. The police dragged one of the Heeley lads, Pete O'Brian, with blood streaming from his head away from the scrap. Another surge forward left me a couple of yards away from some young Mancs. One of them with a basin-cut style haircut pointed at me and shouted to his mates, "Look at him, he's got longer hair than me, get the cunt."

I felt quite proud when I shouted, "Fuck off," as another surge took me away.

The game kicked off. Best, Law, and Charlton might have been displaying their silky skills, but I was on the lookout for flying bottles. The chaos carried on, as older, braver Blades fought to hold their places. I ended up on the floor, with another lad on top of me; it went dark, then all I could see were legs and shoes scuffing my head. I looked round for my mates; they were gone. Panic set in as I scrambled to my feet, only to be squashed again onto a crush barrier. Fuck this, I'm getting out of here. I made my way to the front and snaked along to the safety of the open bit of the Kop, way past the corner flag.

After the match I walked down Shoreham Street to the bus station. All the roads leading into town were packed with Man Utd fans. Even though everybody wore red and white I knew they were all Man Utd, they looked different, and just like any other town, city or ground they visited, they'd taken over. Tomorrow the Blades were playing them at Old Trafford, what the fuck was that gonna be like?

The trip to Manchester would have set my pulse racing, but no way would I have missed it, if I'd had any money, I was completely skint though. Most of the Dronny lads did make the trip, along with a few hundred other Blades. The lads stayed in Manchester for a while after the game, and were ready to board the train back home, when a Man City fan (City played at Hillsborough that day) who they described as a walking mountain wandered along the platform. One of the lads shouted, "Oi ya big fat cunt," as he came wobbling towards them. Alan, one of the Chesterfield lads ran up and booted him, the giant never flinched. The lads scrambled on to the train with the City fan in hot pursuit. They ran into a compartment, and two of them, one on each side, held their feet against the sliding doors to keep him out. He ripped the doors open and slapped the lads around the carriage. Ansh said he'd never been so scared in all his life.

A couple of years later we were talking to some Man City fans in some train station somewhere or other and we told them the story, "Yeah," one of them said, "that's so and so, I used to know him, he's dead now, he got hit with a bus in the centre of Manchester."

"Thank fuck," one of our lads replied. " I bet the bus was a fucking write-off."

The front-page headline caption in the following day's *Sheffield Star*, screamed out at me: VANDALS RUN RIOT ON BLADES TRAIN. It showed a photo of a guard in one of the smashed-up carriages and went on to give a detailed description of all the damage done on the train. All the breakages were listed: fifty light bulbs, ten light shades, three toilet seats, six door frames etc. A £25 reward was offered for information leading to arrests.

Oh, how I'd have loved to have been on the train, loved to have smashed some light bulbs and toilets. The trains British Rail laid on were falling to pieces anyway. Fusty smelling seats covered in dust and toilets that looked like they'd been smashed up already, but it was only just starting, there would be plenty more soccer specials to smash up. The football hooligans were starting to make the headlines. The newspapers called us 'yobs' and 'louts.' I liked being called a lout; it had a nice ring to it.

> **NOTICE !**
>
> The attention of our travelling supporters is drawn to the following in connection with the Watford tie. British Rail ran a special train which conveyed 350 Supporters from Sheffield and a great deal of damage was done on the return journey. We have received a letter from the Divisional Manager which informs us that: 3 Fire Extinguishers were missing, 110 Light Bulbs missing or broken, 17 Light Shades broken, 4 Tables had their vinal covers torn, 4 Toilet Seats were broken and the handles removed from the basin, 6 Toilet Handles were broken, the lino on the floor was ripped in several places and coat hooks in the Toilet were broken off.
>
> This is a disgraceful state of affairs. As the Divisional Manager states, supporters of both Sheffield Clubs, as a general rule, are reasonably well behaved, and trains to away matches have not in the past been subjected to the sort of treatment which is prevalent in many other places. Restrictions have been imposed elsewhere, and in some parts of the country, Special Trains for Football Matches are no longer run.
>
> He warns: "Any further damage to trains from Sheffield can only result in a

**J. W. & M. C.
GREENFIELD**

Managers: Mr. & Mrs. T. H. Ward. Tel.: 45482

Music buzzed through my head every waking hour of every day. The Stones continued to churn out excellent black American rhythm and blues. The Kinks, decked out in flash regency gear or red huntsman's jackets, typified all that was English and indeed England. *Dedicated followers of fashion* told us about the fops and dandies of Carnaby Street, the taxman who took all of their dough: *Sunny Afternoon,* the squalor of being on the dole in *Dead-end Street* (People are dying on Shoreham Street, bottles are flying on Shoreham Street, Shoreham Street yeah, Shoreham Street yeah) and from the same song we sang:

"What are we living for?
To see Wednesday in division four
No money coming in
And Alan Brown is bumming Johnny Quinn."

And for the Kinks enchanting London song *Waterloo Sunset* we changed the words to: "As long as I gaze on, Sheffield United, I am in paradise."

The Who, a tremendous group, oozing style and power churned out a string of brilliant hit singles starting in 1965 with *I Can't Explain,* followed up by *Anyway Anyhow Anywhere.* The teen anthem *My Generation* "I hope I die before I get old" and *Substitute:* "I was born with a red and white scarf round my neck."

Keith Moon the lunatic drummer, performed crazy fills and rolls, pulled mad faces, but kept perfect time as he took the band into overdrive. John

101

Entwhistle picked and slapped his bass like a lead guitar, behind Pete Townsend's surging, wind milling power chords.

The band was fronted by Rodger Daltrey who seemed somewhat amused by the whole shenanigans. They were still the darlings of the mods, even though they now sang about cross-dressing and donkeys on the Isle of Man. Townsend nearly broke my heart every time he smashed up his guitar at the end of a performance. I would have given my left hand to own an electric guitar and this whizzed-up cunt was wrecking 'em.

Bob Dylan told us 'Everybody must get stoned' but I didn't have a clue what he was talking about.

The Beatles, according to John Lennon were more popular than Jesus. Jesus fans were up in arms, burning Beatles records and photos of the Fab Four. Beatles fans retaliated, setting fire to bibles, beating up parsons and torching cathedrals. God intervened, demanded a truce and called it a draw; world peace was restored.

The Small Faces, another mod icon band with the greatest vocalist of all time, Little Stevie Marriott, gave us *Sha la la la lee.* and the classic *All or Nothing.* I didn't fully realise at the time just how amazing these bands were and so many of them. The Animals with Eric Burden's gritty blues vocals and Alan Price's swirling electric organ. The Yardbirds, introduced feedback and distortion for the first time, and at one time or another had arguably the three greatest ever English guitarists: Eric Clapton, Jimmy Page and Jeff Beck in their ranks. The Spencer Davis group with Steve Winwood belting out the marvellous *Keep on Running* and *Gimme Some Lovin.* Manfred Mann, whose main man or Mann, Manfred looked like a 1950s jazz cat. The Troggs kept it nice and simple but had a massive hit with one of the finest rock songs ever, *Wild Thing.* The Hollies a Manchester group named after Buddy Holly had a series of quirky hits with beautiful harmonies. Lesser bands like Herman's Hermits and Dave Dee, Dozy, Beaky, Mick and Titch, a bunch of grinning ugly fuckers who sang the rather suggestive *Bend It* and later, *Legend of Xanadu* with the whip-crack intro. We changed the words to: "That bleak battleground that bears the name of Bramall Lane," and sang it on the Shoreham. Songs flashed through my head like a whirlwind, I didn't have time to take them all in and I didn't always catch the words – not that easy listening to a six inch by three, hissing transistor radio. The beat, the rhythm and the guitars seemed more important.

The British Beat boom that conquered America in 64-65 was now in full swing, making London the style, music and fashion capital of the world. British guitar bands had always looked to the States for musical inspiration, particularly to the black American artists like Little Richard, Bo Diddley and Chuck Berry. Americans were now casting their eyes and their ears over to these shores.

In 1965, Folk Rock was the new trend in America. Dylan's *Mister Tambourine Man* and *All I Really Want to Do* were given the jangley 12-string Rickenbacker treatment by the Californian band the Byrds. It would be a couple more years before I would tune in to the master himself – Bob Dylan. Pop music was all I needed at this time. Many of the pop songs found their way onto the terraces,

"Sha la la la Summerbee," sang the Man City fans. "Who the fuckin hell is he?" was returned back at them.

Poor old Wednesday, there were so many songs made up about them from Blades in the mid-60s. It seems a bit strange though, that they never retaliated, and that lads from the same city could never come up with any original songs of their own, and sadly that's still the case to this day. Wednesday manager Alan Brown and centre forward John Ritchie came in for most of the stick. It was rumoured that as a child, Ritchie suffered from polio and spent some time in an iron lung. Blade songsmiths picked up on this and gave the poor fucker hell. To the tune, *Sorrow:*

"With your iron lung and your legs of plastic
Something tells me you're a fucking spastic
Ritchie, Ritchie"

Keith West's *Excerpt from a Teenage Opera:*

"Count the days into years, John Ritchie's eyes are filled with tears
Yesterday his iron lung broke down
His arms his legs don't feel too strong
Because his iron lung's gone wrong
Opens windows in despair
Tries to breath in some fresh air
The Wednesdayites send their children out
To Alan Brown's house to scream and shout
Alan Brown, Alan Brown
Is it true that Ritchie's iron lung broke down?
Oh no, no"

The Move's *Flowers in the Rain:*

"Woke up one morning half asleep his iron lung was in a heap
And L.S.D. was scattered all around"

The Kink's *Autumn Almanac:*

"Oooooo, John Ritchie's on the rag, yes, yes, yes, yes John Ritchie's on the rag."

And the classic: "Ritchie, Ritchie, Ritchie the bush kangaroo."

It was all crazy harmless shit – I loved it.

Unfortunately for Alan, the Wednesday manager, Brown rhymed with down (going down) and clown, "Let's all drink to the death of Alan Brown" and even if the Wednesdayites had been imaginative or witty enough to pen any anti-Blade ditties they would have had a job to get anything to rhyme with Harris, the United manager.

We were very topical in our choice of songs. When the foot and mouth epidemic broke out in 67 we sang to the tune of *We Shall Not Be Moved:*

"Don't go to Hillsborough you'll get foot and mouth." Then some wag came out with: "Don't come to Bramall Lane you'll get foot in mouth." It was then changed into Sheffield lingo: "Don't come to Bramall Lane thar'll get foot in gob."

What a time to be into the football scene, what a time to be young.

The beat groups though, vied for the number one spot with the likes of Ken Dodd, Petula Clark and Engleburt fucking Humperdink. It was supposed to be us, the teenagers who bought the records, so how come shite like that could get into the charts? Were our mums and dads, grandmas and granddads sneaking into the record shops, buying and playing them on the old wind-up gramophone in the front parlour or in the privacy of their own bedrooms while we were out? Surely not.

I was getting a bit better on the guitar; I learnt a few more major, minor and bar chords and even a few twiddly, lead bits. Weird really, considering I was now playing nothing more than a hollow log of wood with strings on it. I bought the guitar off Bezz for a quid, paying him half a crown a week for two months. The strings were raised about half an inch from the fret board. The pressure used to fret the strings made my fingertips as tough as shoe leather, so hard in fact, I could shove sowing needles through them, I would have loved to have seen Slow Hand Clapton attempt a solo on that fucker.

While I lived for Saturdays and the days out with the big boys, I was still just a little fifteen-year-old kid. Most weekdays were spent (after at least an hour playing football) scrumping apples, garden hopping, carving my initials on trees, scrawling UP THE BLADES on bog walls, reading Batman and Superman American comic books and manking with young strumpets in Dronny Park.

When the park gates shut at sunset we hung around the bus shelters on Dronny Bottom defending our turf. We sprawled out in shop doorways, high on the world, chatting about girls, football and music. Sometimes we stayed out until midnight when the electric 'gas lamps' clicked off for the night, leaving us to walk home in pitch darkness.

A wet, winter Wednesday evening, laid out in the Co-op doorway back then, beats any booze, weed and coke fuelled weekend of today, hands down.

It was open house at my mothers' – the house forever full of kids. I came and went as I pleased. A left-open, back window meant I could get in anytime, day or night. We sang songs and composed football chants, played cards and games of billiards and snooker.

My Uncle Chris bought me a 3-foot by 6-foot snooker table when I was about ten; many happy hours were spent on it. My Unk tried to teach us the tricks and skills he learned as a youngster at the old (now derelict) snooker hall at the back of Dronny bug hut. He told us about Joe Davis, the greatest player ever. Joe once knocked up a ten million-point break at billiards by getting the red and the white ball wedged in the jaws of one of the pockets, and repeatedly tapping the cue ball against them for three weeks in a series of cannons.

"Put some side on it, bottom on, to stun the ball, think about your next shot," he'd say, all to no avail. We just slammed the balls into the pockets. Who knows, if we had listened to him we could have become world champions.

Although we never had much money or snap in the house, Mum would cook up and bring us in plates of chips with bread and scratchit. It didn't matter how skint we were, we never missed having the full mashings Sunday dinner. Mum had a slate at the grocers and the local butchers and would cook up plenty of grub on Sundays in case I brought a couple of mates round.

Life was simple and slow, there was no shit in my life, no pressure at home, I believed what the TV told me, and I didn't have to think too much about

Desolation Row. Whenever at a loose end we dossed around the front room listening to music. Mates brought round their record collections to hear them at full blast. We listened to any kind of music we could find. Mum sometimes came in to have a singsong with us. She weren't a bad singer me old Mam. In her teens she'd been part of an amateur song and dance troupe playing the theatres and cinemas in the Sheffield area.

A combination of the birth of our Terry and a condition called phlebitis, which made her legs swell up, so bad that sometimes she could hardly walk, put paid to that. She belted out the golden oldies from her youth including Dean Martin's *Memories Are Made Of This* with Tiny and me doing the backing: "Ah-um, sweet, sweet, the memories you gave to me, ah-um, can't beat the memories you gave to me, ah-um." We laughed so much at the end of the song it made Mum fart, "Stop it," she'd shout, "you're making me trump," which made us laugh even more.

She also loved some of the modern stuff. We dueted and harmonised to Donovan's *Catch The Wind* – her favourite and the Stones *You Better Move On*.

Mum often bought home piles of old 78 records from jumble sales. We sifted through them and checked them all out. Jazz, Be-Bop and big band music from the 30s and 40s, vintage rock and roll from the 50s. One gem Mum picked up was The Big Bopper (J.P. Richardson) L.P. from the late 50s entitled *Chantilly Lace*. "Heeelloooooow baby, you knooooow what I like."

(The Big Bopper died in a plane crash along with Buddy Holly and Ritchie Valens in 1959.) We all loved the album and played it constantly. One of my mates even nicknamed my mum 'Chantilly' and always called her by that name.

Jumble sales were me mum's passion; she went, mostly through necessity, but sometimes for pleasure. It was a morning out, with the other jumble sale Queens, for a gossip, a natter and a bargain. When I knew she'd been to one I would always her ask her: "Did you get me owt from the jumbo, Ma?"

"I got you six pairs of socks and a good pair of pyjamas," always a good pair of jim-jams: she wouldn't buy me any shit. By the time I reached twenty-one I had 365 pairs of socks and 76 pairs of pyjamas in various stripy colours. She was good at dropping subtle little hints, were me Mam. She once came home from a jumbo and handed me brand new canvas snap bag.

"What ya trying to suggest, Mother dear?" I said.

I started going to the jumble sales with me Mam. I'd been with her many times as a nipper and by then I was used to wearing jumbo clobber, but I hated getting dragged round the church halls and the scout huts. The main reason I went was for the records. I couldn't believe people chucked their records away.

There was an air of insanity surrounding the jumble sale scene. Unsmiling bargain hunters, pushed and evil-eyed each other up as we waited outside. Mum used to mutter things like, "Look at her, she's always bleedin here she is, always at the front. I bet she's been queuing since last night." As the time ticked down to opening the chatter got less, the excitement and anticipation grew to fever pitch. I joined the stampede as the doors flew open, trampling over collapsed Grannies in the corridor… no room for compassion at the jumbos.

I would head straight for the record stall, while Mum battled to the front trying to find a place at the tables where the clothes were piled high. There was always a record stall at the jumbles. Usually the records were crap, The King And I, The Sound Of Music, Strauss waltzes and Mario Lanza operas. Every now and then though there would be some classic Rock 'n' Roll.

Amongst the stuff I picked at the jumbos, all on 78s were *Blueberry Hill* by Fats Domino, *Bird Dog*, by The Everly Brothers and *Rave On*, by Buddy Holly. There were sometimes some early 60s discs on 45 r.p.m. but mostly just the old 78s.

At the end of the jumbo they would sell everything off for next to nothing and I'd buy heaps of 78s for a few pennies. I kept the ones I liked and skimmed the others down the backfield.

Sometimes I joined my mother at the clothes stalls, rabbit punching pensioners as I fought my way through. Mum was a seasoned veteran in the art of rummaging and would have stacks of garments already stuffed in carrier bags or laid at her feet. It's amazing what some folks throw away and every now and again I could pick up some decent clobber. There was always the fear though that someone would shout out "Fuckin hell, I gave that coat to the jumbo last week."

Into the new year of 1967 and January's third round FA draw couldn't have been better. Charlton Athletic away would see us back in London to sample the delights of the capital. Parton, Tiny (his Southampton experience now long forgotten) and me, set off thumbing on Friday night, reaching London in the early hours of Saturday morning.

I took along my new, red silk flag, small in comparison to my banners. It measured about four foot by four with the words SHEFF UTD EL SUPREAMO (the wording stolen from an Everton banner) stuck on in white sticky tape. We headed for St Pancras where we met the suities, Ansh, a few Chesterfield lads and other Blades who'd travelled down on the midnight train.

Around twenty of us hung round the station supping tea and chatting until about nine o'clock, then we caught the train out to the East End. We arrived at Charlton around ten o'clock to pissing down rain and sleet.

Most of the lads found a café to escape the weather, but a few of us decided to explore The Valley (Charlton's ground). We scaled a wall and entered the deserted stadium. We climbed to the top of a huge open terrace on a par with the Holte End at Villa and the North Bank at Wolves and gazed down miles on to the pitch.

Large puddles of water lay across the surface and we were worried the game might be called off. Across from the terrace stood a small stand that didn't even stretch the length of the touchline. One end of the ground was covered, the other open. We walked back out through an unlocked gate and went to the café to find the other lads.

By this time, I'd started to use the boozers. Boozers sold ale and little else except crisps and cigs. As soon as I entered a pub I could smell the beer. There were no whiffs of lasagne or chicken in a basket wafting out of a back kitchen, just beer – strong beer. The old saying: 'He could get pissed on a whiff of the barmaid's apron,' wasn't far from the truth.

Public houses were all high ceilings, nicotine walls, brass bar-rails and ornate ringing tills. Not many pubs back then and hardly any of the back-street ones had jukeboxes. Pub sounds were, laughter, the mumble of a hundred mixed up conversations, thuds in a dartboard and the shuffling and rattle of plastic dominoes.

Being so small I didn't always get in, but when I did I usually found a quiet corner while one of the older lads went to the bar to get my drink. When the pub opened I piled in with the rest of the lads. The landlord didn't seem bothered, probably thinking twenty thirsty Northerners would be spending a quite few bob. I got talking to two older Blades who I hadn't seen before. They told me they were arrested the week before for fighting with some Stoke fans on the Kop at the Lane; they were each fined the huge sum of £1.

One of the Chesterfield lads handed out three or four wooden knuckle-dusters he'd made at work. I grabbed one and slipped it over my fist, punching my other hand with it, thinking I was hard; I had no intention of using it. The suities and the other older lads were complaining about the shit London beer. It all tasted shit to me.

Although it was great sat in the pub chatting with the older lads I couldn't wait for the match to start. A few of us left and hung about outside the ground. Blades started arriving from the morning trains and from S.U.T. and supporters' club buses. It was 'Up for t' Cup': hundreds of Blades mingled around waiting for the turnstiles to open. We went into the covered end, Charlton's Kop, and gathered behind the goal, at the back. A young Charlton fan stood close to us said, "You'll not be stood here when the big lads come in."

Sure enough just before kickoff a group of Charlton fans came in and got behind us, forcing some of the Blades out of the way. We pushed our way up to have a look. There were some big lads amongst the Charlton mob. One of them, who looked like a bigger version of Steve Marriott wearing a full-length leather coat pulled out a metal knuckle-duster and slipped it onto his fist. Ah, so they had the fuckers as well did they? We all got our dusters out, put them on and held them up so everybody could see. It didn't seem to bother the Charlton lads much.

Away fans were now more and more starting to infiltrate the home ends. The home fans massed together to defend them. I don't think it was even done intentionally most of the time. Taking ends was just in its early stages, but nobody, with perhaps the exception of Man Utd and the Merseyside clubs had a reputation. Crewe could be as bad as Chelsea, Bury worse than Millwall: the only way to find out was to go there.

The covered ends or Kops were chosen because a greater volume of noise could be generated under the corrugated iron sheds. At most of the grounds one end was covered, the other open, and fans could walk round from one end to the other.

In these new times, songs, chanting and supporting your team were far more important than fighting. If you were going to fight, you had to able to fight. One on one, nobody else joined in, nobody else helped you. That's why the older kings of the Kop did the fighting. There must have been exceptions obviously, but, from what I'd seen, two lads slugged it out while the rest stood around shouting encouragement, just like a schoolyard scrap. I didn't want to hit or hurt anybody, and I certainly didn't want anybody to hit me, I just liked to be as close to the action as I could. Usually a handful of police on duty in the ground tried to break up or prevent the fights. Pushing each other was tolerated.

A last-minute Mick Jones goal put us through to the next round and we sang his praises to a tune from a new American, manufactured pop sensation (the first ever boy band?), The Monkees', *I'm A Believer*: "Then I saw Mick Jones, now I'm a believer."

As I waited to jump the midnight train back home, I joined scores of other Blades in a mass 'Hokey-Cokey,' which went on for a good fifteen minutes on the concourse of St Pancras.

Punton, you little beauty. After being laughed at and booed by the Wednesdayites at the February 4th derby game, the Bald Bombshell scrambled one in from six inches to give the Blades a 1-0 victory. I don't think the ball even touched the back of the net, but it sparked off wild and crazy celebrations on the Shoreham. For years after, anyone we knew, or even saw with a bald-head was nicknamed Punton in honour of the great man.

Fulham away in the FA Cup 4th round, and it's back to London again, this time on the morning train. Another good Cup following saw a couple of thousand Blades occupy the covered Hammersmith end at Craven Cottage. The Fulham fans certainly liked throwing tin cans and many came over in our direction, until one hit the girlfriend of a rather large Blade. He ran over to the small mob of Fulham fans stood in front of us and battered the lad who threw the can. No more cans were thrown.

At half time with the Blades kicking towards the open end, some of us walked round and perched on the top of a wall at the back of the open terrace. A twenty-foot drop behind us meant we had to be careful. Another Mick Jones goal saw a somewhat muted celebration due to our position. Some thirty years later on a Match of the Day video, I could clearly see myself waving my scarf in front of me like a girl.

Before the game we'd found the legendary Carnaby Street, but much more interesting was a badge shop on a side road just off it. Like many of the other lads I'd started collecting football supporters' club pin badges, which were displayed on the fronts of our bush jackets.

We just stumbled on to this shop due the window display; it showed all kinds of badges. There were anti-American, Vietnam slogans such as 'Vietcong,' 'I am an enemy of the state,' 'LSD not LBJ, ' 'Make love not war,' 'Ban the Bum.' and shit like: 'Save water – bath with a friend.'

One with vampire teeth, saying: 'Drinka pinta blood a day, ' and one that particularly tickled me: 'Eating people is wrong.' We really thought they were so cool and robbed loads of them. The poor bloke behind the counter went mad and tried to push us out shouting, "You little facking baaarstards, get out of my shop."

We ran off laughing. The badges then adorned our jackets next to the footie ones and some of the slogans were felt tipped onto our coats.

Hardly any of the lads bought a ticket for the tube trains. We just pushed past the ticket collector or leapt the barriers. It was just as easy jumping the trains home when we had hitchhiked to away games.

After the game we spent the night trawling the pubs around St Pancras. We didn't even have a drink in most of them. In one of the boozers, Johnny Hall nicked a bloke's bowler hat off his head and ran outside with it. The bloke shot out after him and we all followed. The poor fucker got in a bit of a tangle running around trying to retrieve his hat as we skimmed it to each other like a Frisbee.

On the train home, Fordy and some more of the Dronny lads, told us they'd been in a boozer in Soho, and inside was no other than the famous comedian (and I use the term comedian loosely) Arthur Askey himself. The lads started shouting out Arthur's catchphrases 'Hello Playmates' 'Before your very eyes' and 'Ay-Thang-Yaw.' Fordy said Arthur didn't smile or respond, so they all started dancing around the pub singing *The Bee Song*: 'Busy Bee Busy Bee' which pissed him off even more. 'Big Hearted Arthur' my arse, miserable cunt.

A couple of goals from the legend that was Bill Punton saw Fulham off in the replay, was there no stopping the man?

The 5th round draw took us back to Chelsea for the third time in less than a year.

The Dronny and the Chesterfield lads were out in force on an early morning packed special train from Sheffield.

The magic of the FA Cup, the thrill and expectation of a good Cup-run. Making it to the semis, the final even. Groups of laughing old blokes in their thirties and forties stood around the station suffering from a dose of Cup fever. They'd gone mad for the day and wore rosettes and *Daily Express* cardboard hats with 'Up The Blades' printed on the side. Newspaper sellers outside the station gave these out free. Young boys, wrapped in scarves, waved home-made banners. Bugles swathed in red and white ribbons blew and bells rung. Some fans carried tin foil replica FA Cups on the end of sticks. This year we're gonna do it, we really are.

Bush jackets were the dress code today and tucked in the top pocket of my coat was the knuckle-duster from Charlton. A new lad appeared for the first time with the Chezzy boys. A full blown, back to the 50s, rock and rollin, blue suede-shoed, drape-jacketed Teddy boy who was in his mid-twenties. We nick-named him Elvis.

The now familiar sight of the massive arched glass dome at St Pancras station welcomed us once more. We swarmed off the train, chanting "United-United," and followed the suities to the Skinners Arms pub located on a side Street off Euston Road.

"Standing six foot six and weighing two forty-five, big Gordon."

Big Gordon, a Heeley Green monster was a few years older than us lot. He later gained his fifteen minutes of fame by having the names of his entire pub darts team (plus a dartboard and set of darts) tattooed on his forearm – which was like a leg. The *Sheffield Star* picked up on the story and printed an article and a photo of him proudly displaying his tat. Pint in hand he strolled over to our table. Gordon looked us up and down and said, "I'll bet any of you lads two bob, I can down this pint in one swig." Well, being young, naive little whipper-snappers and not used to the drinking habits of giants we looked at each other thinking, no fucker can do that.

"All right," Tiny said. "I'll bet ya."

"Get ya money out then and put it on t' table," Gordon said. Tiny took a two-bob lump out and put it on the table, Gordon did the same. With a smile and a wink, he picked up the pint and put it to his lips. It vanished in two seconds flat. Tiny's face dropped. Gord picked the money up and walked away laughing.

A year later in the Howard Hotel pub in Sheffield, while waiting for the train to take us to Leeds for a Cup game I witnessed him do even better. Seven pints of bitter were lined up in front of him. In the space of five minutes he'd downed the lot, pausing only briefly in between to let off a series of thundering belches. Each one was timed on a watch, totalling thirty-six seconds, making it about five seconds for each pint. The big fucker could certainly sup 'em.

The Beatles *Penny Lane* blared out from the jukebox, "Bramall Lane is in my ears and in my eyes," the whole pub sang in unison.

We left the pub and headed off to the match. We leapt and barged through the ticket barriers at Fulham Broadway and marched up to the Bridge. Gordon hoisted me up onto his shoulders; it was like sitting on a walking settee, I could see for miles up the street. I held out my scarf above my head as we chanted and sung our songs.

Kick off time approached as we entered at the corner of the Shed. The Chelsea mob packed behind the goal swayed forward. Many of them held walking sticks above their heads.

Seeing the Blades massed on the open end we made our way round. A good three thousand made the trip down. Some of the Blades looked the worst for wear and a few nursed head wounds. We were told that the walking stick carrying Chelsea lads attacked small groups of Blades who'd unknowingly entered the Shed. The game ended 2-0 to Chelsea, with centre forward Tony Hately scoring one of the best headed goals I'd ever seen.

With 40,000 fans leaving the ground it took us some time to walk back under the stand towards the Shed. With the suities and big Gordon at the front we feared no one. By the time we reached the Shed it was all but deserted, so we walked out into the streets.

Parton paced up and down on a mission looking for the big Ginner who'd clipped him back in November. Beetroot and Johnny Hall looted a programme shop outside the ground. They turned the counter over and threw bundles of programmes into the street where young kids fought each other to scoop them up. We walked in the opposite direction to the Tube station looking for trouble – or rather looking for the suities to start some trouble.

A young mini-skirted girl came out of a shop carrying a pint of milk. I went over, stuck my hand up her frock and squeezed her slice. She screamed as the bottle flew in the air and smashed on the pavement, everybody cracked up.

The Chelsea fans, so keen to attack us and try to nick our banner a few months earlier must have gone home. No one came near us. We hung around the streets for a good half hour before making our way back to the tube.

Despite the defeat we spent another brilliant night in the West End around Trafalgar Square, Piccadilly Circus and the streets of Soho. We tried to steal the red and white maple leaf flag from outside the Canadian embassy, but we kept sliding down the flagpole.

I stole a black lacy bra from a sex shop, put a couple of street lamps through and was thrown out of a pub with saloon style doors for being underage by a bloke with a hair-lip who talked down his nose. I stood in the street arguing with the bloke, curling my lip up like Elvis, (Elvis the king that is, not Elvis the Chesterfield Ted) trying to mock the way he spoke.

"You're not eighteen."

"I fucking am eighteen."

"No you're not."

"Yes I am." The rest of the lads came out and joined in the row, all talking down their noses.

"Lerrim in ya cunt he's eighteen." This went on for a few minutes until we couldn't talk for laughing.

After the pubs shut we made our way back to St Pancras. Approaching from Euston Road, the station, with its black pointed spires and towers, looked like some haunted, Gothic, medieval castle.

Late night train travellers were treated to another rendering of the Hokey-Cokey before we boarded the midnight train home.

Two coppers walked into our compartment. About six of us, including Elvis sat inside.

"Right lads," one of the coppers said. "We've had a report that a lady on this train has had her purse stolen and we're searching everybody, so if you don't mind will you all turn your pockets out and put your belongings in front of you."

Three things flashed through my mind as I started emptying my pockets. First, the knuckle-duster, second, the stolen bra, third and so trivial (but I didn't think so at the time), a packet of ten Park Drive cigarettes. My reasoning being that I had paid half-fare for my train ticket. Under fourteens paid half; sixteen was the legal age for smoking. I thought if the coppers saw my ticket and my cigs I'd be in some shit.

Elvis stood next in line to me, so I threw my cigs on to his pile; he picked them up and in a slow retarded voice said, "These aren't mine, why have you thrown them on my stuff? I don't smoke, they're yours." Fucking hell I thought, you thick bastard, here's me fifteen years old and looking about twelve and him in his twenties and he's not twigged on. The coppers sifted through our stuff then began searching us. The copper pulled the bra from my pocket and said, "Where did you get this from?"

"Well," I answered, "I got off with this bird tonight and she gave it me as a souvenir, something to remember her by, like."

The copper smiled saying, "She must have thought a lot about you then."

"Yeah she did," I said. He patted the breast pocket of my coat and fished

111

out the duster, slipping it onto his fist he held it up to my face saying, "What's this then? Did your bird give you this as well, this could do a lot of damage, where did you get it from?"

"Don't know," I said. "I found it."

"Found it did you? Right I'm arresting you for carrying an offensive weapon, get your stuff and come with us." I tried to tell them it was a bridge off my guitar, but they were having none of it. Shit I thought. The coppers took hold of me, one on each arm and led me off the train, the stolen purse now fuckin forgotten. A drunken old Blade dressed in a flat cap and a long rain mac with a huge rosette pinned to the front, staggered up the platform.

"Gerroffhim ya bastards," he shouted as he tried to pull me away from the coppers.

"Get away now or we'll arrest you," the copper told him.

"Fuck off," he shouted. "I'll fucking kill the pair of ya."

He wobbled backwards – throwing punches and shouting obscenities. Some more Blades jumped from the train and tried to reason with the coppers, but they were having none of it. I fought hard to hold back the tears as they lead me to the police room further down the station.

Rodger Fanshaw, 29 Green Lane Dronfield, 12th of the 4th, 1953 (making me thirteen) that's what I'll tell them, I thought, when they ask me my name, address and date of birth.

"Right what's your name? And don't think of giving me a false one or you'll be in more trouble than you're already in now."

"Ronald Sharpe."

"Age?"

"Fifteen."

"Address?"

"132 Stonelow Road Dronfield."

They grilled me for a while, threatening everything from jail to execution, demanding to know where I'd got the knuckle-duster from.

In between sobs (for the benefit of the tape Ronald Sharpe apprentice football hooligan is now weeping) I told them a lad I'd never seen before, gave it me at the match and I only had it to show off.

They left me in a locked room, with just a table and chair for company, for what seemed like hours. The bastards never even gave me a cup of tea. I kept dozing off for a few minutes with my head resting on my arms and then wakening with a jolt. The realisation I was in some deep shit now started to kick in. At that moment I could have done with me Mam.

The coppers came back in, charged me with carrying an offensive weapon in a public place and attempting to defraud British rail by paying half fare for my ticket. I was bailed to appear at Camden Town juvenile court. The charge sheet, signed, sealed and delivered by Sergeant Louis Platt of the London Metropolitan Transport Police.

I was released at about 7 a.m. Sunday morning.

To   **Ronald SHARPE** (Born 12.4.1951)

In the County of London and in the Metropolitan Police District   And to   **Ann SHARPE**

of   **132 Stonelow Road, Dronfield.**

Information has this day been laid before me, the undersigned, by **Sergeant Louis PLATTS** of **British Transport Police, Euston Station**

that you **Ronald SHARPE**

being a ~~child~~ *young person under the age of seventeen years*, on the **11th** day of **March,** 19 **67**, at **St. Pancras Railway Station** in the County and District aforesaid, did **without lawful authority or reasonable excuse, have with you in a public place, an offensive weapon, viz: a wooden knuckleduster.**

Contrary to **Sec 1(1) Prevention of Crimes Act** **1953**

And information has further been laid by **Sergeant Louis PLATTS**

that you the said **Ann SHARPE**

are the ~~parent~~ (guardian) of the said ~~child~~ (*young person*)

CAMDEN Juvenile Court, sitting at :- 163A, Seymour Place, W.1.   You are therefore hereby summoned each of you to appear before the **Camden** Juvenile Court

on **Tues** day, the **16th** day of **May** 19 **67** at the hour of **eleven** in the **fore** noon, to answer to the said information.

Dated this **5th** day of **May** , 19 **67** .

C.Y.P.1

SUMMONS to child or young person (and to parent or guardian)

Offence

M.P.-63-73526/6M
w117 (2)

Justice of the Peace for the County of London

I now faced the small problem of getting back home. The police kept my train ticket as evidence and I only had a few pence left. I thought for a moment about thumbing it back, but had no idea how to get to the motorway or even which direction it was in.

Fuck it, I would have to jump the train back. I checked the timetables and found out a train left about 8 a.m. I sat on a bench feeling utterly pissed off and sorry for myself. I bought a platform ticket and boarded the train. It was all but deserted; I found an empty carriage and stared blankly half asleep out of the window.

A middle-aged, bald-headed bloke wearing a pinstriped suit came into the compartment. He carried a brief case and carrier bag and took the seat across from me nearest to the door. The train set off and the bloke started chatting. He asked me why I was on my own. I told him I'd been arrested and locked up all night; he seemed somewhat overly concerned about my dilemma.

Taking a pack of sandwiches and a flask from the carrier bag, he offered me a ham sandwich and a drink of hot, milky coffee. I was starving, I hadn't eaten since the day before and I gladly took them. Feeling more relaxed with some snap inside me, but still a bit worried about having no ticket I settled down for the journey home.

The bloke carried on talking and asked if I'd ever been to Soho. I told him I had. He stated telling about the prostitutes he visited there and what he did with them. I had no idea what was happening. He took a Health and Efficiency type nuddy book (the ones with the fannies air-brushed out) from his brief case and handed it to me. I flicked through the pages still not twigging and got slightly aroused looking at the bare women and listening to him talking about shagging whores.

"Is your cock getting hard?" he asked. "Let me have a look."

Fucking hell, the crafty bastard was grooming me. I was in grave danger of being bummed. I shot out of the carriage fearing for my bottom and ran up the corridor. I moved past the first-class carriages, which were all empty, but I reasoned that if I went in one, I was more likely to get my non-ticket checked. I found an empty second class one and for the next ten minutes looked down the corridor to make sure the bloke hadn't followed me. Feeling somewhat uncomfortable, but relieved to be out of a tricky situation I again settled down for the rest of the journey.

"Come on son, this is a far as we go," a British rail guard said as he shook me awake. Thankfully he didn't ask to see my ticket. I left the train and staggered still half asleep up the platform.

I looked around – it didn't look familiar. No wonder: I was in Leeds. I'd slept from just outside London and missed the stop at Sheffield. There was nothing else to do but wait for another train to take me back.

An hour or so later I arrived back in Sheffield. I now had to get through the ticket barrier. Easy enough when twenty or thirty lads barged past, but not so easy on my own. I tried to run through, but the ticket collector grabbed me and shouted a guard over for assistance. I explained I'd been arrested, and the London transport police had my ticket. They took my name and address and after a few minutes let me go.

I had just enough money for the bus fare home and arrived back in Dronny about half past two. I knew my mates would be playing football in the park and took a detour there. The game stopped, and all the lads gathered round to listed to my tale.

My Mum was just glad to see me back home, even when I told her I had been arrested. Uncle Chris lay snoring on the settee in drunken oblivion after his usual Sunday dinnertime session. I would have to tell him when he awoke around teatime.

A few weeks later my Mother received a summons to accompany me to court, with me being a minor under the age of sixteen. My mum sent letters to the police and the court saying she couldn't travel to London with me as she was registered disabled. The days turned into weeks, the weeks into months as we waited for a reply; none came. I can only assume that there was some legal technicality involved in my arrest. Maybe they shouldn't have locked me up all night; with me being under age. I never heard any more about it. That was the first of many times I used my mum's disability to get me out of the shit.

"Telly's gone again, Mam."

During the mid-60s we had more televisions than Wigfalls.

The TVs were forever breaking down or blowing up. We bought cheap ones that exploded after a couple of months, or scrounged them off friends, relatives and neighbours.

We had the pay-weekly ones, which were taken back if we missed a couple of payments, and the coin slot ones. I soon sussed out the slot tellies and everything from steel washers to lumps of plastic, cut into the shape of a two-bob bit went into them. Trouble was, when the telly bloke came to empty them they were repossessed.

Frank Turner, Turnip's Dad, lived a few doors on from us. Frank was a pleasant, quiet bloke until Saturday nights, when he went off on boozing missions around Chesterfield. He always caught the last bus from Chezzy which arrived back in Dronfield at half past eleven. I was sometimes hanging around Dronny Bottom when the bus pulled in.

"Come on Ron," he'd shout. "I'll walk up wi thi."

Frank had now turned into the singer Frankie Vaughan, who he strongly resembled. It could take us a good half an hour to walk the ten-minute journey onto Stonelow Road, as he stopped and treated passing strangers to renditions of Frankie Vaughan and Dean Martin songs:

"Gimme the moonlight, gimme the girl and leave the rest... yes, leave the rest – to – me"

"When the moon fills the sky like a big pizza pie, that's... amore"

One night I was helping him to walk along Stonelow, when I happened to mention we hadn't got a telly. Frank, who swore a little when he was drunk, said, "I've got a fuckin telly tha can have Ron, there's nowt up with the fucker except the fuckin channel changer's bust, but tha can change channels with a pair of fuckin pliers, come on, we'll get the fucker." We wobbled down his path and spent five minutes trying to get the key in the door. We picked up the telly, one on each end and managed to reach the top of the path, Frank said, "Put the fucker down a minute Ron and listen to this."

"There's an old piano and it's playing hot behind the green doo-ar." As he said "Doo-ar, " he kicked his leg into the air and staggered backwards. "There's nowt wrong with this fuckin telly Ron, but tha's got to change channels with a pair of fuckin pliers." We finally managed, after ten minutes of singing and laughing to get the telly into our house. He put his arm around me Mum and serenaded her a while before staggering out. He left us with: "It's a fuckin good telly Annie, but tha's got to change channels with a pair of fuckin pliers."

The next day I plugged the telly in, switched it on and it worked okay. As

Frank said, the plastic knob on the channel changer had broken off, leaving just the steel bar. Right I thought, I'll try changing channels and hunted out a pair of fuckin pliers from the outhouse. As I touched the steel bar a blue flash and a crack blew the pliers out of my hand.

The next Saturday Frank fell off the last bus and shouted to me, "It's a good fuckin telly Ron, the only thing what's up with it, is the fuckin channel changers bust and tha's got to change channels with a pair of fuckin pliers, but don't forget to switch the fucker off first, or tha'll get a fuckin electric shock... Gimme a shady nook, gimme a babbling brook and leave the rest – to – me."

Whenever I saw Frank in one of his stupors he'd ask me how the telly was going and remind me I needed a pair of fuckin pliers to change the channel. We had the telly for a good couple of years, sometimes I forgot to turn it off and when I changed channels it nearly blew my hand off. The steel bar was now pointed at the end like a dart and it needed a good grip to move it. Mum and Uncle Chris wouldn't go near it and watched whatever channel it was stuck on. Remote controls eh... I've shit 'em.

Leeds came to the Lane in force on Easter Monday 1967 for a night game. This time the old women stayed at home and sent their grown-up sons instead. A few scary looking fat monsters fronted the Leeds mob and the suities had their work cut out holding it together.

The Leeds fans stood behind us at the back of the Shoreham and they made a few surges to the front. Missiles rained backwards and forwards in the darkness between the two groups and fighting took place all through the game. After the match I saw a fleet of at least thirty Wallace Arnold coaches (some minus their windows) drive down Shoreham Street.

The night after I caught the train to Leeds along the Heeley lads. The suities were also aboard, all in a buoyant mood chatting amongst themselves saying they were certain to get a scrap tonight. There weren't many others on the train, a hundred at most. Maybe the reason being that we had been stuffed 1-4 the night before, but more likely the Leeds monsters had put a few folk off. When we arrived the suit boys as usual headed for the nearest pub and the rest of us caught double decker buses up to the ground, which were parked near the station.

We went on the open Gelderd end and were all but lost in a 38,000 strong crowd. The Leeds mob occupied the almost minute, but wonderfully named 'Scratching Shed.' It couldn't have been more than a dozen steps high but was packed solid from one corner flag to the other with swaying masses of yellow, blue and white.

We left the ground after another defeat. I saw no trouble in the crowded darkened streets outside. Nevertheless there's always something scary about walking the streets around unfamiliar football grounds late at night. We huddled together with our scarves stuffed under our jackets until we caught the bus back to the station and boarded the train home. The highlight of the trip was a rather obliging hair-lipped, Heeley Green bird who'd come along with the Heeley boys just for the ride, so to speak.

Four days later, Manchester City were the visitors. Although they didn't have the numbers of their United brethren, a couple of thousand or so City fans stood at the back of the Shoreham. The *Sheffield Star* described the events of the day as 'The Battle of Bramall Lane.' This was the first time 'Battle of Bramall Lane' was used by the press; it had a nice ring to it. It wouldn't be the last.

'Vicious hand-to-hand fighting took place all through the game. Bottles, bricks, knives and an assortment of other weapons including banner poles were used. There were many injuries and many arrests. Dick Wragg the United chairman said, "I saw the riot and some of the injured people and they were not a pretty sight, some had knives taken away from them, one man was held on the floor while four others kicked him, and another was hit over the head with a bottle."

Mr Wragg also said the club were thinking about banning banners. Good old Dick, he wanted us to keep the bottles, bricks and knifes and ban the banners.

Injured fans during the first 'Battle of Bramall Lane' against Man City in 1967.

On April the 8th, four days before my sixteenth birthday we were off to Blackpool for a day beside the sea. I was well lumped up having sold a batch of footie programmes for a fiver. It would turn out to be some day. As with all the trains travelling west we departed from Victoria station to change trains at Manchester. A dozen or so Chesterfield and Dronny lads joined the Groom mob, the Heeley lads and an assortment of other Blades, including a few of the suities.

After being on the receiving end of them at Chelsea, quite a few of us carried walking sticks (football fads caught on fast). On the train from Manchester to Blackpool I sat in a carriage with some of the Groom lads.

The Groom mob took their name from the Horse and Groom pub at Gleadless where they hung out at night. One of them who I'll call Stan (cos that was his name) carried a flick knife. The week before at the Man City game, Stan had jibbed a City fan. Bragging about his exploits he pulled the knife out, flicked

117

it open and made a few mid-air thrusts. Everybody moved back, but he accidentally caught Drabs in the top of his arm. Drabs pulled his sleeve up shouting,

"Fucking hell Stan ya daft bastard, watch what you're doing."

There didn't seem to be any damage, just a scratch then suddenly it opened up like a small cunt. Blood squirted a good six inches out of the wound. Stan fainted. Somebody pulled a hankie out to stem the flow as Drabs squeezed his arm. Stan was still out cold on the deck. The bleeding slowed and after a couple of minutes Stan came round. At first he didn't realise what had happened and wondered where the fuck he was. He couldn't apologise enough, but the embarrassment of passing out must have haunted him forever.

Little Terry, one of the Chesterfield lads who'd moved to live in London met us at Blackpool station. He had hitched up the night before and slept in his doss bag on the beach. Terry had started to watch West Ham and we all wanted to know (particularly Sinny) what the Hammers mob were getting up to. Drabs went off to hospital to have the wound looked at, telling the doctor he had caught it on a nail.

We moved off to the ground and were stopped outside by the coppers who confiscated all our walking sticks. They told us we could collect them after the game. I started limping, telling a copper I'd twisted my ankle and I needed the stick to walk, but maybe because it was decorated with red and white sticky tape he told me to "Fuck off."

We joined a few hundred Blades on the Kop. A mob of fifty or so Blackpool fans posing no threat stood over to our right. Just after kickoff a group of twenty or so rockers, wearing red and white scarves appeared at the back of the Kop. We thought they were Blades at first, until they walked over and stood with the Blackpool mob chanting "Manchester."

There was a certain air of menace and danger associated with the cult of the rockers. Folk stepped to one side when the rockers walked past. They frequented greasy back-street cafés that usually housed a jukebox, their bikes lined up outside. They wore black leather jackets with the skull and crossbones motif or sometimes the ace of spades or clubs design on the backs. Their studded belts could easily be whipped off and used as weapons. Some wore their hair longish, others still had the Elvis, Gene Vincent, Brylcreemed quiff and side-burn style: very American, very scary.

Rocker birds always seemed to be gorgeous, oozing sex appeal. They looked like Joan Jett and Suzi Quatro; they were (I thought) certain shags.

So, not only had a bunch of rockers turned up, but a bunch of Man Utd rockers. Everybody by now knew about the Man Utd fans, their reputation went before them. Panicking like Corporal Jones, a few of us went over to the Blade rockers shouting: "Fucking hell, Man Utd's here; they're all rockers what we gonna do?" One of the Blades grabbed me by my lapels saying, "Look, don't come running to us every time something goes off; go and fucking do something about it."

As he pushed me away I felt a lump come into my throat. I'd been shown up and thought, I'll have to do something to save face. So instead of losing

118

myself and hiding in the middle of the mob I walked over and stood near to the Blackpool/ Man Utd lads. From close up they looked even more frightening, but it was something I had to do. More of my mates came over to join me. We were making eye contact, no one said anything, but we were nearer to the front line than we had ever been. It had to start sometime and today was the day.

The match passed without too much trouble; there were too many Blades for the combined mob to shift. About twenty of us young 'uns walked round to the police room at the other end of the ground to get our walking sticks back. A different group of rockers about ten strong stood on a street corner eyeing us up. The coppers told us they were keeping our walking sticks and after arguing for a while they again told us to "fuck off or be arrested." The rockers had gone when we came out. We headed off in the direction of the beach.

We hung around the South pier for a while wondering what to do. Other small groups of Blades milled around doing their own thing. We then walked down the Golden Mile heading for the Central Pier. We went under a subway, where at the far end it was either a left or right turn. Everybody turned left.

"It's this way," I shouted, turning right. Having been there the previous summer I knew where I was going. The lads carried on walking left, until they were nearly out of sight. I emerged from the top of the subway and as I looked to my left I saw the Man Utd rockers and some Blackpool fans sat on the railings at the sea front. I thought my heart was pounding outside Stamford Bridge, but it was going twice as fast now. They were only a few yards away; I had no chance of running or turning back. Within seconds they'd surrounded me. One of them pushed me on the shoulder and shouted a young lad about ten-years-old over.

"Get his scarf," he said. The little bastard walked up and dragged the scarf from my neck. He gave me a "what are going to do about it then?" look. I started walking away, fuck my scarf. One of them kicked my trailing leg onto the other forcing me to stumble, they all laughed. Suddenly a Blackpool lad stood in front of me, pushed both his hands into my chest and said,

"I remember you, you got on our coach at Sheffield."

I'm in some deep, deep shit now, I thought.

"No, it weren't me," I said.

"It fucking was you," he said. The punches rained in from both sides and I was knocked to the ground.

It's said that instinct makes you curl up in the foetal position when taking a kicking. Well, I can say that's true. I'd never had a kicking before, but that's what I did, arms over my head trying to protect my face, knees up tight to protect my little bollocks. The boots came in from all angles. "Kill the cunt," they shouted. The booting carried on until somebody said, "That's it, he's had enough."

It stopped, and I opened my eyes, another boot landed on my back. I jumped to my feet and not even glancing over my shoulder, ran like Alf Tupper on his final lap. I crossed the road into an amusement arcade, then straight out of the back door. I came back out from a side street further up the sea front and jumped on a bus heading towards the train station. I didn't feel too bad really; a few grazes and bumps, but supple young bones can take it. I licked my wounds and smiled to myself; fuck-em, I was okay.

119

I made my way to the station and hung around waiting for the others to arrive. They came back in dribs and drabs, some minus their scarves. The lads who'd been with me in the subway came back, they knew what had happened. One of the Groom lads, Ro, got split up from the others. He stood a few yards away pretending to read his programme and had seen my kicking. There was nothing he could have done to help; he'd have copped for it as well. Quite a few Blades got clipped that day. We swore revenge, until someone pointed out that Blackpool were already relegated so we wouldn't be playing them next season.

We caught the train back to Manchester and spent the rest of the night walking the streets around the city centre. Manchester was great, but it didn't have the same buzz as London; we arrived back at the station to catch the last train to Sheffield.

A lad from the Manor estate, who wore a tangerine and white pit helmet stolen from a Blackpool fan, and me, got chatting to two girls on the platform. The girls were from the Burngreave area of Sheffield. They'd been in Manchester for a night out. They were dressed identically, both wearing three-quarter length leather coats, over op-art black and white checked mini-dresses, their hair styled in the short elfin mod cut, both were seventeen years old. My instinct told me I could be in for something really special. We boarded the train and ushered the girls into an empty compartment. After a few minutes snogging and feeling around, the door burst open and half a dozen mates dived on top of us. Many pairs of hands groped the girls.

"Fuck off," I shouted, trying to drag them away. I have to say it was all done in good humour and we were all laughing, I would have done exactly the same thing if the roles had been reversed.

It calmed down a bit until the door opened and Wailsey, one of the pissed up suities came in, "What the fuck are you doing kissing her?" he said to me. "Get her fucked."

He joined the rest of the throng mauling the birds, who squealed and screamed, but were clearly loving it. I thought, hang on in there son and I did. The rest of the journey I spent fighting off my mates who just wouldn't stop trying to get into the girls.

We arrived back in Sheffield and walking hand in hand with the girls, came out at the Wicker Arches entrance of Victoria station. My mates were persistent in their quest to fuck it up for us. They came up behind grabbing the girl's arses, squeezing their tits and trying to pull them away saying, "Don't go with him love, he's crap, come with me." Again it was all done in fun and we were all laughing. The girl asked me if I fancied staying out all night. I certainly fucking did. We finally got shut of the rest of the lads by turning down a side street off the Wicker.

"Go on, fuck off and leave us then you jammy bastard," the lads shouted as we walked away. Staying out all night was nothing new to me: I'd done it many times before, but never with a girl. That little part of everybody's brain which contains unknown quantities of amphetamine, acid, marijuana or any other drug known to man, kicked in, years before I would even start to take it. Stay out all night? I could stay out for a fuckin week.

We explored darkened doorways, narrow alleys, derelict buildings and each other until I thought my young stang was about to drop off. It looked like a piece of string with a radish on the end of it.

About two o'clock in the morning we went to the bowling alley on Queens Road. 'The Alley', a mod hangout, stayed open all night. About a dozen scooters were parked up outside. Sometimes there were bouncers on the doors at the alley, where long hair was frowned upon. To gain entrance I had to tuck my hair behind my ears and down the back of my shirt collar. This time I got in with no trouble and we went to the coffee bar for a drink and a sandwich.

Every mod in the place seemed to know the two girls; they moved off to talk to a group of them and I thought that was it for the night. After five minutes or so they came back and introduced us to some of the lads. We went back out and although I didn't think I had any more left in me, carried on where we had left off.

We left the girls at their bus stop about five in the morning, ships in the night never to cross paths again. The Manor lad went for his bus leaving me in Pond Street bus station where I had nearly an hour to wait for the first bus back home. I went into the underground bogs and stood warming my hands on the hot air hand dryer. I heard footsteps coming down the stairs of the toilets and the chant of "Wednesday." Fucking hell I thought, this is all I need.

Digger Dickinson, Ginner Hyels and Nidge Cousens, three Wednesdayite mates from Dronny walked in.

"Hey-up Ron, what the fuck are you doing here?"

"Long story," I answered. They'd just arrived back on the midnight train from the 6th round Cup match at Chelsea. We all caught the bus home together.

"What did I tell ya about them walking sticks at Chelsea?" I said.

It had been a grand day out, quite a lot to take in, a bit of stabbing, a bit of fainting, football, getting shown up, getting battered half to death and getting shagged half to death, what more could anybody want? Up the fucking Blades.

I finally crawled in bed about half six and slept until I was shouted up for my Sunday dinner at two. I went back to bed and slept through till Monday morning… in two days' time I would be old enough to smoke… yippee.

The Sheffield and Hallamshire County Cup competition took place every year between the South Yorkshire clubs: United, Wednesday, Rotherham, Barnsley and Doncaster.

In the late 40s early 50s crowds of 40,000 plus were not uncommon when the Sheffield teams met. United were playing at Barnsley in the County Cup final on the 8th of May 1967.

Apart from being a small town seeped in the tradition of mining, not much was known about Barnsley or indeed any of the 4th Division teams or fans of that period.

I had been sacked that very Monday from an apprentice painter and decorator's job which I'd held for a good four or five weeks. I walked to the train station dressed in my works gear, splattered in paint, my cards and fifteen shillings or so paid-up day's wages in my pocket.

Wafer and Faggot, the Attercliffe boys and a few others lounged around outside. Faggot as usual wore his leather rocker jacket with Sheffield United painted on the back in white letters. Both were a bit younger than me, making them about fourteen-fifteen years old.

Wafe, a tallish, slim, happy-go-lucky young chap with long, straight blond hair, had the gift of the gab and a pair of bollocks the size of cooking apples. We liked the same sort of things, football, music, long hair, chasing girls and staying out all night. The songsmith of the outfit, Wafe had at least a couple of new Blades ditties usually plucked from the pop charts every week. Sometimes the whole Shoreham picked up on the songs and they were belted out on the Kop. Other times only the dozen or so chosen few sung them in the boozers or on the trains and coaches at away games.

Wafe once told me the story of how he first met Dinky Dawson. Dink, a rocker, Blade and a good mate, came from the Wybourn, a sprawling rough-arse council estate, just behind the Hyde Park flats. Dinky was as gentle as the sweet Lord Jesus, but had the look, and a face that would scare a vampire. Dink and Wafe were in a café somewhere in Attercliffe one night. They didn't know, but had heard of, each other. The two gunfighters sized each other up for a while until Dinky mosied over, spat on the floor and said to Wafe: "I hear you stay out all night?"

Wafe coolly replied, "Yeah, I might do."

"Well I stay out all night as well," Dinky said. "And if you're staying out all night tonight I'll stay out with you."

"Okay." Wafe said. So they both stayed out all night and that was that.

Cool kids stayed out all night, not doing owt in particular, just walking the streets talking, laughing, hanging in shop doorways or on park benches, taking in the night and watching the stars shine until daybreak. You weren't really a lad unless you'd stayed out all night!

Dink went down in Blades folklore years later for an incident at a friendly at Saltergate Chesterfield. He ran on the pitch wearing a red T-shirt with FUCK OFF lettering across the front. The game was underway, and Ernest even managed a diving header. He dodged a squad of slipping coppers like a matador to the cheers of the crowd, until he was finally caught and dragged away.

The short journey into Barnsley took less than half an hour and we arrived about half past five-six o'clock just as the pubs were opening. On the train Wafe told a captive audience about the terrible time he and a few others came in for at Maine Road the previous Saturday, where they were chased round the terraced streets of Moss Side by a mob of Man City fans. They only managed to escape by jumping over a wall, dropping fifteen foot and running miles up a canal towpath.

I was now getting more of a taste for the ale. Three or four pints got me merry, gave me a little buzz, the giggles and a bit of confidence. Any more than four though would see me retching and spewing in the gutter. There was only mild, or bitter, (no puffy lager back then). The beer cost about two shilling a pint – one hundred pints for a tenner eh! It was a penny cheaper in the taprooms.

Taprooms were silent, sparsely furnished, lonely places that gave out an aura of doom. Ancient flat-capped snuff junkies usually frequented them, alongside sad-eyed old darlings, gazing back at a distant past while swigging bottles of Gold Label Barley Wine (the strongest beer in the world at the time). We found a pub and sampled the delights of a couple of pints of Barnsley bitter. On leaving the pub we noticed small groups of unsavoury looking Barnsley characters lounging on street corners.

We reached the ground and joined maybe a hundred Blades on the covered Pontefract Road end, (Barnsley's Kop) about the same number of Barnsley fans stood to our right. As usual both groups, pushed, postured and sang their songs trying to out-do each other.

Just before kickoff, Barnsley's scruffier version of our suities came in. This gave Barnsley the edge, they pushed over towards us with their fighters at the front; none of our suit boys were there.

A pair of six foot tall identical twins with bright ginger hair and both wearing combat jackets came into view. These lads seemed to be the kings of Barnsley's Kop. It was bad enough with one, never mind two of the fuckers. They laid into the nearest Blades moving them back, none of us fancied tackling the big bastards.

A few police came in and briefly restored order allowing us to hold onto our place. We were forced forward as more Barnsley attacked from the back. The gingers and the rest came through the police who were trying to separate us. We held on for a while but were forced down towards the front. Some Blades melted away onto the covered side terrace to our right, after a while we joined them and assembled near to the corner flag.

The Barnsley mob didn't follow us, they didn't have to, they'd proved their point by shifting us off the Kop. We left the game before the end (most of the Blades had already gone) and walked back to the station, with shadier looking post-Teddy boy, rocker type youths eyeing us up. We joined a group of about fifty Blades stood outside the station.

The top of the station approach filled with bodies. The Barnsley mob charged down the road and a hail of bricks sailed towards us. We retreated into the station, then across the train lines as they swarmed onto the platform. There was nowhere else to run. We jumped back onto the tracks picking up stones and chucking them back. Barnsley retreated, so we ran back over the lines lobbing more stones. A few police arrived and restored order, but after a few minutes the coppers simply disappeared. This was the cue for us to gather up more rocks and start smashing the waiting rooms and any other windows in the vicinity.

So this was Barnsley, this was the 4th Division, just as rough and as dangerous as any of the 1st Division grounds I'd visited. I was learning fast not to underestimate anybody. Barnsley were added to the ever-growing revenge list.

The final game of an eventful, eye-opening season took us back to London, and White Hart Lane, the home of Tottenham Hotspur.

Bri Thurman, a Dronny lad who was only fourteen years old at the time, set off hitching with me late on the Friday night. We arrived in Chesterfield around midnight both wearing our footie scarves and bush jackets. Perched on Bri's head was a cowboy hat with a Blades rosette pinned to the front. On the inside of the hat, he'd stitched a small pouch concealing a flick knife.

As we walked through the near deserted streets a group of about four or five youths walked towards us. As they got nearer they stopped talking, a bad sign.

"Watch these cunts," I said to Bri, "keep talking." Bri slipped the knife from his hat. We chatted away as if we weren't bothered. I was streetwise enough not to put my head down and I looked one of them straight in the eyes as they passed in silence.

"Don't look behind, keep walking." I said. We carried on walking and talking until we were way past them; then took a quick glance over our shoulders to make sure none of them were following. It was okay, what could have been a tricky situation had been avoided. Chesterfield could be a very dodgy place; the lads from Chezzy didn't like foreigners, especially those from Sheffield, or Dronfield for that matter.

After an all-night hitch we landed in London around mid-morning. We mooched around for an hour or two then caught the Tube up to White Hart Lane, arriving about one o'clock. The streets around the ground were congested even at this early hour. We had a wander around looking for fellow Blades (we didn't see any) then entered the ground at the Park Lane end turnstiles. We received a voucher as we paid the entrance fee, giving the holder first priority for the sale of FA Cup final tickets. Spurs were playing Chelsea in the final the following Saturday.

Straight away we were surrounded by a group of young Tottenham fans. At first we thought we were in some shit, but all these lads wanted were our vouchers, which we gladly handed over as they were of no use to us. The Spurs lads were quite friendly, and we chatted for a while. Seeing Blades fans mobbing behind the goal at the Paxton Road end we walked round across the Shelf to our right, some of the Spurs lads came with us to try to get some more vouchers.

Half a dozen coach loads of Blades turned up plus a few more from the train including Tiny and Ansh. Again Blades fans gladly handed over their vouchers to the Tottenham lads making it all quite a friendly atmosphere. About ten Chelsea lads, also there for the vouchers got talking to us. They were all about our age, except for one who to my amazement was twenty-three years old. I couldn't understand how anyone as old as that could be so much into the scene and be on the same wavelength as us. The Chelsea lads stayed with us all through the game and offered to show us the sights of the West End after the match.

Despite a 45,000 crowd there was no trouble inside or outside the ground; we walked back to the Tube along with the Chelsea boys, who were fascinated by our accents. They stayed with us for most of the night and we all departed friends... until the next time.

Something was happening in the Haight-Ashbury district of San Francisco USA. Love and peace was in the hair and flowers were in their air.

The Hippy society of peace, free love, marijuana and LSD peaked in the summer of 1967. Doctor Timothy Leary, a professor from the green pastures of Harvard University, who according to the newspapers and telly was some kind of Guru, told the world that LSD was a type of western yoga to expand the consciousness and that everyone should, "Tune in, turn on and drop out." All fine and dandy for Tim, who no doubt had a ready supply of acid at his disposal in some sun-drenched Californian, penthouse retreat.

On a lesser scale something was also happening in Dronny Park, or to be more precise, at the entrance to the grounds of Charlotte Ward's mansion house about fifty yards down the road.

The stone pillars, walls and steps where beautiful people congregated after the park closed were decorated (by us) with brightly painted rainbows, flowers and slogans. 'Make love not war,' 'Hippies' and other shit covered the walls.

A group of girls we'd met in Chesterfield made the six-mile pilgrimage north, at weekends and even on some weekday nights. They wore dazzling dresses, bells, flowers and beads. We hung out in the warm evenings, stretched out and relaxed on a carpet of ivy that grew at the top of the steps.

My acoustic log, bought for £1 in 1966, it's now a collector's item… a refuse collector's item.

I sometimes took my guitar and strummed out the latest naff shite by the Flowerpot men, Scott McKenzie and other manufactured twaddle.

Jimi Hendrix had just burst onto the scene and he'd blown fans, and fellow musicians alike, away with his amazing and unique psychedelic guitar style; but my feeble attempt at *Purple Haze* twanged out on the acoustic log didn't sound quite right. Maybe we missed the Hippy point altogether. Maybe the reason that the movement took off in the States was the escalating Vietnam War. Kids not much older than me we were being drafted and shipped out to the Far East to put the Commies in their place. Press-ganged into fighting a war they knew fuck all about and cared about even less.

It was America's war though, and fuck all to do with me. The 'Free Love' bit… now that made sense and I was a willing disciple. Most of us had long hair anyway and looked like the Hippies, but the English version of the movement consisted of student types and the middle classes, not the working-class kids from council estates. Long hair to me, meant rebellion, rock and roll and the Rolling Stones. I was also a fledgling football hooligan so fuck all this 'love and peace' shit. By the winter of 67 the Hippies were old hat.

125

One ingredient though, and the most important ingredient of all eluded us. 'Pot' as it was quaintly named, never ever surfaced in this remote corner of North East Derbyshire. Even the older lads amongst us had never seen it, let alone smoked it.

The only drug I'd ever seen (apart from Hodgy's Bombers) was a Purple Heart that one of the lads nicked off his Dad and brought to school. He broke it up into about six pieces and the braver lads amongst us swallowed a microscopic lump each. Nothing happened; it was probably a fucking love heart anyway.

The haunting cathedral like, religious swirling organ kicks in. "We skipped the light and dangled, turned cartwheels across the floor." At least that's what I thought was the opening line of Procol Harem's *Whiter Shade of Pale.*

It sat at number one in the charts when Hodgy died. Every time I hear the song it reminds me of him. His motorbike collided head on with a car and left him almost broken in half, he was eighteen years old. Hodgy was one of my best mates; his death hit me like a hammer blow. I knew nothing of death. I didn't understand it. How could someone so young and so full of life be taken away like that?

We all went to the Hyde Park pub on the day of the funeral, dressed up, wearing black ties. We got half drunk and then stood outside the small packed-out Hill Top chapel where the service was held. As the coffin arrived one of the lads shot out a stream of spew onto the church wall. I too felt sick, and we all fought hard to hold back the tears, but no one cried.

For months, years even after his death, I had these recurring dreams. Hodgy would come back and talk to me.

"I can't stay for very long" he'd say. "I have to go back."

"Back to where?" I'd ask him.

"I can't tell you," he'd answer. "But I don't want to go."

"What's it like where you are?" I'd ask.

"It's fucking horrible. I don't want to go back. I want to stay here, but I have to go."

He'd then back away saying, "I'll try and come and see you again."

I'd awake in a cold sweat, terrified and had to sleep with the light on for the rest of the night.

The summer of love saw the release of The Beatles' *Sergeant Peppers Lonely Hearts Club Band.* I first heard the album the day after its release, babysitting with a 14-year-old little cracker called Jilly, who'd queued up the day before to buy the record. My prejudice in the Stones-Beatles feud meant I'd missed out on a lot of the Beatles stuff. *Sergeant Pepper* though was an excellent, crazy musical adventure where Indian themes of the east fused with the rock of the west. The songs conjured up weird images of circus performers on trampolines, tight rope walkers, trapeze artistes, somersaulters diving through hoops of fire, tangerine trees, marmalade skys and newspaper taxis. It made me shudder for a split-second, wondering what it would be like in a million years' time when I hit the age of 64. I listened to it whenever I could. Buying it though was a different matter.

A great effort I must admit and far better than the Stones attempt at psychedelia with the rather disappointing, *Their Satanic Majesty's Request*.

My favourite album of 1967 (although it was released at the end of 66) was the Who's *A Quick One*. I borrowed the record off Bri Thurman in the summer of 67 and played it constantly.

All the Who members had a bash at writing the songs. John Entwistle wrote the haunting *Whiskey Man* and the totally bizarre *Boris the Spider*, Roger Daltrey, *See My Way*, even Keith Moon chipped in with *I Need You* and the crazy instrumental, *Cobwebs and Strange*.

The last track, *A Quick One While He's Away* (the first ever Rock Opera) written by Pete Townsend, consisted of six mini songs all interlinked, telling the story of 'Ivor the dirty old engine driver.' This was climaxed by the amazing *You Are Forgiven*, which showcased the Who's trademark power chords and harmonies.

Many years later, I saw the Who steal the show, performing the song live on the Rolling Stones film, *Rock and Roll Circus*.

The relegation season of 67-68 started off on August the 12th with a friendly at Norwich City.

Three of us: Johnny Hall, Bri Thurman and me set off thumbing early on a scorching hot Saturday morning. There were no motorways on the route to East Anglia, just a series of A and B roads. None of us really knew where we were going; we just kind of headed south-east.

From Worksop, a lift on an opened back lorry took us as far as Sleaford in Lincolnshire; we were stuck there for a couple of hours.

We managed to get another lift taking us to a small village about twenty miles from Norwich. It was now 2 o'clock in the afternoon, the match kicked off at three. Reading the timetable at a bus stop, we found out the next bus, would get us into Norwich at four-thirty. The route must have been via Southern Yemen. The game finished at twenty to five, giving us ten minutes to find and get to the ground, to maybe catch the last kick. Fuck it! We turned round and started hitching back, and it was just as difficult trying to get home.

Undeterred we decided to try to thumb a lift to Skeggy so as not to waste the day, but no luck. We arrived back in Worksop around seven-thirty in the evening and due to our bush jackets, a gang of locals followed us around the town. We managed to lose them in the bus station and caught a bus to Chesterfield and then another back home. It was one of only two occasions I failed to make the game on a hitch-hiking expedition.

Sheffield Wednesday, the old enemy were due at the Lane for the third home game of the season on September 2nd. A meet was arranged for midday at the Howard Hotel. Fifty or so Blades stood outside the pub with more holed up inside. Half a dozen Dronny lads joined the throng. The Sheffield lads were buzzing, confident and cocky.

"We're gonna fuckin kill the bastards today."

Word was out the Wednesdayites were meeting at the same time in Fitzalan Square, only a few hundred yards away in the centre of town. Some more lads turned up saying there were loads of Wednesdayites up at the Square. It never crossed any of our minds to go up to the Square to confront them; the fighting would be done inside the ground.

After an hour or so we moved off towards the Lane. An assortment of weapons: bricks, lumps of wood and iron bars were collected from behind buildings and back yards as we made our way up Shoreham Street towards the ground.

On arriving we found more Blades sat outside the turnstiles on the corner of John Street. More Blades arrived in ones and twos and small groups boosting our numbers to around 200. None of the turnstiles were open, so all we could do was wait. Word came in that a big mob of Wednesdayites had been seen marching down the Moor.

A mass of blue and white filling the road appeared at the far end of John Street and walked down towards us, their numbers roughly the same as ours. Blades leapt to their feet and as one, sprinted towards them. Both mobs reached the players' entrance halfway down. At this point the Wednesday mob turned and scampered back down the road. Nobody followed or chased them, nobody said 'let's do this,' or 'let's do that,' there were no leaders, and no one was in charge. None of the older suities or rockers were with us; I don't think anyone was over the age of eighteen. The hatred everyone felt towards Wednesday had fired us all up. It was the first time we had done it on our own, we were coming of age. We turned, walked back and sat down again.

It was a natural instinct to do what we did; we were there to defend our Kop, a bunch of young kids playing war games. It never even entered my head I might get hurt.

The Wednesday lads didn't run far, they congregated outside the Lane end turnstiles, still on John Street and still in our view. A few minutes later they tried it again, this time they didn't even reach the halfway line before turning and running again.

The turnstiles opened about half past one. We piled into the Kop, but instead of going to our usual place at the front behind the goal, we lined up along the back. Whether this was planned or not, I don't know, but nobody dished out orders; again I think instinct took us to the high ground.

I didn't have a clue what was going through the heads of the Wednesday fans, whether they had leaders or what, but having been run twice in the space of a few minutes, back they came and began queuing outside the Kop.

From the top of the steps we could see out into the street. Everyone expected them to try and walk up the back steps to enter the Shoreham and that's where we all congregated.

The first twenty or so through the turnstiles came in for a barrage of rocks and lumps of timber. They retreated behind a wall to the right, then underneath some steps leading to another entrance. This led to the bottom corner where the fenced off kids pen was later built

More and more Wednesday fans entered the stadium, but they were fucked.

No matter which way they tried to get into the Kop, we had the higher ground and showered them with stones and other missiles. So where were the coppers while all this was going off you may ask? The simple answer is, well... nowhere. There were one or two dotted round the ground, but that was it. They obviously didn't fancy the prospect of tackling a few hundred, armed to the teeth rampant teenagers.

Four, five, six times the Wednesdayites tried to reach the back of the Kop and each time they were forced back to the bottom corner.

Somebody, somewhere, must have been in charge of the police operation that day and after half an hour or so of chaos a squad of coppers finally arrived. Around twenty or so police surrounded the Wednesday fans and the combined mob of pigs and pigs walked up the steps towards us. We charged down throwing everything we had. The coppers were just as bad as their new mates, they turned and ran. More police arrived and tried a new tactic, pushing us back, mingling in with us and nicking those they saw throwing missiles. This allowed the rest of the police to bring the Wednesday mob up the Kop and deposit them at the back to the right hand side of us.

Sergeant Plod to PC John Law: "What do you reckon John? We've got two hundred U-bleedin-nitedites, throwing bricks and going mad and a couple of hundred Wednesdayites cowering in this corner.

"Well, sarge, why not put the Wednesday fans on the terrace or even take them round to the Lane end, that should stop the trouble."

"Nay lad, the Wednesdayites have every right to stand where they like, we'll take them up to the back, two yards from the Blades mob, form a line in between and try to protect them." Policing at its best, eh?

The ground started filling up, with more lads from both sides joining their own mob, only a few feet away from each other. I'll say one thing for the Wednesdayites; they were quick on the uptake. The missiles that had been raining down on them for the best part of an hour were now being returned into the Blades ranks.

Macduff was the second eldest of the now six Cardwell brothers (three were Blades, three were Owls). At fourteen years old, he already stood head and shoulders above me. Mac got his nickname from the tall, thin comic book character Lofty Macduff. Mac wore a white pith helmet, (the type African white hunters wear) borrowed from me. My mother had bought it from a jumble sale, and I had painted BLADES in red paint onto the six segments of the hat. Mac staggered backwards as half a cheese brick smashed into the cork helmet, leaving a large dent in the side. Injured fans from both sides were led away to be treated by the St John's ambulance brigade stationed at pitch side.

There weren't too many black lads at the games back then. One of the Heeley Green mob, and the only Wednesdayite in their crew, was a black kid called Mick Grudge. Mick, at the forefront of the Wednesday mob, laid into any Blade who came near him. Seeing this, Herman, Scanno, Mouse and the rest of the Heeley lads, even though he was their mate, steamed in, forcing him back into the crowd. There was only one black lad in the Blades mob I can remember. A lad named black Arthur, he wasn't really black though, just mucky.

In our ignorance we were terrible racists at the time. There were no black people at all in Dronfield. The only black men we had ever seen were on the Tarzan films at the Bug Hut and the Abbeydale school cricket team.

We were even scared to death as kids when told, "If you don't behave, a black man'll get ya," or "Weer's me Mam?" "She's run off wi a black man." It was quite acceptable for Alf Garnett on Saturday prime-time telly to call them 'Darkies, Wogs and Coons.' Nobody complained.

Attercliffe, with a large immigrant population was supposed to be the place where all the black men lived. "I'm gonna tell ya where the black men live, they all live down Attercliffe."

We sang awful songs about the Ku Klux Klan nailing niggers to the door and Paki's eating Kitty-Kat and Kenomeat. A variation of the Zigga-Zagga chant, "Nigger-nogga, nigger-nogga-wog-wog-wog," was often chanted at the matches.

In 1968 Enoch Powell's 'Rivers of blood' speech stirred up even more racial hatred. "Enoch, Enoch send the wogs home," could be heard at most football grounds.

Well into the 70s they still copped for it. In the Comedians TV programme, everyone from black people, to thick Irishmen and spastics were fair game, again no one ever said it was wrong. I'm not quite sure if Charlie Williams, the black Barnsley comic, inflamed, or made the situation more acceptable by taking the piss out of his own race.

We really didn't know any better and just went along with it. No one thought it was wrong, and none of us had the balls to do anything about it even if we had wanted to. It wasn't until the early 70s we started meeting and getting to know black lads at the games and in the pubs and clubs around town. The shouts of black bastard were then reserved for coppers and referees.

Anyway, at the Lane kickoff approached, and with 36,000 fans in the ground the fighting continued. Both managers made loudspeaker appeals for calm. Like anybody gave a fuck! We were having a good time. Every now and again lads from both sides would recognise a friend, workmate, neighbour or relative and shout out a greeting.

"Nar-then Steve how tha going? See ya t'neet" before laying back in again.

The Wednesday mob, lucky to be on the Kop in the first place, didn't try to make any inroads and stayed over to the right. With the game now underway things calmed down slightly, but missiles continued to fly back and forth. Lads were arrested or thrown out of the ground, some of the injured fans were treated on the spot with the more serious cases whipped off to hospital.

Even before, 'Iron lung, legs of plastic,' John Ritchie scored a late winner for Wednesday, their fans started drifting off.

We left the ground and did the usual march up the Moor into town, trying to find the Wednesdayites. We were pissed off obviously about the result but pleased that a bunch of young lads had successfully defended the Shoreham end.

The front-page headline of the Saturday evening sports paper the *Green 'Un* read: SIX HOSPITAL CASES MAR RITCHIE'S DERBY WINNER. It went on to give a detailed account of the all the trouble. The paper got to know about the meeting place of both mobs by interviewing young lads. Their names, ages and the districts where they lived, were printed in the paper. It told of the Blades mob gathering stones from outside the Howard and the Midland station. 'The Scrap' on John Street before the game (which wasn't really a scrap, just a chase) and how the Shoreham Street end had been turned into a battlefield. It also said 'By 2.15 five teenagers had been taken to hospital and at least another dozen had been treated on the spot for head injuries. Amongst the weapons seized were a large piece of lead, which had struck a boy in the face, jagged tins and house bricks. One fan said his friend had been struck on the head by half a house brick'

The quote of the day however came from the United chairman who dismissed the violence as just 'Unfortunate pre-match excitement.' The Monday morning nationals picked up on the story, where Sheffield United topped the league table of arrests and shame. Fucking great stuff, I thought, top of the league at last.

The day after I was walking along Stonelow Road with a couple of mates when Paddy O'Brien's father – also called Paddy O'Brian – came staggering home from the Sunday dinner session. Paddy, a staunch Wednesdayite shouted, "What about that then Sharpy, ya little cunt. Up the Owls. What have you got to say about it? Ya not so fuckin clever today are ya? Up the fuckin Owls." Now this wasn't a bit of friendly banter. He was drunk, granted, but from the way he spoke I knew he was after some trouble.

"Fuck off, ya drunken old cunt," I shouted back. Paddy slipped off his coat, took his false teeth out and put them on a garden wall, which was about two foot high. He held up his fists in the Queensbury rules style.

"Come on then Sharpy. I'll fuckin kill ya, you little fuckin bastard."

Well, Paddy was a bloke in his forties. Men were old in their thirties back then, and at forty they were fucking ancient.

I was only sixteen and a little bit scared, but he'd called me a bastard and I didn't like being called a bastard and besides, he could hardly stand up. I walked over and with one punch knocked him over the wall. My fist sunk well into his face; it was like punching a sponge pudding. He lay sparked out in the front garden. We all walked away laughing.

Ten minutes later we went back for a look, he was still out cold, maybe more from the beer than from the punch.

Manor Blades in the Claymore pub 1978

Chapter 4

(Steel toe-capped) boots of Spanish leather

Mick Jones had always been mine and many other Blade fans favourite player. So his transfer to Leeds United for £100,000 on Friday September 22nd, 1967 somewhat pissed me off.

Tiny and Ansh came round to our house at teatime and suggested we go down to the Lane to protest. We arrived at the ground about six-thirty and joined the Bramall brothers, Jagger and Pete and another dozen or so Blades outside the players' entrance. They'd obviously had the same idea as us and just turned up to see what was going on.

Rumour had it that Jones hadn't really been sold as someone had seen him go into the ground ten minutes before we arrived. Apart from that, we'd signed (the day before I think) an inside forward from Carlisle United named Willie Carlin, who according to the papers had signed for United to lay the goals on for Jones and his partner Alan Birchenall.

"I'll tell you what," said a lad I'd never seen before, pulling a foot-long carving knife from his inside coat pocket. "He's not fucking going anywhere, especially to Leeds, cos when he comes out I'm gonna kill the cunt."

The lad looked like he meant it. We hung around a while longer and out came Jones with two or three other blokes (I've no idea whose they were) carrying his boots and a few personal belongings.

"'As tha' gone then Mick?" someone shouted. Jones stopped and spoke to us for a few seconds saying he didn't want to go, but it wasn't up to him.

"Fuck off then, ya cunt," knife boy shouted and that was that, off he went.

"Right, we're off to the Skates," said one of the lads. "Your lot coming?"

"Skates," I said. "What's that?"

"It's the Silver Blades ice skating rink on Queens Road," he answered.

"Fucking ice-skating, we can't ice skate."

"You don't have to. Thing is, there's a bar there that will serve anybody, it's a penny to get in and the best thing… its full of birds." That was it, we were sold and off we went, little knowing I would spend the best part of the next two years visiting the place at least once and sometimes three times a week.

The Silver Blades was housed in the same building as the bowling alley and a casino. A nightclub called the Heartbeat made up the complex; the entrance fee either a bob or two bob, depending on the night, but once a month – on a Friday they held 'the penny pop night.'

In the queue I said to Tiny and Ansh, "I'll get these; you can get the beer in." As I peered over the barrier onto the ice, the cold from the rink hit my face. The place was packed, but with maybe only a hundred or so bodies skating and falling about on the ice and about five hundred others walking round as spectators.

We had no trouble getting served in the bar upstairs, where you could see out through the large windows overlooking the rink.

A DJ spun the latest pop sounds from a stage, that was actually housed on the ice, bang opposite the bar. I'd never seen so many girls in one place; Quasimodo would have pulled in there.

We introduced the rest of the Dronny lads to this paradise and the Friday night ritual began. The six o'clock bus into town, three pints in the, long since demolished, Montgomery boozer on the corner of Queens Road, and then into the Skates at half past seven.

Accents have always fascinated me. I don't know if it's the same in other parts of the country, but within say a fifteen-mile radius of Sheffield, the language is so diverse. Chesterfield, just twelve miles to the south has a dialect poles apart. Dronfield, slap bang in the middle is perhaps a cross between the two. Rotherham folk, six miles to the north of Sheffield, speak in a slightly different tongue and the Barnsley accent is well... as bloody common as muck.

The Sheffield lads we met at the Skates and the Lane constantly took the piss out of the Dronny lads, saying the town was upper class and we talked posh. If they'd have seen Cammell's Row they wouldn't have thought we were posh.

In the 60s and even more so in the 70s and 80s, many well-to-do Sheffield families moved to the town. It was seen as a step up the ladder, moving from Yorkshire to the more tranquil and up market County of Derbyshire. Sheffield folk trying to be posh, eh! Impossible.

The day after my first visit to the Skates, the Blades played Newcastle United at home. We all gathered at the back of the Kop for the first time since the Wednesday game and sat down in protest against the sale of Mick Jones. Willie Carlin scored on his debut, so fuck Mick Jones, we had a new hero; plus we still had Sherman the Tank Birchenall... for another two months anyway.

Two days after the Newcastle game we were off up to Hillsborough for a testimonial game against Wednesday. We met up in town, around 100 strong, but instead of walking, caught a couple of the fleet of special buses from Flat Street in the city centre.

We entered the ground at the Penistone Road end and joined hundreds of Blades at the back of the Kop. Again the Wednesdayites standing behind the goal at the front copped for a barrage of missiles. They knew we were coming and what had happened last time, but they didn't have the gumption to occupy the high ground. After the match we walked en-masse back to town, with the Wednesday mob at the other side of the road.

An article in the *Sheffield Star*, entitled 500 'FOOTBALL ROWDIES TERRORISE THE STREETS,' later described the events. It told how 500 youths had brought traffic to a standstill and intimidated passers-by on Penistone Road. Irene Boydon prosecuting, told the court: 'Two large groups of football fans, one wearing red and white, the other blue and white clashed after a game at Hillsborough. The red and whites charged the others, starting fights, and chaos followed'. Fans from both sides who were arrested were named and shamed.

One fifteen-year-old Blade (who could not be named for legal reasons) was seen carrying a length of chain; he told the court he had it, 'To protect himself from Wednesdayites' Some of the fans were banned from the games and had to report to police attendance centres for six weeks from three o'clock to five on match days. They were made to sweep up around the police station and wash the coppers cars.

Parton fronted the charge, swinging a piece of lead pipe around his head. Wednesday, in the space of one year had been pelted with eggs, chased off the Shoreham, and burned with acid. They'd been seen off once again and were becoming something of a joke. I almost felt sorry for them.

I'm not going to say too much about the acid incident in respect of the lads involved. It did happen though, once, at a testimonial game and was never repeated. It is however part of United's hooligan history and I'll leave it at that.

Two weeks later a dozen or so young Blades, all aged around fifteen-sixteen and proudly decked out in their colours walked into the Skates. They were catching the midnight train to London; the Blades were playing at Tottenham the following day. Tiny and me had arranged to hitch it, but for a change we were setting off early on the Saturday morning. I told the lads about my visit to Spurs six months earlier and how friendly the Tottenham fans were. When the Skates shut they left for the train in high spirits.

We set off about 7 a.m. the next morning, reaching White Hart Lane just after the kickoff. We'd been stuck halfway down the motorway for hours, but a great lift in a lorry dropped us off on Tottenham High Road close to the ground. We entered at the Shelf turnstiles and seeing a small group of Blades behind the goal on the Paxton Road end went across to join them. Only a couple of coaches made the trip, plus a few more on the morning train. The lads from the midnight train, looking a bit worried, greeted us. Their scarves now hidden away under coats or stuffed down trousers, they told us they'd been chased outside the ground and threatened with a pasting after the match.

"Fuck me Ron," one of them said. "I thought you said it was okay here."

"It was last season," I replied.

A group of nasty looking Spurs fans were already gathering to our left. They were a lot bigger and older than us, maybe they'd come round to thank us for last season's Cup final vouchers?

Midway through the first half United were awarded a penalty and we celebrated like we'd already scored by dancing around and swaying forward. Spurs fans packed behind the goal at the Park Lane end swarmed across the Shelf towards us. There was a delay for treatment to the injured Blade player and by the time Bernard Shaw stuck the pen in the bottom corner the Tottenham mob were massed behind us. Some Blades anticipating what was about to happen moved away. As the ball hit the back of the net our celebrations were somewhat muted. The Spurs fans moved down from the back and from the side. I knew what was coming, we all did. Nobody would be making a stand, we were all crapping ourselves, but no one wanted to admit it.

It was now every man for himself, we melted into the crowd and I ended up alone near to the right-hand side corner flag. The Spurs lads snaked through the crowd trying to seek us out; I was shitting myself as a group passed close to me.

134

My main concern now was getting out of the ground in one piece. I managed it just after half time by persuading a bloke to open up an exit gate. I decided to catch the tube to St Pancras. I had no idea where everyone else had gone, but reasoned to myself that's where they would head for.

On arriving I found most of the lads already there. Again I came in for some stick; one lad saying that far from it being okay, Tottenham was the worst fucking place he'd ever been to. We'd made it out unscathed though and the scarves were back out. We hung around inside and outside the snack bar. Some more lads arrived making our numbers around twenty. The game had ended, and we laughed and joked as if nothing had happened.

A mighty roar and the thunder of a hundred pair of boots echoed through the station. The noise and the fear of those few seconds will live with me forever. Oh fucking hell, I thought, as the Spurs mob stampeded towards us. We scattered in every direction. One of the Hackenthorpe lads, Bob Pixsley, and me ran down a subway that came out on Euston Road. I glanced over my shoulder to see a dozen Spurs boys ten yards behind and closing. Bob slipped off his scarf and dropped it to the ground. The front Spurs lads stopped, scrambling and fighting over the scarf giving us a few seconds breathing space. We shot across the road dodging traffic and ran down towards Kings Cross. A quick glance behind, assured us that the chase was over. We stopped, and laughed that ridiculous laugh, a mixture of panic and relief while holding on to each other gasping for breath. Not really knowing where to go or what to do, we gave it five minutes, and walked back slowly and cautiously towards St Pancras. We peeped round a corner into the station and saw that the Tottenham mob had left. Most of the lads were still there, the ones inside the snack bar had been unable to escape. They'd been clipped and had their scarves taken. No one was injured, but we were told that a couple of our lads had been interrogated. The Tottenham mob found out we were catching the midnight train home and would be returning to get the rest of us later on. Fuck it, I thought, there're not spoiling my night out, they probably wouldn't come back anyway.

Things were beginning to change on the football scene. Six months earlier at Tottenham there'd been no trouble whatsoever, but today we'd been lucky to get away alive. We hadn't tried to invade Tottenham's end, we hadn't threatened anybody or tried to show off, but still they'd tried to get us. Not only that, they knew which railway station we were leaving from. The violence, which had been confined largely to the terraces and surrounding streets was now moving miles away. The defenders of the ends were changing tactics and no matter where you stood in the ground or even outside it, you had to suffer the consequences.

Twenty or so 15/16-year-old little boys in the big bad city with no one to protect them had to grow up quick if they were to continue to play the game, but we were learning fast... we had to. What I'd noticed about the Tottenham boys, apart from them being a lot bigger and older than us, was that many were wearing boots, some with steel toe-caps. The birth of the boot boy was dawning.

We hung around the front of the station and saw groups of lads in red and white scarves appearing from Midland Road at the side of St Pancras. We knew they weren't Blades as there were far too many of them. Some of them came over and inquired, "Are you Boro?"

"No, Sheff Utd," we answered, "we've been at Tottenham, where you been?"

"Charlton," one of them answered. More and more Middlesbrough fans came into view; six coaches were parked down the street. We got chatting to a group of young lads about our age who were from Redcar. We told them about the hard time we'd come in for, both at White Hart Lane and at the station, we also said that the Spurs fans were coming back to get us,

"We'll see about that," one of the Boro lads said, "We're all from Yorkshire (before the 1972 Local Government Act Middlesbrough was part of North Yorkshire) and Yorkshire folk stick together, were not leaving till midnight so if they come back, we're with you."

Cheered up by the fact that we had some reinforcements we enjoyed the rest of the night along with the Redcar boys and some more of the older Boro lads. At 11 o'clock St Pancras station heaved with red and white. Mainly the red and white of Middlesbrough, but more Blades turned up; they were from the S.U.T. coach that had stayed over until midnight. It was parked on Midland Road at the side of the station along with the Boro coaches. Everyone knew that the Spurs fans were supposed to be returning. Some of the Boro lads were huge blokes in their twenties and thirties and I hoped and prayed that the Tottenham mob would reappear.

For a few brief seconds I thought they had as everyone ran towards one of the entrances to the station. Someone said about thirty lads appeared, took one look and ran back out again. I didn't see them, so I don't know, but it was probably was the Spurs lads, I can't think who else it could have been. By midnight I was sat on the train home, I didn't have a ticket, but I didn't give a shit. We said farewell to our Boro brothers in arms. It had been an eventful day, lessons had been learnt, and more would follow.

A week later Man Utd were back at the Lane. Half an hour before kickoff Macduff and me entered the ground at the bottom right hand corner of the Kop. The Man U. hoards stretched from the behind the goal at the bottom, to the back of the Kop, a good 5,000 of them at least.

To the left, in the spot where the Wednesdayites had been forced to stand a couple of months earlier, stood about a hundred or so Blades. "Fucking hell," Mac said, pointing up at the Blades, "They've not brought many."

"That's us, Mac." I replied.

Sherman Birchenall was sold to Chelsea in November 67 making Sheffield United the first club in history to sell two players for £100,000. The two leading scorers had been flogged and it was the start of the Blades becoming known as a club that sold all its best players, fuck the fans, eh? No wonder we were destined for relegation.

Over the next year or so the arrest figures started to grow, and I was getting a bit of a criminal record. At the home game against Wolves, along with a few other lads I was dragged from the Kop and ejected from the ground. None of us were charged, but our names and addresses were taken, and we were told by the police, they'd be keeping an eye on us. Drinking under age at the Howard Hotel cost me a fine of £1.

For no reason whatsoever the coppers came into the crowd, nicked me and about half a dozen likely looking lads at the home game against Coventry City. I had to attend the juvenile court with my mother in tow; I was again fined £1.

The next one came when Macduff and me damaged some council property and threatened the park keeper in Dronfield Park. We were caught scraping the letter C off the closed sign on the putting green hut with a penknife. We had to travel six miles by bus to Eckington, then walk a couple of miles to the court, held at Renishaw, Derbyshire. The panelled courtroom smelled of old wood and polish. Three magistrates, looking like demon headmasters sat in a raised area in front of a giant coat of arms, peering over their glasses at us. I swore a solemn oath to tell the truth the whole truth and nothing but the truth, and hoped God wouldn't strike me down dead. We stood side by side in the dock, hands behind our backs, afraid to look at each other for fear of cracking up. The Parky took the pledge, pointed to Mac, and said, "I asked him his name and he told me to fuck off." I bit the inside of my cheeks, looked at the floor and could feel my shoulders rocking. Mac's Mother jumped up and shouted, "You lying bleeder, my lad doesn't use language like that." She was warned by the magistrate and told to sit down. The Parky carried on, he pointed at me and said, "Then I asked him his name, and he replied… Harry Arsehole."

We doubled up laughing, as did most of public gallery and were given a ticking off by the magistrate. We were found guilty and fined ten bob each but were ordered to pay £5 costs (which was a fortune) for the damage. The *Derbyshire Times* wrote up the case. It said Sharpe, cross-examining, (we defended ourselves) asked how come it cost £5 to have a 2-inch letter repainted on the sign. A spokesman for the council replied, saying they had to pay a sign writer to repaint the whole sign. Fucking madness. The fine was eventually paid off at half a crown a week.

I was then nicked for assault causing actual bodily harm after a fight with a Dronny lad who I didn't know on the last bus home from Sheffield. This was a bit more serious and I received three-year probation sentence. Probation was terrible. I had to go the church hall every Monday at 5 o'clock along with three or four other youths for a session with the probation officer – Mr Herd, a big burly bastard with a broken nose.

Macduff, (burglary) and Curly Pear, the cigarette thief – who had been on probation for most of his life also attended. Mr Turd (as we called him) had once been a heavyweight-boxing champion in the army and he took a particular dislike to Macduff. When it was Macs turn to go in, Turd would come out into the corridor where we all sat and start sparring up to him saying, "Come on Cardwell you're a big lad, do you fancy your chances?" He would then punch Mac a few times on the shoulders pretending he was messing about, Mac would mutter under his breath, "Fuck off ya big bastard."

"What did you say?" Turd would shout.

"Nowt sir," Mac would reply, as Turd dragged him in the room by his ear.

He wasn't too bad with me, if I was working (which wasn't that often).

"You know where you're going don't you, Mr Sharpe?"

"Yes, sir. Borstal sir," I'd answer.

"Don't think I can't have you sent there, because I can you know." He always threatened me with Borstal. "If you haven't got a job by next week that's where you're going."

I must admit the prospect of Borstal scared the shit out of me. My cousin Kenny Raynor had done a stretch there and he told me the screws were a set of sadistic bullying bastards. Some his fellow inmates, he said, were even worse. I knew Turd couldn't have me sent away though, unless I was taken back to court for committing the same offence.

Cousin Kenny Raynor, circa 1960. Who according to my Mum was, "Too bloody good looking for his own good and had kids all ovver place."

The first league game of 1968 in early January took us to Hillsborough.

We again walked, mobbed up, along Penistone Road and entered the Kop unopposed. The two mobs stood side by side with a line of police separating them. The usual pushing, shoving and fighting took place, but nowhere near as bad as the game at the Lane.

After a Mick Hill (the new hero) cracker in a 1-1 draw, we walked mobbed-up back into town with the Wednesdayites nowhere to be seen.

By the time Man City (who we had bumped into many times in various ways over the last few seasons) arrived at the Lane for the first home game of 68, the Blades mob were firmly established at the back of the Kop. City, who went on to win the First Division title that year, as always brought a large following and were stood to the right of us. Again a squad of coppers stood in between trying to keep us apart.

City scarves, sky-blue with small maroon and white bands running horizontally across, were (along with Leeds scarves that were the same design) the most sought-after trophies among the scalp hunters of the day. I already had a Leeds scarf, along with a Villa, Wolves, Burnley and a couple of blue and white ones. In one of the surges into the City ranks I managed to grab a scarf. It was the new trend to wear the scalps hung off the shoulder straps of our combat or bush jackets.

After the game a large mob of us were on our way up to Victoria station to confront the City fans. A young City fan aged about fourteen walked round a corner straight into us. The poor little fucker had tears in his big brown eyes as the mob surrounded him. "Leave him alone" I shouted. "For fucks sake he's on his own and he's only a little kid." I then kicked him up the arse and nicked his scarf (only kidding). I put my arm around him and he told me he was lost and was trying to find the station.

"I think it's called the Exchange," he said.

"Is it the Victoria?" I said.

"Yeah that it" he said.

I walked him up and left him at the bottom of ramp leading up to the station. A large group of coppers ran down from the station and chased us off.

We were drawn away to Watford in the 3rd round of the FA Cup. Beetroot, Fruitbat and me, met at the Coach and Horses to thumb it into town to catch the special.

I wore my combat jacket with all the scalps attached, steel toe-capped boots and a cardboard pirate hat with the skull and crossbones motive on the front. The other lads just wore their red and white scarves.

A car pulled up virtually straight away, we jumped in and the elderly driver asked: "Where you going lads?"

"We're just going into town to the train station; we're off to Watford to watch United."

As soon as I got in the car I noticed Wednesday stickers on the windows.

"Well, well, well, look at this," the driver said, laughing his head off. "Three Unitedites in my car and me a Wednesdayite, who would have thought it eh? And all these Wednesday stickers, we can't have this can we? We better take them down, eh!"

In one swift movement Fruitbat grabbed an Ozzie Owl sticker, pulled it from the window, screwed it up and threw it on the floor. He was already on the next one when the bloke shouted, "No, no, I didn't mean it, I was only kidding." Beetroot and me cracked up as Fruitbat tried to unravel the sticker and stick it back on the window, it kept falling off.

"Just leave it," the bloke shouted. He didn't say another word and we were in pieces as he huffed and puffed all the way to town. He let us out near the Howard. We thanked him, but he just grunted and drove off.

As we walked down towards the station a bloke approached us with a camera saying, "Do you mind if I take your photo?" We stopped and stood close together saying, "Yeah go on."

"No, I just want you" he said to me "It's for the *Sheffield Star.*" Fuck me I thought, I'm gonna be famous. The others moved, and I stood there posturing, trying to look hard. I fully expected my photo to be in Monday's paper, but it wasn't, the lying bastard.

Thousands of Blades took over Watford, and another Mick Hill goal put us through. After the match on the way back to the train station I nicked a Watford scarf off this slightly balding, bespectacled, smallish youth.

Arriving at the station the lad appeared with two coppers. "That's him," the lad said. The coppers grabbed hold of me and marched me into the police room inside the station. The scarf was tied on my jacket with the rest of the scalps. I protested my innocence saying it was a Wolves scarf and I collected scarves by swapping them with other fans and I had two Wolves scarves. The lad insisted it was his.

"How old are you?" the copper asked me.

"Fourteen," I replied (thinking about my half fare ticket).

"How old are you?" he said to Watford lad.

"Seventeen," he answered. "Well," the copper said, "He's a lot younger than you, so I don't think he'd have taken your scarf,. Go on (to me), get on your way."

Sorry about that Elton.

Even though we won the game, the special train was demolished on the way back. In the next home game's match programme, British Rail called us animals and a set of bastards. All the damage was listed, even the amount of stolen bog rolls. They said they were having serious reservations about putting on special trains for United fans in the future. Great stuff.

Things started to change on the fashion front. Although I had never been a real mod (impossible with a Rolling Stones hair style), I wore – especially during my school years – the more affordable mod gear: button down and tab-collared shirts, op-art ties, hipsters, Cuban-heeled and desert boots. Many of the young Dronny lads now embraced the cult of the rockers. I don't remember why or how it came about or who started it.

I managed to pick up a leather jacket for a couple of quid and had the misguided view that covering it in studs would make me hard. The jacket felt good though, it hung just right. I didn't need to spend loads of money on clothes to look good. At seventeen years old I was a skinny as a young racing snake and felt confident and comfortable dressed in faded Levi's, T-shirt and leather jacket.

It was back to Renishaw Magistrates again when I was arrested again for riding a mate's motorbike with no tax, insurance, licence or L-plates. As I leapt a fence to try and make my escape from the police, the local copper, Constable Bunting, shouted, "You might as well come back Sharpy, I know it's you, I've got ya this time you little bastard." Once again my brief gave the court a sob story about me being a really good lad and having to look after Mum. The fine totalled twelve quid and the sympathetic magistrate added it to ones I was already paying.

Constable Bunting was a big fat fucker and one of those good, old-fashioned beat Bobbies that we all look back on with fondness. Hard but fair… not quite, just hard. He introduced himself to us one night by lifting me off the ground by my lapels and slamming me into the side of the telephone box at the bottom of Green Lane where we hung out most evenings.

A chance of a bit of revenge came when we drew Blackpool at home in the 4th round of the Cup. They'd been relegated, and I didn't think we would be seeing them again for a while, so this was a bonus. A few hundred fans travelled and gathered behind the goal on the Lane end.

Halfway through the 2nd half I saw (from the Kop) Wafe and two or three others walking round past the cricket pavilion towards the Lane end. Wafe had a large Union Jack flag tied round his shoulders; it dragged on the floor behind him. They ran straight into the Blackpool mob and ten seconds later were on their way out chased by about thirty youths.

After the game I went on a mission, hoping to find the lads who'd clipped me in Blackpool. Outside Jack Archer's sports shop on Bramall Lane, Rocket (who also copped for it that day), recognized one of his attackers in a group of about ten others. He decked the lad and the rest scattered. Around fifty of us chased them towards the Moor where they turned down a back street and managed to scramble on coach. The coach sped off as we put the back window through.

Tottenham, who we had another score to settle with were the next visitors for a midweek night game. Not many away fans travelled long distances to night games at the time and hardly any Spurs fans turned up.

An eighteen-year-old, blond haired, inside forward signed from Watford scored on his debut that night. His name— Tony Currie; but would he justify the massive £26,500 transfer fee splashed out for his services? Only time would tell.

The 5th round Cup draw took us to West Ham. Tiny had bought a car and five of us: Tiny, Ansh, Andy Ellis, Wuss and me drove down to London. The Hammers' mob had quite a reputation. Little Terry, the Chezzy lad who'd moved down there, kept us informed about their exploits on his occasional visits back home. Terry told us about the game against Man Utd on the final day of the 67 season. Man Utd had to win the game to secure the championship and thousands flooded into the East end. The Man Utd hoards took over the South Bank (West Ham's Kop) as well as most of the ground. Terry said the West Ham mob had a good go but were no match for Man United's superior numbers. He also told us that a large group of Man Utd fans on the South Bank carried brush staves with barbed wire wrapped around them.

We arrived at Upton Park around two o'clock. Ansh and me found a boozer near the ground and the other lads went to a café. A good following of Blades massed on the North Bank saw United do the business on the pitch winning 2-1 with reserve forward, Phil Cliff, scoring both goals. Quite a few Blades including Tiny, Andy and Wuss went on the South Bank.

We found out later there was trouble at the Tube station after the game, and on the way back to St Pancras a mob of Tottenham fans attacked some Blades. A girl with the Blade group was badly injured. Tottenham were beginning to piss me off.

The quarter-final draw took us to Leeds United at Elland Road. As I walked to the bus stop on Dronny bottom, a bird – it must have been a giant wandering

Albatross – dropped a large black and white dollop, covering my left shoulder and splattering onto my hair. It stunk like, well... shit. My mates, amidst bouts of laughter danced around me holding their noses.

"Ne'er mind Ron," one of them said. "It's supposed to be good luck if a bird shits on you; we're forced to win today now."

"No, it's only lucky if it shits on your right shoulder," somebody else said.

"No, they have to shit on your head for good luck," another mate said. So, all of a sudden everybody's an expert on the luckiness of bird shit. I nearly spewed as I grabbed some grass and managed to get most of it off.

After witnessing Big Gordon demolish seven pints in record time at the Howard we caught one of the special trains to Leeds. We were allocated 13,000 tickets for the open Gelderd end. Everybody was out for this one including all the Dronny and Chesterfield lads. Steve Cardwell, even though he was a staunch Wednesdayite came along for the crack. Steve brought along a small steel catapult and a pocketful of ball bearings.

I sat next to Gordon on the train and could hear the contents of his stomach churning around like a washing machine.

A girl I'd seen at the games quite a few times, and whom I'd been meaning to get acquainted with, brushed past me on the packed train. Without saying a word I took her hand, led her down the corridor into the toilet and locked the door behind us. All my mates followed, hoping to get a bit of the action. Making sure the girls head faced to the right, I knee-trembled nearly all the way to Leeds with the lads outside banging on the bog door, shouting: "Lerrus in, ya bastard." No chance, I smiled to myself. Just before we arrived in Leeds I opened the door and in the mad rush and crush outside, Ansh scrambled his way in and managed a quick pop before we pulled in at the station.

We caught double-decker buses up to Elland Road. Outside the ground we had a little scuffle with a group of Leeds fans led by a Catweasel look-alike weighed down with scalps. There were so many scarves hung from his combat jacket it was a wonder the scruffy bastard could even walk, let alone fight.

During the game the chant of "Sheff Utd hallelujah" went up. Ansh and me started this off for a very good reason. Everybody raised and shook their hands in the air making it impossible for any hawk-eyed coppers to spot who was throwing missiles. Ansh let fly a full-sized red snooker ball at the Leeds goalkeeper Gary Sprake. The ball sailed through the air and headed straight for Sprake until it smacked against the crossbar.

If the ball had connected, Ansh, maybe at this very moment would be wondering if the next meeting of the Armley parole board would be considering his release.

Leeds won the game 1-0, so the albatross turd hadn't brought me much luck, but at least I'd had a shag. After the game we swarmed down the banking at the back of the Gelderd, throwing everything we could pick up at the Leeds fans on the streets outside.

We again caught buses back to the station where we ripped out light bulbs and fittings throwing them out of the windows at the Leeds fans on the streets. Hundreds of Blades, held back by the coppers massed outside the station. A huge mob of Leeds, 500-600, appeared and the two mobs threw missiles at each other. Steve fired a volley of ball bearings into the Leeds fans. The police restored order and we were allowed into the station. Small groups of Leeds fans began entering the station; Blade scalp hunters attacked them.

A giant twenty stone Leeds fan wobbled towards us. Little Drew, the smallest by a good foot of the Dronny lads got behind him, leapt on his back like a flea and tried to grab his scarf. The Leeds monster was far more agile than he looked. He caught hold of Drew, lifted him above his head and slammed him onto the floor. We heard the air leave Drew's lungs as he hit the deck.

About six of us ran in booting and punching. My steel capper sunk into his rop and almost disappeared. He windmilled into us knocking two of the lads down. We danced round him throwing wild kicks. The big bastard just wouldn't go down. Another lad jumped on his back and hung onto his neck. Giant grabbed him and swung the lad to the ground. We looked at each other wondering what to do.

Two coppers came running over and the Leeds fan, still holding on to his scarf, ambled off. Lucky for him I thought, don't mess with us again. Drew was still on the deck panting for breath, he looked like he'd been in the ring with Mick McManus. We picked him up saying, "Fuckin hell Drew, why don't pick on some fucker a bit bigger next time?"

On the train back home I went in search of the girl in the hope of second helpings. I found her with her tongue stuck halfway down the throat of a fellow Blade. Shit I thought, I was thinking of proposing marriage.

I'd been to Leeds twice now and scored both times, which was twice more than United had done. Seven days later, who did we play? Yeah, it was Leeds away again, this time in the league. I gave this one a miss, and so did everyone else. The crowd of 31,000 was 17,000 down from the previous Saturday. Did United manage to score? Did they fuck.

My seventeenth birthday fell six days later on Good Friday.

The Blades played at Liverpool and came back with a surprising 2-1 victory; all was not lost in the fight against relegation. I spent the night at the Skates and got drunker than I had ever been in my life.

For the final game at the Lane against Chelsea we needed to win to have any chance of staying up. Everybody was out for this one. We hoped Chelsea would turn up this time; not many had travelled to the night game the previous season. Chelsea brought a few hundred fans and they went on the Lane end.

The Blades duly fucked up again, losing 1-2. After the match hundreds of Blades swarmed down Bramall Lane. The Chelsea fans had already left the ground. Before the subways were built at the end of Bramall Lane, a grass covered traffic roundabout occupied the spot. As we reached it we saw around fifty or so Chelsea lads, some were stood, and some were sat or sprawled out on the grass. It looked as if they were waiting for us. They didn't seem in the least bit bothered as we ran towards them.

The ones who were sat down jumped to their feet in readiness. I don't think they realised just how many they were up against. Not only that, we had a few scores to settle and were fired up to fuck, as we'd just been relegated.

More and more Blades came into view and at first Chelsea tried to make a stand, the front lads trying to hold the rest together. Then they all turned and ran. We chased them all the way along Bomb Alley, where they stopped a couple of times for a few brief seconds and again tried to make a stand before finally scrambling to safety inside the station where a squad of coppers held us back. So that was it, Second Division football to look forward to next season.

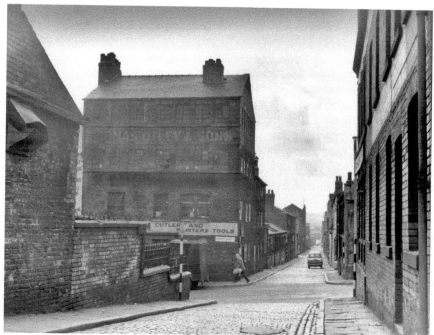

Eyre Lane 'Bomb Alley.' The alley ran from just past the bottom end of Bramall Lane to Howard Street opposite the Midland train station, a route we often took in the mid-late 60s to get to the away fans who'd travelled by train.

I had a longish spell of employment from late 67 to the summer of 68, working at the Dronfield Woodworking Company making cutlery boxes. The wages, £8 a week. Again half went on board, but four quid spendo went a long way back then. The main reason I stuck it so long I think, was the coming of Radio One. In the shop where I worked a giant old wireless covered in dust and cobwebs sat on a shelf. The old hags who glued the satin lining inside the cutlery boxes had it tuned to the Home Service or Radio Two where they listened to Jimmy Young and other shit.

"What's the recipe today Jim?" I soon put a stop to that crap. I kept tuning it in to Radio One.

The women, who'd been there for years and years complained to the gaffer. He tried a compromise, saying we would have half an hour on one station, half an hour on the other. That didn't last long. After a while the old fuckers got fed up of me switching stations and Radio One blasted out all day, except when it shared airtime with Radio Two.

I always listened to the Tony Blackburn breakfast show before setting off to work. Blackarse, a dim-witted cunt, didn't even know what day it was, but he played all the latest pop stuff: I suppose he had to really. It sempt to me like he didn't really want to play any rock stuff. He'd stick a Cliff Richard or Des O'Connor song on, or any other shit that nobody else, only him, wanted to hear, and say, "Oh, I really like this one; it's one of my favourites." Fuck off Blackarse.

It's really weird, and somewhat scary, how it's all come full circle. How I shout at my teenage daughters when they're tuned into Radio One to: "Turn that crap off."

"Go on then, Dad," they answer back, laughing, "Put your old-man station on."

In late summer, early autumn of 68, I started work as a labourer at the William Lucas malleable iron foundry on Dronny bottom.

Macduff, who had just left school, started a few weeks later.

The foundry was a dark, filthy, noisy hell-hole. Iron foundries had intrigued me ever since I wandered into Prestwich's at the age of four, looking for my uncle Chris; I could smell and almost taste the iron. Passing them on dark winter evenings with the flames and sparks shooting from the furnaces always reminded me of bonfire night. They were exciting and dangerous places where hard-working, honest men grafted.

I'd worked as an apprentice moulder at Butlers Iron Foundry in the winter of 66-67 when I was fifteen. It didn't last long, three or four months maybe. It was quite interesting to start with. This old bloke trained me up and taught me how to make the moulding boxes. I can't remember the exact procedure, but I do remember shovelling black sand into the steel cased moulding box, ramming more black sand around the pattern, sprinkling some cocaine type white powder on top, flipping the box over and ramming in more black sand around a tube. The tube was removed leaving a hole for the iron to be poured in.

It took a few weeks to even get it half right. Sometimes the whole lot collapsed, and I had to start all over again. When I got the hang of it, I carried the finished box – weighing about half a hundredweight, from the bench to the foundry floor to wait its turn be filled with white-hot molten iron.

I was the youngest there and had to sit in the gloom with the old moulders at snap and dinnertimes. They never had much to say and spoke only about work or maybe their gardens. I saw hairs sprouting from their ears and growing out of the ends of their noses and I thought, I'm never gonna fucking end up like that.

In between hiding and skiving, our gang of about half a dozen labourers at the Bottom Yard, as the foundry was known, did all the shit jobs. We loaded and unloaded lorries, moved stuff around the foundry and shovelled heaps of sand from one place to another, for no particular reason. We helped the moulders drag red-hot castings from the moulding boxes. The castings were pulled out with long handled pincers, then whacked with hammers to knock off the surplus

145

sand and flashings. The red-hot sand hit our eyes and faces, and if we weren't careful the castings burnt our legs. The moulders wore steel capped moulding boots with thick leather covers over the front to stop any molten iron from spilling down the lace holes.

There were two casts a day, one in the morning, and one in the afternoon. Sparks and flames shot out from the rotary furnace and clouds of steam and choking acrid smoke engulfed the factory. The moulders stood in a line under the slowly rotating furnace. They carried pots attached to long-handled ladles, lined with a clay solution to stop the molten iron from melting through. As soon as their pots were full, they ran like their lives depended on it, to pour the iron into the casting boxes before it cooled.

At the end of the cast the white-hot slag – the shit from the lining of the furnace was tipped out onto the floor. Some of the moulders had frying pans and would cook up an egg or a couple of rashers of bacon for their breakfast on the slag while it was still hot. When the slag cooled, it was our job to break it up with sledgehammers and crowbars, load it into hoppers and transport it on an electric bogie (a small truck) to be dumped. Even though the bogie's top speed was only about five m.p.h. we piled it up many times.

Mac and me worked half an hour's overtime during our one-hour dinner break, charging the furnace for the afternoon cast. We loaded ingots of pig-iron, by hand into a hollow tube about ten feet long. This was housed on runners that ran into the furnace. It was pushed in and dropped, by turning a large wheel (a bit like a ships steering wheel). As we got close, the heat from the furnace scorched our faces. It was hard, hot, backbreaking work. If we rushed we could get the job done in twenty minutes.

Dripping with sweat, we nipped out to the Rock Tavern boozer across the road, where my Uncle Chris (who also worked at the foundry) would have two pints of foaming Stones Best Bitter, lined up for us.

As with every job I've ever had, I soon got bored and started messing about. Even though Mac and me were a pair of bastards, the gaffer – a Mr Cassey, for some strange reason took a shine to us. The first of our three sackings came when he caught us asleep in the shower room/bogs where my Uncle worked, part-time as the toilet attendant. A week later he sent a message (via my Uncle) saying that we could come back as long as we behaved ourselves. We returned to work and knuckled down for a few weeks until boredom took over once again.

We had many hiding and sleeping places around the works. One was a tunnel underneath a stone bridge at the far end of the foundry. A large hole in the wall, led out to some wasteland at the side of the railway tracks. Across the road from the foundry stood the derelict St Mary's Catholic Church.

In broad daylight we robbed the lead from the roof, windows and parapets and humped it across the road to the tunnel. We had the bright idea to melt it down and dragged a hefty old casting pot through the hole in the wall. We built a fire, stuck the pot on the top, loaded in the lead and waited. Nothing happened. Cassey's head appeared through the hole, he almost apologetically sacked us on the spot.

A week or so later we were hung on a street corner, kicking our heels when

146

Cassey pulled up in his car. He had a chat with us and ended up giving us one last chance, had the man gone mad? We started back, and again towed the line for a while.

The core shop girls were a bunch of forty/fifty-year-old cackling hags. They made some kind of sandy things, that went inside the moulding boxes. Because we didn't give a shit about the job and our cheeky attitude they had no time for Mac or me.

We were sent to sweep out the core shop, along with an, older, big, hefty labourer who we'd nicknamed Fat Mattress. Mattress was from Skegness. He'd married a Dronny woman, who he'd met in a whirlwind romance while she was on holiday there. We swept round the machines and stacking racks, fucking about and laughing. Mattress fancied himself with the ladies, he chatted them up, flirted and the old bags loved it. Mattress stood in front of the women, lifting their frocks up with the brush handle, pretending it was an accident, saying, "Ooooh, I'm sorry, I nearly saw your pants then." They squealed, giggled and tippy-toed around, limp-wristed like little dancing mice. Mattress got a bit bolder and lifted one of the crone's dresses way up, till we could see her bloomers. This had the fuckers in hysterics until I shouted at the top of my voice: "SHOVE IT UP HER FUCKIN FANNY."

It went silent apart from Mac's roar of laughter. The hags downed tools, stormed out as one, and returned two minutes later with Cassey, who sacked me, and even though Mac's only crime was to laugh, sacked him as well. Mattress, who'd started all the shit in the first place kept his job.

. . . seen at Huddersfield
Nothing is so untidy and ugly-looking
as the scrawls and daubs fans make on club walls and gates.
This lot disfigured the Huddersfield Town ground after Sheffield United had paid a visit.

147

Chapter 5

The motorcycle black madonna two-wheeled gypsy queen

By the summer of 68 we were well into the rocker scene. Some of the Dronny lads now rode motorbikes, but for every rocker that had a bike, there were two or three others that didn't.

The Dronny lads with bikes, plus their pillion riders rode to the Skates on Friday nights and parked up alongside the mods scooters outside the bowling alley. The rest of us went by bus. Sometimes fights or arguments broke out between the rivals and sometimes the rows of bikes or scooters were kicked over while one of the groups was inside.

As well as the Alley, other mod hangouts included Down Broadway on High Street in Sheffield city centre. The small basement bar with four mirrored walls made it seem massive inside.

The Highway 61 club at Heeley and The Speakeasy at Darnall were the other main mod hangouts.

The DJ at the Skates, regularly played the post-psychedelic, Bubblegum music, that took over the charts and the airwaves in the summer of 68.

Ohio Express's *Yummy Yummy Yummy*. The 1910 Fruitgum Company's *Simon Says*. Gary Fuckit and the Union Gap's *Young Girl. Mony Mony* by Tommy James and the Shondells. The Lemon Pipers *Green Tambourine* and Love Affair's *Everlasting Love*. The hordes of more than willing teenage lasses, who hung-out at the Skates, loved this cheesy shit and looking back, I don't suppose the music was all that bad.

It's the first thing that springs to mind when I think back to the Skates and 1968, and no matter what era we live in, there's always gonna be a bit of feel-good pop around.

After the disappointment of *Their Satanic Majesties* the Stones were back to their blues roots and back to their best with the release of the marvellous *Beggar's Banquet* album. *Sympathy for the Devil* and *Street Fighting Man* were the best-known tracks. My favourite, however, was the excellent *Stray Cat Blues* a rather risqué R&B number that told of the pleasures of forbidden fruit.

A new self-proclaimed King of the Kop arrived on the Shoreham and he even took over Willie Ward's rallying cry of Zigga Zagga. Eskimo led of a gang of rockers who hung around the Pond Street bus station. The Pond Street Mob came mostly from the Wybourn and Manor estates. A well-built, stocky lad from the Wybourn, Eskimo, had long, straight, jet-black hair and a round face with Inuit features. He looked like Nanook of the North, had a team of pet huskies, paddled down the River Sheaf in a kayak and never ate yellow snow, hence his nickname.

Not to be outdone, his lieutenant, a lad from the Manor called Butlab was a

Wednesdayite and had christened himself 'King of the Wednesday Kop.' There were usually about a dozen or so lads who hung around the bus station, but a number of hangers-on could double the size of the mob.

The Pond Street mob would start fights for no other reason than they regarded the area as their 'Turf.' At weekends thousands of people used the bus station. The refreshment kiosk known, as 'The Threepenny Bit' was the meeting place for courting couples, and dozens congregated around the booth hoping their dates would turn up.

Up to 11 o'clock at night, just before the last buses left, hundreds of folk stood around the station, chatting, laughing and singing as they waited in the queues. Any lads, alone or in groups who passed through and got a bit too loud or gobby, or even just made eye contact copped for it from the Pond Street boys.

I knew Eskimo and his sidekick, Little Jimmy, from the matches and would stop and have a chat to them if I passed through the station. I was always a bit wary of the rest of them, as it didn't take much for them to kick off. Pond Street Nora, a six-foot-tall vagrant, lived and slept on the benches or the inside bogs at the bus station. Nora wore a long dirty rain mac and size twelve plimsolls. Her head resembled a donkey, which she tried to partly cover by always wearing a headscarf. She carried all her worldly goods in a couple of shabby shopping bags. Nora smoked discarded dog ends and the poor woman could often be seen foraging for food in the litter bins. I always felt sorry for her but couldn't help laughing at the crazy things she used to shout: "Carrots and pays (peas) carrots and pays, barrel organ, barrel fuckin' organ, I know thi mutha an I know thi fatha," followed by a stream of obscenities. Young kids or innocent passers-by were terrified of her; as for no apparent reason she'd often leap from a bench and attack or insult them. The Pond Street mob, bless 'em, saw Nora as part of their turf and anyone who took the piss or got too lippy with her were quickly dealt with.

Many years later at a mate's flat I sat with a dozen or so fellow marijuana smokers (mostly strangers); it was the early hours of the morning and we'd been smoking all night. The conversation somehow turned to Nora. Everyone had a story or a recollection about the old dear. I sat listening, straight-faced, waiting my turn to strike. In the first lull I jumped to my feet and shouted, "When you've all fuckin' finished, that's my Aunty you're talking about."

I sat back down with my head in my hands. The ten second silence that followed sempt like an hour. I slowly lifted my head back up grinning like a lunatic.

"You bastard Sharpy," one of my mates shouted. The place erupted in laughter.

I borrowed an LP from a girl at the Skates called *Another Side of Bob Dylan*.

I'd listened to, but never really heard Dylan's commercial hits, *Blowing in The Wind*, *The Times They Are A-Changing*, *Like A Rolling Stone* and perhaps the first ever 'Rap' song, *Subterranean Homesick Blues*. They were all okay, I thought, but that was about it.

Another Side came in an unassuming white cover with just a small photo of the man himself on the front. I didn't get too excited about the record, but thought I'd give it try.

On arriving home I dropped the needle and after a few crackling seconds, beautiful, amazing lyrics swept out and smacked me straight in the face. Dylan's acoustic guitar, clear and sharp, rang out like a bell. A weeping Harmonica blew long, wailing, timeless notes. It was incredible. I played it constantly trying to take it all in. The record had been released four years earlier in 1964; why hadn't anybody ever told me about it? Maybe... no certainly at thirteen years old I wouldn't have been ready to hear it. I conjured up my own visions of what Dylan sang and was absorbed and lost in the music for weeks and weeks.

I needed more, so I nipped into town one Saturday morning to Violet May's and bought *The Freewheelin' Bob Dylan* first released in 1963. This was even better.

On the bus back home, I read all the back-cover notes, but it was front cover that grabbed my attention. It showed Dylan, dressed in blue jeans and a short beige, suede jacket walking down a snowy New York street. His shoulders hunched up against the weather, his girlfriend, Suze Rotolo, clung tight to his arm; it looked so real, I could almost feel the cold. Nobody told me it was a New York street, I just knew it was, and it was like they were going somewhere, I didn't know where, but I knew it was somewhere special.

I couldn't wait to get home and after playing the album non-stop all afternoon, I wouldn't have cared if I never heard another record again.

I became addicted to *Talking World War Three Blues*, a song that lampooned the West's cold war cat-and-mouse games with the Russians, but also gave out an alarming message of what the whole world must have been feeling and thinking in a somewhat uncertain and daunting period of modern history.

I played it so many times, listening intensely to the words and at the same time trying to copy Dylan's flat-picking country blues guitar style. Mam was on the verge of a nervous breakdown; it was the closest she ever came to hitting me.

"For Christ's sake put summat else on," she'd shout through the front room door. "I wouldn't mind if he could sing, its nah-nah-nah, nah-nah-nah all the time, it's sending me bleeding mad, if you don't stop playing it I'll chuck it through the bloody window, I swear to God I will, I'm bloody sick on yer, why don't you piss off out?"

Good old Mam, God love her.

After months and months of listening and practising I started getting close to the flat-picking guitar style. I taught myself the left-hand hammer-ons and pull offs, but the secret lay in the wrist action of the right hand. Moving from the bass to the high strings using just the pick required speed and coordination. It eventually all fell into place and I didn't even have to look at my right hand, it just sort of came naturally.

I was going backwards, and the next Dylan LP I bought was his first; titled *Bob Dylan* recorded in 1961.

I rambled into New York town and froze right to the bone as the wind blew the snow around. I pictured B-movie gangster dives and steam rising from the gutters in the winter streets. I took a rockin, reelin, rollin downtown subway ride, to the Greenwich Village coffee houses: Cafe Wha? The Gaslight and Gerdes Folk City. I imagined fingerpickin Hill-Billies and wailing blues harmonica players. I heard freight train whistles blow and held on tight to a gospel plough.

So here I am, at home: I'm listening to songs about Martin Luther King, nuclear fall-out shelters, banned cannonballs, pellets of poison and racial tension in Mississippi.

At the Skates, it's yummy yummy yummy I've got love in my fuckin tummy and Simple Simon telling me to put my hands on my head and let my backbone slip... weird shit man.

I bought a harmonica, hooked it up to a metal coat hanger and hung it around my neck. At first it was level with my forehead and then my chin. I twisted and adjusted it and finally got it close to my lips. I figured out that to produce a scale, the instrument had to be alternatively sucked and blown. I blew one note and it fell off. I tried tying it on with string and elastic bands, still it kept moving to one side or falling off. I gave it up as a bad job, stuck a Dylan record on and tried to play along to it holding the harp in my hands. It didn't sound right, I was baffled. I didn't realise harmonica's came in different keys, so if the tune was in, say the key of C, the harmonica had to be the same. If that wasn't confusing enough, the blues notes were sucked out, so again a different key was needed. Mind-boggling shit. Another thing I realised is that a mighty fine pair of lungs is needed to be a good harp player.

I stuck at it and eventually worked things out by trial and error, but it would be a few more years before I would buy a proper holder. In the meantime I learnt some carols on the harp and earned a few bob playing them outside posh houses at Christmas.

It was around this time that I realised my singing voice left a lot to be desired. I could just about growl out a tune all right but couldn't hold a note longer than one second. If (albeit uneducated) folk reckoned Dylan couldn't sing then what chance did I have? Still – keep plodding on son, I thought.

The 68-69 Second Division season started with a home game against Aston Villa. The 12 o'clock Dronny to Sheffield bus travelled through Heeley Bottom and from the top deck I spied a dozen or so of the Heeley Green mob all clad in leather jackets turn on to the top end of Shoreham Street. Along with a couple more Dronny lads also dressed in leathers, I jumped off at the next stop and ran up to join the Heeley boys. We greeted each other like long-lost brothers and set off towards the Howard.

Passing the football ground at the junction of Shoreham/John Street, a Villa coach pulled up about twenty yards away. As the supporters piled off we ran towards them screaming and shouting. The coach sped off with half the passengers still aboard. The Villa fans that left the bus scattered in all directions. We didn't even bother chasing them. A good start to the new season.

At the game the Blades went 3-0 up early in the match. Villa bought a good following of a couple of thousand and were massed on the Lane end. When the third goal went in the Villa mob swarmed towards the cricket pavilion heading for the Kop.

A five-foot high fence to stop the crowd from changing ends had been erected at the open bit of the Kop level with the corner flag. This proved no obstacle as the middle of the Shoreham emptied, scaled the fence and flocked towards the Villa fans.

A wooden gate around four feet high was now all that stood in between the two mobs. As we arrived a group of about twenty Blades mods were already over the gate and running towards Villa. The Villa mob stopped dead in their tracks, turned and ran back to the Lane end. Job done in two minutes flat.

A certain amount of friction existed between the Blades mods and rockers. Nothing serious, but the two groups never mixed together except when the fighting started. At half time most of the mob left the Kop and stood on the back steps or hung around the snack bar. Small groups of lads from both groups eyed each other up, but usually kept themselves to themselves.

The half time chat generally centred on what would be happening after the game, or whether it was worth trying to get round to the Lane end to confront the away fans. At the end of the game we all left the ground together and after hitting town, went our separate ways.

Fans from most clubs who we met on our travels, in train stations and on the road, were usually quite friendly. We'd swap tales about the grounds we'd visited and what we'd been up to at the games. It was rumoured on the football grapevine that although they didn't have the largest mob, Millwall were one of the roughest set of fans in the land. The Millwall fans I met on the motorway on the way to Chelsea, and the lads on the train, coming back from Rotherham were all sound, but when the teams faced each other it would be a different story.

I jumped off the bus outside the Earl of Arundel boozer at the top of Shoreham Street, as about forty or so drunken Millwall lads spilled out into the road. I hung well back and followed at a distance as they made their way up to the ground. They were a mixed bunch of lads, some mods, some with long hair and most looked to be older than us, in their early to mid-twenties. They entered the turnstiles at the corner of Cherry Street/Shoreham Street. I followed a few yards behind as they made their way along the walkway towards the back of the Kop.

They gathered in the far-right hand corner and immediately the Blades mob moved from the middle of the Kop and swarmed towards them. These lads didn't give a fuck and in the fight that followed, gave as good as they got.

The coppers were in straight away trying to keep the mobs apart.

In one of the surges, a young Millwall lad got stabbed. As might well be imagined, this incensed the lad's older brother who went absolutely crazy, decking Blades from all angles. The stabbed lad was taken away for treatment and his brother went with him. All through the game we tried the move the small mob, but a combination of police and determination from the Millwall lads meant they stayed for the duration.

One of the Dronny lads, Hippo, heard a conversation between a couple of Blades: "Fucking hell," one of them said, "these fuckers are hard bastards."

"Yeah," the other one said. "There're all Dockers." Hippo picked up on it, we adopted the term, and 'The Dronfield Dockers' were born. It was all done tongue in cheek at first, but some of our lads painted it on the backs of their leathers. It was felt penned inside bus shelters, the bogs in the boozers and walls and buildings around the town.

The lads from the village of Unstone – a mile down the road from Dronny got in on the act. The half a dozen or so rockers who lived there called themselves 'The Unstone Leather Kings' and painted the letters ULK on their jackets. The Unstone lads knocked about with us so there was no hostility between the two gangs. Old Dronny lads to this day, still speak of, and call each other Dockers.

At the recent 2006 World Cup finals a Union Jack flag hung from the wall in one of our locals, the Bridge Inn, with the words Dronfield Dockers splashed across it.

The first game of 1969 in early January took us to Mansfield in the FA Cup. On the Friday night before the match a group of about twenty Blades left the Skates to walk the twenty-odd miles through the night into North Nottinghamshire. They must have been mad.

I set off thumbing alone, early on the Saturday morning. A couple of miles from the town I passed the group of Blades as they trudged up a hill, looking somewhat pissed off. They still managed to give me a cheer as I hung my head out and waved from the lorry window.

We'd been allocated about five thousand tickets for the game, which were sold in a matter of hours. The Cup matches were always special occasions, and everybody wanted to be there. We assembled on the open end of the ground about half an hour before kickoff. A line of coppers stood pitch-side looking up at us. A few Blades scaled a small wall at the front and the police tried to hold them back but were overwhelmed as hundreds swarmed over and ran across the corner of the pitch onto the larger side terrace.

We moved along to the far end, near to Mansfield's covered Kop. The police reassembled at the front; they knew what we were up to. Another charge and scale took hundreds of us over the wall and onto the Kop. The Mansfield mob, gathered at the back behind the goal scattered as we swarmed onto their end. We occupied the spot where the home fans had stood, chanting, "Easy, easy."

I noticed a bit of commotion behind me and gaps appear in the crowd. A huge Mansfield fan, who wasn't that tall, but about four feet wide stood alone, arms outstretched offering to fight all-comers. No one seemed willing to take him on. A couple of us forced our way through, as he whipped his stang out and started squirting jets of piss on those closest to him. He was swamped before we reached him. He went down under a sea of boots and punches. The police came in and dragged him, ragged, bruised and bleeding, out to safety. All fine and dandy to mess with the Shoreham boys pal, but piss on em… at your peril!

After four pioneering years on the terraces I was learning how to look after myself and survive, not only in the football environment, but also in the pubs, nightclubs and on the streets. I'd never been that good at fighting, lacking the power to put someone on their arse.

I could front it though; I had a bit of lip and could hold myself together in tricky situations. I didn't back down and approached battles with a smile on my face, especially when I'd had a few pints. I could gee the lads up saying things like, "Come on, we're not gonna run from these fuckers." I reasoned that if a little cunt like me was going to stand his ground then everybody else should. I wasn't scared about getting hurt, that's not quite true: I wasn't bothered about getting hurt, but I didn't want to get hurt too bad!

The buzz came not from the fight itself – but from the seconds and split seconds before it, when my heart nearly exploded. Let the cavemen do the decking. I loved seeing the enemy back down and run, and I hated having to do a runner. I took no pleasure in hurting anybody or chasing them for miles. It didn't always work like that though. A boot in the bollocks that took my breath or a sidewinder to the head that made my ears ring, brought it all back home, but it was all part of the game, and what a fucking game it was.

Most of the time it never even came to blows as one side or the other backed down and ran. Two mobs could pass each other on opposite sides of the road and nothing but verbals were exchanged. Not many opposing fans ventured on the Shoreham now we were in the Second Division. We did however manage to get on a good few of the home ends at away games.

It wasn't the same every week. Different circumstances meant different responses. Sometimes it was straight in without even thinking about it. Other times, hang back a bit and not only size up the enemy, but also look at the reaction of our own troops to see who was up for it. Sometimes my shoelaces suddenly came undone as we advanced towards our rivals and I had to stop for a few seconds to tie them, everybody knows you can't fight with a loose shoe…

We were the boys now; we'd hung on to coat-tails of the suities, learning the trade. Now it was our turn to defend the Shoreham end, seek out the away fans at home games, give them a hard time, chase them back to the station or brick their coaches. We accepted the same to happen to us at away games. We were under no illusions about where we stood in the league table of football hooligans, nor did we care. Nothing was organised; we just turned up at the train station or the S.U.T. depot for away games. Sometimes hundreds, sometimes even thousands, sometimes only fifty or so.

For the home games we usually met up at the Howard. Like the team we supported, sometimes we won, sometimes we lost, sometimes getting chased, sometimes doing the chasing, that was the way it was, no big deal. Back then and way into the 70s it was more than often a home and away thing.

It's hard to generalise but, say in a mob of a hundred lads, there were maybe a dozen or so front-line scrappers, a couple of nutters who didn't give a shit, a few arse-twitchers who openly whinged, saying things like: "We're gonna get battered today," some comedians who lightened things up, lads who crashed the cigs and bought rounds of beer, scroungers who were always skint and hangers on, who kept themselves in the background.

You didn't have to be a good scrapper to belong, but it helped. Most lads

154

were there every week. Some were nowhere to seen at tough away games. I knew most of the lads and most of lads knew me. Some of us were 'faces,' minor celebs like, and there were always one or two groupies knocking around, either at, or after the games who were up for a shag.

We were a group of teenagers doing what most working-class teenagers did: trying to look and dress good, fight, drink, and shag as many birds as possible. We walked with a swagger associated with members of a gang, but this was football, and much bigger gangs could be lurking just around the next corner.

More than anything though, we were all passionate Unitedites, true Blades. Our love for the Blades was unconditional. We sang, shouted, chanted and cheered the lads on, all through the game, no matter what. We never slagged off the players or called for the manager's head, even after relegation.

Arthur Walker was about 3-4 years older than me. Arthur had been a Teddy boy ever since I first met him in the early 60s. He still wore the drape jackets, brothel-creepers, boot-lace ties and shit, and he still wore his snow-white hair in the quiff at the front, ducks-arse at the back style. Arthur had a small (20-30 houses) window-cleaning round in Dronny.

One night in the Midland boozer, he asked me if I wanted to earn a few bob, helping him on his round. I arranged to meet him the next morning, and he arrived, carrying a pointer ladder (these were used to clean the downstairs windows), two buckets and a couple of chamois (Davis Junior) leathers.

"First thing we've got to do, Ron," Arthur said, "is to nick a big a ladder, some cunt's had mine away. Come on, I've seen one on Holborn."

So, we robbed this ladder from a back garden on Holborn Avenue and we were off.

The trouble with Arthur's round, was that the houses were dotted all over Dronny, and we had to walk miles to get to them.

Arthur, a small, skinny geezer, had a wicked smile, a twinkle in his eye and was a proper ladies man. He told me stories about all the women he'd shagged on his round. I must admit, I did get a bit worked up about the prospect of shagging the women, but I'd been doing the round for a couple of months and although he flirted a lot, I'd never actually seen him go in anyone's house for a session.

"I fucked her, the other week Ron, when I called round for the money," he used to say.

"When I'm doing bedroom windows, some of 'em come upstairs and cloth off," was another one.

"Can I do some of the upstairs Arth?" I asked him.

"Oh no, Ron, we don't want you tippling off a ladder and breaking ya neck, do we?" he said.

We did the round, sometimes on a Thursday, sometimes Friday, to get a few bob for the weekend.

I'm in the Midland one Thursday night, sat with Big Dung, when Arthur strolls over and says, partly to me and partly to Dung, "I've got summat on tomorrow, Ron. Can you do the round on your own? And don't forget, her at that big house on Hill Top Road, she pays wi her body, so you can fuck her if ya like."

I saw Dung's face light up.

"Yeah I'll do it Arthur," I said.

Dung's straight in. "I'll come and help ya, Ron. Don't want paying or owt, just get me a couple of pints, eh?"

"Yeah, ok. Come round to our house about nine," I said.

Next morning, I awoke to thuds on my bedroom window.

I glanced at the clock, it read 10 minutes to 8. I opened the curtains as another snowball thumped against the window.

I could just make out a lone figure, stood in a snow drift, with a blizzard raging around him.

"Come on Ron, let's get going," Dung shouted.

"We can't clean windows in this weather," I shouted back.

"Come on, we can do it Ron, we can do it."

"Fuck off back to bed ya daft cunt," I shouted back.

In early March I boarded a train with about 50 or so Blades to Aston Villa. We arrived at Witton station and walked the short distance to Villa Park. By kickoff another two or three coaches arrived, so there's about 200 of us stood behind the goal on the open Witton end.

Ten minutes in to the match, Stan Lake and me get chatting to two birds, who happened to be Birmingham City fans.

I noticed to my right, around 50 Villa lads moving towards us. Blades ran over to meet them, and the Villa lads backed off, but didn't move far, and stood about twenty yards to our right. More Villa lads appeared from behind the stand to our right, scaled the fence and joined the lads already there. Again, Blades moved towards them and backed them off.

We were getting on well with the girls, the Blades were doing OK, so there was no need for Stan and me to join in.

Looking over to the Holte End, I saw masses of Villa fans moving over to the stand on their left. A few minutes later, 100s were already over the fence, with more scaling it. This time the Blades didn't move. The Villa mob gathered behind us and within seconds they waded in. The other lads to our right, steamed in, making it a two-pronged attack. Blades started to melt, there was far too many to handle.

This left a few Blade normals, Stan, the Blues sisters, me – and dozens of Villa prowling around the gaps the Blades had left, looking for stragglers to chin. Now you always want United to score, eh! No, not always, so what did they do? They fuckin scored. There was about twenty Villa fans stood just behind us and when the ball hit the net. The Birmingham birds went crazy, jumping up and down hugging each other and us. Stan and me didn't move.

"Don't you celebrate when you score? We go mad," one of the birds said.

"No, we just stand still and say nowt," I answered.

Brian Jones, the true Rolling Stone and the genuine rebel of the band, died in the summer of 69. He was twenty-seven years old. Jones really didn't give a fuck. His sex, drugs and rock 'n' roll lifestyle finally caught up with him. Just weeks after being sacked by the Stones, he was found dead in the swimming pool of his home in Sussex. Jones had always been my favourite Stone. How could they sack him? Brian Jones founded the band, named it and recruited all the other members. His good looks, arrogant attitude, his style and stage presence did much to uphold the bands radical image. Although he didn't write any of the bands hit songs he was a multi-instrumentalist who gave the band its blues feel. He experimented in new sounds and instruments and was the heart and the soul of the band. The group I grew up with and loved more than any other had included Brian Jones. The Stones were never quite the same without him and in my view after *Let It Bleed* or maybe *Exile On Main Street* they never made another decent album or single for that matter.

Macduff persuaded their Steve, who worked at a warehouse that stocked spray paint, to nick us some cans. We set out on a painting and decorating mission on Dronny Bottom, armed with a can of red paint each. We sprayed Blades, Shoreham Bootboys and Sheff Utd on every white wall on the main road, on the footbridge and in the waiting rooms at the now shut down Dronfield train station.

After spraying BLADES in two-foot high letters on the rendered gable end of a row of terraces on Alexandra Road, the old woman who lived there came out and caught us. We tried denying it, but the can was in my hand; the paint was still wet and stunk like fuck.

"I know your names," she said. "And if you don't clean it off, I'm fetching the Bobbies." She brought out a bucket of water and two scrubbing brushes and stood and watched while we scrubbed it off. So there we were, two of the big hard Dronny Dockers dressed in leathers with a four-foot-tall, seventy-year-old lady, poking us in the back, shouting, "Come on, put some bloody elbow grease into it." The outline was still visible ten years after.

A few days later all our handiwork on Dronny Bottom had been desecrated with the word OWLS sprayed over it in large blue letters. Word came via the grapevine that a Wednesdayite called Spider had done the dirty deed. Spider, a small weaselly lad with ginger hair, freckles and steel-rimmed, round National Health specs, laid low for weeks as the word went round we were after him. He couldn't have known Mac and me had done the spraying or he'd never have dared to ruin it. I can just imagine him bragging, "It were me that sprayed 'Owls' over that Blades graffiti," then hearing: "It were Mac and Sharpy who did it." I bet the poor lad nearly shat his pants. We finally collared him one night outside the Midland boozer.

"Spider ya little cunt," Mac said, grabbing him by the neck. "I've been looking for you for ages."

Spider pleaded innocence but guessed what was coming as he removed his glasses. Mac started slapping him saying: "Don't-fuckin-ever-fuckin-spray-over-our-fuckin-spraying-a-fuckin-gain... Cunt." Each word was followed by an alternate flat hand, then backhand slap around Spider's ear holes. For the word

"Cunt." Mac spun him round and booted him up the arse, helping him on his way as he ran for his life along Dronny Bottom.

Years later Spider was jailed for manslaughter. After being attacked by his next-door neighbour he picked up a lump of wood and smashed the bloke over the head, killing him stone dead.

September 1969. After a night at the Skates, Macduff, a lad Mac knew from Chesterfield and me made our way up to Tinsley in the east end of Sheffield. The M1 motorway had by now finally reached civilization. We arrived about midnight and stood on the slip road trying to hitchhike south to Watford. About three hours later we were still there. We decided enough was enough and slunk off to walk back to town.

We found an unlocked, parked-up lorry and managed a couple of hour's cat nap until the buses started running. We made our way back into town and hung around the Pond Street bus station café, supping tea while planning our next move. We decided to catch the S.U.T. bus. We boarded one of six coaches and arrived in Watford around one thirty. Three of the buses pulled up at the ground together.

A lone skinhead stopped dead in his tracks as he turned a corner a few yards in front of us. With a look of terror on his face he turned and shot off down the street. Blades piled off the coaches like marauding buccaneers, screaming, "Fucking skinhead, get the bastard." Dozens of Blades chased the poor lad until he finally escaped through a back garden.

Although most of us had heard about the skinheads, I don't think any of us had ever seen one. It was like an alien from outer space had just landed, but we were way-behind-the-times Northern monkeys.

Last season's Cup game here had been a piss-take with thousands of Blades taking over the town and the ground. This time there were only a few hundred of us, but no one expected any problems. We gathered on Watford's Kop just to the left of the goal and ten minutes before kickoff a few more lads from the supporter's club coaches increased our numbers to about three hundred. A couple of hundred Watford fans stood to our right with the obligatory line of police in between.

By kickoff more Watford fans appeared, boosted by a group of rather large West Ham lads, some wearing claret and blue scarves and some sporting the new skinhead look. Whether these lads were West Ham fans who lived in Watford or they'd just come along for the crack, I don't know, but they swung the balance in Watford's favour. The police didn't help our cause by grabbing many of the Blades front line boys and removing them from the ground. We managed to hang in there until the end of the game. Once again lessons were learnt that day. Don't underestimate anybody, anywhere.

A few weeks after the Watford game the first skins started to appear at the Lane. Sinny and couple more of the Chezzy boys ditched the leathers, shaved their heads, donned the boots and braces, Ben Sherman's shirts and Levi Sta-press kaks. A few more Blade rockers also went from one extreme to the other, but it was mostly the mods, or the hard mods, who started to evolve in 68 that

158

picked up on the new movement.

Not only had a brand-new culture arrived, with it came a new style of music that few had even heard of, let alone listened to. Jamaican Reggae and Ska-fast, punchy up-beat Ska. The 'Rude boy' sound, played only at illegal West Indian Blues parties could now be heard on the radio, pub jukeboxes and in some specialised nightclubs. Rude came from the Jamaican slang for cool. The Rudies wore smart black suits, white shirts, with slim ties, topped off with pork pie hats, later called bluebeat hats. The bluebeat hat soon became a must have fashion accessory for the new skinhead trend.

Prince Buster's superb *Al Capone*, recorded two years earlier, but now resurrected, made me want to leap on the dance floor, lift up my knees and stomp my feet like a madman. The array of horns, trombones and saxes, the lone bass drum and the chic-chicka-chic-chicka-chic-chicka, marimba vibe, sounded as if fifty speakeasy musicians were enjoying the biggest party there'd ever been: "Don't call me Scarface, my name is Capowne, C-A-P-O-N-E. Capowne" – but I was a rocker and I wasn't allowed to like this kind of music. I thought the opening words, as the gangster's limo screeches to a halt and the machine guns let rip were: "Al Capone's guns don't hurt you," and wondered why the fuck that was? Did he aim to miss? Were there no bullets in it? I felt a fool when somebody eventually put me right.

Harry J Allstars catchy instrumental *Liquidator* made the top ten in 69. Desmond Dekker hit the charts with *Israelites*. I didn't have a clue what he was on about, but couldn't help but enjoy the jumpy, reggae groove. "Get up in the morning same thing for breakfast, so that every mouth can beeee fed. Oh-oh, Unitedites," I sang. Symarip's *Skinhead Moonstomp* became the skins anthem. The Boss skinhead shouted, "I want all you skinheads to get up on your feet, put your braces together and your boots on your feet and gimme some of that ooooold moonstompin."

The cultures we belonged to dictated the music we listed to. The mod sounds were strictly soul and Tamla-Motown and not for the uncouth ears of the rockers. Mods wouldn't be seen dead listening to the Rolling Stones, Bob Dylan or Chuck Berry. Music is music though and it formed a large part of my growing up. Always there to lift me up and to keep me going. From 1950s Skiffle and Rock 'n' Roll and, eventually (due to the film *A Clockwork Orange*) Lovely-Lovely-Ludwig-Van Beethoven. I loved 'em all. "So I say thank you for the music, for geeeving eat to me."

In later years Wafe and me were sometimes the only white kids in the all-night Blues party's held at the Pitsmoor, Burngreave and the Havelock Square districts of town. Spliff in one hand, can of Red Stripe or Special Brew in the other, we took a walk on the wild side, through a government yard in Trenchtown surrounded by dreadlocks, taking in the pounding, Rocksteady and Ragamuffin sounds until daybreak.

The skinheads represented a kind of masculine, street-style, English working-class image that was perfect for the terraces. If I'd have had a bit more bottle, I'd have gone that way for a while but, back then, my hair was my crowning glory. It hung in waves and ringlets and attracted the ladies, which at that time was far more important than any fighting image.

At the age of eighteen I would have crawled on my hands and knees through a cesspit full of hungry sewer rats just to fondle a bare breast... well perhaps not. I was maybe a bit of a skinhead in spirit though. The gutter press kindly informed me the skins were my new enemy. I'm sure they had no intention of stirring up trouble. It seemed the younger generation just couldn't win. A few years earlier long hair had outraged parents, politicians, the clergy and the establishment in general. Now young kids were being sent home from school and battered by their parents for having their hair cut. What the fuck did they want? It cracked me up watching a Panorama TV documentary on the new craze when a reporter asked a young skin, "Why are you a skinhead?"

"Cos it's elfey init," he replied.

As if to counter the new skinhead movement, the rockers, or Grebos and Greasers as they were now more commonly known, stepped up a gear. Many embraced the more sinister, darker sub-culture of the Hell's Angels. Seaside resorts saw the return of the mid-60s bank holiday battles, but this time they involved the Angels and the Skins. The Angels started out life in California in the 1940s. They didn't surface in Britain until the late 60s. The urban myths and tales of their legendary Harley Davidson, chopped hog 'runs,' chronicled in Sonny Barger's autobiographical book *Hell's Angel*, and Hunter S Thompson's *Hell's Angels*, were a must read for any inspiring Angel or rocker. The books glorified the motorcycle gangs, booze and drug fuelled exploits, hyping up the Angels fighting, drinking and sexual prowess. Hundreds of outlaws clad in Nazi regalia took over whole towns and communities.

The girls who ran with the gangs were regarded as the property of the menfolk. The Mamas were available to any member of the chapter who fancied a shag. The term 'Pulling a Train' was used when multiple members of the chapter took it in turns to screw one of the Mamas or some slag who'd wandered into one of their hangouts. The Old Ladies belonged to one member alone and no one else was allowed to fuck them. All fascinating, mind-blowing shit. I flirted and fantasised with the idea for a while. I admired the Angel's day-to-day freedom and rebellious lifestyle. The thought of shagging all the Mamas certainly appealed to me, but wearing Levi's (Originals) covered in oil, shit and piss, biting live swans heads off and going down on menstruating birds didn't.

I did try an experiment though. The pith helmet Macduff wore at the Wednesday game was redesigned. I knocked out the dent, cut off the rim leaving just the head part. I made a new rim out of thick cardboard, glued it to the top bit and filled in the joins with plaster of Paris. It now slightly resembled a German helmet. I painted it black and when it dried, painted swastika's in white on both sides. It looked okay, but I never had the arse to wear it, fearing it might fall to pieces as I hit town on the seven o'clock bus.

Herman, Dinky and Wafe did make it into the Angels though. Herman bought himself a Harley, rose through the ranks and eventually became President of the Sheffield chapter.

I changed the design on the back of my leather on a regular basis.

160

Sometimes a pattern in studs, other times I painted on different motifs. All sorts of shit adorned the jacket, skull and crossbones, a devils head and a scull wearing a winged Viking helmet. When I fancied a change I just painted them out with black paint.

I'd read the Hell's Angels book and saw the name of a splinter group of renegade Angels… 'Satan's Henchmen' That's rather fucking cool, I thought, and painted it in dripping blood-style red letters on the back of my jacket.

A few weeks later I started a new job at William Lee's iron foundry. As with any new job the first day was always a bit daunting. I'd worked in the foundries before, so I knew the crack, but this time I was on my own and didn't know anyone else who worked there. At the morning snap break I sat down with a group of blokes all older than me, late twenties, early thirties, I'd seen a few of them knocking around Dronny, but didn't know any of them to speak to. We got chatting and they asked me shit like where I'd worked before etc, so at least they were talking, and they all seemed okay. One of them asked where I went boozing. I told him, the Midland on Dronny bottom (our local at the time).

"Oh the Midland," he said. "I was in there last week and there were a gang of fucking rockers stood about thinking they were right good and ya never gonna guess what one of the cunts had painted on the back of his fuckin jacket."

Oh no, I thought, please don't say it, please don't say it. I could feel my face colouring up. He dragged it on.

"Fuck me," he said. "I couldn't fuckin believe it."

"Come on," one of the others said, "What did it say?" Oh shit I thought, I could feel my mouth falling open revealing a gob full of dry bread and haslet.

"Satan's fuckin Henchmen," he shouted out.

"Satan's fuckin Henchmen," one of the other blokes said. "What a cunt, Satan's fuckin Henchmen." I thought I was going to die; my face must have been as red as a baboon's arse. I knew had had to say something before I exploded. When the laughter died down I said: "That was me."

"What was you?" the bloke said.

"That was me, in the Midland."

"Yeah, I know you go in the Midland you just said you did."

"No, that was me with *Satan's Henchmen* on the back of my jacket."

"Yeah, I know it was you," he said, his face breaking out into a grin, "That's why I said it! Only having you on son, welcome to Lee's."

The rest of the men rocked with laughter, I'd been stitched up good and proper. Nice one, you bastards. Welcome to Lee's indeed. Nevertheless as soon as I got home the black paint pot came out.

For a League Cup night match at Leicester I set off thumbing, alone, around mid-morning. A series of good lifts got me there around 3 o'clock just as the pubs were closing. I hadn't expected to arrive so early and had four and half-hours to kill before the game.

I wore the usual gear: leather jacket, Levi jeans, steel capped boots and woolly Blades scarf. I made my way to the train station to check out the arrival times from Sheffield and found out a special train would arrive around 6.30.

To be on the safe side I removed my scarf and went for a walk around the city centre. I returned to the station after half an hour or so, slipping my scarf back on. I figured it would be safe to do so in the station area.

I noticed a long-haired lad about my age, leant against a wall looking over at me. He wore the same gear as me, except for a Levi cut-off, worn over his leather jacket. We stared at each other for a while until he strolled over and asked, "Are you from Sheffield?" I told him I was, and we started chatting. He said he was a Northampton Town fan and to prove the point, took off his cut-off. Painted in white lettering on the back of his leather, the words: Northampton Town, along with the names of some of the players.

He told me although he supported Northampton, he lived somewhere in between the two towns and often travelled to Leicester to watch the games. He said he hated Leicester and always stood with the away fans and that tonight he'd be supporting the Blades. We went for walk up to ground and chatted away, telling each other our exploits and what we'd been up to at the games. He said Leicester had a large mob of skinheads and being a rocker he hated the bastards. We went back to the station where we hung around killing time until the special pulled in. A hundred, maybe a hundred and fifty or so Blades piled off the train on to the station forecourt. Most of the lads came over to greet me. The Northampton lad was well-impressed.

"Fucking hell," he said. "This is a right mob, we're gonna take Leicester's Kop tonight easy."

It didn't take him long to muscle in. It was now 'We.'

We marched off in the direction of the ground doing the usual shit, running up and down the streets, chanting, fucking around and scaring the innocents. The Northampton lad loved it, geeing everybody up shouting things like, "Leicester are shit," and "C'mon, we're gonna take their Kop."

As we neared Filbert Street the roads leading to and around the ground became more densely populated. I was on the lookout for Greg, the Leicester rocker, who I'd met back in 66. We'd sought each other out and met up two or three times both at the Lane and at Filbert Street, had a good chat, a laugh and parted friends. Near the ground I noticed a group of half a dozen Leicester skins stood on a street corner. Fuck me; one of 'em's Greg.

"Fucking hell, what happened to you?" I said. Unsmiling, he answered: "It's the new thing." I sensed he didn't want to talk to me. He asked if we were going on the Kop. I said we were. His parting shot, just one word: "Right." He turned and walked away followed by the rest of the skins.

It surprised and somewhat saddened me that a clash of cultures had put an end to our friendship. It was okay when we supported different teams, but as he said, 'the new thing' had come between us.

I heard a roar as we reached the Kop. Blades charged towards a wooden exit gate and began booting the doors. Another surge forward saw the gates burst open as we poured through on to the Kop. We swarmed in taking the Leicester mob by surprise. They backed off as we reached the centre directly behind the goal. In the commotion, I'd lost the honorary Northampton Blade.

I realised straight away it had been a bad move. After the initial shock of seeing us race in, the Leicester mob regrouped to our right. More appeared behind us, then a group of skins came at us from our left. We were surrounded and after a brief thirty-second brawl we were forced down to the front and then into the far-right hand corner. Blades started to scale the small fence to the perimeter of the pitch, then over another fence to a little covered terrace to our right. A few of us stuck in the bottom corner tried to hold on, but were overwhelmed. As I stood on the fence ready to jump to safety I saw the Northampton lad, now wearing a blue and white Leicester scarf screaming death threats at us. I aimed a final boot as I fell backwards landing awkwardly with my foot caught in the railings. I tried to get up, but my ankle was fucked, and it wouldn't take my weight.

The police and ambulance men were now on the scene. I was helped round the pitch by the ambulance men and taken down the player's entrance to the medical room. They strapped my ankle up and after a few minutes I was allowed back on to the side terrace to join the rest of the Blades.

There was no big inquest about us getting run, it was just one of those things, we half expected it to happen at away games, especially the night matches when fewer fans travelled. A few words were said though about the sneaky Northampton bastard, but you live and you learn, eh!

I got a lift back with a van-load of Hackenthorpe lads. We cruised the streets around the ground for a while, gaining a bit of revenge by jumping out and attacking any small groups of Leicester fans we came across.

In mid-November, Macduff and me arrived in Sheffield at the last minute and just managed to catch the last of fourteen S.U.T. coaches for the trip to Bolton. We took our seats on a half empty bus of normals. All the other buses had already left. We had to stop twice for an elderly couple to go for a piss which fucked us off because we hadn't had a drink.

In a built-up area on the outskirts of Bolton I nearly shat myself as a car came out of a side street and smashed straight into our side of the coach, near to where we sat. The bus nearly turned over on impact. We jumped off to see what was happening. A woman driver leapt out of the car. She wasn't injured but was obviously suffering from shock. She ran up and down the road screaming and crying, shouting: "I'm sorry, I went for the brake, but it didn't stop." The car, with its bonnet up and its radiator steaming was embedded in the side of the coach. The coppers arrived and after ten minutes or so of taking details and checking the damage, decided the bus was okay to continue the journey. As we drove off, the still hysterical woman was being helped into an ambulance.

We were dropped off outside the ground around 2 p.m. Mac and me strolled into a pub called the Wagon and Horses. The place was packed with rockers, many wearing red and white scarves. Bolton's colours were navy blue and white. At first we thought these lads were Blades, but I couldn't work out why I hadn't seen any of them before. We both wore leather rocker jackets and our scarves, so we didn't look out of place. A rousing chorus of a song I'd never heard before filled the air. I heard the words "Bolton" then "Wanderers." We were just about to sup-up and slip out, when a couple of the rockers walked over and asked, "Are you from Sheffield?" Fuck me I thought, we've had it. We said we were and prepared for the worst. Maybe if we had tried to deny it or mumbled some excuse it would have come on top, but I'm certain our long hair and jackets saved us.

The lads were sound though. We chatted for a while and stayed for another drink. The Bolton lads shouted some more of their mates over. They told us that quite a few of their lads also went to watch Man Utd (which could have explained the red and white scarves?)

In the 60s, Lancashire was a hotbed for rockers. As well as Bolton, Blackburn, Preston, Burnley, Blackpool and both Manchester clubs all had groups of Grebos among their followings. The further south we travelled it was more than likely to be the mods that we came across. We left the lads in the pub and parted on good terms. It was ten minutes or so before kickoff and we headed for the ground. We could hear Blades chants coming from the covered Lever end, so in we went. A mob of about 500 Blades stood at the back of the Kop just to the left of the goal. To the right, only a few yards away the same amount of Bolton fans gathered. A line of coppers stood in between. The Blades mob seemed to have the upper hand. A group of Blade skins on the front line pushed forward, making threatening gestures. I noticed a couple of Bolton rocker birds stood near the front. Mac and me moved down and moved in. A choice between wrestling with large hairy men and a couple of curvy birds... well, there was only going to be one winner.

Just after kickoff the lads we'd seen in the pub (around fifty strong) charged in. The tide turned and the skins, along with the rest of the Blades started backing off. For a split-second we pondered about going back up to lend a hand, but the prospects of a possible shag soon put paid to that idea. The girls seemed well up for it. The police restored some kind of order, but the Blades were on the back foot. The fighting and pushing continued all through the first half. At half time the lads we'd seen in the pub came down for a chat. They said they were only interested in the skinheads. Near the end of the game the Blades mob retreated into the far left hand corner. I saw Sinny and a few more skins climb over a fence to the safety of the side terrace.

We left the game just before the end and the girls accompanied us back to the coaches. We managed a five-minute grope and tremble on a side street in view of the buses. As the coaches revved their engines ready for the off, we made a last-minute dash to jump on board. The piss-couple complained about us being late. We gave them a duel "FUCK OFF" and sauntered up to the back seat.

On the radio on the way back we heard a report that Blades fans had terrorised Bolton town centre before the game, smashing shop windows and causing mayhem. The Sunday papers also did a story claiming Blades fans had beaten up innocent Bolton fans and that some had lighted cigarettes pushed into their faces.

As the end of the 60s loomed, I was arrested after the home game against

Leicester on the 6th of December. After what went on at Filbert Street in the League Cup game I was out for revenge.

After the game hundreds of Blades marched to the train station. We stormed on to the forecourt, trying to get to the Leicester mob. Police dog handlers forced most of the Blades back. I was grabbed and thrown into the back of a meat-wagon along with three or four other Blades. A lad I knew from the Birley district was inside the cop van. He looked like he'd been through a shredder. His coat and jeans were ripped to fuck, and there were dog bites to his arms and legs. As the doors opened to put me inside the lad tried to force his way out but was thrown back in by the coppers. He spent the rest of the short journey to Water Lane charge office screaming death threats to the cop dogs while booting the back doors of the Maria.

We were held for an hour or so, charged with threatening behaviour, bailed and released. The Birley lad left with us, released with no charges, but still swearing vengeance on the coppers and their hounds. I pleaded not guilty, but the case was proven, and I was fined a tenner.

Even though the arrests were piling up, it didn't bother me too much, nor did it bother any of the other lads. Arrests or even just ejections from the ground gave us more credibility. We were quite proud when half page spreads in the local rag, named us and wrote up our escapades. 'Bad publicity' aided our reputation.

The final away game of the 60s took us to Huddersfield on Boxing Day. I set off on a fine, crisp morning with the grand total four pence in my pocket. I thumbed it into town and hung outside the station scrounging a tanner here, a bob there, until I had enough money for the train fare.

Another whip round on the train raised the admission price and enough money for a few pints. This procedure I repeated many times over the next ten years. When I was flush though I always chipped in to help out mates and even lads who I didn't know; we all did.

Thousands of Blades swarmed into Huddersfield and hundreds invaded the Cowshed end. Only the large police presence prevented a complete rout.

"This is my generation; this is my generation baby." The 60s had been an incredible decade. I was a teenager growing up, just the same as others before, and others after. Everybody's teenage years are special or should be special. It just so happened that mine were slap bang in the middle of a cultural, sexual and musical revolution like no other. It was an amazing period of freedom and discovery.

So what would the 70s bring? Flying cars and rocket ships to Mars? Would football fans stop being silly, start growing up and getting on together… maybe.

Chapter 6

Eternal circle

As I finished this little reminisce, England, with only one player in the entire squad who had the bottle to use both his feet, had just lamely exited in the quarter final of the 2006 World Cup. Every player did his job, but nobody dared to make a mistake or take any risks. They showed no flair or imagination, no smiles, no sportsmanship and no enjoyment of the once 'Beautiful game.' Their wage packets and media profile were far more important.

With the exception of maybe the African nations, every team are now connoisseurs in the new art of diving, cheating and trying to get their fellow professionals sent off… but that's the way twenty-first century football has gone and it's only going to get worse. Get ten men behind the ball and don't lose – for fuck's sake don't lose.

A game of chess the soccer pundits call it. Boris Spassky, Bobby Fischer and Karpov, part of a flat back four. Soccer pundits? Don't get me going on them bastards. Alan fuckin Hansen; nobody would ever score a goal again and every game would end up 0-0 if it were up to him.

"Where was the marking? Terrible defending. There's no one on the back post. They were all ball-watching." Then the cunt explains how the goal – that could and should have been prevented – was scored. We fuckin know, Hanson. We were watching it.

Mrs Higginbottom of 63 Snape Hill Crescent, her neighbour, Mr Jones, and the rest of the hundreds of houses on the estate where I live have removed the St George flags from bedroom windows and specially erected giant poles stuck in their gardens. If half a dozen of them have even seen a game on the telly, let alone attended a real match, I'll stand bare naked on the town hall steps and shout: "Up the fuckin Owls."

Tacky 50 pence St George flags, blown off cars, litter the streets.

Cheap, replica England shirts worn by every brainwashed sheep, their relatives, pets, babies and girlfriends with no brains to wash, can now be chucked or mothballed away until the next multi-million-pound rip-off. Who can really blame them though, for being swept along on the tidal wave of patriotic mass hysteria stirred up by the gutter press and the media? I shudder to think what would have happened if England had won the World Cup.

Knighthoods for Sven, David Beckham and Sammy Lee? MBEs for the rest of the squad? OBEs for every player who's pulled on an England shirt in the last two years? Ten million student arseholes jammed into Trafalgar Square to welcome the team home? A week-long public holiday? I would have stayed in for a fucking month.

Football was mine, for me and for people like me. A bunch of mindless imbeciles? Yeah right, but we knew the game and we loved it. The Blades reached the promised land of the Premier League. Admission prices along with the player's wages continued to soar.

So what's it's gonna be then, eh? I asked myself. One more season, just one more. Swear to god our kid, swear to god.

A terrible lout with shoe missing, being escorted past the John Street Terrace

PART TWO
A 70s Trip

Foreword

Ah but I was so much older then, I'm younger than that now.

Saturday February 7th, 2009

It's Derby day, Wednesday at the Lane and a heavy Friday night session's left me feeling like shite. I crawl from the sack at 7.30 am to try to get myself together for the match that kicks off at noon. Hangovers are getting harder to handle, so fuel's needed to kick-start me into action and to see me through a long day. I rustle up a full English, but after one suck on a sausage, it's scraped into the dog's dish. It's nothing to do with nerves; everything tastes like cardboard these days. Our Rip spins round licking his lips, he can't believe his luck. A magpie hops around the branches in the tree at the bottom of our garden.

"Fuck off, or fetch one of ya mates," I shout at the bird.

After a shower and gum brush, I get dressed, sup three cups of tea, smoke six roll-ups, force a bowl of cornies down my throat and then defy the laws of gravity by splashing half a gallon of diarrhoea around the upper rim of the bog.

I check my stuff, money, bacca, Rizlas, filters, a bag of privet, King Size Rizlas, half a gram of Charlie, a couple of Es… all purely medicinal of course, and last but not least a clean hankie: well you never can tell. I slam in my weekend teeth, flash a swift grin at the mirror, Worzel Gummidge's handsome head smiles back at me, and I'm ready for the off.

It's snowed over and freezing outside. As usual, the first flakes of winter have caused chaos and brought the whole country to a standstill. Stories of havoc and turmoil dominate the national news programmes. Outside broadcasts show tobogganing children whose schools have been forced to shut. Councils are running out of grit, power lines are down, cars, lorries, and snowploughs are left abandoned, and a state of emergency's been declared. This is England in the 21st century, God help us if we ever have to face a nuclear war.

I leave the house at ten bells and slip on the best six quid I've ever spent: a three-quarter length heavy leather duffle coat bought from Chesterfield flea market. Like a pensioner scared of breaking his hip, I navigate the iced-over steps leading down to the bus stop, and there's enough time to roll another cig before the bus arrives.

Dec Bates and his missus, Carole, on their way to the game pull up and give me a lift into Sheffield. I walk from the Earl of Arundel boozer on the corner of Shoreham Street up onto Bramall Lane. It's only 10.30 am, but riot police are already positioned around the, now closed down, Cricketers Arms and on the corner of Denby Street ready to repel any side street Blades attacks.

Located in the heart of Bladeland, just yards from the away end turnstiles, the Cricketers had been a thriving sanctum of hooligan activity for close on forty years.

But, like many boozers in the area and like hundreds of others in every part of the land, the smoking ban, cheap supermarket ale and the recession took its toll. The old place now stands derelict and empty, and only the ghosts of long-dead, chain swinging Shoreham Bootboys haunt its dark and dusty corridors… amen.

I amble up to the Lord Nelson (Fanny's) where Herman's waiting with my match tickets. Fanny's is bursting at the seams, and my glasses steam up as I push my way to the bar. It's so packed I can't even move my arms from my side to wipe them.

Five minutes later, I finally manage to attract a barmaid's attention through the mist, and I'm sipping the first pint of the day, a pint I don't even want. Herman's sat in the corner with his granddaughters, Mick Scanlan and Fredrik and Lina, two GAIS Gothenburg fans who've travelled over from Scandinavia for the game. The Swedish couple has adopted the Blades as their second team.

I try to get outside for a smoke, but I'm stopped by the lad on the door. He tells me, "Sorry, pal you can't take your drink outside today, coppers orders." I balance my pint on the edge of Herman's overflowing table, and he joins me outside to sort out the money for the tickets. Twenty-nine fuckin quid for mine and a fiver kids' ticket for my eighteen-year-old daughter, Riki.

Now Herman and I are of an age when we should be discussing the benefits of fish, blood and bone fertiliser, or giant marrow growing down on t' allotment, but we chat about what the young BBC lads are likely to do to the Wednesdayites – if they dare to show. Fifty years of hatred shows no sign of cooling.

In the corresponding game at Hillsborough four months earlier, around eighty BBC lads took over Legends boozer on Hillsborough corner and hung a flag in the pub window to announce their presence. Wednesday would have to pull off a similar stunt today to regain any credibility. No chance. Blades have been patrolling the area around the Lane since 9.00am. Jail sentences or three-year bans mean nothing to this new breed of modern-day Blades. Despite an overwhelming police presence using up-to-the-minute technology, these young bloods try to keep over forty years of terrace culture alive and kicking.

Over the last week, the internet message boards have been rife with rumour. It's been suggested the Wednesdayites, too scared to run the gauntlet along Bramall Lane have been digging a secret tunnel all the way from Hillsborough.

'*Swinging a pig*' a song from my old CD drifts out from the open pub window. It's eleven bells, and I'm meeting Riki at half-past outside the Sportsman. The first pint's gone straight through me, and it takes me a few minutes to squeeze my way through the crowd to the bog at the back of the boozer. My stomach's rumbling and I can feel a liquidised turtle's head bubbling near the surface. Thank fuck, no one's in the shithouse, a rare occurrence in these cocaine days. I've made it just in time. I check the bog roll holder, it's empty, so it's either back through the crowded bar to ask for a closet roll or hold it in. I spy a neatly folded towel, hung next to the sink, praise the Lord.

I head off to the Sportsman to see the front doors bolted shut. The back yard, however, is heaving with Blades. *"We hate Wednesday"* rings out from over the wall. I lean up against the window ledge at the side of a dozen, faceless RoboCops clad in regulation riot gear and roll another cig.

Riki arrives, and as we walk to the ground she says, "How long is it since Wednesday won at the Lane, Dad, forty years is it?"

"Forty-two Rik," I tell her.

"We're gonna lose today, aren't we Dad?"

"I've got a nasty feeling we are lass," I answer.

We enter the Bramall Lane end upper tier and make our way to the bar area. It's £3.20 for a plastic bottle of lager. No smoking signs are everywhere. I light one up anyway.

We take our seats ten minutes before kickoff. On Riki's strict orders I'm sober and straight. Its derby day and every single Blade should be behind the team, but we're surrounded by the watchers and the whingers, whose idea of support, is to shed a tear for the TV cameras after a play-off final defeat or wear a fuckin away shirt at home games. Instead of being deafened by the crowd, horrible, pounding, repetitive, drum and bass muzac blasts from the sound system. Gary Sinclair, the Bramall Lane DJ and announcer does the job he's paid to do. He puts on the spiel and tries to whip the crowd into a frenzy. All this glamorised, Americanised, plastic razzamatazz reminds me why I'd fallen out of love with the game which had always been a massive part of my life.

The Wednesday fans are seated below. I can hear, but I can't see them. Mesh netting has been erected all the way across the stand to prevent objects being thrown. The netting stops the bottles, but not the piss inside them.

Finally, the terrible music stops and a half-hearted rendering of *'Greasy Chip Butty'* doesn't exactly lift mine, or the players', spirits as Wednesday move down the pitch towards the Kop end and slam in a goal after only thirty seconds.

Bastard, I knew it. United scramble an equaliser four minutes later, and the old, terrible *Tom Hark* theme greets the goal. Why do they have to play that crap? But somehow I know it's not going to be our day. Wednesday and their fans seem more up for it. Wednesday score again with a fluky thirty-yard pile driver and lead 1-2 as the half-time whistle blows.

It's back to the bar to queue for another bottle of overpriced lager and a soft drink for Riki. We spend the half time interval chatting to Dinky Dawson and his son Reece – named after the Blade legend Gill Reece. Dinky toyed with the idea of naming his son after another 60s Blades legend, but luckily for young Reece, Dink decided against it: Kettleborough Dawson wouldn't have sounded quite right. Dinky and Reece join us for the second half.

The Blades huff and they puff, and they hoof. Long balls and throw-ins are pumped into the Wednesday penalty area to the three Blade dwarves playing upfront. The six-foot-tall Wednesday centre backs simply head them back out. The master tactician patrolling his technical area in front of the Blades dug-out can't understand why United can't score. Twenty-seven thousand Unitedites can.

Then it's all over and not only had Wednesday won at the Lane for the first time since Engelbert fuckin Humperdinck topped the charts, but they've also done the double over us for the first time in living memory. We move towards the exit and Rik says to me, "Promise me, Dad, you're not going to do anything outside."

"I'm not going to do owt, Rik, honest. I can hardly bleedin walk these days let alone fight."

I light up a flip as we make our way down the steps onto Bramall Lane. I hear a voice behind saying, "You're not supposed to fucking smoke in the ground and that cunt in front smoking."

I feel like turning around and putting the cig out in the bastard's eye. A quick glance over my shoulder reveals the biggest, meanest looking fucker who ever walked. Lucky for him I'd promised our Riki no trouble.

Riot police are stationed all along Bramall Lane. The mood is sombre, but not really hostile as the coppers try to keep thousands of Blades on the move. Groups of lads, congregated around the Cricketers are pushed up John Street by the police.

We walk up to London Road and through the back door of the Barrel Inn. The pub's packed full of pissed-off Blades, some are debating about what went wrong; others just stare blankly into space. Rik and I stand in the iced-up back yard sipping dry apples. We drink up and walk back down to Bramall Lane to put Riki on the bus home. The bus stop is outside the Lane end, and just two middle-aged Blades dressed in managers' jackets are stood there.

The Wednesday team coach drives down Bramall Lane, and as it passes, I stick up my fingers and shout, "Fuck off ya Wednesday bastards." The two blokes shoot me a look of disgust; Riki just shakes her head and says, "Daaaad."

"Never liked the bastards. Have you?" I say to the two blokes. The managers don't answer.

The bus arrives; I wave Rik off and make my way back up to the Barrel.

Stocksy's stood at the bar, his phone rings and I hear him say, "We're in Barrel." "It's Clink," he says to us. "He's on his way."

I'd not seen Clink for a few weeks. He'd upset his missus, who'd banished him to the settee to sleep under the quilt for a month. After an all-day drinking session, he'd stumbled into the Steel City tattoo parlour on London Road. You might think fifty-four years old is a bit late on in life to get the first tattoo, but it didn't stop Clink having SUFC tattooed on the one hand and BLADES on the other. Clink's mate, Brownie, whose leg had been amputated only a few months earlier went one step further. With a lovely touch of irony – Brownie had SHOREHAM BOOTBOYS in half-inch letters scrawled across his neck.

Clink's still not arrived so after a pint I walk down to the Albion. Scores of coppers and half a dozen riot vans line both sides of London Road. Groups of lads stand outside boozers and on street corners wondering what to do.

The Ganja posse, assembled in the back yard of the Albion pelt the police with snowballs. A riot could be only a shot away, but the coppers don't respond. After half an hour or so the police move off and leave us to it.

It's only 3.00pm, so there's all afternoon, evening and night to drown our sorrows. We huddle around heaters in open-sided smoking shelters, swigging, snorting, smoking and swallowing, trying to numb the effect. Lads arrive and relate post-match Wednesday clipping tales.

Into the evening and more lads, who've been patrolling the city centre trying to seek out them 'dammed elusive Wednesdayites,' arrive, but as usual there's no pig fans in town. Frustrated Blades have even been fighting each other.

It's 10.30pm when I fall out of a taxi and stagger into the Bridge Inn on Dronny Bottom. Jock, a Blade bitch wearing tartan underpants, and Louise, a Wednesday wench dressed in an Owls shirt, square up to each other at the bar.

"Rip her fuckin' tits off, Jock," somebody shouts. The crowd gets in between, leaving them pointing fingers and exchanging insults.

Time for bed, I think.

Unstone St. The cobbled back-wack in-between The Cricketers and The Sportsman pubs. Where we launched 2 prong attacks from John Street and Denby Street on the away fans leaving Bramall Lane

Chapter 1

Everybody must get stoned

1970 tiptoed in with barely a whisper, no fanfare of trumpets, no mass celebrations and no extravagant firework displays. I had no plans, no expectations and no resolutions. The 60s had set a precedent, music, fashion and culture wise; it would be a hard act to follow. This had been the time to be young, the time when teenagers ruled the world, but I had no idea I'd lived my teenage years through one of the most exciting decades ever, because nobody spoke about the 60s until the 70s.

Six months earlier the Yanks won yet another race. American astronauts turned on by Symarip, stomped around the old lunar in galactic Doc Martens.

Nothing else had changed much though, the two decades just merged into one. The steelworks, iron foundries and the coal mines in our area, as well as the textile, shipbuilding, car-plants, engineering and other heavy industries throughout the land, were still in full production and anyone who wanted work could easily find a job. The shops still shut at bang on 5.00 p.m. every weekday and closed for half a day on Wednesday afternoons in Dronny and Chezzy and Thursdays in Sheffield.

No shops opened on the Sabbath, except beer offs during pub licensing hours and the new-fangled Chinky chippys – who allegedly served up Alsatian, Tomcat and portions of curried rat. The credits at the end of TV shows ran slow enough to read, beer hovered around half a dollar (12½ p) a pint and sausages had meat in them.

If more than a dozen cars were parked on the same street, either a party or a funeral was going on. At home, we still didn't own a fridge, a washing machine, a phone or a front room carpet. A colour telly was a distant dream and I'd yet to don my first pair of undercrackers. The Hippies and the street fighting men students who were preaching a revolution in the 60s were now well on their way to doing what they were always destined to do. Fashion designers, architects, brain surgeons, heads of light entertainment and junior government ministers, just didn't have the time or the inclination for weekend uprisings.

As ever, art students waited in line to be the next generation of rock stars.

And the football, the good old football, the football's never gonna change. Refs still wore black, and goalies' jerseys were always green (except against Plymouth Argyle.)

Shorts might have been an inch shorter, hair an inch longer, but the players were all men, real men, all except the Wednesday team, who were a bunch of fuckin pansies.

Thousands of football fans in every corner of the land, full of a mixture of anticipation and excitement tuned their radios to the BBC for the live FA Cup draw broadcast on Monday at 12 noon. Did I want a 4th Division club away?

Man Utd, Leeds, Liverpool at home? Let's have an easy 'un, eh? Hartlepool's at home, or even more comfortable, Wednesday away.

You could hear the black balls rattling around the velvet bag: "Number 37... Sheffield United... will play... number 15...Everton." Everton, top of the First Division, now that could be a bit tricky.

The first game of the new decade was declared all-ticket, and a few of us went down to the ground early when the tickets went on sale. We found hundreds of Blades already queuing. The cold, wet weather couldn't dampen our spirits. It's the magic of the FA Cup again; the old fever's upon us, so fuck Everton, this year we're finally going to Wembley. Everybody in the queue chatted and laughed; no strangers here, we were all Blades, all brothers. I clutched on to my half a dollar juvenile Kop match ticket like a bull-week wage packet.

On the day of the game, a hundred or so Blades are packed in the back room of the Howard.

"Fuck me," somebody shouted. "Look at this lot." We ran to the windows to see a huge mob of Everton: five-six hundred strong, swarm out of the station. A squad of coppers herded them towards the bottom end of Shoreham Street. No one suggested we should go out to confront them. Street battles before the game were rare; the fighting took place inside the stadiums and in the surrounding streets, usually after the game ended.

We marched up to the ground and squeezed our way into a packed and swaying Shoreham. I expected the Everton fans to be on the Kop, but they were massed on the Lane end.

Everton took the lead with a penalty, but United came back with two great headed goals from Colin Addison and Gil Reece, sending us crazy and putting us in the next round.

Moose Mulligan, the third son in the Cardwell dynasty, started out life on the dark side. Along with his elder brother Steve, Mulligan spent his early years watching Wednesday. When he reached fourteen, I showed him the error of his ways by taking him to the Lane to see a proper team. Hallelujah! Moose saw the light and took the path to righteousness.

Round four of the FA Cup took us to Derby County. Macduff, Moose, Dick Dung and I travelled on a packed train, arriving at about one o'clock. Macduff and I both wore our leathers and steel cappers. In true Hell's Angels style, I'd cut up a biscuit tin with a pair of snips and made two swastikas which were fastened with thin strands of copper wire to the front of my jacket.

We headed to a boozer straight across from the station, Moose and Dick were only fifteen years old, but they got in with no bother. Wafer sat alone perched on a stool at the front of the bar. We greeted each other as footie lads do.

"Fuckin hell what thar doin here?" Wafe told us he'd been in the pub since opening time.

An old darling who must have been forty-odd at least sat opposite us. Forever the charmer, Wafe whipped out one of his prize cooking apples and rested it on the stool in front of him.

"Oi Missis, look at this fucker," he shouted. The granny squealed and spat out her Barley Wine, we doubled up laughing. More Blades arrived, and after an hour of singing and boozing, we headed for the ground.

We moved through a built-up area, crossing a busy main road to a narrow alleyway with corrugated iron walls. I remembered a pitched battle taking place at the end of the alley a year earlier.

We'd played Derby the season before on Easter Monday. Mick Spear, a mate from the Batemoor estate in Sheffield, and me, set off thumbing early, reaching Derby before the pubs opened. We walked around the town centre killing time when we noticed a bloke eyeing us up. This big, mean-looking fucker, looked to be in his mid-twenties. He wore a thick woolly black and white scarf, knotted at the neck and a full black beard covered most of his face. We stopped and pretended to look in shop windows, and every time we stopped, Black Beard stopped just a few yards away. He moved closer, looking in the same window as us. Mick and I looked at each other. I'm thinking, shall we do a runner or what? Gimme a sign, Mick. Black Beard walked up to us and said, "How many are you bringing today?"

Oh he wants to talk, I thought. "Don't know," I said, "a couple of thousand, maybe."

"Are you going on the Pop side?" he asked. I assumed the Pop side was Derby's equivalent of our Shoreham end.

"Probably," I answered.

"Well don't," he said. "Chelsea came last year with 13,000; we had 9,000 on the Pop side. Chelsea thought they'd took it, but another thousand Rams, all carrying sawn-off shotguns came in and blasted Chelsea straight back off, nobody's ever took the Pop side." He spoke so fast I could hardly make him out. Mick and I looked at each other thinking… what the fuck!

"Who's your king?" Black Beard asked before we could answer he said, "I'm the king of the Pop side, I only fight other kings, I fought Birmingham's king the other week. We fought for half an hour, and I beat him, then we went to the pub, and he bought me six pints. I bought him four, so who's your king?"

"Eskimo's our king," I answered.

"Eskimo! I'll fight Eskimo, where is he?" Black Beard said.

"Eskimo'll be here later," I told him.

"I'll fight him when he comes then," Black Beard said.

"Who's coming to help you today?" was his next question.

"Help us, what do you mean?" Mick said.

"We've got four thousand Man Utd fans coming to help us, who's coming to help you?" Black Beard said.

"Well, nobody's coming to help us as far as I know," I said.

"A thousand Leicester fans are coming to help you," Black Beard said, "Leicester hate Derby, so they're coming to help you, I'll fight their king as well, I only fight kings."

I got this terrible urge to say, "I'm a king." just to see his reaction but thought better of it. After another ten minutes of ridiculous bullshit, we managed to give the Black Beard the slip. Later on, we made our way up to the station to wait for the train mob to arrive. A group of about a dozen lads, some in blue and white scarves stood outside the station. We went over for a chat.

"Who are you lot?" I asked.

"We're Leicester," one said. "We hate fuckin Derby; we've come to help you."

Fuck me, it's all true. I just wondered where the other 988 Leicester lads were and when the 4,000 Man Utd fans would be arriving. Mick Spear, bless him, eventually moved to Humberside and joined the 'other firm': the Kingston upon Hull police force.

We came out from the end of the alley into a long terraced street with cramped back-to-backs on both sides and followed the crowd. The Baseball Ground appeared from out of nowhere squashed in between the houses. Inside it seemed, poky, small, almost claustrophobic. We took our places in a 40,000 crowd on the Pop side terrace. A brand-new double-decker stand with standing underneath replaced the old corrugated iron-roofed terrace we used last season. A metal fence halfway along segregated the Pop side. We pushed our way through to the fence; Derby's mobs stood a yard or so away on the other side. Meat pies, Bovril, green-hangers and other missiles flew backwards and forwards. Confrontations on open terracing usually ended with one side backing down or running. Still, the steel barrier separating the two mobs made everybody feel a little bit braver, giving lads on both sides more confidence. Seeing our leathers, a Derby skin shouted, "You fuckin greasy, rocker bastards, get a fuckin wash."

"Fuck off ya skinhead cunt," I shouted back. Insults shot back and forth.

"You're fuckin dead outside, you ugly cunt. Me and you, one on one, It's a good job this fence is here, or I'd fuckin kill you, ya wanker." This carried on all through the game.

The Cup dreams fucked for another season when United go three goals down. Ten minutes before the game ended, we squeezed our way out, hoping to get a bit of action. No Derby fans were around, so we headed back towards the station. We hung around the town centre for a while, making nuisances of ourselves. I shinned my way up a white marble monument of an ancient soldier on a horse and sat at the back of the rider whooping like a cowboy. Two coppers appeared and beckoned me down.

"What do ya think you're doing up there?" one said.

"Nowt," I said, "I'm just messing about." He pulled one of the tin swastikas off my jacket and pressed it hard into my cheek.

"You're going to use this to cut somebody's face open, aren't you?" he said.

"No," I said, "it's just decoration for my jacket."

"Well it looks like an offensive weapon to me," the copper said. The coppers pushed me around for a while, threatening arrest. One of them ripped the other swastika off my jacket and crushed it under his boot.

"Now get off home or be arrested," he told me.

'Shovel face' (he looked like he'd been smacked in the mug with one) Gerry

Young became a Blade favourite when he fucked up in the 1966 final to hand Everton the FA Cup on a plate.

Wednesday eventually forgave him and set up an end of season testimonial match against United, up at Hillsborough. Around two hundred Blades met in Fitzalan Square at dinnertime, ready to give Gerry, and the Wednesdayites some abuse. Wednesday had been relegated a few days earlier.

I'd been to the game at Hillsborough and stood in the pouring rain with Steve Cardwell to watch Wednesday join us in the Second Division. Man City didn't even look interested and played the game at half pace. The City had two shots on goal, and both the fuckers went in. I don't know how I managed to keep a straight face. Wednesday were shit, and even though the City did all they could to let Wednesday win, they couldn't handle it. I left the ground with a pissed off Steve, drenched to skin, but smiling like I'd just won the pools.

Mac and me, both dressed in leathers, as usual, got chatting to a couple of Blade rockers at the meet in the Square. They told us the night before they'd had a pre-arranged scrap with a mob of skinheads up at Gleadless.

"The Dronny Dockers turned up to help us," one of the lads said.

"Who's the Dronny Dockers?" I asked him.

"Haven't you heard of em? There's a right fuckin mob, all ride Harley's they do." Mac and I just smiled at each other.

After half an hour or so we set off on the march up to Hillsborough. Halfway up Penistone Road, we passed a large patch of rubbish strewn wasteland surrounded by scores of pigeon cotes balanced on sloping banks at the back of Langsett Road. I hated Hillsborough; it felt alien, like a different town, not part of Sheffield at all, a fuckin horrible place where, just like the site of Auschwitz, songbirds refused to sing.

We stopped off at a couple of boozers en-route, reaching the ground around half-past two. We joined another couple of hundred Blades on the Kop and laughed at the small mob of a hundred or so young Wednesdayites stood to our right. It would have been no achievement in bullying a bunch of kids.

By kickoff there were considerable gaps in the stands, the Leppings Lane end's deserted, and there are bigger gaps on the Kop. Only around 10,000 fans bothered to turn up, maybe the Wednesdayites couldn't forgive old Shovel Face after all. The game ended, and nobody gave a fuck about the score as we swarmed out into Penistone Road for the usual unopposed walk back to town. Macduff noticed one of the groupies who hung around the football scene; he nipped over for a chat. Little did he know I'd had words with her at a night game at the Lane, a few days earlier.

"Where's Mac?" she'd asked me.

"Oh, he's picked up a dose; he's at the pox clinic tonight," I told her. I saw the girl, pointing at me and snubbing Mac.

"You little bastard Ronald," Mac shouted.

Most of the Dronny Dockers still wore leathers, but they'd traded in their motorbikes for cars. We now cruised in style, usually about a dozen of us, sometimes more, in Ford Anglias and Minis. We travelled all around the area watching bands or to listening to the latest rock and pop sounds at pub discos.

The Centre Spot at Basegreen, the Old Harrow, the Birley Hotel, the John' O' Gaunt at Gleadless all had large concert rooms where the turns performed.

The Black Swan on Snigg Hill in Sheffield City Centre was the best live music venue in the area. Many up and coming bands who went on to bigger things played the 'Mucky Duck.'

Our favourite haunt was The Blue Bell at Hackenthorpe, known locally as 'the Palladium of the North.' We called in the Bell a couple of times a week and just about every weekend. Live bands played to packed crowds, and the Friday and Saturday sessions sometimes ended in mass brawls which the locals just took in their stride. I knew a few of the Hackenthorpe lads from the Blades games, so there was never any trouble between us.

Marijuana played a big part in 1960s folklore; everybody smoked marijuana... yeah right. I'm sure all the rock stars, the showbiz personalities and the beautiful people who hung out on Carnaby Street could easily pick up the gear. It was also available to the middle-class students who moved in college and university campus circles. Still, to the vast majority of working-class teenage lads and lasses in every UK town and city, marijuana was pure myth. Now it wasn't like I was some kind of recluse, I was out every night doing pubs, night clubs, watching rock bands and mixing with crowds who looked like they should be smoking marijuana, but I was nineteen years old before I even saw, let alone smoked the fucker.

Returning home from the Bell one Friday night in the spring of 1970, I sat in the back of Spiv Hoyland's Anglia flanked by a couple of rocker birds. Tad Hadley sat next to Spiv in the front. One of the girls asked me, "What bands are you into? I'm into Led Zep, Deep Purp, Black Sabb and Frank Zapp."

"I'm into Black Frank, Led Purp, Deep Sabb and Zep Zapp," I answered. The girl looked slightly puzzled. The light blue cotton, loony type pants I wore didn't impress this tart.

She told me she only usually went with lads who wore faded Levi's, but I'd got great hair, so she'd made an exception. Well, lucky me, I thought.

"If you want to see me again," she said, "Make sure you're wearing Levi's."

"Oh, I will," I answered.

After an unsuccessful shagging attempt we dropped the birds off and headed back to Dronny. We pulled up at the top of a country lane on the road home. Tad opened a small paper bundle full of squashed up green leaves. Fuck me; it's marijuana. Bush, Tad called it.

"Don't say owt to anybody about this, Ron... promise," Tad said.

After I swore a vow of secrecy Tad wrapped one up. I'm sure the word 'Joint' wasn't mentioned as joint, spliff, roach were hippy words and Dronny Dockers were far too hard to use puffy hippy words, so we probably just called it a fag.

We passed it around and waited ten minutes; nothing happened. Maybe I should have inhaled? I might have been a bit of a rebel, but I'd always been a little bit apprehensive about getting involved with drugs. Would I become an addict and suffer the dreaded reefer madness? Or maybe get hooked on the demon weed, grown (so the scaremongers would have us believe) in Beelzebub's allotment, guarded by Cerberus, the three-headed hound? But I thought... well, this is fuckin shit.

"How ya feeling Ron?" Spiv asked.

"Fuck all's happening man, it ain't groovy," I answered.

We decided to go to my house to smoke some more drugs.

My Uncle Chris would have been in bed since 9 p.m. He always hit the sack early and rose at 5 a.m. This habit, from the days when he'd worked down the pit, had never left him. 'Early to bed, early to rise, makes a man healthy, wealthy and wise,' he used to say.

His daily ritual of 'getting the fire going' started as soon as he'd supped his first brew. The ashes from the night before were scraped out from under the fire grate and shovelled into four sheets of newspaper. Along with the dust swept up, the paper was folded into a parcel and emptied in the dustbin. Then it's out to the coal house for a log, and on to the back step, where he chopped it into sticks with a hatchet sharper than a cut-throat razor. He criss-crossed the sticks on a bed of squashed up newspaper, before arranging small pieces of coal to the pile. When the fire got going, larger lumps from the scuttle were placed on top. He then balanced the coal-shovel between the grate and the top of the fireplace. Next, he added a double sheet of newspaper over the shovel creating a vacuum to draw in the air. All this had to be timed to perfection. He watched the newspaper until it began to scorch and whipped it off before it caught fire.

The thought of Uncle Chris's fire lighting often stops me in my tracks when I'm hurling abuse at the gas fire if the bastard thing doesn't ignite on the first click.

When we arrived at our house, Mum was still up, watching telly in the kitchen. We went into the front, room and I stuck a Dylan album on while the lads wrapped another fag up.

"Take a big drag, Ron, and hold it in your lungs," Tad told me.

After a few, drags, I began to feel rather lovely. I picked up two snooker balls, one red and one white and started rubbing them together. Fucking hell, I'd had these snooker balls for years and never realised just how beautiful they were. I held them about six inches from my eyes, rotating them around and around. I could hear them scraping together in time to the music. They were red and white, Blade colours; they were the most fantastic thing I'd ever seen. Whoooo! this is it; far out, I'm splitting the cosmic atom baby, there's 'buses out of Monticello and everything's cool.'

"Look at these fuckers," I said to the lads, passing them the snooker balls "There're fuckin great." This set us all off laughing. I laughed so much, I nearly bust my stomach open. The lads went home after an hour or so. I went off to bed still feeling rather good. I had a wank to end all wanks: "Ooooh Black Frank." I shouted as it shot out like a length of string.

I awoke the next morning and thought, what a damn fine experience, but it wasn't no watershed in my life. I'd no intention of ever buying any bush and becoming a drug fiend, but if any come my way again, I'd undoubtedly smoke the fucker. I didn't need weed or anything else though to get any higher; I was flying already.

Blues clubs in the dodgy red-light district of Havelock Square at Broomhall or the mainly black Pitsmoor/Burngreave areas of Sheffield were the only local places where you pick up a bit of bush. Tiny, Macduff and I once wandered into a blues party at Havelock Square after the night clubs had shut. We had to make a swift exit when Tiny started bouncing around the room, walking like a chicken and talking like a Rasta. We spent the next half an hour driving around the Square shouting, "Can I fuck you for nowt?" at prostitutes stood on street corners.

It must have been a good couple of months before I had another smoke. Tad, however, was never the same again. Although always quiet, he went, in the space of about a year, from being one of the lads to a silent, smiling zombie. He moved away from Dronny and lived alone in a Sheffield bed-sit. He progressed onto the harder stuff, and a couple of years later at the age of twenty-one, he died of an overdose.

Uncle Chris fell ill in the summer of 1970. He flatly refused to go to the doctors, saying he didn't want any fuss. He spent most of the time laid up in bed supping whisky. When his weekly pension money ran out, he'd send me up to our Joan's who lived at Lowedges to borrow money for the pain-relieving whisky.

I sat chatting in the bedroom with him one evening, and he told me, "I'm going home Ron lad." I knew exactly what he meant, but I didn't want to believe it. Eventually, we persuaded him to see the doctor, and after tests, he was diagnosed with lung cancer and admitted to Walton hospital in Chesterfield.

I missed the Tuesday night visit to see him as the Blades played Leeds at the Lane in a League Cup tie. Macduff and I entered at the Lane end side, near the cricket pavilion just in time to join hundreds of Leeds fans swarming from the Lane end towards the Kop. None of us wore colours, so we mingled in with the Leeds mob okay.

The Blades mob moved from the covered bit of the Shoreham onto the open part waiting to face them. Steel railings ran from top to bottom, but access to the Kop could be gained through a gate on the walkway at the back. A couple of coppers usually guarded the entrance and locked it when the game started. We kept quiet, and I could hear the Leeds fans saying stuff like, "Come on; get ready, straight into them, nobody run."

A Gap of about twenty yards formed between the two mobs, caused by normals moving out of the way before the trouble started. The Leeds mob, with Mac and me squashed in the middle about ten yards from the front, slowed as they reached the gateway. The coppers were pushed aside as they funnelled through the gap. Seeing this, the Blade mob advanced towards them. Dick Dung, dressed in his familiar dogtooth checked blazer, appeared at the front. Dung might have only been a little fucker with no meat on his bones, but he held no fear. He ran alone from the Blade ranks, through no-man's-land straight into the Leeds fans.

In a split second, the roar went up and the Blades steamed in. The front Leeds fans, trying to retreat, were stopped by Leeds fans trying to advance. Mac and me, now only a yard or so from the front threw snidey, sidewinding punches at confused Leeds fans. Not only were they getting fucked, it now seemed their own lads were hitting them. We made it through onto our own side and turned to join the final charge.

The wire mesh fence at the back of the Kop gave way due to the pressure of retreating Leeds bodies, and dozens slid down the steep banking. Some Leeds fans tried to hold it together screaming, "Don't run... fuckin stand," but once we had them on the back foot, there was no stopping us. The police arrived and restored a bit of order by pushing Leeds fans back towards the Lane end. The Blades also did the business on the pitch, winning the game 1-0.

The following evening, along with all the family, I went to see my Unk, he seemed okay, and we chatted about the match.

"United did well last night eh, Ron?" he said.

"Yeah they did Unk; Currie scored a right cracker, thirty-yarder." I answered. It was the last time I spoke to him. The following day, returning home from the iron foundry at Heeley where I worked at the time, I saw all the curtains in our house drawn. I knew straight away he'd died. I didn't know what to do with myself; I was devastated. I just couldn't stay in the house, so I jumped in the bath and headed for the Midland pub to drown my sorrows, but when I reached the boozer, I couldn't go through the door. I knew if I tried to speak to anyone, I would have broken down. I sat on a bench across the road for a good half hour until Locky, one of my mates, walked past. He shouted from across the street, "What the fuck are you sat there for, Ron? Get yasen in the boozer." I tried to answer him, but the words wouldn't come out.

"Fuck you then," he shouted. I wanted to go into the pub to explain to Locky I wasn't being ignorant, but I just couldn't do it. I sat there a while longer until Hippo pulled up in his car. I managed to blurt out, "My uncle Chris's died." Hippo suggested we should go for a cruise round to try and get my mind off it. We called at a few pubs, but I couldn't get myself together.

Back home, I stayed awake all night. In between sobs I kept saying out loud: "So long, Unk. So long."

My uncle Chris meant the world to me, he'd been ten times better than any dad could ever have been. So now it's just me, and my owd Mam left to take on the world.

Mum soon got into the routine of rising at five bells and lighting the fire.

Chapter 2

He puts his cigar out in your face just for kicks

On the route to the Peak District and the gateway to the Derbyshire Moors, stands the sleepy, rural village of Holmesfield. This small backwater, a couple of miles from Dronfield consists of a council estate, large private houses, a few farms and half a dozen clique boozers, frequented by three-eyed inbreds, ten-bob millionaires, real millionaires and red-necked, red-faced farmers. The residents of this little horse-shit smelling hamlet stand about ten years behind Chesterfield folk in the fashion stakes.

Four of us: Ricardo, Big Dung (who bore more than a passing resemblance to the comedian Marty Feldman) Macduff and me, jumped in Ricardo's car to set off for a boozing session out over t' moors. We decided to stop off for a swifty in Holmesfield at a pub called the Horns Inn.

The Friday night in-crowd, clutching personalised pewter tankards engraved with shit like 'North East Derbyshire master manure maker 1956' and 'Daisybelle, the cow of the century' froze and stood open-mouthed as the four long-haired aliens strode into their territory. We ordered drinks and the barflies stood around the counter fell silent as we waited to get served. The landlord looked us up and down, but never said a word as he pushed the drinks towards us, making sure he spilt a bit.

All eyes were on us as we moved through the crowd. We found seats at the back of the pub next to a group of half a dozen blokes dressed in their father's de-mob suits. All these fellas were older than us, but only maybe in their late twenties, early thirties. I sat nearest to this group and sussed out the main mouth straight away. He nudged the others and nodded his head in our direction. The group – although not looking directly at us – muttered some snide comments and gave out a few little limp-wristed gestures and girlie whoops. Out of the corner of his mouth, Ricardo said, "Let's sup up and fuck off." Dung agreed with him. Mac and I were having none of it, we just smiled, and we didn't even have to tell each other to get ready.

The main man leaned over and whispered to one of his mates as if to say, "Watch this." Tapping me on the shoulder, but still shooting glances at his mates for encouragement, he said, "Excuse me; a flea just jumped out of your hair and landed on me."

I heard exactly what he said, but I couldn't quite believe he'd said it, so just to make sure I said, "What the fuck did you say?"

The bloke answered, but this time he looked me square in the eyes: "A – flea – has – just – jumped – out of your – hair – and – landed – on – me." His mates banged their hands on the table and rocked with laughter.

Still seated, I answered him with a swift right hook. "Come on then ya fucking bastard," I shouted as I waded into to him. I knew Mac would be with me. In seconds his mates and most of the blokes in the pub were into us. I saw

Ricardo and Dung scrambling through the crowd like a pair of girls, heading for the exit.

The landlord ran from behind the bar and caught Mac with a beauty. Mac staggered backwards, and as he hit the wall, a brass plate fell off and banged like a gong on his head. If we hadn't been in so much shit, it would have been hilarious, but nothing quite beats the thrill of a good old-fashioned bar-room brawl, even when you're losing. The noise of overturning tables, scraping chairs and the sound of breaking glass gave me a boost like an injection of adrenaline. Mac scrambled to his feet, and we waded back in, punching and booting anything near us, but we were getting overpowered.

It's time to retreat. We wind-milled through the crowd and made it out through the door, followed by half of the pub. We turned to face them, which stopped them in their tracks. Everybody wanted to kill us, but none of them wanted to be the first one in. We bounced around the car park, laughing and shouting, "Come on then, ya fuckin rubbish, what the fuck was that? Ooooh, you're dead now ya bastards, the Dronny Dockers are coming back to get you, you're all fuckin dead."

The two cowards sat shitting bricks in the car. Ricardo revved the engine like he was ready to start the Monte Carlo rally.

"What the fuck did you run for, ya fuckin yitten (Dronny slang for scared) bastards?" Mac shouted as we jumped in the back seat.

"We'd have got killed." Dung said.

"Like fuck," I said, "if we'd stuck together we'd have done the cunts." As we skidded out of the car park, I wound the window down and shouted, "Don't go away ya bastards; we'll be back in half an hour." We did think about going back with a few more lads, but pub brawls kicked off pretty regular, and as usual it was all soon forgotten.

We did, however, make sure all the lads got to know about the two bottlers.

Fifteen years later; Mac and I are stood at the bar in the Bridge Inn one Sunday night when Big Dung walks in. Dung had married and moved out of the area, but Mac had seen him hundreds of times since the Horns incident. We began to reminisce about the good old days. We laughed and chatted away for a good ten minutes until Mac, without warning, pushed a lighted cig into Dung's cheek. Dung screamed in agony shouting, "Fuckin hell Mac, what did you do that for?"

"For fuckin running off that night in the Horns," Mac said.

"It was years ago," Dung said. "We were only kids."

"I don't give a fuck," Mac said. "I'm like a fuckin elephant me, I don't forget owt." Dung shot out of the pub.

"Fuckin hell, there's no need for that Mac," I said.

"Fuck him," Mac said. "I never liked the cunt anyway, and if I ever see fuckin Ricardo again, he's getting the same." I couldn't help but smile when I said to Mac, "You're a fuckin bad man. MacDougal."

"I fuckin know I am, Ronald," Mac said.

The 70-71 season started with a home game against Swindon Town. For some reason, I left the ground early, a few minutes before the final whistle. A couple of coppers hung out at the top of the steps, and a few more early leavers trickled away from the ground. I walked alone down the back steps of the Kop.

Four suedeheads, dressed identically in navy-blue Crombies pushed past me. Three of the lads wore red and white scarves with the Sheffield coat of arms cotton badge stitched on the front and a red and white cardboard strip in the top pocket of their jackets, the other wore a blue and white scarf with the Wednesday crest and a blue and white stripe in the top pocket.

"Narthen, cunt," I said to the Wednesday lad, tapping him on the shoulder "Take that fuckin shit from around your neck." All four stopped, and one of the Blades said, "He's with us and who the fuck do you think you are? Ya long-haired twat."

"I don't give a fuck if he's with you," I answered. "He's got a fuckin Wednesday scarf on."

"We'll have him one on one," one of the other Blades said.

"Come on, then, lets us two go for a walk where there are no coppers," I said.

"No, lets fuckin do it here," the Wednesday lad said.

"Fuck that," I said. "There are coppers all over, let's go for a walk."

We carried on arguing until we were out on John Street when one of the Blades took a swing at me; I saw it coming and jumped back. The others moved forward, forcing me to back off. Shit, maybe I should have kept my gob shut.

The game ended, and John Street started to fill up. I spent the next few seconds dancing and dodging kicks, hoping some mates would turn up. Seeing the commotion, sections of the crowd stopped, and a significant gap formed, with the five of us sparring and jigging in the middle. A big lad from Arbourthorne, whose name I can't remember, appeared at my side: "All right, Ron, what's up?" he said.

Before I could answer, Dec Fields, Sinny and a couple more mates arrived. I didn't have time to explain.

"Right," I shouted. "It's fuckin even now, come on."

The four lads turned and ran on to Shoreham Street. Most of the Kop mob were now out on the street, smelling blood, but, probably thinking it was Swindon blood, they joined the chase. When we caught up with them near the post office, the Wednesday lad had taken his scarf off. The Blades lads now tried to play it all down, insisting it had all been a mistake and they were 'Blades.' All four were given a few clips before they slunk off, I never saw the three Blades again.

I'd been to Hillsborough in the mid-late 60s quite a few times with Steve Cardwell, and he'd been to the Lane with me. Neither of us was stupid enough to show off our colours. I suppose it was commendable for the Blades to stick up for their mate, but what the fuck was I supposed to do? A culture clash, it seemed, came before football loyalties.

I loved playing football just as much as I enjoyed watching it and even

185

though it would be a wrench to miss the Blade games, I signed up (along with some of my old school mates) for the Dronfield youth club under 20s team. We played on Saturdays in the Sheffield Junior League, so the only time I could get to see the Blades was the night matches.

We trained twice a week in the gym at Gosforth School and on youth club nights played 5-a-side games on the floodlit asphalt tennis court at the side of the youth club. After a couple of months of training and playing, I felt as fit as fuck.

Saturday the 3rd of October 1970, I don't think we had a game, but if we did, I must have feigned injury to be at the Lane for the derby against Wednesday. Nothing in the world would have kept me away from this game.

Half a dozen Dronny Blades dressed in leathers, faded Levi's and steel-capped boots, jumped on the number 12 Chesterfield to Sheffield bus. We joined the same number of Chezzy Blades already aboard. Sinny and Podge (their heads shaved for the big occasion) are clad in the latest skinhead gear. Black Harringtons, cream coloured Sta Press kayaks and Cherry Red Doc Martens.

After a few pints in the Howard, along with another hundred or so Blades, we leave the boozer and head towards Shoreham Street. We join thousands of fans, draped in contrasting red and white and blue and white, flocking up to the stadium. Expectations are high, but the fear of defeat, or worse still, humiliation, lurks at the back of everyone's mind.

This game and the return match at Hillsborough are the highlights of the season. These are two games we can't lose, nothing else matters, just beat the Wednesday bastards that's all we ask.

It's about fifteen minutes before kickoff when we enter the ground. We sprint up the back steps four at a time, eager to taste the atmosphere. Sinny shouts, "Right lads, get fuckin ready, It's our skins against their grease and their grease against our skins today."

Now I don't quite know why; could it possibly be, this nineteen-year-old who'd been playing football for a few weeks had learnt some discipline and grown up a little bit? I'm thinking; fuckin hell, what's he saying? He's twenty-three years old, and he's talking like a little kid. This unexpected mature moment vanished as the anticipation kicked in and volume from the Kop increased. It's that unique, incredible, war-like roar that can only be heard at a Sheffield derby. It's not a chant; it's more like a growling, neck vein-bulging scream that starts in the pit of the stomach and extends from the bottom of your heart.

"Ya-ni-ted" – all three syllables delivered with equal venom. "Wens-dee – Ya-ni-ted – Wens-dee – Ya-ni-ted – Wens-dee" echoes around the stadium as Blade and Owl try to out-shout each other. It's not for the team, there're not even on the pitch, it's for us, the mob, the Blades mob, we've got to be louder than our greatest rivals. We squeeze into the Blades mass, where we screech, we yell, and we bawl, we're the fuckin loudest, and we're the fuckin hardest.

Thousands of Wednesdayites occupy the right-hand half of the Shoreham, screeching, yelling and bawling just as loud as we are. Where the fuck has this lot come from? How did they get in?

Three years ago they were stuck in the corner, heading house bricks, surrounded by police, but today they're here in force. Crombie-clad skinheads and hard-mods dressed in checked Shermans and short-sleeved Fred Perrys jostle for position on the front line. Brutal fuckers, confident, gesticulating, screaming threats, standing firm and more than ready to fight. Who the fuck are they? I've never seen any of them before, strangers from our own city. These bastards are well up for it, so we've got to match them, got to be a little bit braver, got to defend the Shoreham end at all costs.

The two mobs stand only a yard from each other. The front row boys from both sides throw punches past a line of police trying to separate them. The new buzz word on the terraces is: Aggro, aggression, aggravation,

"Ay-Gee-Ay-Gee-Ar-Ay-Gee-Ar-Oh – Aggro."

The odd missile flies back and forth, but that's not good enough, everyone wants to get in close, feel a face at the end of their fist and a bollock on the tip of their boot. The mood is pure hatred, they're invading our end, but this is as far as they're going, this is our bit, this is where we stand, directly behind the goal, we're not shifting.

40,000 voices roar out the teams, and both sets of fans take their eyes off each other for a few seconds to welcome them. They sway and surge forward, waving scarves and banners, celebrating like a goal's gone in. The Blade ranks swell as latecomers from the boozers join the throng, and the force of fifty new bodies collapses the police line; yes, the nutters are here.

Wednesday win the toss and opt to kick towards the Lane end. This means the Blades attack the Kop in the first half, a slight disadvantage as tradition dictates the Blades kick toward the Shoreham end in the second half, "It's worth a goal start int it."

The crowd settles down slightly to focus on the game, but every few seconds, Blade eyes glance to the right, Owl eyes to the left, watching and listening for the roar of confrontation.

The Blades kickoff, spraying lovely passes around the early season still green turf. By January the grass will have disappeared from every part of the pitch, except around the corner flags.

United are well on top, and Eddie Colquhoun sends us crazy, by giving the Blades an early lead.

"Eddie Colquhoun, Eddie Colquhoun, Eddie."

When Billy Dearden nets number two, we're delirious and the chant of, *"Poor old Wednesday can't play football, we play football, Wednesday's fuck all... Easy, Easy, Easy"* echoes around the Shoreham. This sparks off more fighting and the police are finding it hard to keep control.

The half time whistle blows, and the Blades are cheered from the pitch. Halfway there I'm thinking, fuckin come on United don't slip up now.

Into the second half and Wednesday pull a goal back. This gives the Wednesdayites new hope, and they spring back into life. Their team responds, and my heart sinks as the bastards draw level. Now the game is finely poised, the atmosphere, electric.

So here we are, *feeling sad, feeling blue, United 2 Wednesday 2'* then... *On to the pitch comes John Tudor hurrah-hurrah.'* Substitute Tudor's through on his own, one on one with the goalie, he's got loads of time and loads of space, there's not a Wednesday defender in sight.

The Wednesday keeper runs out narrowing the angle, Tudor's got to score, got to dribble around him and put the ball into an empty net but, no: what's he doing? He shoots, low and hard, straight at the goalie – shit… but the ball goes through the goalie's legs into the net.

"Yeeeeeeeessssssssssssss" three fuckin two, get in there. Incredible noise and celebrations greet the goal.

"King of kings and Lord of lords, for he shall reign forever and ever, Hallelujah, King Tudor, King Tudor, Hallelujah king Tudor king Tudor."

The Shoreham boys are having a fit. We hug, kiss, dance, surge forwards, sway sideways, fall down, get back up, its sheer chaos, its absolute delight, it's party time.

Wednesday fans look dejected, the goal's knocked the shit out of them, but it gives us an adrenaline boost that takes us punching and booting through the police lines. For a few brief seconds the Wednesday fans back off, but the coppers re-group and order is soon restored.

The Shoreham's in full voice now, not just the mob, the flat caps standing in line with the corner flags are joining in. The noise can be heard from Hyde Park flats to Wadsley Bridge. My heart's in my mouth every time Wednesday move into the Blades' half. For fuck's sake bring the ball-boys into the game, boot the ball down the fuckin cricket pitch and let them have a game of keepy-uppy for a few minutes.

Then it's all over, the final whistle blows to a roar to end all roars. There's no need for feet as the momentum of the crowd carries me down the steps on to John Street. We march onto Shoreham Street three hundred strong, singing, laughing and jigging. The Wednesday fans have split and melted, they walk alone or in small groups staring at the pavement.

A derby day defeat destroys the soul, their desire to fight has disappeared. We don't want to fight either, we're so happy, we've beaten the old enemy, we've beaten the Wednesday bastards, let's get into the boozers to sing and drink the night away.

We walk through Pond Street bus station, and the chant of *"Ya-ni-ted"* nearly lifts the roof off the main terminal. Blades congregate around the Threepenny bit kiosk, congratulating each other. The boozers'll be open in ten minutes, "Let's get fuckin bladdered."

The day's events got me thinking, did I really want to give all this up to play football? But it wasn't like this every week, the exceptional buzz of a derby match only happens twice a season. The other thing that made me think was the vast numbers, and more importantly, the actions of the Wednesdayites. We'd more or less had it our own way since the mid-60s.

Could this be the same set of lads who'd been humiliated inside their own ground on 'Egg Day' four years ago? Only six months earlier we'd swanned around Hillsborough like we owned it, but today they'd matched us for fervour, hostility and aggression. A bit of a shock really, I didn't like to admit it, but it looked like things were starting to even out on the Sheffield hooligan scene.

Chapter 3

It's alright, Ma (I'm only bleeding) – Spring 1971

It was one of them moments; you know, them moments that only happen on rare occasions, a moment when you look just right… no, better than just right, exactly right, spot on, fuckin perfect. I'm dressed to the nines in a freshly ironed, sweet smelling ice blue Ben Sherman, navy blue Levi needle cords and black, flat-heeled Chelsea boots. After a fortnight on the Clearasil lotion my spots were healing up nicely and with a little pinkie end dabble of Mam's foundation they were almost invisible. My hair, shoulder-length, hung in waves and ringlets. As I step back from the mirror, I think, yes, you handsome cunt; some lucky little darling's in for a treat tonight.

Downstairs, Mam, dressed in a brightly coloured pinafore, Parky in hand, sits in her comfy chair in front of the telly soaking her corns in a bowl of warm water, laced with bicarbonate of soda. Park Drives had always been my preferred choice of fags, probably because, from the age of ten, I'd stolen 'em off Mum and Uncle Chris. I got used to Parkys and if anybody gave me a cig with a filter on, I always ripped the tip off. The tobacco companies still used every media outlet to bombard us with advertising campaigns. They assured us it was still pretty cool to smoke. Embassy (and later Players Number 6) encouraged, and tried to kill, us even more by introducing free coupons that could be exchanged for an array of classy gifts. You only needed 500 for a top of the range, imitation mother of pearl shoe-horn. A thousand bought you a pair of (made in Sheffield) stainless steel toenail-clippers. Clothes were also available from the Embassy catalogue, and as the famous old song goes:

"I'll never forget the night that we met you had your new suit on.
The one that you got by saving a lot of Embassy coupons."

Outside I hear a car horn pippin; the lads are here.

"See ya later Ma," I shout, and I just catch the first bit of: "Behave yasen and don't slam the bleedin… " from Mum as the door rattles on its hinges behind me.

Don Hippo's sat at the wheel of his Vauxhall SL (Super Luxury) blasting the hooter. Little Fred's in the passenger's seat, Young Mott's lounged in the back. I jump in at the side of Mott and we're off.

A mate's told us about a Thursday night disco boozer on the other side of Chesterfield, swarming with loose and willing women.

"If you don't get a fuck there," he said, "There's summat up with ya."

At eleven bells we stagger out of the pub, legless and birdless. Little Fred and me wrestle to get in the front seat, I win. Why I wanted to sit in the front I'll never know, because in the space of a year, Hippo went from the safest, slowest driver in the world, to a mad cunt.

I'd had a bad car crash a couple of years earlier when Grunter and me, both aged seventeen and pissed out of our minds, raced one of the Dronny bikers along Stonelow Road.

Grunt hit the causey edge and the car overturned. It slid along on its roof for a few yards, sparking like a grinding wheel. In the following seconds everything went dark. I thought, oh fuckin shite, I'm dead. What a bastard, I'm only seventeen years old and I'm dead. My eyes opened and focused, I'm upside-down, but I'm alive, I'm fuckin alive, get out before the fucker blows up, I thought, and I scrambled out through the boot.

I escaped with just cuts and bruises, but Grunt spent a few days in hospital nursing a head the size of a barrage balloon. The crash really shit me up, so I rarely sat in the front seat unless drunk.

"Slow down, fuckin Stirling Moss," I shouted to Hippo as the car sped down the steep slope of Hady Hill towards Chezzy town centre at 60 m.p.h.

Hippo just grinned as he swung the car right, overtaking a crawler about 100 yards from a right-hand bend. Fifty yards away a double-decker bus appeared, looming high and wide and heading straight for us. Hippo swung back left but lost it as the car skidded on the wet surface and drifted sideways. He straightened up too late as we ploughed into a wall. I shot forward and felt the cold, wet fresh air hit my face as my head went through the windscreen. I jumped from the car shouting, "Fuckin ell, I've got some fuckin glass stuck in my gob, get the fucker out." but it sounded like, "Guckin ell, gav got gum guckin glass guck in gi gob, get gu gucker gout."

The impact had broken my front tooth in half and knocked the remaining bit up into my gum. I could feel my lip hanging down and blood running from my forehead into my eyes. The other lads, tried to calm me down. I paced up and down in shock, leaning forward to try to stop the blood dripping on my clothes, shouting, "Get this glass out of mi gob; it's stuck in mi gum."

"It's all right Ron calm down," one of the lads said.

"Is it bad?" I asked.

"No, it's not bad, just a few little cuts."

"But I've got some fuckin glass stuck in my gum, can't you pull it out?"

A green M.G. sports car pulled up behind us and a young couple jumped out. They helped me into the car and shot off to the hospital. I sat on the girl's knee in the two-seater.

I kept saying, "Sorry, I've got blood on ya."

"Don't worry about it," the girl said. They took me into casualty and stayed until a nurse came and took me into one of a line of cubicles surrounded by plastic curtains. I heard a voice coming from the next cubicle, "Help me, somebody help me, please help." This went on a while, and I thought this bloke must be badly injured, so I got out of bed and pulled the curtain back. I could see a small cut on the man's forehead.

"Somebody hit me with a bottle," he said. "I'm in so much pain."

"Shut up cunt, thiz nowt up wi thi," I said. A doctor came and stitched me up and I managed to get a ride home in an ambulance

I climbed in through the back window and looked in the kitchen mirror at my smashed-up dial... oh fuckin shit. I nipped upstairs and tapped on Mum's bedroom door. I knew she'd still be awake, reading and whittling until I rolled in.

190

"You better prepare yourself for a shock, Ma," I said, opening the door. A look of horror came to Mums face as she saw me.

"Oh my god, what's happened to ya?" Mum shouted. "You've been fighting again, look at the bloody state of you." Mum began to sob. "I'm fed up with this; oh I am, I really am, you'll be the bleedin death of me you will."

"It's all right, Ma. Don't start roorin, I've not been fighting, I've had a car crash, I went through the windscreen, I've been to the hospital and they've stitched me up, I'm okay, don't worry."

Not even having the slightest inkling I'd just scared my mother half to death, I crawled into bed. After feeling sorry for myself for five minutes, I slept like rat until late morning.

I awoke feeling like I'd grown another head and peeped in the mirror to make sure it hadn't all been a bad dream. A fat purple face covered in congealed blood stared back at me, my bottom lip looked like a stewed prune. I replayed the crash in my head and thought, ah well at least I'm not dead.

Mum must have calmed down a bit because her voice sounded ok when she shouted, "Are you coming down for cuppa Ron? I've just mashed." I went downstairs, but when Mum saw me, she started wailing again.

I comforted her by saying, "Bleeding hell, Mother, don't start again."

A while later Mum said, "Come over to Mrs Kay's Ron; let her have a look at you."

Mrs Kay, a wily old fucker with a head the size of a shire horse, was well in her seventies, but she still had all her marbles. She was Mum's best gossiping mate and lived in the pensioners' bungalows across the street. The two old buggers spent hours tittle-tattling about the neighbours. Even though I felt like shit I thought I'd go over as Mrs Kay always used to get her purse out and give me a couple of bob for a pint.

We went in and Mum said, "Just look at the bloody state of our Ron, Vera; he's gone through a car windscreen. Have you ever seen owt like it in your life?"

"Ooooh, Ron, what have ya bloody done, come here, let me have a look," Mrs Kay said.

"I've had a car crash, Mrs Kay. I went through the windscreen."

Mum and Mrs Kay hummed and arred and oooohed and tutted.

"Come over here, near fire, have a warm, Ron. Weers me glasses, Annie? I can't see bugger all without 'em. I can never bloody find 'em." Mrs Kay shuffled the contents on the top of the coffee table until she found her specs. She perched them on the end of her nose and said, "Lean over Ron, I can't see right. Let me have a look at ya." I leant over until my face was about a foot from hers.

"Ooooh my bloody god," Mrs Kay said.

Then without warning she moved forward. Grabbing my balls in one hand she gave them a squeeze, which made me jump, and said, "I bet you haven't got much of a cock on you this morning, Ron, have ya lad?"

Me Mam and Mrs Kay sat there cackling like two tripping witches: the fuckers.

Later on in the evening all the lads came round to our house with a couple of Watneys Party Sevens which I swigged through a straw. We watched *The*

Comedians on the telly and I laughed so much a couple of stitches came out of my lip.

The day after, the lads came round again and despite my protests they bundled me in a car, drove me into Sheffield and forced me to have my picture taken in the photo booth in Pond Street bus station. I lived on soup for the next few days. I wasn't too worried about the state of my clock, because I knew it would eventually heal up. A deep cut in my forehead just below the hairline needed five or six stitches, about a dozen or so were inserted in the corner and the inside of my lip, and a couple more in the bridge of my nose. The rest were just tiny lacerations all over my face. I'd always taken pride in my perfectly straight set of zoobies, now one of them's smashed to fuck and it really pissed me off.

A couple of days later, Hippo called round. He told me the car was a complete write-off and his dad wanted to have a word with me.

We went to see his dad, who shoved a piece of paper in front of me and said, "Sign that."

"What is it?" I asked.

"Oh it's just to say you won't be claiming any compensation from our Donald's insurance." The thought never crossed my mind. I didn't even know I could claim any compo. I signed the paper anyway; Hippo looked a bit embarrassed.

Hippo's dad, Horace, weren't short of a few bob, he owned a grocery shop on Dronny High Street and he'd bought Hippo the brand-new car. He also paid for the insurance and didn't want the payments to rise.

I went to see a dentist who told me the tooth would have to come out and be replaced with a false one. He took some impressions by ramming a gumshield filled with evil tasting sloppy cement into my mouth, but never explained why. It took months for the National Health appointment to come through.

When the day arrived the dentist told me I'd be having an injection to knock me out, the injection wasn't covered by the N.H.S and would cost £3. Three fuckin quid, that's more than a day's wages. I told the dentist I didn't have the money and he said I could pay it off weekly, I still haven't paid it.

I awoke gagging and heaving. It felt like a lorry had parked up in my gob. I managed to ask the dentist, "What's in my mouth?"

"It's a plastic pallet," he answered in a broad Scottish accent. "For a whale you'll feel like ya have the wh-ooooole of Glasgee in ya mooth, but you'll soon get used tay it, och-eye the noo, wee laddie."

I'd imagined the tooth would be taken out and a false one, somehow wedged in, I had no idea it would be attached to half a yard of plastic.

The dentist told me to take out the pallet after meals to clean it.

"Dinnie ever sleep in it," he said, "If it falls oot, it could choke ye to death."

Fucking marvellous, I've got to put up with a Jock city in my gob for the rest of my life and the fucker might choke me to death.

This made me think what a really nice chap Horace was. I felt I deserved some compo for all this shit. Maybe I should have clunked clicked, but there was no seat belt law at the time and I'm not quite sure if the car had them fitted anyway.

After tea I managed to prise the nasher out, but couldn't get it back in, as I kept heaving when it touched the roof of my mouth. I left it soaking in a cup of water all night.

Next morning, I went back to the dentist carrying the tooth in my pocket. I took it out, covered in fluff and strands of tobacco and handed it to the dentist saying, "I can't stand this in mi gob." He rinsed it under a tap and slammed it back into my mouth, telling me I'd just have to get used to it.

The following Thursday, seven or eight of us (two cars loads) walked into the Ozzie Owl night club, housed in an upstairs room at Wednesday's football ground. Steve Cardwell worked there as a bouncer, so we all got in for nowt. There was only a few dozen folk in the club, it would liven up in half an hour or so when the boozers shut.

The DJ spinning tunes from a podium on a raised platform announced a special treat; Mighty Melvin the famous cross-dressing go-go dancer would be making an appearance. Always outrageously funny and camp, Mel dressed in extreme flimsy costumes, flirting, pouting and flickering his ginger eyelashes. Melvin could turn up at any city centre disco pub or night club, leap on the dance floor and cavort like a demented goblin. He eventually became a bit of a local celebrity.

His stang had either been lopped off or taped up under his legs because there was no noticeable bulge. When he became well-known he travelled around the circuit with some of the DJs doing regular gigs. Melvin, standing fully five-foot-tall, on pink-skinned, red-haired legs, wore skin tight gold coloured satin hot-pants with a matching top, barely covering his nipples.

The lights went down, and the spotlight hit him as he pirouetted onto the dance floor like a ballet dancing orang-utan. The crowd roared and cheered him on as he went through his routine. Two shit-hot, scantily clad go-go dancing girls appeared, one on either side of Mel, rubbing their bodies onto his and stroking his freckles. I didn't know whether to laugh or spew up.

Amidst all this merriment the club filled up. Groups of lads eyed us up and pointed fingers in our direction. We were in the heart of Wednesday territory and knew it would only be a matter of time before it kicked off. We moved things along a bit by singing a rousing chorus of: *"We are the Shoreham Bootboys."* before steaming into a group of a dozen or so lads at the other side of the dance floor.

The music stopped, and the house lights came on as the DJ shouted for assistance. I copped for a sidewinder which dislodged my zoobie. I saw it skim along the dance floor and disappear amongst a mass of girl's legs and handbags.

"Hold on a minute," I shouted, "I've lost mi tooth." It surprised me when the fight stopped for a few seconds as I crawled on my hands and knees searching for the tooth. I found it, stuffed it in my pocket, jumped to my feet and shouted, "Right, I've got the fucker, on we go."

We were well up against it by now as most of the lads in the club joined in. We were forced towards the exit and smacked and booted down the stairs. Steve and the other bouncers were now on the case and they ushered us through the front doors onto the forecourt.

The lads inside tried to force their way out, while we tried to force our way back in. We danced and bounced around exchanging threats, promising we would be returning next week with reinforcements. We congratulated each other for our efforts, laughing and saying stuff like, "Did you see me drop the big twat?" "There were at least three fuckers on me and they couldn't put me down." None of us were badly injured, just a few lumps, bumps and grazes.

The following Thursday, five cars carrying around twenty Dronny lads pulled up outside the club; my pallet, now held firmly in place courtesy of a squirt of Sterafix denture glue. We'd purposely arrived after the pubs shut, hoping to catch the same bunch of lads inside the club.

"Oh fuckin hell," Steve said, but still managed a smile as we swarmed up the stairs.

"You're wasting your time though lads, there's no fucker in." We looked around, but none of the lads from the week before were inside. We hung around for half an hour or so, intimidating the few punters dotted around the club. We decided to fuck off and come back another time when no one expected us, but after a few weeks we'd forgotten all about the little skirmish.

The 1971 return derby at Hillsborough took place on the 12th of April, Easter Monday, my twentieth birthday.

I remember starting off in Dronny when the pubs opened, but little else until I staggered through the turnstiles just before kickoff. I joined thousands of Blades on the Kop, but I don't recall any of the 0-0 draw or any of the fighting. There were numerous arrests before; during and after the game, but I was oblivious to it all.

Saturday 1st of May 1971, I awake to blazing sunshine and a hangover from hell. My grass-stained, hedge-ripped clothes are strewn around the bedroom floor. Macduff would probably be feeling a lot worse than I did, as today was the day he'd chosen to tie the knot.

At the same time as McDougal pledged his troth at the altar, the Blades kicked off against Watford at the Lane in the final game of the season, needing a point to gain promotion to the First Division. What a day to get married. The wedding was a low-key, family only affair, I was so glad I wasn't invited.

The night before, a mob of us did a stag-do tour around the Dronny boozers. Closing time approached as we pushed our way into the chock-a-block best room at the Bridge Inn. We didn't use the Bridge very often, for the simple reason the pub at the time was a spit and sawdust, rough and tumble, traditional old-fashioned joint. The landlord refused to install a jukebox, probably with the intention of keeping us young 'uns out.

At weekends though, the pub's very foundations shuddered to the boom of Alf Butcher's drums and the tinkle of his wife Gladys's honky-tonk piano. Every Friday and Saturday night, old-time music hall revellers packed out the best room. They banged lumps of wood on the tables; shook tin tea-caddies filled with dried peas and rattled brightly painted Spanish maracas and castanets in time to ancient melodies.

The band was jumping, and the joint began to swing as we forced our way through to the bar. *"Daisy, Daisy give me your answer do."* echoed around the room. We thought we'd join in the spirit of the fun by giving them a song of our own and belted out a rousing chorus of, *"He's getting married in the morning."* A song, perfectly appropriate for the occasion and one that fitted in nicely with the sing-along theme of the evening, but the mostly middle-aged Bridge posse didn't take too kindly to us muscling in on their act.

A suited-up old bloke in his forties, stood behind us, shouted, "If you don't shut ya gobs, he'll be getting fuckin buried in the morning." That's quite amusing, I thought. Mac however didn't and punched the bloke in the face. So here we go again, another full on Wild West, saloon-style, bar-room brawl; fuckin brilliant.

The music seemed to grow louder as the battle took off. Gladys pumped up the volume on the old ivories and Alf whacked the drums like Keith Moon on acid. As usual most of punters were into us. The blokes threw haymaking punches and screaming women tried to beat us to death with various makeshift percussion instruments.

It was all a bit half-hearted on our part; we didn't really want to hurt any of the Bridge crowd as most of them were familiar faces. We made a strategic retreat, helped through the door by the landlord. Outside we fell about laughing and then some fool (possibly me) suggested we end the night – for old time's sake, with a garden hop.

We chose Park Avenue, a nice posh street with plenty of exotic shrubs and bushes to destroy. After ten minutes rampaging around the grounds we staggered home to sleep it all off.

At the match nearly 39,000 Blades roared the team to a 3-0 victory.

With the score at 0-0, Stewart Scullion, the Watford left winger, had us all cacking our pants when he rattled the crossbar from thirty yards. The Blades manager, John Harris must have noticed the potential of Scullion because he signed him a week later.

We drove back in Little Fred's car where we planned to party the night away. The first action of the evening came outside the Victoria boozer when we spotted 'Ferret' a fifteen-year-old Dronny groupie. Ferret's pert little breasts stuck out just below her neck, she'd been my hoe for the last eighteen months.

"Gerrin here Ferret, ya little fucker," I shouted. She's in the back seat before I've finished talking, Ferret didn't need no urging. We drove out towards the Derbyshire wilds and pulled up at a patch of bracken on the road to Toad's Gob. Ten seconds later, Ferret's little black hot pants dangled from a branch and her feet pointed to quart to three.

Fred dropped Ferret off, parked his car somewhere and we headed for the Greyhound pub to meet up with a few more mates. Young Mott hits the top shelf and after an hour or so he'd sunk a dozen double vodkas. We decided to move on and head off to a party at Caroline Roper's mansion up at Dronfield

Hill Top. Caroline's parents are loaded, the shorts cabinet is well stocked and there's always a selection of fine wines ready for consumption. Outside, someone noticed Mott was missing, we just assumed he'd drunk too much and wandered off home. It turned out he'd gone for a piss, fell down and crawled into the pub coal shed where he fell asleep on top of the coal heap. He woke up on Sunday morning covered in cuts and coal dust.

August 1971 and eight of us, Big Fred (little Fred's older brother) Bucket Allen, who greets everybody with a kidney punch from behind, Titch Garbutt, Johnny Cobb (a few years later Johnny, at the age twenty one would take his own life, sat in a garage with an hosepipe attached to the car exhaust), Don Hippo, Spiv Hoyland, Killer Bennet (what a nickname to have to live up to) and me, set off for a week of sun, sex, sea and beans in Newquay, Cornwall.

We leave the Greyhound at closing time on Friday night in two cars, packed with three tents, a camping stove, a couple of frying pans, six dozen eggs and twenty tins of Heinz baked beans.

It's around 6 a.m. on Saturday morning when we reach the resort. After parking up in a lay-by just outside the town centre we head for the beach. It's a hundred-foot drop from the road above down to the shoreline, but it's raining so hard we can't even see the ocean.

I was back on the dole and, after forking out for the petrol, I'm left with around a tenner, just over a quid a day. I've got it all worked out, the beer costs about twelve to fourteen new pence a pint (this decimalisation shit is doing my head in) that's enough for about five or six pints a night, leaving a few bob for cigs and snap. I reckon a tin of beans, an egg and a carton of milk every morning for brecky, a bag of chips for dinner and another one at teatime should see me through the week.

By mid-afternoon the weather's cleared up and I've already spent nearly a quid at the dinnertime session. The pubs shut at three so it's back to the cars for an hour's kip, a change of clothes and a wash in the public toilets.

We're back on the town for six o'clock. Thousands of young revellers cram the streets around the town centre; this is going to be great, I can feel it. Seeing as we're in Newquay one of the lads suggests a session on the old Newky (Newcastle) Brown. I check the price at the bar, "Twenty-four pence a bottle. The day I pay twenty four pence, nearly five fuckin bob for a pint of beer is the day I stop fuckin drinking." I shout. Even the bitter's seventeen pence a pint in this sea-front bar, let's fuck off and find somewhere cheaper."

"Get thi hand in thi pocket Sharpy, ya fuckin Jew," one of the lads shouts "Fuck off, I'm not Jewish," I shout back.

We trawl the pubs and by 10 o'clock I've got the superman buzz. Groups of lads and lasses party in every pub and jig around the streets. Everybody's chatty and friendly, everybody's out for a good time. Then I'm out on the street alone, fuck – where have they all gone? I've lost everybody. Fuck it, I'm sound on my own anyway, I don't need anybody. It's around midnight, and Trojan sounds drift out into the night from an open upstairs window of a club called simply 'Discothèque.' The Upsetters, *Return of the Django* blasts out of the sound system

196

as I enter the upstairs room. Moonstomping girl and boy skin and suedeheads fill the small dance floor. Even though my hair's hanging on my shoulders nobody gives me a second glance as I make my way to the bar.

I stand on the edge of the dance floor, bobbing my head and raising my knees in time to the music like a dancing fool, nobody in here knows me though; I'd never do this in front of the lads. A couple of skins walk over, one of them says, "Hello mate where ya from?"

"Sheffield," I answer.

"United or Wednesday?" he says.

"There's only one team in Sheffield pal," I say.

Not wanting to commit himself he says, "Which one's that?"

"United," I answer. We all laugh.

"We're from Coventry – City fans."

"Yeah, I've been. Not a bad mob, Coventry." Let's keep it all nice and friendly I think. I'm pissed, but I can sense the atmosphere, everything is relaxed, no culture clashes here; we're all young kids in our prime, on holiday and having a fantastic time.

Me and Bucket Allen at Newquay 1971

I mingle and chat to lads and lasses from all parts of the country; it's all smiles, back pats and kisses, kinda like being loved-up but without the 'E's.' Throbbing Jamaican ska sounds bounce through the room. It's like I've known this crowd all my life. Then it's 2 o'clock and it's all over. The last waltz is the classic *Al Capone* by Prince Buster, everybody's up moving and grooving, it's a special, unique moment in time, one to look back on when I'm old and grey. I leave the club arm in arm with a spiky-haired little beauty wearing a green mohair cardigan and monkey boots.

We spent the days bumming around the beach, watching the surfers and exploring caves. I couldn't swim further than two yards, but it didn't keep me out of the sea. I'd only ever seen the grey waters of Skeggy, Cleethorpes and Blackpool, but the ocean here's a nice shade of green: proper sea water. I'd wade out until the water reached my neck, before jumping up into eight-foot-high waves which took my feet off the sand and threw me backwards like a rag doll.

By Wednesday my funds are running low. We've already been moved on by the coppers and told to find a proper campsite. We just pitch the tents further up the road.

Wednesday night and its gone midnight, the rain's hammers down on the

197

sides of our two-man tent containing four bodies. We lay in our doss bags, blowing bean farts and chat about all kinds of shit in the pitch darkness.

"What's your middle name, Ron?" Titch, matter of factly, asks me.

"Ampt got one, Titch. Just plain Ronald, me," I answer.

"What about you, Cobbo?" Titch says.

"Me anall," Cobbo says. "Just John."

"What about you, Donald?" Titch says to Don Hippo.

"Not telling ya," Hippo said.

"Come on, cunt. What's up with ya?"

"No, I'm not saying owt, you'll all laugh," Hippo says.

"We won't laugh, honest, Don. Come on tell us."

"No, you can fuck off, I'm not telling ya."

"Come on were not gonna let it drop until you tell us."

"Oh fuckin hell, all right," Don said. "It's Horace."

"Fuckin Horace," we all rocked with laughter kicking our legs in the air. "Fuckin Horace, Donald fuckin Horace, oh my god. Fuck me."

"All right ya cunts," Don said. "I knew you'd laugh."

Half an hour later we've calmed down and we're getting ready for some kip when we notice torch lights outside the tents; the coppers are back. Hippo's the nearest to the flap as it opens up.

"I've told you once to move on," the copper said. "You better be gone by the morning or you'll be in serious trouble. Now I want all your names and addresses. You first," to Hippo.

"Donald Senior" Hippo said.

"Middle name," the copper said. That's it, we're in bits. "Oh you think it's funny do you?" the copper said. We held on to each other, nearly pissing ourselves. "Come on," the copper said to Don "middle name." Don couldn't answer for laughing and we're all in hysterics. "This is your last chance, I'm not going to ask you again," the copper said.

"All right, all right, it's Horace," Don managed to blurt out. I thought my stomach was gonna bust. The coppers take all our names and addresses amidst more bouts of laughter.

I woke up next morning laid in a river. The rain's seeped through my sleeping bag and I'm soaked to the skin, it wouldn't be so bad but I'm down to my last pair of clean jeans. We all squelch out to discover we'd pitched the tent inside out. Fuck the beans and milk this morning; I need some proper food. We jump in the cars and shoot off to find a café. I spend most of my remaining stash on a full English.

On Thursday morning we packed up our stuff and set off for Torquay. We hung out of the windows, throwing the remaining eggs at each other cars as we overtook and swerved along weaving country roads. When we arrived in Devon both the cars were covered in yolk.

All of us wore our hair shoulder length, except Big Fred, who'd recently gone against our rocker values by opting for the skinhead look. Some of the livelier seafront pubs had 'No Skinheads' signs on the doors, so we had trouble finding decent bars where we could all get in.

I pulled a Scottish bird on the nighttime session and left the others for a walk round with the girl. Trouble was I didn't have a penny to my name. The bird bought my drinks for the rest of the night, and they reckon Scottish folk are tight, eh! I scrounged fifty pence off Hippo and met her again on the Friday night.

We set off early on Saturday morning to make it back home for the first game of the new season against Southampton at the Lane.

The spring of 71 saw the first inklings of a new pop culture that would dominate the single charts for the next three or four years. T-Rex, were probably the band who pioneered the new movement of 'Glam Rock.'

Marc Bolan, sprinkled in glitter and stardust and clad in satin and velvet, had thousands of young teenybopper girls (and boys) swooning and creaming their undergarments. As well as having the advantage of being Bolan's best mate, Micky Finn was the worlds most talented and accomplished bongo player. It's a great shame and one of the biggest injustices in the history of rock, that on every T Rex recording, Finn's haunting voodoo rhythms are lost in the final mix.

T-Rex might have looked flash, but there was nothing flash about their music. The band went back to the basics, just good old fashioned, three-chord, three-minute, bongo inspired, gooey rock 'n' roll. There was nothing really innovative about the glam rock scene though. Pop and rock stars had been flamboyant from the very beginning, Little Richard wore make-up in the 50s, the psychedelic mid-60s saw Hendrix dressed in rainbow costumes and the Stones (circa *Jumping Jack Flash*) with glittered up faces.

The pick of new bands for me were Roxy Music and David Bowie. Roxy Music's unique, eerie, futuristic sound fitted their space age look of silver suits, stilted boots and weird, spiky hairstyles perfectly. Bowie had the same kinda star-man guise, but his semi-acoustic sound and his Dylanesque/Lou Reed style lyrics gave him a more laid-back, arty image. Gary Glitter, and later, Suzi Quatro just belted out tribal 4-4 rhythms the children couldn't help but chant along and boogie to.

Now this would have been the perfect time to get myself a job, save up, buy an electric guitar and amp, glue some stars on my spots and find myself a rock 'n' roll band. But I was having far too good a time to get rich and famous, and besides, would I be able to handle all them gruelling world tour schedules? And which would be better, playing in front of thousands at Shea Stadium? Or swaying along with thousands on the Shoreham? Not much in it really.

I still kept plugging away on the guitar, though, and I could pick my old acoustic log like a *Deliverance* hillbilly, but I needed some new inspiration and some new heroes. I'd fallen out with the Stones after Brian Jones's death and Bob Dylan had just about lain dormant since the motorcycle crash. Dylan, who'd been my musical salvation, lost me, and no doubt many others, when in the late 60s and early 70s he brought out albums like *Nashville Skyline, New Morning and Self-portrait*. What the fuck were they all about?

I discovered an antidote in the English folk singer, Roy Harper's classic *Flat Baroque and Berserk*. Album. In the song *I Hate the White Man*. Harper launches a scathing attack on the establishment. He blames his own race for the fucked-up state of the world. He sings about the *'Crazy white man and his teargas happiness.'* *'I hate the white man and his plastic excuse; I hate the white man and the man who turned him loose.'* Stirring stuff.

Macduff was having none of it. When I played him the song he shouted, "What the fuck's he on about? Is he a fuckin nigger or summat?"

"No Mac," I told him. "He's white."

"What's the cunt singing I hate the white man for, then?" I couldn't be arsed to explain. When the chorus came in, Mac drowned out Harper's vocal, bellowing: "I hate the fuckin black man."

We did get to listen to some Dylan stuff though, when Johnny Hall befriended a lad in the Wapentake pub who had access to the secret world of 'Bootlegging.' This was the very beginning of the bootleg era and nobody knew too much about them. The albums, imported from America were all different coloured vinyl, in red, orange, green and blue. They were amazing; we'd never seen anything like them. Most of the songs were from the early 60s before Dylan became really famous. All original acoustic stuff we'd never heard, along with some obscure country-blues covers, from obscure artists. There were out-takes, where Dylan would crack-up halfway through a song, even telephone conversations. Some of the recordings were terrible and sounded like a pan of bacon was frying in the background, others were spot on. The lad who did the bootlegs was very cagey about the whole business and it took Johnny months to gain his trust and allow him to see, and eventually buy the records.

Through listening to these songs and reading up on Dylan, we discovered his influences and his heroes. Dylan turned us on to Woody Guthrie, Leadbelly, Big Joe Williams, Roy Acuff, Hank Williams, Big Bill Broonsey and many more.

We searched the shelves in Violet May's and the Wicker record shops and managed to root out some great albums.

Praise the lord, the three-year probation sentence I received in 1968 was about to end, but, shit, with only a few more weeks to do, I'm nicked for fighting again and charged with the same offence – assault occasioning actual bodily harm. The fight happened on the night of Big Fred's birthday bash.

At this point I must explain how lads with older or younger brothers were named. In Big Fred's case, Fred wasn't big, just older than his brother, Little Fred – or Young Fred. The same with Young Mott or Little Mott, who had an older brother called Big Mott. But when it came to the Young family, things started to get a bit confusing.

There were four Young brothers, the oldest Young being David. His nickname at school was Flung Dung, so he was known as Big Flung or Big Dung. The next in line Richard – or Dick was called Little Flung, Young Flung or Dick Dung. Nip, the next one down was known as Flung Dung the Younger or Nip Dung and the youngest Young-Alfie was called Young Flung Dung the youngest, complicated shit, eh!

We'd been up at Fred's house before the pubs opened for a Saturday afternoon session on his home brew. I didn't sup much for the simple reason: it tasted like shite. Sass (Timothy Guy Mitchell Ward, and that ain't no shit, man), however, got well stuck in to the free ale and by the time we'd hit the boozers at opening time he was just about fucked. We did the pubs at the top end of Dronny first, the Green Dragon, the Blue Stoops and the Victoria. Then we moved on to the Greyhound (the Dog) and the Bridge Inn.

I helped Sass out of the door as we left the Bridge and all but carried him down Chesterfield Road on the way to our next port of call, the White Swan (we were all barred from the Midland at the time). About a dozen or so of the other lads were still in the pub; they said they'd catch us up in a minute.

As we neared the laundrette, Barber Dunham (the local Sweeney), and his son David, who I knew from school, appeared about twenty yards in front of us. As they reached us, Sass swayed across the pavement, barging into them. An argument followed and within seconds I was fighting the pair of them. Sass, who wouldn't have been much help even if he'd been sober, just propped himself up against a wall. The rest of the lads came around the corner and seeing me brawling, steamed in and booted Dunham and son all over the street. We left them in a heap and went along our merry way.

Half an hour later three coppers stormed into the Swan and dragged me outside. After a struggle they managed to prise me into the back seat of the Panda. The lads were straight out and surrounded the car. The car rocked from side to side. The driver skidded off to the sound of boots hammering on the side panels; he did his best to try to skittle the lads at the front. I arrived at Beetwell Street cop shop in Chesterfield, where they grilled me for half an hour, but I wouldn't give any names. They put me in a cell for an hour or so to 'think about it.'

When the last bus back to Dronny left Elder Way at eleven bells, I was charged, bailed and released; I walked the six miles back home. All the lads said they would chip in to pay my fine, but would it be a fine? I knew I could get sent down for breaking my probation, but with only a few weeks remaining on the order, I felt, with a little bit of luck, I might be okay.

Mr Turd, my first probation officer had been replaced about six months earlier by a bloke called Mr Stockley. Stockley, a placid, quiet chap had eyes so far apart; they were nearly on the sides of his head. He always wore the same clothes, a Harris Tweed jacket, a Burberry-style check shirt and a dark green, hairy, thick-knotted tie. I couldn't believe the difference between the two probation officers. Turd, the horrible, nasty, old-school, military type bully, thought the only way to keep his teenage reprobate charges in check was to bring back the birch and restore capital punishment. Stockley, on the other hand didn't give a shit. The sessions rarely lasted longer than a couple of minutes. It was: "Hello, how ya doing? Keeping out of trouble? Yes? Good. See you next week."

When I told him I'd been arrested, he said, "Well you're nearly at the end of your sentence, so I wouldn't worry about it too much."

At the next session Turd's sat there at the side of Stockley. What the fuck does he want?

"Ah Mr Sharpe, Mr Sharpe," Turd said. "You just couldn't do it, could you? I knew you were a wrong 'un the first time I saw you. Well you're in big trouble now, lad. I told you where you'd end up, didn't I? It's prison for you this time boy." I'm thinking, what the fuck has it got to do with you, ya big cunt, you're not my probation officer any more, but I just stared down at my feet. Turd laid into me again, Stockley never said a word.

By the time the trial came around at Renishaw Magistrates my probation had finished. I'd arranged to meet my solicitor for a last-minute briefing before we went in, but he hadn't arrived. Fuckin hell, its Turd again, he comes marching along the corridor with a prison officer at his side. He grabs my arm and pushes me into a small room, with just a desk and few chairs inside.

"This is Mr (whatever his name was)" Turd said. "But you better get used to calling him sir. He's a prison officer from Stafford Young Offenders Institute, that's where you're going today, Mr Sharpe. I rang the jail this morning to make sure they had a place for you."

I didn't know what to say; I could feel my mouth drying up and my heart pounding. The prison officer spoke, "You'll be okay, lad," he said. "It's a young offender's prison, all the inmates are around the same age as you." They gave me a few more minutes shit, all about what to expect in jail. Fuckin bastard, the prospect of prison scared the shit out of me.

My solicitor turned up and I told him what Turd said. He stormed into the room and laid into Turd: "You've got no right to even speak to Mr Sharpe. He's no longer on probation and even if he was, you're not his probation officer." Turd's attitude changed immediately, he went from bullyboy to a timid wreck.

"I'm only trying to do what's best for Ronald," he told my brief. The bastard couldn't help himself when he added: "But spell in prison, in my opinion would do him the world of good, don't you think so?"

"Don't worry," my brief said. "You're not going to prison."

I wasn't so sure. I agreed to plead guilty beforehand. My solicitor must have thrashed out a deal with the prosecution, because the case was read out without too much fuss and finger pointing. The head magistrate asked me if I had anything to say. I apologised for my behaviour and promised it would never happen again. My solicitor gave the court the usual spiel about me being a really good lad, who looked after his Mummy, did all the housework, the cooking and the shopping. He said the fight hadn't been my fault and I was only trying to help my drunken friend.

The magistrates huddled and whispered for a few seconds, before asking the prosecution: "Anything known about the defendant?"

"No previous convictions," the prosecution answered. Fuck me, I had at least five. This was too much for Turd who'd been eyeing me up like a hanging judge all through the proceedings. He jumped to his feet and shouted, "No previous convictions? He was still on probation for assault when this offence was committed. I used to be his probation officer."

"Are you Mr Sharpe's probation officer now?" my solicitor asked Turd.

"No but, but... " Turd mumbled

"Well, I'll thank you to keep out of this; it's got nothing to do with you." Turd sat back down, his nostrils flaring. My solicitor and the prosecution had a confab for a minute and spoke to the magistrates who retired to consider the sentence. I began to imagine what they were saying, "Mumble, mumble, prison sentence? Mumble, mumble, fine?" "Mumble, he looks after his mother." Yes, fine me ya cunts; I look after my mother you know.

They came back out after a couple of minutes and fined me a tenner with five quid costs, fifteen quid. Yes, what a result. Turd's head looked like exploding as I flashed him a cheeky grin across the courtroom.

Fifteen quid, I thought. There were about fifteen of us out on the night, so it's a quid each. Two of lads gave me a quid, the rest of the cunts forgot all about it.

I spent seventy new pence (about seventeen shillings and sixpence in real money) out of the two quid on the first haircut I'd had in years, a latest style, Rod Stewart feather cut. When I left the salon I looked more like Rod fuckin Hull. He was a vindictive fucker that barber, Dunham.

At the start of the 71-72 season, the Blades took the First Division by storm. I'd packed in playing football and returned to the fold after one pretty successful and enjoyable season. Dronny youth club finished runners up in the Sheffield junior league, just missing out on the title.

Playing delicious, attacking football in front of bumper crowds, United went twenty-one games unbeaten and topped the table until early October. The Blades defence looked comfortable and confident, even though the goalie, John Hope, sporting a truly horrendous haircut, could be a little suspect. Len Badger, oozing class and style, and steady Teddy Hemsley held the fullback positions. Eddie Colquhoun, a Jock centre half was solid at the back and chipped in with a few goals from corners. Frank Barlow and John Flynn made up the half back line

Trevor Hockey, who looked like the president of the San Bernardino Hell's Angels, ferreted around the centre circle stamping on rival midfielder's toes. He won the ball by fair means or foul – usually foul and tapped it a yard or two to Tony Currie who danced around baffled opponents before spraying beautiful forty-yard pinpoint passes to Woody on the right or Geoff Salmons, Gill Reece and Stewart Scullion who contested the left wing spot. Billy Dearden, a ten-grand bargain buy from Chester proved he could find the net in the First Division, just as he'd done the season before in the second. The joke at the time… 'United's got one Deard 'un, Wednesday's got eleven.' Rival fans sang, *"Hockey is a werewolf."* So what, he was a fuckin werewolf, we joined in and even started the chant off.

It had always been a pleasure to watch the Blades, always a joy to stand on the Kop and to sing our hearts out for the lads, no matter how they played. This was a special time though, the team actually gave us something to sing about; they played some beautiful football.

The match-day experience kicked in as soon I woke up on Saturday morning. The expectation of what would lie ahead, the tingle of travelling to a dodgy away match, the sights and the smells of strange new cities. The tingle grew into a buzz as soon as the floodlights came into view. Would we get run? Would we run them? Would we make it back to the station alive? How many would the away team bring to the Lane? Would they come on the Kop? Would they try to take it? Would they take it? Would they fuck.

With Dronny train station now shut down and derelict, we caught the red painted single-decker Booth and Fisher dinnertime bus to the home games. And that's how I felt: I was home.

The Boothy bus dropped us bang outside Jack Archer's sports shop on Bramall lane. The streets and pubs around the ground felt safe and comfortable, just as the streets and pubs around Hillsborough felt unpleasant and alien. The excitement and anticipation grew as we entered the turnstiles. Full of energy and bravado we galloped up the back steps that led to the Shoreham. It was the only place to be. *'Shoreham Street where it is magnifique, where all the Wednesdayites lay dead at our feet.'*

With latest style silk scarves tied loosely around our necks or tightly around our wrists, we squeezed our way into the mob, where we swayed, sang and taunted the away fans on the Lane end.

The fenced off cricket square and the old Victorian cricket pavilion with its giant clock and tin-plate scoreboard all added to the character of Beautiful Downtown Bramall Lane.

I got back from Torquay in time for the first home game against Southampton and as I entered the ground just before kickoff at the Cherry Street/Shoreham Street turnstiles I witnessed the Blade mob running the Southampton fans off the Kop.

Leeds were slaughtered 3-0 on the following Tuesday and in a repeat of the League Cup game a year earlier, their mob, who again came round from the Lane end in an attempt to take the Shoreham, were seen off without too much fuss.

The first away game on the following Saturday took us to Everton. Just before closing time on Friday night in the Dog, Young Mott and me decided to thumb it to Merseyside. We robbed a box of twenty-four packets of crisps from the boozer's stockroom in the back yard. Pissed as two farts, we caught the last bus into Sheffield with twelve bags of crisps each secreted about our person. Mott scoffed about six bags before we reached town. As we trudged along Glossop Road he turned a Norwich shade of yellow and collapsed in a bus shelter.

"I can't go any further Ron," he said. "I'm fucking badly."

He really did look rough, but we had a togger match to get to, so I said, "Come on Mott, it's just a spot of jaundice you'll be all right in a bit."

"I think I'm dying," Mott said.

"You shunt have eaten all them fuckin crisps, it's fucked you up," I said. After ten minutes or so Mott spewed up and came round a bit, so we carried on.

A car containing two lads and a bird, who all looked drunker than us, pulled up. We shot off towards Manchester and screeched into the city in record time. The two lads and the bird were sound and pointed us in the right direction by dropping us off near the East Lancs Road. Another lift took us within ten miles of Liverpool, where we met two Man Utd fans, thumbing home to Preston. They'd been to Anfield to watch Man Utd play Arsenal. Man Utd were forced to play their home games on Fridays at a neutral venue for a while, after the FA closed down Old Trafford due to crowd trouble. They told us the Liverpool and Everton fans turned out in force and teamed up to have a pop.

We hit Liverpool as dawn broke and were dropped off in some kind of slum clearance area. In the half-light we could make out rows and rows of half-demolished terraced houses, cranes with dangling steel balls and smoking ruins. Some of the houses looked like they were still lived in, as the curtains were still up, and the chimneys were smoking.

We nearly shit our pants as a pack of at least twenty barking, growing wild dogs came around a corner and started ripping lumps out of each other. It was like we'd landed in fuckin hell. We made our way to the city centre and hung around the shops for a while. After sharing a hearty crisp breakfast with a mob of seagulls on the waterfront, we made our way up to Goodison Park. We plotted up in a boozer near the ground and went in just before kickoff, joining a small group of about fifty Blades behind the goal. We saw Pete Fagin who told us he could get us back on his coach, so we were sorted for a lift home. We lost Pete and in an effort to find his bus, we left the ground before the end, missing Woody's late winner. On the way to the coaches we got stuck in the middle of a huge mob of Everton fans, out for blood.

There must have a good fifteen coaches lined up outside Stanley Park. Where the fuck were all this lot in the ground? Familiar faces looked out at us, banging on the coach windows and waving. Fuckin hell, the thick bastards are gonna get us killed. We stuck our fingers up at the Blades so as not give the game away.

We found Pete's coach, jumped aboard and gave the Everton fans some abuse when we knew we were safe.

A new set of lads, mostly skin and suedeheads began to appear on the front line at the matches. Big Herman John Darbyshire, was more of the Munster than the Hermit variety – our Herman was now known as Little Herman. There was Lefty, Walt Williams, Walt's younger brother Ray, Kenny Ball, but none of his jazz men, Young Wafer (Alex), Basil Fox, Junior, Big Bret Speddings, Sam Pointer, Scuffles, Spot, Salty and Big Senny.

The Heeley Green, The Groom mob and most of my mates who'd stood together on the Shoreham since the mid-60s were still bang at it.

The first season back in the First Division saw some epic battles and hundreds of arrests at the Lane. Tottenham, Chelsea, Leeds, Man City, Newcastle and Man Utd all attempted to take the Shoreham, only Man Utd, with a mob of about twenty thousand, managed it.

If I wasn't thinking about football I was dreaming about it. I'd have given anything to see the Blades play in the Cup final. I had this strange recurring dream about Wembley. I'm stood on the deserted tunnel end of the stadium huddled in the corner with fifty other trembling Blades. The other end of the ground is packed with swaying blue and white masses of Leicester fans. The tannoy announces, "This is the lowest attendance ever for a Cup final, 23,000 and only fifty Sheffield United fans have turned up."

Big Brett Speddings 1969, courtesy of top Sheffield photographer Mick Jones

I'm laughing, because I think – well at least they can't get us on this end, when Wembley turns into a giant dance hall. Now there's only the dance floor between us. There's no escape as 22,950 Leicester fans walk across it and start dancing on our heads.

An even worse, terrifying dream, saw me walking on the Kop at the Lane dressed in nothing except a short string vest that only reached to my belly button. I kept trying to pull it down to hide my walnut ball sack and shrivelled up stang. The Kop's full of settees and armchairs with thousands of Wednesdayites sat on them, all pointing and laughing at me. Was this a nightmarish vision of the future? The shape of things to come? It surely couldn't happen could it? Seats on the Kop!

Much hype and controversy surrounded Stanley Kubrick's new film, *A Clockwork Orange*. It had me well worked up before I'd even seen it. When I did go to see the film at the ABC Cinema on Angel Street in Sheffield, I had no idea it would almost blow my head off and change my life forever.

The opening shot hooks me instantly as the camera slowly pans out from a close up of our anti-hero and humble narrator... Alex. A tilted black bowler hat rests just above his false-lashed right eye. The manic half-smirk on his face radiates pure evil. Alex lounges in the futuristic 'Korova' milk bar, toasting his audience, us, with a glass of milk.

His clothes are white, but a kind of, off white, a mucky white. He wears a collarless shirt, with bleeding eyeball cuff-links and trousers held up by wide, white 1930s style braces. The shot zooms out further to Alex's three 'Droogs' all dressed in the same clobber. Alex's heavy black boots rest on a table, fashioned in the shape of white plastic sculpture of a backward-squatting; open-legged, nude woman wearing a green wig with matching slice hair.

More sculptured tables come in to view; each girl wears a different coloured wig and matching pubes.

Fantastic words; Moloko Plus, Moloko Synthemesk, Moloko Vellocet and Moloko Drencrom are splashed across the milk bar walls. Purcell's dark, foreboding *Queen Mary's Funeral March* dirges in the background. The combination of this sinister music and the frightening image of a not too distant future work perfectly. I sit open-mouthed, my pulse racing. Alex speaks for the first time.

"There was me, that is, Alex, and my three Droogs, that is, Pete, Georgie and Dim and we sit in the Korova milk bar trying to make up our razoodocks what to do with the evening.

The Korova milk bar sold milk-plus, milk-plus Synthemesk, or Vellocette or Drencrom, which is what we were drinking; this would sharpen us up and make us ready for a bit of the old Ultra-violence."

What's he saying? It makes no sense, but somehow I know exactly what he means. This is the coolest thing I have ever seen or heard; it's so good I feel like crying.

I sit through the film in a trance. I'm turned on to Ludwig Van Beethoven's synthesized devil trombones and angel trumpets, Rossini overtures and Elgar symphonies. I've got no idea what I'm listening to, but again I seem to be able to relate to it.

I floated out of the cinema, my head full of marvellous music and wonderful visions.

Two days later I'm back to see the film again and it's just as good. Another couple of visits in the next fortnight and I'm starting to pick up phrases and bits of lingo. Fuckin hell, to think I used to laugh at Turnip when he went to see Cliff Richard's *Summer Holiday* sixty-eight times.

A Clockwork Orange was based on the novel by Anthony Burgess, first published in 1962, and written in the fascinating language of 'Nadsat', a teenage jargon (part Russian, part Cockney rhyming slang) of a not too distant future. I borrowed the book from Beetroot and became even more obsessed. An appendix glossary in the back explained every crazy word. I read the book three times in as many weeks and I had to keep flicking to the back to decipher the words.

I was working the night shift at Gunstones bakery in Dronfield at the time with a mate called Deeks, who'd also seen the film. We marched around the factory dressed in white overalls with a malt loaf stuffed down the front of our bollocks, shouting: "Great bollshy yarblocko's to thee and thine." "Come and get one in the yarbles, if you have any yarbles, ya eunuch jelly thou." "I'll tolchock your rot and knock your zoobies out."

When the film soundtrack came out, I bought the album and played it constantly. It was better than the Stones and Dylan put together. I even bought unabridged versions of Rossini's *Thieving Magpie* and lovely, lovely Ludwig Van's *'Glorious 9th Symphony'*

The *Thieving Magpie* sempt vaguely familiar: a distant memory maybe from my junior school days, but now I associated this powerful, stirring piece, that builds to a tremendous crescendo, with gang warfare. The kettle drums were the stomping of boots, the violins the adrenaline rush and the cymbal crashes sounded like bottles, smashing into the heads of Billy Boy and his Droogs.

I started speaking Nadsat. "Put us a drop more moloko in me chi will ya Ma? My malenky petitza," I said to my Mother.

"What ya bloody talking about, Moloko, chi? Ya daft bugger," me mum said.

"I'll razzrezz your glazzies and tolchock ya gulliver," I answered.

"I think you've gone bleedin mad," Mum said.

Gangs of teenagers dressed in toned-down versions of the gear (white overalls and bowlers) began to appear at football matches. Then the film was gone, withdrawn from circulation in 1973 by Kubrick himself when incidents of copycat violence were reported up and down the country.

The film was re-released after Kubrick's death in 2000. As soon as it came out I dragged our lass off to see it. Shaz soon got pissed off when I blurted out every line before it was spoken.

Talking of 1973 films: well, I don't really want to talk about it, but after seeing *The Exorcist* that year, I slept with the bedroom light on until 1975.

Performers at the Great Western Rock festival at Bardney near Lincoln, included, Roxy Music, Slade, Joe Cocker, Rod Stewart and the Faces, Genesis, Status Quo, Sha Na Na, Rory Gallagher, Stone the Crows, Wishbone Ash, Santana, the Incredible String Band, Sutherland Brothers, Lindisfarne, the Beach Boys, Focus, Atomic Rooster, Humble Pie, Nazareth, Buddy Miles, the Strawbs, Alexis Korner and Don McLean. The four-day show (Friday to Monday) was held on the bank-holiday weekend at the end of May 1972.

I can't remember exactly how much the tickets cost, but I think they were £6.00. To put it into perspective, I was working, cash in hand, for a landscape gardening company and earning £3 a day, so the tickets were the equivalent of two days' wages. According to the New Musical Express, the organisers were expecting in excess of 50,000 at the concert.

Willie Marples, Beetroot and me, set off hitching in the wind and rain around teatime on Friday. Buying tickets at that price never even entered our heads. We planned to either sneak in somehow or bust down the fences, but we took enough money to pay at the gate if things got desperate. We took a sleeping bag each, but no tent or change of clothing. I wore a woman's shiny, black PVC mac. You know: the ones 1960s Dolly birds wore in the fashion magazines. Fuck knows where it came from; it must have come from a jumble sale. This covered a terrible brown and yellow quartered football shirt I'd nicked from school. I'd felt-penned the words BOB DYLAN on the front of the shirt. I must have looked fuckin incredible.

Forever the optimist, I thought we would walk onto Dronny Bottom, stick out our thumbs, the first car would pull up, drop us outside the festival entrance, give us free tickets to get in, and we'd be bang at the front when the first band took to the stage for the evening session. It didn't quite work out like that.

I've got no idea where we ended up, but we didn't get very far. I think it was a small village somewhere between Chesterfield and Derby. We'd been stood for hours on a lonely country road, where a car passed every ten minutes or so.

We eventually walked off and found a railway station. The trains had stopped running, but the waiting room was open, so we dossed there until the trains started again next morning. We got a train to Derby then one into Lincoln, landing around 10 o'clock Saturday morning. There were quite a few rain-sodden, pissed-off looking, hippy-type souls hanging around the station.

As we left the train we were approached by three lads who looked like swamp monsters. They asked if wanted to buy their tickets for £3 each as their tent had blown away in the middle of night, they were drenched, and they'd had enough. The tickets were like plastic credit cards, so we knew they were genuine.

Well-pleased with the half-price tickets; we hit a boozer at opening time and got chatting to a couple of lads from Bradford. They were football lads: Bradford City fans and we had a good old chin-wag, swapping football stories. It turned out these lads worked at the festival doing security on one of the gates.

They said they could get us in for nowt and we were a bit pissed off having just bought tickets. "Don't worry about that," one of lads said. "There's loads of people outside without tickets, you'll be able to flog 'em easy."

We left with the Bradford lads, as they had to get back up to the festival to start work in the early afternoon; we caught one of the special buses up to Bardney.

As the lads said, there were hundreds of people milling around outside the main gates looking for cheap tickets, or maybe waiting for everyone to get revved up enough to bust down the fences. The festival area was surrounded by corrugated tin sheeting about 12 foot high.

We flogged our tickets for £3 each and went in with the Bradford lads, who were guarding a service gate about fifty yards from the main entrance. It must have been the Bradford lads who came up with the idea of selling pass-out tickets. Anyone who wanted to leave the festival grounds were given a pass-out at the main gate, the pass-outs were the credit card tickets used to get in. Once inside, we went straight to the main exit gate and were handed tickets as we went out.

Outside we sold the tickets for £2 each, walked back, banged on the Bradford gate and were back in. We shared out the money, gave it ten minutes and did the same again. After an hour going in and out we had a nice wad each.

We decided to give it a rest and stay inside to watch some of the acts and get drunk-to-fuck in the beer tent. We walked through a waist high sea of foam to get to the main area. As we approached I could see bodies disappearing when they reached the middle of the foam, which was the about the size of half a football pitch. We raced in, and as we hit the middle we realised why. Our legs shot from under us as we hit a six-inch-deep patch of mud. We emerged from the other side pissing ourselves laughing, covered in this orange-coloured slimy shit.

Due to the on-off rain and the constant wind, the atmosphere sempt a bit subdued. Bits of straw, blown from bails placed all around the main concert area to soak up the mud drifted through the air. Bedraggled looking hippies, wrapped in plastic sheets and ponchos plodded up and down through the sludge. Juggling circus performers, uni-cyclists and dwarfs on stilts tried to cheer up the crowd.

Groups of Hell's Angels hung around inside and outside the beer tent. From the colours on their cut-offs I could see that most were from the Wolverhampton chapter. The Angels, as Angels did, fucked about, pushing each other in mock fights, trying to look hard and intimidating. It was their kind of duty to try and scare the innocents, but they weren't really causing too much shit.

We had so much cash we didn't have to watch the pennies and got well stuck into the ale. Now you might think, with so many bands playing that the lasting memory would be the music. On the Saturday, though, the only bands I can really remember were Rory Gallagher, who got the crowd rocking and was amazing, and Stone the Crows, with Maggie Bell, who were even better.

Rod Stewart and the Faces were the last band on, and the Faces, when they were the Small Faces had always been one of my all-time favourites. Maybe it was a combination of not much kip and a full day on the ale, but after the first couple of songs I was curled up in my sleeping bag, bang out till the next morning.

The folk tent blew down during the night and was now probably wafting its way towards Skeggy.

Foam bath at The Great Western Express Festival, Bardney, Lincoln 1972

On Sunday morning we went to see the Bradford lads and were back outside doing the pass out sketch again.

With only two days of the festival left, the crowd outside was a bit thinner, but the tickets still flew out at a quid each, leaving us with another nice wedge. Sunday was an even bigger blur than Saturday, even though Slade, Status Quo and the Beach Boys played. The only act I can vaguely remember were a band called Brewers Droop. I even remember one of their songs *"It's not the meat it's the motion"* where the singer pranced up and down the stage brandishing a giant, erect, polystyrene stang.

After another night laid in a bed of mud and with no dry clothes to change into, we decided we'd had enough and after the dinnertime session in Lincoln we caught a train back to Sheffield, arriving home on Monday evening with more money than we'd set off with.

In the winter of 1972 the miners went on strike. Picket lines were set up at power stations, ports and coal yards. Schools, dependent on coal-fired heating were forced to close and factories laid off hundreds of workers. The grave diggers joined the strike, so nobody was allowed to die. It was quite exciting at first when the lights and the telly went off during the power cuts.

Mum and me sometimes sat in the candle-lit kitchen, singing songs to the accompaniment of my guitar. Boozers with electric beer pumps were forced to close when the power went off. Coal was in short supply, not for us though as a seam from the old Silkwood colliery ran at the back of Frith Wood, just a few hundred yards from our house. Macduff and me, armed with sacks and shovels dug out the coal from the banking on a bridal path at the side of the wood. The coal was a bit crumbly and discoloured, but it burned okay. As we dug deeper into the seam the coal became more solid. After a couple of days our coal sheds were full to the roof.

I'd been brought up with Labour Party principles and quite a few of my family, including my Granddad, my brother Tony, Uncle Chris and many more cousins and Uncles once worked down the pit, so I was sympathetic to the miners' cause. But Mac and me were a pair of unscrupulous bastards, and entrepreneurs that we were, we came up with the bright idea of selling the coal.

Remembering our Cammell's Row trolley building skills we hammered a cart together and attached it to an old pram chassis. The cart held four/six sacks, but it was still hard work dragging it through the paths in the wood. Once we reached the roads it became fairly easy.

We knocked on doors and the coal flew out at 50p a sack. The trouble was though, when we emptied the coal down the cellar grates it disintegrated when it hit the bottom.

We arrived at the bridal path one day to find half a dozen blokes digging out the banking. They'd cleared all the mud and clay away and were a good couple of yards into the coal seam. Pit-props held up the banking above the seam. The coal coming out now was like proper coal, black and solid. We got chatting to these blokes and found out they were striking miners. One of them said, "We've heard somebody going round the streets selling coal, if we find out who it is we'll kick their fuckin heads in, pass your sacks down lads, we'll fill them up for ya."

The Penthouse, another Pete Stringfellow enterprise was, as the name suggests housed on the top floor of a building on Dixon Lane in Sheffield city centre. Three flights of steep stairs with rock-star murals painted on the walls needed climbing to reach the club.

I'd been there a couple of times in 69-70 when it first opened, but I never really got on with the place. It was an up-market joint with dress restrictions, frequented by a mostly clique crowd of toffee-nosed birds and poseurs who were probably the last remnants of the Mojo set after it closed in 67. In 1972 the Penthouse changed owners and opened up as a rock club. With no dress code and a more relaxed atmosphere it attracted, let's say, a more down to earth clientele.

The DJ played a good mix of classic rock tracks, chart songs and a lot of the Glam-Rock stuff that peaked in 72-73. Live bands also performed in the nightclub. Our leather jackets and steel capped boots were now consigned to the wardrobe of history, replaced by satin coats, flares, sixteen button shirts with fly-away collars and platform shoes.

Not only did Austin's on the Moor sell all the latest gear, it also accepted provident cheques, so I usually shopped there. Just around the corner from Austin's, stood a great little boutique called 'Some kinda mushroom.' The shop sold some weird and wonderful shit. I owned three satin jackets at the time, a turquoise one that knocked me back about a tenner, a navy blue one – eight quid I think I paid for it. The best one though, a lovely gold-coloured little number scrounged off a mate, cost fuck all,

Clothes were really important, and I still got that unbeatable buzz of jumping out of the bath after work on a Friday evening and slipping on a brand-new latest style shirt or pair of kaks. But no way would I have a stayed in for a week or saved up to buy the trendiest stuff.

We were street, pub, club and terrace-wise, and when you're high on confidence you don't need to spend ten quid on a jacket or a new pair of platforms to pull a bird – and that's what nights out were all about: birds, booze and music. Birds could even be pulled in the boozer after an eight-hour stint in the steelworks or an afternoon shift down the pit; it weren't what you wore, but what you were.

Talking of platforms, Cuttsie, my next-door neighbour went off to Leeds to buy a pair of platforms, they cost him, wait for it… thirty-three quid.

"Ya must have gone fuckin mental," I said to him.

Our Friday night routine started at opening time (6 o'clock) in the Green Acres. 'The Ackers' as we called it, was a new boozer situated in a shopping precinct on the Green Lane end of Stonelow Road. The precinct was built on the very spot where the 'Crick-crock' our old football pitch once stood. The pub had only been open for two years and I'd been banned for one of them for fighting. A spot on, up to date juke box, made the Ackers *the* place to be; all the young kids used it.

At half seven, Moose, Sass and me pile into Johnny Walker's car for a lift into town. "Get Alvin on, Corn Merchant." I shout (Johnny's dad owned a shop in Unstone called Walkers Corn Merchants). Johnny doesn't need telling, he's already slipping the cassette into the player. It's Ten Years After recorded live at Woodstock. The Woodstock MC announces: "There are buses going out of Monticello everything's cool, everything's cool all around… ladies and gentlemen, Ten Years After." *I'm Going Home* blasts out from the car stereo.

After an unaccompanied guitar solo opening, nine minutes of pure, no fucking about, one hundred miles an hour, twelve-bar Rock 'n' Roll, kicks in.

To a thumping backbeat, Alvin Lee ad-libs lyrics from classic Rock tracks. *Blue Suede Shoes, Boom Boom, I Gotta Woman, Whole lotta Shakin and Baby Please Don't Go*. Halfway through, the track winds down. The band seems to be taking a rest and the handclapping Woodstock crowd are audible in the background. Just when you think it's all over, it takes off again into a blistering Gibson lead guitar solo finale that has us bobbing our heads like the Wayne's World dudes digging *Bohemian Rhapsody*.

"Look out baby I'm coming to get ya, one more time… going home."

We've barely got our breath back as Johnny drops us outside the Buccaneer on Leopold Street in Sheffield city centre. Johnny doesn't stay; he skids off to meet his bird. If the Penthouse is the club of time, the Bucc is the boozer. Housed in the basement of the Grand Hotel, this really is the place to be. The cave like arched entrance opens up at the bottom of a flight of stone steps. The décor in the dark subterranean bar is similar to the old Esquire club. Its swashbuckling pirate themes, fishing nets, mermaids, compasses, thick ships' rope, cutlasses and Jolly Roger's. 'Yo-ho-ho and a bottle of fuckin rum.'

Watney's Keg Red Barrel served in plastic glasses tastes like warm piss, but who gives a fuck? The atmosphere and the music is first class. The DJ must have every classic record ever cut. All the great 60s rock stuff from the Stones, the Beatles, the Who and Dylan. Obscure Pink Floyd tracks, weird shit from Van Der Graff Generator, Frank Zappa and the Grand Funk Railroad (Funky Train, Moose called them). The Velvet Underground, the Alex Harvey band, Family and the newer stuff from Bowie, Roxy Music and the likes. After an hour or so of swaying and fighting to get served, it's off on the circuit.

The Minerva, a fabulous rough and tumble old joint at the bottom of Charles Street sometimes had live bands playing on weekends. McCloskys Apocalypse, a popular Sheffield group consisting of three spaced-out, but musically accomplished nutters often played the Minerva. The singer, and electric

213

violin virtuoso, got up to all kinds of mad shit on stage including biting chunks out of pint pots. Moose, Sass and me squeezed in one Friday night at the back of the concert room as the band belted out a brilliant version of the Who's, *The Seeker*. *"I asked Bobby Dylan, I asked the Beatles, I asked Timothy Leary, but he couldn't help me either."* The front row of the audience sat only a couple of feet away from the stage. The band knew how to work the crowd and the Minerva buzzed as the singer pranced around the stage; he produced a bottle of petrol and took a large swig. Whipping out a cig lighter he blew out a stream of petrol and lit the fucker. A long-haired lad sat with a group of mates on the front table copped for it as one side of his hair went up in flames. The lad's mate emptied a pint over his friends head extinguishing the blaze. Then the lad whose hair caught fire (who now looked like Phil Oakey in an early Human League incarnation) lobbed his pint at the singer. The bass guitarist leapt off the stage and steamed into the group of lads and a full-scale brawl erupted. Moose, Sass and me held each other up, we were laughing so much.

The Nelson, another hairy, hippy haven on Furnival Gate boasted the best juke box in the northern hemisphere. As the Glam Rock scene kicked in, more and more Bowie freaks dressed like Spiders from Mars, happily mixed with the Zeppelin, Purple and Sabbath head bangers who frequented the joint.

We sometimes called in the Barleycorn, the only puff boozer in town. Big Doreen always propped up the bar. He wore thick-rimmed black specs with milk bottle bottom lenses. He might have talked like a queen, but he could kick like a mule. Nobody fucked with Doreen; well they did, obviously, what with him being a Perry Como, but nobody 'fucked' with him if you know what I mean.

The Albert stood bang across the road from the City Hall. Lumps of plaster hung from the walls and the toilet smelt like a swamp, but like most of the boozers on the route, the poky old dump had another excellent juke box. We'd hit the Penthouse before ten thirty, mainly for the free admission and cheap drinks. At that early hour though, most of the punters were girls; the lads usually arrived after the pubs shut.

The Penthouse walls are painted black, the seats, black, plastic-coated benches. It's loud, it's dark, it's dirty and it's dangerous, just as a nightclub should be. Roxy Music's swirling synthesized *Virginia Plain* purrs in the background like an alien spacecraft, *"Baby Jane's in Acapulco we are flying down to Riooooh."* Fuckin beautiful.

Our usual strategy was to chat up a couple of birds and arrange to meet them later. If nowt better could be pulled, the '2 o'clock emergencies' could be called on at the end of the night. Wafe and his younger brother Alex were usually in the club plus a few more lads we knew from the matches. If nowt could be pulled we'd jump a taxi back home; after a while the taxi drivers refused to take us to Dronny unless we paid up front. Moose and Sass didn't bother with taxis; they robbed cars for the journey home. They even stole a taxi one night.

'Chop' an old Blade buddy who I'd known since the 60s was the resident DJ at the Penthouse. One of Chop's fingers had been lopped clean off in an accident at work – hence the nickname. I always had a chat to him when I went in the club and I'd dropped his name on many occasions to gain free admission. You know the crack, "Has Chop put me on the guest list tonight? No? Well, he usually does; can you go and tell him Sharpy's here?" That did the trick, cos whoever was on the pay-in counter didn't want to scale ten thousand steps up to the nightclub. Chop, a small friendly, funny geezer was a ringer for Joey 'The Lips' Fagan, the laid-back horn player from the marvellous film *The Commitments*. Chop had all the patter you'd expect from a good DJ.

It's Thursday night in late 72, Moose and me are stood on the stage where the DJ's booth is housed, chatting to Chop about the Blades or some other shit, when Chop says, "Fuckin hell, look who's just walked in." We turn to see Gary Glitter with an entourage of about dozen followers entering the club. (I've got no idea what Gaz was doing in the Penthouse, maybe he'd done a gig in the area, but the drummer in the Glitter Band came from Sheffield, so it could have been him who brought them in.) With one hand already searching for Gazza's hit record, Chop grabs the microphone, turns down the music and turns on the spiel. Pointing to the bar area he shouts, "Rock 'n' Roll, Rooooock 'n' Rooooooll, a celebrity graces the Penthouse tonight… ladies and gentlemen… Gary Glitter." All the Penthouse punters look towards the bar where Gaz, his mates and a few groupies are stood. Gazza nods his head towards Chop and raises both his hands in a victory salute. Moose and me raise our hands in a 'fuck off' salute and give Gaz the rods, shouting, "Fuck off Glitter, ya fuckin wanker, fuck off." Gaz turns away.

"Fuckin hell, ya pair of bastards," Chop says, trying not to laugh as the drumbeat from *Rock 'n' Roll part one* kicked in. "You'll get me the fuckin sack." Would we have done the same if Dylan or the Stones walked in? Probably not, but I always knew there was something dodgy about that Glitter fucker.

Tiffany's night club on London Road with its pagoda style front entrance is a pretentious kinda place that tries to be up-market but fails miserably. It's plastic palm trees, fake fountains and shitty, rubber chicken in a basket type meals served in the exclusive Treetop lounge. The club employs a strict dress code of jackets, trousers, shirts and ties for the blokes. There's no restrictions for the birds though, a strand of cotton covering the slice is all that's required.

Like an early version of Roxy's 'Grab a Granny' night, on Thursdays, Tiffany's attracts a wide variety of loose ladies aged from fourteen upwards. There's married birds out for a quick shag, teenage tarts out for a slow one, ageing wallflowers desperately seeking romance and divorcees on the lookout for new dads to bring up their offspring. Mexican-tashed vultures dressed in crushed velvet jackets and flared beige slacks hover around the dance floor believing they're capable of pulling Miss Universe.

We'd been going to the club for a few weeks, for the simple reason a shag was almost guaranteed. We certainly didn't go for the music, the resident house band droned out classic shite, like *Knock Three Times On The Ceiling If You Want Me* and *Chirpy Chirpy Cheep Cheep*. Birds went to Tiffany's to get fucked; lads went to Tiffany's to fuck 'em.

In November 1972, I met a twenty-one-year-old divorcee there, called, how's about... Tiffany. Tiffany lived with her two mixed-race boys aged one and two, in two-up two-down terraced slum, not too far from the Lane. She shared the house with another divorcee who had a mixed-race young girl. The house can only be described at best, as a festering, stinking cess pit. It was fuckin disgusting. There were dirty nappies, tins of rotting food, half-full bottles of sour, green milk and other shit piled up and strewn around every room. It made our old house on Cammell's Row look like a display room at Ponsfords. So what did I do? Like a fuckin idiot, I got involved.

There was something about Tiffany, though, something dark, dangerous, and exciting, something that fascinated me, something that made me look past all the shit, the stink and the squalor surrounding her. Could it have been the twinkle in her roving eye? Her voice maybe? She spoke with a lovely middle-class accent. Sex-wise Tiffany had been around the world, I'd been to the bottom of our garden, maybe that had something to do with it.

It was strange and maybe a little sad how she'd sunk as low as she did, as she came from a well-to-do, respectable family who lived in the Midlands. She'd had a strict Catholic upbringing and attended convent school. At the age of eighteen on a family holiday she'd met a lad from Sheffield. She just left everything, never said a word to her parents and eloped with the lad. He dumped her after a few weeks, and she dossed around in various shit-holes. Her parents spent weeks looking for her until she finally contacted them to tell them she was safe.

She started hanging out in an Arab cafe where she met and married a Somalian/Arab. The A-rab, she told me, treated her like shit when he was in a good mood and knocked the fuck out of her when he wasn't. He dumped her after she became pregnant for a second time. What the fuck was I thinking about? I had no reason whatsoever to get involved, I was having a great time, out every night boozing, fucking and fighting. I'm twenty-one years old, going on fifteen. I knew nothing about women and even less about relationships; the longest I'd ever stayed with a bird was about an hour and a half, now I'm mixed up with a tattooed divorcee with two kids – two black kids and I'm still a little kid myself. Even though I knew black lads from the matches and downtown, the stigma was evident and racism (especially in Dronny) was still rife. White bird, tattoos, black kids and what have ya got?

Months later when I eventually ventured out with Tiffany and the kids, I still felt ashamed the kids were black. I tried to dilute the embarrassment by telling my mates she'd been married to a half-caste; I emphasized the word married, so it didn't seem as bad. Paranoia set in, I could sense people looking at me and talking behind my back. Fuck knows what my mates thought about it or why none of them said, "What the fuck are you doing with her?" But I wouldn't have listened.

When Tiff's Mum, Dad and family got to know me, they treated me like royalty. They saw me as the white knight who'd rescued their little girl from the evils clutches of the infidels. I must have been semi-serious because I took her up to meet my Mam. After a chat with Mum in the kitchen we went into the front room, playing records and passing time until we could get down to the business on the settee. Mum always went to bed when the telly finished around midnight. 12 o'clock rolled around and I nipped in the kitchen and said to her.

"In't it time ya went to bed, Ma?"

"I'm just having my hot milk," Mum said. Ten minutes later I heard her shuffling around, so I went back in. "I'm just having a tidy round," Mum said. You crafty old bugger I thought. Another ten minutes passed, and I heard her shut the kitchen door, she's on her way to bed at last. The front room door opened and just Mum's head popped round.

"Don't forget to take your false tooth out before you go to bed, Ron. I don't want you choking to death in the middle of the night. I'll say goodnight then. Goodnight," Mum said as she closed the door. Tiffany and me doubled up laughing. Luckily I'd told Tiff about my zoobie or I think I might have choked my Mam to death in the middle of the night.

Inside the Bucc

Chapter 4

Take me for a trip upon your magic swirling ship

Shites McGregor invited me to a party at his mate's house up Dronfield Woodhouse. I'd known Shites for a few years through our love of music and he often came up to our house on Sunday afternoons for a jam session on the guitars. Shites told me to bring my guitar as there'd be a few lads there who played, and we could all have a jam. Tiffany was staying at our house for the weekend, so I took her along.

The place was rocking when we arrived; all the rooms in the large house were packed to capacity. The party-goers were the kind of freaks you always seemed to see at early 70s party's. Student, post hippy, anti-war demonstrating, army greatcoat wearing, raggy bearded, Pink Floydy, Rick Wakemany types.

Digger Dickinson a mate I'd known from the mid-60s turned up at the party. I'd not seen him for a while, as Digger was a wanderer. He'd announce out of the blue, "I'm fucking off for a bit next week." Digger travelled alone to whatever destination took his fancy. He'd just throw some things in a bag and shoot off for a few months to anywhere in Europe or places further afield. In an amazing coincidence Digger once decided to go to Australia, where he'd lived as a youngster. He hitched down to Southampton and boarded a boat to the other side of the world. On board he bumped into two other Dronny lads (one of them is now my brother-in-law) who were doing the same thing. They all stayed for over a year.

Digger and me had a good old chinwag, mostly football banter as he was a staunch Wednesdayite. Two lads were strumming away in one of the downstairs rooms. One of these lads was shit hot. His fingers glided along the fretboard producing some marvellous licks. I joined in and started playing some 12-bar blues. Shit-hot picked up on it straight away and we jammed along for a good half hour.

Someone in the room rolled a joint and Digger and me took a few tokes. At the time I hardly ever smoked dope. Weed, known then as 'grass' or 'bush', wasn't too potent and half the weight was made up with hemp seeds. The stronger resins of Paki or Afghan Black and Lebanese Red were usually used by students and the middle classes. Cannabis use amongst the footie lads was rare; although Herman, Dink and Wafe, through their association with the Hell's Angels had the gear on occasions. After ten minutes Digger and me chilled and sat giggling in the corner. A lad came in the room, picked up my guitar and attempted to play. The strings on my old log were raised about half an inch from the fretboard, no one, unless their fingertips were made of plate steel could play it.

"I can't play this," he said, "The strings are too tight." He looked like he was about to burst into tears. This reduced me to fits of laughter. Another lad came into the room carrying a bottle of gin and offered it round. It came to me and I said, "No thanks pal, I don't like gin; it tastes like perfume."

"This is special gin," he said. "You'll like this." I took a guzzle and passed it on to Digger. There's nowt fuckin special about this I thought, it tasted like shit. Everyone left the room leaving just Digger, Tiffany, myself and the bottle of gin. The bottle still held an inch or two of liquid and Digger and me both grimaced as we took another swig, Tiff said she didn't want any.

We finished the bottle, the room filled up again and another jam session started. After half an hour or so things started getting a bit weird. I'd stopped playing the guitar and stared intensely at a picture on the wall; the figures in the painting sempt to be moving. The empty gin bottle lay on the floor between Digger and me. Digger brought me out of my trance by saying, "Pass me the bottle Ron."

"It's empty," I said.

"No, it's full," Digger said.

I passed Digger the bottle, he held it to his lips, tilted it back and took a long imaginary swig. "See," Digger said. "I told you it was full, have a swag." I took the bottle and did the same.

"Have you ever seen a bottle as full as that Ron?" Digger said.

"No, I haven't Dig. It's the fullest bottle I've ever seen," I answered. We passed the bottle back and forth making gulping sounds as we supped the invisible spirit.

"Oh bottle of gin, you are so full," Digger said.

"You are the fullest bottle of gin in the world," I said. Tiffany looked at us as though we'd gone mad and indeed we had. We carried on paying homage to the gin bottle until the laughter took over. Now this laughter was like no other laughter I've ever experienced. Stomach clutching, rib busting, eye running, snot dropping hilarity. I crawled out of the room on my hands and knees to escape it. I caught a fleeting glimpse of Shites as he floated past me in the hallway. The laughter stopped, and I needed another fix, so I crawled back into the room. Digger's eyes turned an intense shade of blue, he looked almost serene. It was like I was in the presence of some higher being. As soon as he saw me, Digger burst into laughter, which broke the spell and set me off again. I scrambled back out and now faced a dilemma: I didn't want to be on my own, but I really thought if I laughed any more it would kill me. I made it back into the room and then the fear started.

Tiffany spoke to me, but I couldn't make out what she said: her voice sounded like a 45-record played at 33. Her mouth seemed to have moved from the centre, to the right-hand side of her face, it looked like she was having a stroke. What the fuck's going on? I'd smoked marijuana before, but I'd never felt like this. I held on a while longer hoping this terrible feeling would disappear, but it got worse.

Digger's still sat on the floor with a spaced-out grin on his face.

"I've got to get out of here," I said. Tiffany didn't want to leave, but I said, "You do what you want, I'm fuckin going." Tiffany and me walked out and Digger followed. Out in the street I looked at Tiffany and it was like I could see inside her mind. Now I don't really know if she was just smiling, but I said to her: "What the fuck are ya laughing at me for?"

"I'm not laughing at you," she said. Her mouth twisted to one side again. All I could think was, she's fuckin evil, she's the devil.

"Get away from me, you evil bastard," I shouted.

Digger piped up with, "It's the old, old story; it's the old, old story."

We walked onto Carr Lane where a Transit van full of mates who'd been boozing out in Derbyshire pulled up at the side of us.

I was still shouting, "Keep away from me you evil cunt," at Tiffany and Digger was still mumbling, "It's the old, old story."

The lads told us to jump in for a lift into Dronny. Inside the van things got worse. I had this horrible feeling Tiffany was going to push me out of the back door. I'd be laid bleeding to death in the road while she went off and fucked all my mates. I pressed my back hard against the side of the van, so she couldn't get behind me. Lads were dropped off one by one and Digger left us with, "It's the old, old story." This made me feel slightly better, because the fewer lads there were in the van, the less would be able to fuck Tiff. We were dropped off outside our house and I felt relieved to be still alive. I shouted, "I knew what you were planning, you evil bastard but you didn't get did me did you?"

Fuck knows what Tiffany must have been thinking. We went in our house and into the front room. I shouted Mum in and said to her, "Look Mam, you've got to tell me the truth." I pointed to Tiffany and said, "Is she evil?"

Mum looked at Tiffany for a few seconds as if she was sizing her up. "Yes she is," Mum answered. So I hadn't gone mad, my Mam could see the evilness as well.

"Oh no," I sobbed. "She's the devil." Again, what must have Tiffany thought with my Mother saying she was evil?

"He's been smoking cannabis," Tiffany said to Mum. My mother's mouth seemed to distort as she said, "Have you been taking drugs?"

"Fuck off, both of you," I shouted. "You're the devil," I said, pointing to Tiffany. "And you're in fuckin league with devil," I said, pointing to Mum. That was the first time I'd ever said fuck in front of my Mum. I moved to the corner of the room, wailing like a little kid and sat with my back to the wall so they couldn't get behind me.

"I'm phoning the doctor," my Mother said. We didn't have a phone, so Mum went round to our next-door neighbours to phone the doc.

After what sempt like hours, but was only maybe half an hour so, a pissed-off looking Doctor Green – who'd never smiled in his life arrived. I'm still sat in the corner rambling on about devils, demons and shit. The reefer madness I'd always feared had taken over. Tiffany told Greenhanger about the cannabis.

"Are you sure it's all he's taken?" he asked Tiffany. She said it was.

"He must be having a psychotic reaction to the cannabis; it should wear off in a couple of hours." The really strange thing about the whole situation was, Tiffany and my mum were now talking to each other like they were best mates, while earlier Mum accused her of being evil, or did I imagine it all? My fucked-up head conjured up terrible notions, they were communicating through telepathy, planning to whisk me off to hell.

220

I sat in the corner until it came light in the morning. My mother had gone to bed and Tiffany was dossed out on the settee. My sanity returned, and I couldn't apologise enough to Tiff. I spent the whole of the next day (Saturday) feeling slightly fragile and embarrassed. I swore an oath I'd never touch cannabis again.

Shites came up to our house on Sunday afternoon and brought back my guitar I'd left at the party. I told him what happened.

"Fuckin hell," he said. "I can't understand it; you didn't have any of that gin that was going around did you?"

"Yeah I did," I told him.

"Fuck me, it was laced with Acid," Shites said. "One of my mates had a swig and he put his head in the washing machine for three hours, we couldn't get him out, he said it was incredible."

So that was L.S.D? Yeah, right, fuckin marvellous. Where were all the love vibes, butterflies and rainbows? It would be quite a few years until I took another vacation.

Trains to Blades away games late 60s

Chapter 5

(Golden) boots of Spanish leather

A double page article entitled, 'When the gold and silver boots crash in,' appeared in the *Sunday People* or it could have been the *News of the World*. The write-up told of a group of Blade hooligans who wore gold painted Doc Martens and Wednesday lads who wore silver ones. The story was hyped up and sensationalised as you would expect from a Sunday rag. I'd noticed a few lads at the Lane – no more than a dozen or so, who wore the gold boots. They were mainly young, mixed-raced suedeheads from Attercliffe and Darnall. The boots looked cool enough, worn by the right people with the right gear, Crombie's and turned up Levi's.

A few weeks after the story broke we played Derby County away. Everybody turned out for Derby. I arrived at the station just before dinnertime and couldn't believe the number of golden boots stomping around the concourse. We weren't catching the train until about one o'clock, so about ten of us decided to go and have a look in the Claymore to see if there were any Wednesdayites about. One of the lads brought along his mate, who I'd never seen before. This geezer really looked the part, standing over six feet tall and weighing in at around sixteen stone. He wore the hooligan attire of the day, scarf tied around his wrist, another hung off his belt and, on his feet – yes you've guessed it – a pair of size fourteen shiny golden Doc Martens.

No one was in the Claypit, so we walked back past the Top Rank and along the graffiti-covered walkway under Arundel Gate which came out at the top of Howard Street. Halfway along a group of a dozen or so Wednesday boys walking towards us came into view. They were about twenty yards away and I saw them ready themselves and start bouncing. I was at the front and as you do, I glanced over my shoulder to make sure everybody was ready.

I saw big golden boots stop dead in his tracks, whip off his scarves and push them under his jacket. Who the fuck have we got here? I'm thinking. This could have easily unnerved us and given the Wednesdayites a boost, so I shouted, "Fuckin come on," and ran towards them. The other lads were with me and I saw the first three or four Wednesday stand firm, but the others started to back off. As the front Wednesday lads saw their mates retreat, they turned and ran.

"What the fuck ya doing? Ya fuckin useless cunt," I shouted at golden boots. With his knees still knocking he muttered some feeble excuse. Another fuckin passenger.

Over the next few weeks it got ridiculous, every fucker wore golden boots. The boots were barely visible under some of the Kop singers' twenty-two-inch bottomed flares. Fashion conscious trendies wore them to complement their 50p-a-pair 'Bobby Washable' jeans, bought or lifted from Dempsey's clothing emporium on the Park Hill flats precinct. Young chabs, barely old enough to walk, rooted out their dad's five-sizes-too-big working boots, sprayed them up and swanned around the Shoreham thinking they were hard; talk about the power of the press eh?

With the Glam Rock movement at its peak, Marc Bolan became a rock god – the new Elvis. I couldn't help being a bit envious and jealous of the little fucker, who every bird in the world fancied. The whole scene came a bit too late for me and my mates. It wasn't cool to be into bands twelve-year-old girls were screaming and creaming at. We'd had our time; this was the music for a new generation of teenagers. We viewed it as a bit of a joke, especially Gary Glitter. I was never quite sure if Gaz was taking the piss, or if there was something wrong with the cunt.

Pop music always has, and always will be about sex and showmanship, but it didn't stop you wanting to kick some of the fucker's heads in, especially that bass player in the Sweet when he mimed, "We just haven't got a clue what to do," in *Blockbuster* on *Top of the Pops*.

Glam was the music of the time, though; played on the radio, on pub jukeboxes and in the night clubs we visited at least three times a week. Some of the songs were quite good and great fun for the young 'uns, but not something to get too excited about or to listen to at home; that pleasure was reserved for the wonderful Roger Whittaker.

When Slade first hit the scene in 71, their artificial skinhead look didn't seem quite right. Now glammed up to fuck, they were one of the most popular and successful bands around. They were more acceptable to me, mainly because of Noddy Holder's exceptional voice: a bit like John Lennon, only an octave higher. Slade wrote some marvellous stuff in the early 70s; some of the B sides, which I doubt most of the teeny-boppers who bought them ever even heard, were better than the A-sides, but I felt just a little bit too old to be into Slade.

Mud, the Rubettes and Showaddywaddy, all with a kind of parallel-universe 1950's look and sound, sat alongside Alvin (Coo-coo afuckin choo) Stardust, another 1950s throwback at the bottom of the Glam-Rock pile.

The Faces weren't really a Glam Rock band, even though they wore the satins and the silks. Musically they were far more accomplished than any of the others; *Maggie May* still stands out as one of the best singles ever made and I loved their *Gasoline Alley* album. The Faces were proper rockers with a pedigree dating back to the early 60s. They looked and sounded like they were enjoying themselves, having a laugh, a set of mates fuckin about. Rod Stewart was a pretty cool geezer, he looked like one of the lads, somebody from down the boozer, somebody who'd get pissed and probably have a scrap at the end of the night. His football loyalties need to be questioned though. I hated his celebrity-status association with the Scottish national football team; more so, because at the time, the Jock fuckers ran riot and took the piss every time they came to England. Even though his Dad was a Strap, he came from London for fuck's sake. His other teams were Man Utd and Celtic, nowt like edging ya bets, eh Rod? Why not chuck in Real Madrid, Inter Milan and Ben-fuckin-fica?

The Faces, used to be the Small Faces, so in my eyes, even without the greatest vocalist who ever lived, Stevie Marriott, they could do no wrong. The

Faces didn't really give a fuck and I could relate to that.

Maybe Rod should have done us all a favour by calling it a day after *You Wear it Well*. He carried on though and jumped on the mid-70s Disco bandwagon with the truly embarrassing *Da Ya Think I'm Sexy?* Could he have been taking the piss? I hope so.

Over the road from the Souvenir Shop 1970s

Chapter 6

I'm gonna grow my hair down to my feet, so strange, so I look like a walking mountain range

In the mid-60s we'd worn our hair long as a badge of rebellion. The establishment labelled us worthless, good-for-nothing, dirty, stinking, idle, fuckin layabouts. A couple of years later, in an amazing show of hypocrisy the skinhead's copped for the same shit. By 1973, it was quite acceptable, compulsory even, for sportsmen, newsreaders, show business entertainers, TV presenters, county councillors, coppers (excluding chief constables), prison guards, probation officers, doctors, school teachers, borough surveyors, solicitors, dads, uncles and all the rest of the fuckin two-faced system to grow their hair... and boy did they fuckin grow it. Even Bruce Forsyth had wig extensions.

There were still plenty of jobs around, but my stance against the establishment, coupled with me being an idle cunt, meant I spent quite a bit of time on the dole. We had to make do with my unemployment benefit and mum's Assistance money. Mum sometimes earned a few bob doing babysitting shifts, or a bit of cleaning for the neighbours, but there were times when we had no food in the house at all. If there was more than one tin of marrowfat peas in the pantry I thought Mum was stocking up for a nuclear war.

In the spring, summer and early autumn months, I could always earn a few bob golf ball hunting. Since being old enough to walk, I'd foraged around the gorse and holly bush-lined, immaculately groomed fairways of the private and exclusive, no-trespassing Hallows Golf Club. The golf course stood at the top of Hallows Rise (the steepest hill in Dronfield.) As a ten/twelve-year-old in the early 60s, I'd sat in line on the steps outside the clubhouse with half a dozen other urchins.

"Caddy, sir. Please, sir, caddy?"

Like slaves at an Alabama street market auction, our teeth, calf muscles and earlobes were checked out by the golfers. They kept us hanging for a few more seconds before deeming us worthy to hunk a bag of thirty-fuckin-seven clubs around the course for four hours.

The standard caddying fee was five bob (25 p). I soon learnt I could root out a dozen or so golf balls in half the time it took to caddy, earn more money and not have to listen to middle-class shite spouted by the golfers.

Well into the 70s, Moose and me paddled around the two small, evil-smelling, stagnant ponds that flanked the 16th hole, fishing out golf balls. It shows the calibre of the golfers up there when most weekends we could collect 50 to a 100 balls. The money from the golf balls funded our away trips or nights out. We sold the balls to Willie Marple's dad, Bill, who sold them on at a profit.

Bill, who earned a few bob teaching the sport, would rattle on for ages about golf. He'd tell us in detail about the day he shot a 66 in 1948 using only a Mashy Niblick and how he taught Arnold Palmer to get out of bunkers. For fuck's sake Bill, just give us the fuckin money before the boozers shut.

We were sat in Bill's front room one evening watching him sort through, grade and price-up the balls. 15p for a brand-new Dunlop 65, 12p for a scuffed one. 10p for a new Penfold, 8p for a Ben Hogan (an American ball, slightly bigger than the English version) 6p for a Slazenger, down to 2p for a remould and a penny for balls that were cut to fuck or had turned black, due to being stuck in pond mud for ten years.

Moose worked at the time as an apprentice at a pork butcher's shop on Whittington Moor in Chesterfield. Moose ate loads of pork, which must have done something bad to his insides, making his farts smell fuckin wicked. Moose let rip a long, slow disgusting fart. Bill ran to the window, heaving and gasping for breath. He went crazy and banished Moose from his house telling him never to return.

The next time I went up, Bill couldn't quite get his head around what Moose had done. He said to me, "What kind of a man farts in another man's house? Don't ever bring him again."

I sometimes did a few days graft with Cisco Morris, a mate who worked as a delivery driver for Gunstones bakery. His shift started at five o'clock in the morning and it nearly killed me having to rise in the middle of the night.

Cisco had a great little fiddle on when we delivered to the big shops in Sheffield city centre. We'd carry in the trays holding a dozen loafs which were stacked onto shelves in the store rooms. None of the shop workers or gaffers ever bothered us, or even gave us a second glance; we were just the delivery boys, dressed in brown Gunny's smocks bringing in the bread, two or three times a week. A foreman-supervisor checked the delivery by counting up the empty trays, a lot easier than having to fuck about counting each individual loaf. If there was say, ten trays, he would pay for one hundred and twenty loafs. The supervisor had no idea we'd slipped in at least one, sometimes two empty trays inside the full trays. So we were paid for twelve or twenty-four extra loafs. We could only do this in shops taking large orders. We obviously couldn't do it in the shops that only took a couple of trays. Cisco sold off the spare loaves to other shops.

We'd finish the round just after dinnertime or early afternoon. Cisco would drop me off with a couple of loaves and two or three trays of half a dozen cakes and pastries, plus a few bob from the fiddle money.

Cisco, a couple of years younger than me, was an ordinary-looking lad, small, about my height, 5'6, maybe a bit smaller. He dressed fairly well, smart, but not too flash. Cisco however was an unlikely-looking fanny magnet. Was it his good looks, his *Hi Karate* after-shave, hairy chest, giant stang, his charm maybe? Was it fuck. Cisco possessed a secret weapon, or, to be more precise, secret weapons that made the ladies drool whenever we hit the night clubs. What were these secret weapons, Ronald? I hear you all ask; well, Cisco had a pair of magic feet. He could boogie better than Fred Astaire on methamphetamine.

Within seconds of him taking to the dance floor, he'd be surrounded by a selection of slice. Keeping perfect time, Cisco-the-Disco twisted and twirled like a human spinning top, while I stood on the side lines feeling like a twat but trying to look cool doing the old toe and heel. Three or four birds vying for Cisco's attention meant some of the fuckers would end up unlucky or lucky as far as I was concerned. I never failed to pull when out on the town with Cisco.

On the way to the Top Rank one Thursday night, Cisco and me called in the Wimpy Bar at the top of Fargate. For all you younger readers out there, Wimpy bars were early versions of McDonalds, but the burgers didn't taste like shit and were strangely addictive. When the burger and chips arrived I looked at the meagre portion of about half a dozen chips and said to the waitress, "Narthen love, you've forgotten the chips."

"That's the set amount," the waitress replied.

"What six fuckin chips?" I said.

"It's one scoop per meal and I don't want to listen to that language," she said.

"Well, fuck off, then," I shouted.

After wolfing down the scran, I thought: right ya bastards, I'm going to put a dent in Wimpey's multi-million-dollar profit margin and slipped the knife and fork into my jacket pocket. I bet the cutlery weren't even made in Sheffield. We left the Wimpy and walked down Norfolk Row towards the Rank. Halfway down, whilst stopping for a piss at the side of a wall, I saw a cop car appear at the top of the street. The coppers saw me pissing and skidded towards me. I thought about the knife and fork in my pocket and ran towards the bottom of Norfolk Row to sling them. As I reached the Holy Chapel of Saint Marie I tried to throw the fuckers over the church roof. The building stood about fifty-foot-high, though, and the knife and fork hit the wall and bounced back into the street.

The coppers caught me and led me towards the cop car. They asked me why I had the knife and fork and why I'd tried to throw them away.

"I must have just picked them up from the Wimpy by mistake," I said.

"Right," the copper said, "you're under arrest for urinating in the street and theft." They put me in the back seat of the cop car, but I opened the opposite side door, jumped out and ran like a bastard back up towards Fargate. They caught me before I reached the top and this time, they handcuffed and rammed me back in the car. For some reason Cisco got in the car and came with me to the cop shop, maybe he thought they were just going to take my name and let me go?

Inside the station they took off the cuffs. What made me flip I'll never know. I'd been here before and was clued up and just about sober enough to keep my gob shut, but one of the coppers who'd arrested me said something, and I punched him in the mouth.

I was wrestled to the ground, kicking and screaming by three or four coppers. I went crazy and booted one of the coppers on his knee. He hopped around on one leg, yelling in pain. They eventually overpowered me and held me face down.

"What are you doing knocking about with him? He's mental," I heard one of the coppers say to Cisco.

"He's not really a mate; I don't know him that well," Cisco lied. Fucking hell Cisco, thanks for the support pal. I couldn't really blame him though.

"Well, he's not going anywhere, so you get yourself off, son," the copper said to Cisco.

The coppers dragged me by my feet into a room at the side of the desk sergeant's counter; I've no idea why they didn't take me to the cells. Inside they laid into me, particularly the one I'd booted. He sat on top of me and pummelled my face in. I tried to fight back and managed to get a few punches in. All the buttons on my white shirt were ripped off and the penny round collar hung by a thread. The scene from *A Clockwork Orange*, when little Alex suffered the same fate at the hands of the Millicent's, came into my head. This gave me an unexpected buzz and for a few brief seconds I actually enjoyed it.

"Come on ya bastards, I'll fuckin kill ya," I shouted.

I can't really remember what happened next, whether I asked for hospital treatment, or the coppers realised what they'd done and just took me there, but there I was, covered in blood, sat in the casualty department of the Royal handcuffed to a copper.

The copper who I'd booted limped along to get his leg looked at. I kicked off again by tugging at my handcuffed wrist and shouting at passing nurses and other casualties of the night, "Look what the bastards have done to me." But it just made my wrist hurt.

"Stop showing off," the copper shouted.

"Fuck off ya cunt," I shouted back. A nurse arrived, took me in a room and put a couple of stitches in my forehead. The scars in the corner of my lip from the car crash opened up and needed re-stitching.

Back outside the copper who I'd booted said, "Look, if you calm down for a minute, we can come to a compromise. You could be in serious trouble for assaulting a police officer. It'll be jail for certain, but I'll not say anything about my injuries if you don't say anything about yours, we'll just charge you with drunk and disorderly and you'll get a fine."

Now hindsight is a fine thing and I should have said, "Fuck off, because you could be in serious trouble for smashing my fuckin face in," but I didn't. I'd started to sober up and I just wanted to get home.

"Drunk and disorderly is that it?" I said. "That's it," the copper said.

They took me back to the nick and locked me up for the night. Next morning I faced the magistrates looking like a war victim. I pleaded guilty to the D and D and received an £8 fine. Not a bad result really, because even though I'd had my head pummelled in I'd managed to injure a couple of coppers.

I'm gonna jump ahead a little here and move into the early 80s, April 1982 to be exact. The Blades were playing Bournemouth at the Lane in the old 4th Division. On my way to London Road a couple of hours before the game, I crossed Bramall Lane onto John Street at the side of the Cricketers. A police van containing about ten coppers pulled up at the side of me. A sergeant sat in the passenger's seat wound down the window and shouted, "Oi, I see your face still hasn't healed up."

"What ya on about?" I answered.

"You don't remember me, do you? But I remember you, ya little cunt," the copper said.

Who the fuck's this? I'm thinking. Then it hit me, it's the bastard who'd battered me all them years ago. I gave him a smirk and said, "Fuck off ya piece of shit."

"Do you fancy your chances?" he said.

"What ya gonna do, get ya mates to hold me down again?" I said. I knew exactly what the cunt was after and I walked away. The van drove slowly at the side of me, with the sergeant and his mates shouting shit out of the window. Don't bite, I thought and crossed the road. The van drove off and I could see the coppers laughing through the windows.

At the game, I'm stood on the Lane end with a few mates. The sergeant appeared on the pitch perimeter and I saw him point me out and guide a couple of coppers who were stood near us towards me. The coppers grabbed an arm each and led me down to the front and over the railings.

"You just can't keep out of trouble, can you?" he said to me. Again, I kept my cool as they led me to the detention room on the corner of the South Stand.

There were no luxuries in the lock up; it was just a concrete room with no seats. I stood with three Bournemouth fans and Gary Kisby, one of the young BBC lads, who'd also been removed from the Lane end. We chatted and had a laugh together and when the game ended we were all released without charge. On the way out, the sergeant pulled me to one side and told me, "I'll be keeping my eye you, lad." Fuckin coppers, eh! Don't you just love 'em?

Dick Dung weighed about six stone wet through, but whether out on the streets, in the pubs and clubs, or on the football terraces he held no fear and would have a pop at anybody.

We're at Filbert Street and it's about twenty minutes from the end of the game when three or four Leicester lads appear across the street from the away end exit gates. The gates usually opened about ten minutes before the matches ended to let out the early leavers. There were always a few young kids stood outside at every ground hoping to catch the last bit of the game for free.

The coppers still weren't clued-up enough to stop mobs of hundreds, walking from one end of the ground to the other and charging in when the gates opened.

The Leicester boys were obviously waiting for more of their mates – and for the gates to open. From the back of the away end, over a wall about 12/15 foot-high we could see out into the street. We exchanged a few threats, and the Leicester lads, thinking they were safe because the gates were shut, were full of it.

"Fuck this," Dick shouted and in one swift movement he's up and over the wall. He splattered on all fours but jumped straight back on to his feet and laid into the Leicester boys. We ran down and forced the gates open, to see Dung chasing them down the road.

In October 73 returning from a League Cup night game at West Brom, I heard for the first time the term 'Pigs' From the late 50s when I first started supporting United, all through the 60s and up to that time I'd never heard either Blade or Owl use the word. Two young Blades sat in the seat in front of me, engaged in conversation kept referring to 'Pigs' I leaned over and asked them what they meant.

"It's Wednesday," one of them said. "There're fuckin pigs."

"Why do you call 'em pigs?" I asked. "Don't know," one of them answered. "But they are fuckin pigs, that's all there is to it."

Over the next months the term became more and more common, and within a year or, so many Blades used it. I even started calling Wednesday mates and referring to Wednesday as pigs.

"What ya calling Wednesday pigs for?" they asked.

"Cos they are fuckin pigs," I answered.

A fanzine called 'The red and white wizard' appeared around the downtown boozers in the mid-70s. One issue showed a photo of the Wednesday team with pig's heads superimposed on the players.

Years, and I'm talking ten/fifteen years later, always quick on the uptake, Wednesdayites started calling Blades fans and the team, pigs. Forever a million miles behind in originality and innovation, a photo of the Blades team did the rounds and guess what? The players had pig's heads.

I've no idea why they couldn't come up with their own insult; 'Blind mole rats' 'Three-fingered sloths' 'Slimy slugs.' Anything, but no, "They call us pigs, so we'll call them pigs." Quite amazing really. The impact of the slur has completely vanished, as thousands of both Blade and Wednesday internet message board gimps use the word (or associated words, like, grunter, swine, snortbeast, truffle hunter and porker) in every other sentence.

Portman Road Ipswich. After smashing up a boozer near the ground called the Sporting Bumpkin, for no particular reason, a few hundred Blades take their places on Ipswich's Kop. Roughly the same number of Ipswich's mob stand a yard or so away with a few police trying to keep order.

"Eye-eye-eye-eye Ipswich Republican Army, wherever we go we fear no foe cos we are the I.R.A," rings out from the Ipswich ranks. Fuckin good song I think to myself, very witty. The I.R.A. at the time were at their peak and everybody knew about the paramilitary group, the Irish Republican Army.

After a few more renderings of the song, one of the Blades bellows out, "Eye-eye-eye-eye Shoreham Republican Army, wherever we go we fear no foe cos we are the S.R.A." We all joined in and sang it for the rest of the game. From Suffolk back to South Yorkshire the song reverberated around our coach. Blatant song theft of the highest order, but fuck it, fans stole songs from each other all the time. Over the next few months the song, but more predominantly the term, S.R.A. Shoreham Republican Army, became used more and more.

It's the new name for the mob: S.R.A. began to appear felt tipped on boozer bog walls and spray-painted on buildings around town. Eternally quick on the uptake, Wednesdayites, who in the early 70s decided in their wisdom to rename their Penistone Road end Kop 'East Bank' (stolen from either Arsenal's North Bank or West Ham's South Bank, take your pick) began to call their mob the 'East Bank Republican Army' how the fuck did they think of that? Well fair enough, we'd nicked it from Ipswich, but swiping songs and terms from your closest rivals, well that's as low as robbing the last threepenny bit from your blind grandma's purse. No Blade would ever dream of singing anything Wednesday sang first.

From the late 60s we were the 'Shoreham Boys' or the 'Shoreham Boot Boys.' Shoreham, a small sea-side resort in West Sussex had nice ring to it, yeah Shoreham: fuckin cool. Shoreham: two syllables, all the best ends were two syllables: Stretford, Kippax, Leazes, Holgate, Boothen, Fullwell, Park Lane Gelderd etc. We identified ourselves with the name of our end and we knew the names of all the other team's ends.

We were lucky the Lane hadn't been built a few yards further down or we would have been called the Charlotte Bootboys. Now it would have been slightly confusing for the Wednesdayites to call themselves the 'Penistone Bootboys'. Penistone, a small village north of Sheffield on the road to Barnsley, no, not fuckin cool.

I'm certain that if Penistone Boot Boys had been sprayed on a wall the 'tone' bit would have been erased, but enough of this frivolous shit. Wednesdayites, unoriginal, copying, dirty thieving, stinking bastards they are, burgled our name, just like they'd always robbed our songs and our chants.

I'd made no arrangements for a meet up with the lads for a County Cup game with Wednesday at Hillsborough in January 74. I'd missed the last home game, so it must have been about a three weeks since I'd seen any of the boys. Hardly anybody owned a phone, so if a meet had been sorted I knew nothing about it. Instead I met up with a lad who was knocking Tiff's married best mate off. I'd been for a drink with him and the birds a couple of times, but he hardly spoke a word. We were both Blades, but that's the only thing we had in common.

A small part of me started to question the antics I was getting up to at the games. At twenty-three years old, I thought maybe I'm getting a little bit too old for all this shit. Most of my Dronny mates packed in getting involved in the trouble and just went to the games to watch the football. I never spoke about the things I got up to at the matches, except to hooligan mates.

I met Chatting Mick in the Penny Black at twelve o'clock and after numerous failed attempts trying to engage him in conversation, I started to get a little bit pissed off. Fucking hell I'm thinking, what the fuck am I doing here? Mick told me he'd arranged to meet two Wednesdayite mates in a pub on The Wicker at one o clock. Well, I thought, even though they're Wednesday they've got to be a bit more interesting than this cunt. After a silence that lasted a good couple of minutes, but felt like an hour, he finally spoke, "My sister's got a dog." All right, here we go, it's not mind-bending stuff, but at least it's a start.

"Oh, as she?" I answered. "What sort?"

"Don't know," he said. "But it's got reight big paws."

"Right," I said, waiting for the follow up, but none came.

One o'clock finally arrived and we set off for the Bull and Mouth. The two Wednesdayites were from the same planet as Mick-gormless oblivion. We caught the bus up to Hillsborough and passed the Victoria boozer on Penistone Road, a few coppers were stood outside. All the windows were missing, broken glass, pint pots and bits of furniture littered the street. This got my juices flowing and I thought what the fuck am I doing sat here missing all the fun?

We reached the ground about fifteen minutes before kickoff and entered the open Kop in the bottom corner (I always wanted it to piss down with rain at Wednesday home games, so the bastards would get drenched.) I looked up to see a mob of Blades numbering 300-400 at the back of the Kop. A bigger mob of roughly 600 Wednesdayites stood to their left. I'd enough of the three stooges and made my way up to join the Blades.

I expected to see Stocksy and the Darnall lads, the Cromford Street boys and the other usual suspects. Moose, the main man, was working away at the time, stitching mail bags in the North Sea Camp detention centre. I pushed my way through to the front line. A squad of thirty or so coppers, truncheons drawn, stood in a line trying to keep the rival fans apart. There were a few familiar Blade faces, but none of the main lads.

The Wednesdayites were in the ascendancy, trying to force their way through the police. Blades had a more laid-back approach, the front line stood with arms outstretched as if to say, "We're here, on your end, come and shift us."

Just before kickoff about fifteen to twenty of what must have been Wednesday's main boys appeared. These fuckers really looked the part and were well up for it. One in particular, a short stocky cunt with greasy black hair, went ape-shit as he tried to force his way through. He didn't give a fuck; the police kept pushing him back, but, egged on by his mates, back he came again and again. This gave the Wednesday mob a boost and more and more tried to break through the police line. The police didn't seem bothered about arrests; they just wanted to keep us from killing each other. I thought we're in grave danger of getting fucked here. I could see a few Blades losing it, moving further back. By this time we're outnumbered by at least two to one.

"Fuckin come on lads," one of the Blades shouted and we made a surge forward through the police. We had to, just to show the bastards we were up for it. We exchanged a few punches before the coppers forced us apart. The coppers waded into the Wednesday mob with batons drawn forcing them back. The main Wednesday boys and their leader were still going crazy, urging each other on, like they could sense the day was going to be theirs. Again I thought, we've got to try to keep it together or we're going to get fucked for certain.

A gap of a few metres formed between the two mobs. Greasy's still stood at the forefront, arms outstretched issuing threats. All eyes are on him; his mates are patting his back and encouraging him, he's invincible... and then, a tallish, but slightly built, blond haired Blade who I'd never seen before, moved along from the top bit of the Kop into no-man's land. He looked like the angel from the film Barbarella. He wore a sheepskin coat and a red and white woolly scarf, folded over at the neck with the Sheffield coat of arms badge stitched on. He didn't really look the part, but never has an appearance been so deceptive. Who's this fucker? I'm thinking and what the fuck is he going to do?

Greasy, his arms still outstretched, sneered and clenched his fists as the angel moved towards him. In one swift movement the Blade shot forward and delivered the most excellent head butt I've ever seen. Johnny Quango – eat your fuckin heart out. The crack was beautiful, it sounded like willow smacking a cricket ball to the boundary. Greasy's legs wobbled, his knees buckled, his eyes rolled and closed as his head slumped forward. His mates managed to hold him up by his arms before he collapsed. The angel calmly walked back into the Blade ranks, even the coppers looked impressed. What made it so much sweeter was the fact that the greasy, gobby bastard had so much front. Fuckin marvellous, I thought, I wish I'd had the balls to have done it.

With their leader fucked, the rest of the Wednesday boys didn't seem quite so keen. Greasy, no doubt seeing stars and little bluebirds fluttering around his shattered ego disappeared from the scene. But it wasn't long before we came under attack again. The Wednesday boys with the numbers in their favour made repeated attempts to get into us, but we hung on in there until the end of the game. The match ended goalless and went to penalties. I didn't give a fuck about the score and I left the ground with about forty other blades before the shootout started. We walked a few hundred yards down Penistone Road and jumped on a bus back to town. I learned from one of the lads on the bus, around a hundred Blades met-up in town and battled at the Victoria boozer, before the coppers came and broke it up.

It had been quite a day, leaving me much to ponder. We'd been on the back foot for the first time ever at Hillsborough, the only face saver being the head-butting angel. That lad alone did what every Blade, me included should have done. If we were going to walk the walk and talk the talk, we shouldn't have to rely on others to do it for us. Next time I promised myself, I'm gonna be a little bit braver.

We'd done well to hang in there, considering the numbers, but where were all the lads? A few hundred at Hillsborough four years ago had been enough, but the times they were a-changing. Our numbers were starting to dwindle, as Wednesday's increased, it needed sorting fast, the question was though, were we capable of sorting it? A few months later at a testimonial game against Wednesday at the Lane, things would get even worse.

Alan Woodward (Woody) a strong and powerful barrel-chested, right winger had been a great servant to the club. He'd joined the Blades straight from school and made his first team debut in 1964. Labelled a bit 'nesh' by the Lane regulars when he first started, Woody soon won the crowd over by scoring some spectacular long-range screamers plus a few straight from corners, as well as laying on scores of goals for the rest of the Blades forward line. Not once, though, in his long and distinguished career had the ball ever touched Woody's silver scone. His testimonial in early May came two weeks after the 73-74 season finished.

I'd not seen any of the lads since the last home game of the season three weeks earlier. No meet up, as far I knew had been arranged, but its Woody's testimonial, surely everybody gonna be out for this one?

I knew I needed to be a bit careful; I was on bail at the time charged with malicious wounding and criminal damage. The fight started at the Hofbrauhaus – our regular Thursday night drinking den.

The Hofbrauhaus, a massive, rip-roaring, German style bierkeller on Arundel Gate held a couple of thousand punters. The only drink on sale was strong Bavarian ale served in heavy stein glasses holding either half or one litre. Fuck knows how the waitresses carried about five of the fuckers in each hand. An oompah band dressed in traditional German costume (kurze lederhosen, white shirts and feathered hats) provided the music. Coach loads of hen parties, stag nights and birthday bashes travelled from all over the region and further afield to dance on the long wooden tables and to party the night away.

The best thing, apart from all the loose women was the free beer. We had the fine art of 'minesweeping' off to a tee. As the punters danced merrily away on the tables, we walked in between them and lifted their ale, I don't recall ever buying a drink in the bierkeller.

Moose, me and four other Dronny lads got into an argument with a group of a dozen or so Wednesdayites who were out on a stag-do. A few punches were thrown before the bouncers broke it up and threw us all out. Despite being outnumbered the fight continued along Arundel Gate and around the corner onto Furnival Gate. We relished situations like this. I knew all the Dronny lads would stand together and nobody would run, no matter what.

A couple of the stag-do boys were already down making the others a bit hesitant. I was at it with one lad when Moose charged forward. His momentum carried all three of us straight through the plate glass door of an amusement arcade. Both my hands were bleeding badly, and blood squirted from a deep cut on Moose's arm, the lad lay unconscious in the doorway.

The sound of breaking glass and the screeching alarm freaked us all. We knew the coppers would be on the scene soon. It was every man for his self as we scattered in different directions. Moose and me ran up towards the Moor where a cop car skidded up at the side of us.

"We've just been attacked by a gang of lads," I told the copper. "They chucked us through a window."

"Get in lads," the copper said. "I'll take you to hospital." The copper sped off to the Royal. We told him a load of bollocks before we arrived in casualty. Moose's arm was in a bad way, still pumping blood as the nurses laid him on a trolley. I sat on a chair at the side of him.

After a few minutes an ambulance arrived and stretchered in the lad who'd gone through the window with us. A few minutes later half a dozen of his mates, along with two coppers walked in. We could see them pointing us out to the coppers. About four of them ran towards us. Despite our wounds we were up and into them. We backed them into the doorway and out to the street. The coppers broke it up and we were taken back inside. More coppers arrived, spoke to the lads and more fingers were pointed in our direction. A nurse took us away to be stitched up, and when we came out the copper who brought us in came over and said, "You've not been telling me the truth, you attacked them, you're both under arrest."

As we were taken out to the cop car we made another surge (ya know, the old bravado surge) towards the group of lads. We were cuffed, thrown in the back of the car and whisked off to West Bar cop station. After a couple of hour's interrogation in separate rooms we were locked up for the night. The next morning we were charged with malicious wounding. They threw in another charge of criminal damage (the glass door) for good measure, before we were bailed and released.

The case came up at the magistrates, where we pleaded not guilty. The court extended our bail and we were sent for trial at crown court. We were told by our brief, the lad who went through the glass door with us (the groom) was so badly injured his wedding had to be cancelled; he also told us we were in deep shit and to expect at least a year in jail. Within weeks Moose broke his bail by getting collared, along with Sass, for car theft. They were remanded to Armley jail until the trial came up.

Half an hour before kickoff at Woody's testimonial I walked alone into the Whetstone (now the Moorfoot Tavern). The Whetstone, one of our main meeting up boozers, was all but deserted. I sank a quick pint and thought I'd move on to the Sportsman.

As I walked along Bramall Lane I expected the street to be heaving with bodies heading for the game, but only a sprinkling of fans, the majority wearing blue and white were moving about. Is it Woody's testimonial or what? I'm thinking.

Denby Street, usually bustling ten minutes before kickoff was nearly empty. I called in the Sportsman but nobody's in there. Where the fuck is everybody? I left the pub as a group of about ten Wednesday lads walked passed. They stopped talking and even though I had no colours on, all eyes were on me. Instead of turning left towards the ground I turned right and walked a few yards up the road. Glancing over my shoulder, I saw them turn onto Bramall Lane before I doubled back. I fuckin don't believe this I'm thinking, everybody must be in the ground.

I entered the ground just before kickoff at the John Street turnstiles and joined a trickle of fans climbing the back steps. A couple of hundred Blades were stood in our usual place at the back of the Kop. A few of the lads were there: Lefty, Walt and Ray Williams, and couple more of the Darnall lads, the Cromford Street lads, Tabby Greenwood, his brother Steve, Razzy and the three Kelwick brothers, Alan, Gozzer, Pat, Bent Nosed Mitch, Gibby, Kingy, Herman, Stocksy and a few more: around thirty lads altogether. The rest were mostly young 'uns and singers, looking a tad uncomfortable as to our right stood a big mob of five hundred Wednesdayites.

The young 'uns, and I'm talking thirteen and fourteen-year-olds here, were a liability, and of little or no use in situations like this. They were well up for it against weak opposition or when the numbers were in our favour, but when it came on top, they panicked and ran, spooking the rest of mob. We'd all done it though, all gone through the learning process, it was all part of the game; their time would come. A large police presence, holding the Wednesdayites at bay were parked in between us. More Wednesdayites were arriving all the time.

So here we have it, Woody's testimonial, every Blade and their fuckin grandmothers should be here to pay homage to the great man, but more importantly to repel the Wednesday bastards, who don't give a fuck about Woody. Their sole purpose is to try to take the Kop. But no, there's thirty or so lads and a couple of hundred chabs who don't really want to be here.

All through the game the Wednesdayites try to advance, and only the large police presence prevents a rout. Blades are melting, and by half time there's around a hundred left. We're not even talking to each other, cos no fucker knows what to say. The half time chat's cancelled; we know if we move, Wednesday's got the Shoreham. We can see the whites of their eyes and their snug faces, stretching their necks and peering past the police.

Near the end of the match, they break through, there're behind us, we move up to face them; no chance, they've broken through at the front, so no matter which way we turn there're behind us. The coppers have lost it and we're fucked.

I notice a familiar face on the Wednesday front line, the big Blade from Arbourthorne who stood by my side after the Swindon game in 1970. The bastard's wearing a blue and white scarf,.

Ted Bear, one of Wednesday's best-known lads comes into view. I knew Ted through a couple of Dronny Wednesdayites. There was no love lost between Ted and me though. When he moved to Dronny, sometime in the 80s we got to know each other and always had the crack and a good old reminisce. (Ted passed on about ten years ago. R.I.P. ya Wednesday fucker.)

Ted's stood with the Walters brothers, a pair of big, mean, black fuckers with only three eyes between them. Ted gives me a nod, not a friendly nod; it's an arrogant kinda gesture as if to say, "We've fucked you Sharpy." Well we are at war after all. We're all still here though, surrounded by Wednesday; it's as if they don't want to write us off, humiliation is enough.

I don't even remember leaving the ground, who I left with or where I went. I do remember seeing Wafe at the end of the game, I don't think we even spoke; we just looked at each other as if to say, "What the fuck's going on?"

We'd seen off the best in the early 70s: Tottenham, Chelsea, West Ham, Leeds, Newcastle, and Man City, plus many lesser mobs, who were a lot better than Wednesday. Only Man Utd and Leeds, both with overwhelming numbers had ever took the Shoreham, but if there's no fucker there to defend it, what can you do? So, the unthinkable had happened, shown up and shit on by Wednesday in our own backyard. A crowd of just over 10,000 turned out, and more than half of it were Wednesdayites. Fuckin shocking. I felt like crying. Blades who stayed away that night should hang their heads in shame for the rest of their lives.

The wounding trial came up a Sheffield Crown Court. I dolled myself up in my best togs and put on a shirt and tie. I was sure I was going away, and there was fuck all I could do about it. I'd got away with loads of shit over the years, but this time it looked like my luck had finally ran out. Tiffany came to court with me. Moose and Sass were shipped over from Armley and waited in the cells under the courthouse.

Our solicitor arrived with the barrister who represented us. The barrister's wig and black gown brought home the feeling I was in some deep shit. We went into a room for what I thought would be a last-minute briefing.

"I've spoken to the prosecution," he told me, "and if you plead guilty they've agreed to a two-year binding-over order. I've spoken to Mr Cardwell and he's agreeable, are you?"

Fuckin agreeable, not many; here's me thinking I'm going down, and this comes out of the blue.

I took the stand; Moose came up from the cells and gave me a nod and a smile as he joined me in the dock.

Our barrister told the court, it had all been a... misunderstanding (nice way to put it). He said both of us were injured and needed hospital treatment, we'd pleaded guilty and saved the court both time and money by accepting a binding-over order. We were both very sorry and both promised it would never happen again. The judge, who looked at least a hundred years old, peered over his glasses at us.

"I think these lads are of good enough character not to be bound over," he said. "Case dismissed." Fuckin hell, he must be mad. I'd slipped through the net once again. Ronald Sharpe the man they could not hang.

Moose stayed in the dock to face the car theft charge. A prison officer brought Sass up to join him and both pleaded guilty. I sat in the public gallery watching the shit. The judge asked the prosecution how long they'd been on remand, and he was told, over two months.

"I think they've been in jail long enough to reflect on what they've done," the judge said, "Case dismissed."

The old fucker must have had his leg over last night. We celebrated with a night out, at the scene of the crime, the Hofbrauhaus.

All through the summer I pondered my future on the hooligan scene. I knew I had to be careful because I couldn't keep escaping jail forever. I always thought I'd pack it all in when I reached twenty-one and became a man, but I'd hit twenty-three and was still at it. Fuck me; I was older than some of the players.

How many more seasons before I called it a day? How many more years before I could sit in the comfort of the John Street stand, flat cap covering my slightly balding head, applauding good moves from both the Blades and the opposition?

I honestly think if the shit at Woody's testimonial hadn't happened I would: not necessarily have packed it in, but maybe calmed down a little bit. It haunted me, though; I couldn't get it out of my head, and I couldn't leave it. I hated the Wednesday bastards more than ever.

At the start of the 74-75 season we drew Chesterfield at home in the League

Cup. I'd always had a soft spot for 'Tairn' as the Chezzy folks called their team and I'd been to a few of their home games in the early 60s and again with the Chezzy Blades in the mid-60s. Two of the Chezzy Blades, Sinny and Podge met some Newcastle lads and took in a few Newcastle games both home and away. No doubt seduced by the marvellous Geordie accent, or could it have been the fact they were joining a bigger mob, the two defecting bastards deserted the Blades and were now fully paid up members of the later to be 'Toon Army.'

Sinny sometimes ran with the Tairn mob and now, being a wanted man by many Blades, it was hoped he would turn up for this game. It weren't no great loss, losing Sinny; although he'd always been there or thereabouts since the mid-60s, I'd never actually seen him throw a punch.

Many, many years later he told me his version of why he'd stopped coming to the Lane. He said Pete O'Brian and a couple more Blade skins went to Chesterfield on Sinny's invitation for a night out. When they left the nightclub, Pete and his mates were jumped by a load of Chezzy lads. Pete reckoned Sinny set them up and swore if he ever saw him again he'd kill him. Sinny gave me his word he knew nothing about the ambush, but he daren't risk bumping into Pete again so he stayed away from the Lane and started supporting Newcastle.

On the night of the match I didn't expect Sinny or any other Chezzy lads to turn up at the Lane. Although Chesterfield had a small mob of, game-enough lads, most of the town's football fans supported Man Utd, Leeds, Liverpool, both Sheffield clubs, or any fucker else who were the flavour of the month. I was a bit shocked to see around five hundred Chezzies mobbed up on the Lane end. All the Man Utd glory hunters and the rest must have turned out for this one. A rumour went around the Kop that Sinny had been spotted coming out of the train station with the Chezzy mob.

At the end of the game we swarmed out of the Kop towards the Lane end. I was shocked again to see the Chezzy mob running full-tilt bouncing and screaming up John Street towards us. We were straight into them and in a matter of seconds they split and scattered in all directions. With the job done I never bothered chasing. As I walked onto Bramall lane I saw a group of mates who said they'd seen Sinny running for his life past St Mary's church.

Moose finished his latest spell in jail and was back amongst the fold... for a while at least. September 74 and its Leeds United at Elland Road.

Fuckin Leeds; a few months earlier, ten thousand of the bastards massed on the Shoreham two hours before kickoff and took the piss. A couple of hundred Blades stuck in the right-hand top corner held on for a while, until overwhelming numbers eventually shifted us. Now none of us would have minded... nay welcomed even, a smack in the earhole or a kick in the bollocks off a Leeds' lad from Harehills, Beeston or Chapeltown, but like a poor man's Man Utd, Leeds were starting to attract the 'Glory Hunters.' They now boasted a huge following, boosted by lads from most of the towns in the Yorkshire region and from towns and cities all over the country. There was the Hull Whites, Barnsley Whites, Rotherham Whites, Cleckheaton Whites, Donny Whites, Bradford Whites, Wakefield Whites, Emmerdale/ Robblesfield/ Hotton Whites, Northampton

Whites, Cockney Whites, and the Plymouth Whites. The most feared out-of-town Leeds mob, however, came from a small South Wales seaside resort. A group of twenty-five stone, big, black, love walrus, mutha-fuckers called... the Barry Whites.

Watch any game today from grassroots Sunday morning level to the Champions League and you'll see players, managers, coaches and substitutes screaming abuse and threats at the officials. This all started over forty years ago with Leeds United and their manager, Don Revie. It was win at all costs with these cunts. The Leeds players, in particularly Bremner, Hunter and fuckin giraffe neck Charlton, couldn't stand a decision going against their team. What really pissed me off though was they were all great players, so they had no need to cheat. Refs and linesmen were harassed and chased around the pitch if they dared to give a free kick or a throw in to the opposition. Bremner could kick the ball out for a throw-in when none of the other side were within ten yards of him and still claim it was a Leeds ball.

The giraffe-necked bastard impeded goalkeepers by holding their arms to stop them catching corners. That's when the spirit and the sportsmanship of the game started to die and escalated to what we see today. Fuckin Leeds United and their arsehole manager, the pioneers of underhand-tactics. I hate the bastards.

Moose, Dick Dung, Wafe, his brother, Alex, Sam Shirt and me, caught an early morning service bus from Pond Street, arriving in Leeds at eleven bells-opening time. Some of the other lads were supposedly catching the train around dinnertime. I knew for certain we were in for a rough ride, but we were out to do our own thing and if the other lads were coming (which I doubted very much) we expected to bump into them somewhere or other in Leeds.

None of us wore colours, we didn't really need to: Moose would let anyone who wanted to, know who we were. We did a couple of virtually empty pubs in the city centre for an hour or so and by the time we were back on the streets there's plenty of scarved-up (but all the lads wore scarves at the time) Leeds fans knocking about.

I'd purposely sunk as many pints as I could to get a bit of the old Dutch before the inevitable happened. Moose was at it straight away, barging into passing Leeds fans.

"What the fuck are you looking at, cunt? Yeah we're from Sheffield, what the fuck are you gonna do about?" The rest of us are trying to look and act as hard as we possibly can.

A small group of Leeds lads, sat on a wall looked us over as we passed through a shopping precinct. One of them, a huge fat cunt festooned in scarves, and sew-on badges covering his denim jacket, jumped up and walked towards us.

"Where are you from?" he asked, arrogant as fuck, in a broad Cockney accent.

"We're from Sheffield, ya fat bastard," Moose answered. "Do ya fancy it, me and you, one on one?" The fat cockney's face dropped.

"Come on, fat cunt. Ya fuckin big enough, aren't ya? Go and fetch your fuckin mates as well," Moose said.

"I don't want any trouble," fat bastard said.

"Well fuck off, before I rip ya fuckin head off," Moose said.

By about 2 o'clock we're still in the city centre and there's Leeds fans, hundreds of 'em, everywhere. I had a word with Moose, who was still at it, saying, "We're gonna have to calm down at bit Mulligan, there's too many of the fuckers, we're gonna get killed here."

"Fuck em," Moose said. "There're all a bunch of fuckin wankers."

Moose reluctantly calmed down a bit and we made our way up to the ground, reaching Elland Road just before kickoff. Wafe, Alex and Sam said they were going in the Peacock boozer for the last 'un. Moose Dick and me decided to go in the ground. We went in the standing bit of the South Stand; the seating part was under construction at the time. We'd only been inside for a matter of minutes before hundreds of eyes were focused on us. Moose clipped at least half a dozen Leeds fans round the head as we pushed our way in, shouting, "Get outa fuckin way, ya Leeds bastards."

I noticed a small patch of red and white on the Lowfields terrace. "Come on," I said. "There's some Blades over there." We moved off, followed by at least fifty, mostly young, sixteen/seventeen-year-old Leeds lads. Moose kept stopping and offering out the ones nearest to us, but none of them would take him on. This was the front to end all fronts; it can't last much fuckin longer.

We reached the group of Blades on the Lowfields to find they were old blokes, women and a few young kids. A good hundred Leeds fans were now on our trail. The Blades melted when they realized what was happening.

The Leeds fans massed behind us and normals moved out of the way leaving us stood in an empty circle. We turned and faced them, smiling, arms outstretched, hearts pounding. This is what it's all about; this is the buzz, if you're not scared in situations like this, what's the point of doing it?

"Come on," we shouted. "There's only fuckin three of us." So what did they do? They started singing at us. No shit: they started singing and pointing at us.

"In their Sheffield slums

In their Sheffield slums

They look in the dustbin for something to eat

They find a dead rat and they think it's a treat

In their Sheffield slums."

Moose's face turned to thunder; the thing was though, he really meant it when he shouted, "Fuckin slums, you saying I live in a fuckin slum? I'll kill ya bastards." Moose ran in, kicking and punching, causing the Leeds fans to domino over. Dung and me followed, booting and stomping on fallen bodies. That was end for us; we were attacked from all sides. Dozens of fists and boots rained into us. We were hammered down to the fence at the front and dragged over pitch side by the coppers. It always amazed me how we came out of these incidents with so few injuries. We gave the Leeds fans a smile and the rods to show them we didn't give a fuck, as the coppers grabbed our collars and marched us around the perimeter towards the Gelderd End.

The Gelderd Enders let rip a deafening chorus of,

"Hey rock 'n' roll. Cloughy's on the dole." (Brian Clough's forty-four-day reign as the Leeds manager had just come to an end.) I thought we were nicked, but the coppers just took us to exit gate and chucked us out.

I looked down at my brand-new pair of snide brogues. Tiffany had bought me the shoes the day before from Rotherham market, six quid she'd paid for them and they were completely fucked.

We were ragged and bashed, but nowt serious. We laughed about the whole incident when I started singing, "In our Dronfield slums." We caught a bus back to the city centre and decided to catch the train home. We reached the station well before the game ended. On the forecourt we saw a group of a hundred or so Blades, mostly singers, normals and young 'uns stood against a wall flanked by three or four coppers and a couple of cop dog handlers. A few of the lads were there, shouting to us. The lads told us about twenty of them came on the special arriving in Leeds at 2 o'clock. As they left the station they were attacked by hundreds of Leeds fans and chased back in.

The coppers did fuck all to protect them, saying they shouldn't have come; they'd been stood outside the station for two hours. The coppers realized we were from Sheffield and tried to push us in with the group. I thought, I'm not standing here for another hour.

"Look," I said to this copper, "we came on the bus this morning, we're going back on the train, so we need to get tickets, and we're going in the station to get them."

"You're not going anywhere," the copper said. "Stand here, you're going back on the special with this lot."

"Are you fuckin thick or what?" I said to the copper. "I've just told you we haven't got tickets." The next thing an Alsatian's got my hand in its gob. I booted the dog, it yelped and let go. My hand was covered in slaver and blood. I went crazy, screaming at the copper.

"I'm fuckin reporting you, ya bastard. I've got your number, eight fuckin three one. You're in deep shit. I've done fuck all wrong. I've just told you we don't have tickets and you set the fuckin dog on me. I've got all these as witnesses."

Everybody shouted, "Yeah we saw it." I really was fuming, and my hand hurt like fuck. The copper looked a bit worried.

"Go on then, get your tickets, but I want you back here," he said.

"Fuck off," I shouted, "and don't think I'm not reporting you, cos I fuckin am."

We went and bought tickets and caught the service train back. My hand was throbbing and bleeding, my clothes were ragged, and my shoes were scuffed and scratched to fuck. Ah well I thought, it's just another day in the life of following the mighty Blades, who'd dipped 5-1, as it happens.

The week after its Liverpool at the Lane. About forty of us entered the Kop just before kickoff; Liverpool's got a mob of three-four hundred on the right-hand side of the Shoreham. There's another few thousand Scousers, swaying and singing on the Lane end.

Seeing the boys arrive, the Blade mob moved from the middle of the Kop over to the right to face them. The usual line of coppers are stood in between.

The Scousers looked confident enough, gesticulating and singing. We had a quick look to size up the situation and somebody shouted, "Come on, up the back steps." We ran back down the Kop steps and turned left, round to the spiral staircase that came out where the Shoreham curved round at the white wall. We waded in from the left and seeing this, the Blade mob attacked from the right. I copped for a head ringing sidewinder that wobbled my legs, but I managed to stay on my feet. After thirty seconds of fierce fighting we got behind the Scousers, forcing them down towards the front.

Panic set in as they tried to escape, pushing each other down and pulling each other back. Those who ended up on the deck were booted and stomped. We were still into them as they scaled the fence onto the pitch. As soon as they were on the perimeter, they got a bit braver, bouncing about with their arms outstretched; you're a couple of fuckin minutes too late I thought. All this caused a rumpus on the Lane end, where the Liverpool fans tried to scale the fences to come and help their mates, but the police held them back.

We gave them a rousing chorus of "E-Eye Addio – they're all going home," as the coppers marched them round to the Lane end.

About twenty of us caught an early train to Stoke on the following Saturday.

The Cromford Street boys (Cromford Street is an area of terraced housed roads standing at the back Shoreham Street, the lads from the district went under the name: the Cromford Street Mafia), Walt Williams, Kenny Ball, Tommy Ridley, Chris Midgley, Stocksy, Schitz, Bent Nose, Bridd, Wandering Walt etc, not the biggest of mobs, but most could be trusted to stick together and not run.

A great article appeared in the Sheffield Star when Schitz faced the court for the umpteenth time charged with football violence. The headline read 'Saturday Schizo' and told of the hard-working painter and decorator family man, who turned into a schizophrenic whenever he went to a football match. Schitz even had his own song; all the lads sang it when he arrived on the Kop: "Saturday Schitzo, Saturday Schitzo, Hello, Hello."

We landed about dinnertime and boozed in the pubs near the station until about 2 o'clock. We expected to see Stoke fans knocking about, but there were hardly any. This surprised me a bit, as Stoke, particularly at home, in my opinion had one of the best mobs in the country. The Stokies always sempt to be one step ahead, a set of fierce fuckers who dressed up to the minute, they were proud of their team and were always ready to fight.

I'd missed last season's encounter at Stoke, where once again the lads copped for a bad time. One of Blade black lads, Phil Knight, tried to dye his foot-high Afro, blond, but it went a bit wrong. The small group of Blades, with Phil standing out a mile were surrounded inside the ground. Phil spent the whole game having to listen to the Stokies singing: "Who's that nigger with the yellow hair? Doo-dar, doo-dar."

We walked up to the ground and neared the Victoria about half past two. A fleet of a dozen or so S.U.T. and supporters club coaches containing mainly normals and singers pulled up outside the ground. A few seconds later I found out where the Stoke fans were. Hundreds of the fuckers appeared from the side streets on both sides of the road and laid siege on the buses. We hung back; it would have been suicidal to get involved as all the Blades were still on the coaches cowering under the seats. The coppers arrived and restored a bit of order, holding the Stoke fans back while the Blades got off.

We noticed a boozer on one of the side streets and nipped in to plan our next move. As always there's a bit of bravado when the danger's passed.

"We should have got into the cunts."

"I'm not fuckin bothered, me. I was waiting for everybody else to start."

"We'll have the cunts in the ground."

There's a very good chance we're gonna get fucked today I thought, but fuck it, it's all part of the fun.

We left the pub and entered the open end just before kickoff. The Stoke fans, hundreds of 'em, abandoned the Boothern and pitched camp where they could confront the opposition. The coppers were starting to get a bit more organised by herding fans, who arrived on the specials or on fleets of coaches on to the away ends. Due to lack of opposition some of the home fans no longer needed to protect their ends. They were changing tactics by infiltrating the away ends, or by standing on the side terraces as close as they could get to the away fans. There was no set of rules for the police to follow though; each police force did their own thing. Sometimes the coppers gave protection; sometimes they didn't give a shit. Their favourite retort being, "Well you shouldn't have come." It was like the bastards were sticking up for their home town hooligans. No such luck with the Sheffield coppers, they hated us.

Around five hundred or so Blades, surrounded by coppers are stood just to the left of the goal. We made our way through the crowd and stood slightly behind the group of Blades at the back of the terrace. We were sussed straightaway, lads instantly know who other lads are. Lefty and about a dozen Darnall lads who'd travelled in a van joined us.

So there's about thirty of us, who's just about ready for whatever happens, the rest of the Blades are huddled together thanking fuck for the coppers. The Stokies are close enough to talk to us; in fact they are talking to us, informing us we're "Fuckin dead." Lefty just laughed at 'em. He didn't give a shit.

Wafer, wearing a Ron Atkinson-style, long leather appeared, and I swear to god he was ready to walk straight past us until I shouted three times, "Wafe, over here, narthen cunt, over here, oi over here," it didn't take Wafe long to weigh up a situation.

"Oh," he said, "I didn't see ya at first," but I bet he was thinking, shit, my cards marked now.

Nobody's taking much notice about the game; all eyes are on the Stokies, who could break through the coppers at any minute.

Stoke's shirts are red and white stripes, the same as ours. I didn't know at the time that the Blades had forgotten to pack their away shirts and were forced to wear Stokes all blue 2nd strip. Blades playing in blue, I couldn't get my head around it. Stoke scored and I cheered, I thought it was us. We scored, and I shouted, "Fuckin offside, are you blind, ref?"

Fifteen minutes before the game ended most of the Blades drifted off, leaving thirty or so hardy souls to face the onslaught. The Stokies were now behind and massed to our right. Hundreds of fingers pointed at us as the chant rang out, "Stokie Aggro, Stokie Aggro, Aggro-Aggro." This is serious shit, how the fuck are we gonna get out of this one? I noticed a familiar face in the mass of Stokies behind us: one of the Rotherham Blades, his face contorted in anger pointed his finger at us screaming: "Stokie Aggro." You crafty bastard I thought, and I was in two minds about grassing the cunt up. "Oi, Stokies, see that cunt there, he's one of us." Lefty bounced about still smiling, ready for anything. The attack came and after thirty seconds of trying to defend ourselves we were forced over to the left. The coppers got in between and we were pushed towards an exit gate in the bottom corner followed by hundreds of Stokies. The coppers somehow managed to hold the Stokies back until we were out of the gate. Lefty and Darnall lads turned left to where their van was parked, and we turned right towards the station. It was quite a trek back to the station, but we managed to make it back in about two minutes flat.

At the next home game I saw the Rotherham Blade. "Look who we've got here lads, Stokie Aggro, Stokie Aggro." I shouted at him; he didn't know what to do with himself. From that day to this, whenever I see him, I call him 'Stokie' and make sure whoever he's with gets told the story. 'If I could turn back time,' eh? He's had to live with bottling it for the last thirty-four years.

A few weeks later we were the last to leave the ground at Filbert Street, Leicester. Around twenty of us deliberately hung back hoping for some action as a squad of coppers escorted a few hundred Blades back to the station. As we passed through the park and reached the road leading to the station, hundreds of Leicester fans swarmed through the park towards us. The Blade mob and the police were about fifty yards up the road as we stopped to face Leicester. Leicester didn't hang about and were straight into us. The coppers ran back down to break up the fight.

After a minute or so of chaos more coppers arrived, herded us together and pushed us towards the station. Leicester were on both sides and in the middle of the road, trying to get to us, it was coming on top. I wore a silk scarf tied loosely around my neck and felt it strangle me as a Leicester lad grabbed it and pulled me backwards. I turned to see this thin, lanky cunt with shoulder length brown hair, dressed in brown baggies, brown tank-top and a penny round collared shirt covered in printed Charlie Chaplin's. I laid into him, but within seconds I was face down on the deck with my arms behind me and a coppers knee in my back. Fuckin shite, nicked again. Another copper came, and they grabbed an arm each and marched me towards a van. Moose and Dick ran over shouting at the coppers, "Come on copper, it weren't his fault, we're getting attacked here and he's only trying to protect himself."

"Yeah," I said. "You saw what happened, he tried to fuckin strangle me." Another fight kicked off and the coppers just let me go and moved to try and break it up. That's me done for the day; I trotted up the road and into the station, thanking fuck for a lucky escape.

So this was it, Saturday after Saturday after Saturday. It went off every week. Hooliganism peaked and peaked again. Thousands of yobs travelled up and down the country and fought in the stadiums, in the surrounding streets, at pubs, coach parks, motorway services and railway stations. Ends needed defending, reputations needed maintaining and trains needed wrecking.

So where did us lot figure in football's grand scheme of shit? Were we real supporters? Loyal supporters? Did we love the Blades, Owls, Reds, Blues, Whites, Millers, Tykes, Spurs, Bees, Hornets, Hammers, Lions, Tigers, Rams, Wolves, Cobblers? Or did we, as the sociologists and anthropologists claim (congratulations for such a fuckin mind-blowing observation) just attach ourselves to a particular football club? No shit, of course we attached ourselves to a particular football club, in probably 95% of all cases our home town football club. That was the whole point.

Along with the other ninety-one English and Welsh tribes we carried on playing the game; a game many of us had played for close on ten years. Badminton, Squash, Polo, stick em up ya arse, this was the only game. There was no precise set of rules in this game though, nothing black or white. Football lads survived the chaos with a mixture of good luck, common sense and instinct, and to survive for many years the timing had to be perfect. To be a real lad, you had to be close enough to the front line to gain respect from your mates, but not too close to get arrested or stranded if it came on top. A close eye to watch your rivals for weapons or for signs of bottle loss was essential. Then there's the inner-eye to watch yourself and your mates for signs of bottle loss, and yet another eye, an eagle eye located up your arse to watch out for the coppers. Many fuckin eyes were needed to be a footie lad.

Lads were expected to perform every week. Terrible hangovers, bouts of influenza, or broken limbs were no excuse, sick notes weren't accepted.

Officers from every police force in the land made up the third team in the contest. Once again the coppers had no specific set of rules to follow. And, again, instinct, luck and a little bit of nous played a big part. You could talk to some of the coppers like they were shit, others knocked the shit out of you. Even if you got nicked, you could sometimes talk your way out of it. There were times when you had to eat shit, grovel, crawl and apologise, but if it kept you out of the courts and out of the nick it was worth it

There might not have been any secret signs or handshakes but being part of the mob was like belonging to a Masonic brotherhood. The gangs gathered every Saturday, packs of grown men who acted like kids, little kids who met up in chosen pubs or on street corners for a full day of fun and frolics. Little kids who went to each other's houses for tea, slept on their settees and fancied each other's wives. But we were hooked. We lived for Saturdays, lived for the match day crack and the camaraderie. We were having a fuckin good time; if we weren't, we wouldn't have done it.

Success on the pitch meant little to us. Now it would have been great to win the League, or get to the Cup final, semi-final even, but we were Sheffield United fans and although we could always dream of achieving some honours, we never really expected it. Next season maybe, eh?

The press labelled us 'mindless idiots' 'louts' (that one always amused me) and 'beer-fuelled yobs' and, then, aided our reputations by printing thug league tables, articles and photos of our exploits. The daft cunts made us famous, made us newsworthy and made the hooligan problem ten times worse. Blame the press, I say. But, fuck the press: they knew fuck all.

We loved football just as much as much as we loved our respective teams. We knew everything about football, we knew all the rules of the game, knew who our rivals' best players were. We admired tricky wingers, battling centre forwards and intelligent inside lefts. Flashes of genius, flowing moves and thirty-yard, top corner thunderbolts by the opposition always received a polite splattering of applause even from the most partisan crowds.

The focal point of every Saturday obviously came at 3 p.m. when the game kicked off (could it have been coincidental to the boozers shutting?) But for the lads, Saturday's often started at 6 a.m. and ended at midnight.

On occasions, Saturdays started on Friday night and ended Sunday morning. For the really unlucky ones, Saturdays lasted three months and ended with a walk out of the 'Big House' gate. The chance of arrest or injury was always there, but these were risks worth taking. The fines were still relatively small and could be paid off at a couple of quid or less a week. Magistrates would occasionally dish out a big fine or a short prison sentence to try and convince the establishment they were tackling the problem.

A young Hackenthorpe Blade, incidentally, held the honour of copping for the first ever £100 fine dished out for football-related disorder. This happened at Derby in the early 70s. The lad appeared on the Yorkshire Television news programme *Calendar* and the fee he received paid the fine.

Anyone who wore their club colours were fair game, no code of conduct existed. Ten lads who turned a wrong corner and bumped in two hundred rivals were written off without a second thought. Even more so than the late 60s, the early to mid-70s was a home and away thing. If the lads got turned over at Stoke, everybody would be ready and waiting for when they came to the Lane. If Birmingham copped it at our place we were certain to get reprisals at St Andrews.

Places we'd explored as chabbies in the 60s were now no-go areas. Only the foolhardy, the brave, Kung-Fu experts or lone drunkards went to Chelsea, West Ham, Tottenham and Millwall. Liverpool, Everton, Leeds, Newcastle, Sunderland and Man City had huge mobs at home and took thousands away.

Man Utd as ever were untouchable, and so they should have been, just like the Grand Old Duke of York they had about ten fuckin thousand men (lads.) As a young fifteen-year-old I couldn't help but be impressed by the Man Utd hordes. But now I couldn't get my head around what they got out of it. And what did the proper Manchester lads think about the thousands of bandwagon jumping, Bay City Roller-clad glory hunters, muscling in on their fame?

Anybody could be a Man Utd fan. Following Man U at the time must have been akin to following England in the 90s. Hundreds of lads from every part of the land converging on towns and cities and running riot. What possible buzz could masses of lads get by slapping a few locals? And what about the home games at Old Trafford, coaches from every part of the country turning up. How the fuck would you know which ones to brick? Nah, no fun at all.

There were the so-called easy places (although you could never tell) like Ipswich, Norwich, Coventry, Luton, Carlisle, Fulham, Palace, QPR. The in-betweeners like Wolves, Villa, West Brom, Leicester, Forest, Burnley and loads more where it could go either way. A few of the big boys tried, but only Man Utd and Leeds, both with overwhelming numbers, had ever took the piss at the Lane.

But there was something special and something magic about every mob, (even fuckin Wednesday). The songs they sung in different regional accents, the way they spoke, the gear they wore. It was a kind of mutual respect that nobody, only footie lads, would understand, and respect at the time was a word no footie lad would ever use or even admit to.

Into 1975; January, and it's Villa away in the 4th round of the FA Cup. It's early Saturday morning and hundreds of Blades hang around Pond Street and the S.U.T. booking office sheltering from the snow and sleet. Transistor radios are pressed to freezing earholes waiting for news of the pitch inspection at Villa Park to see if the game's on.

"Yes, it's on," somebody shouts and a huge roar goes up from the crowd. We walk down to the station to book tickets for the special and retire to the Howard until the train's due.

The train's packed to capacity and we arrive at Witton station close to Villa Park at around 2 o'clock. Our plan is to nip off and try to get a few swifties in before kickoff. Everybody else seems to have the same idea as hundreds of bodies run towards the exit and squash their way through. A large squad of coppers with vans and dogs are waiting at the bottom of a ramp. We're about half way down the ramp when the first wave of Blades hit the bottom. The coppers wade straight in with truncheons drawn, the dogs are snarling and going mental. Blades are grabbed, whacked and thrown into the waiting vans. What the fuck's going on? I'm glad I wasn't at the front. Other Blades remonstrate with the coppers.

"What the fuck are you doing? They've not done owt wrong."

A hail of bottles and coins sail through the air at the police. They back off a bit allowing us to swarm out. Lads fall and are trampled on by fellow Blades. There were far more injuries inflicted on one another when a football special rolled in, than any of the fighting at the games. The coppers are soon back on the ball, nicking Blades and throwing them in the vans. We're herded together and pushed and thumped toward the ground. Fuck me, these West Midland coppers don't fuck about.

Another Cup dream is fucked when the Blades dip 4-1 to Second Division Villa. A few days later I received a letter from Moose who was back in jail. Moose wrote, "Fuckin hell I'm laid here on the top bunk, fuckin freezing, listening to Tony fuckin Blackarse on the radio, me and Sass haven't got a burn between us. I'm gasping for a shag (has tha had any fresh bag lately?) Me Mam sent me a letter and put a quid in it, some bastard's nicked the fucker, and to cap it all, United lost 4 fuckin 1 to them Villa bastards. I'm on the fuckin rocks man."

The Blades unveiled former Notts County chief Jimmy Sirrel as their new boss. Jimmy didn't win any silverware, but he picked up the 1975-76 season's handsomest manager in the world award.

I'd been planning for years to have a United tattoo, but through fear of pain I'd never quite got round to it. The week after my 24th birthday, in a moment of madness, I called in the tattooist on Heeley bottom and paid fifty pence to have the words Sheffield United F.C. scrawled on my right arm.

I met Moose, Sass (both free again for a while) and Hiram in the Green Acres about 7 o'clock. After being two goals down, the Blades came back to beat Everton 3-2 at Goodison.

"What about United eh, Mulligan?" I shouted as I entered the pub.

"Yeah fuckin brilliant," Moose shouted back. "They were losing two nowt as well."

"Look at this fucker," I said, rolling my sleeve up and flashing my new tatt. "I've just had it done; cost me ten fuckin bob it did."

"Fuckin sound," Moose said. "I might get one done next week."

Moose and me carried on chatting about the Blades (Sass and Hiram weren't interested in football). Two blokes we'd never seen before sat with their wives or girlfriends on the table to our left. They both looked older than us, early thirties maybe. Suddenly one them jumped up and leaned over the table in between Moose and me. Looking from one of us to the other, he said in a broad Sheffield accent,

"I'll tell ya summat lads, there always been one thing Wednesdayites are better at than Unitedites."

"What's that?" I said

"Fighting," he answered. He walked back to his table and sat down. Now there was something about this fucker, something that gave me the shits. Sometimes instinct just tells you who a fighter is, and I thought straight away this cunt's one.

He's in our local for fuck's sake, calling the shots, dun't he know who we are? It took a lot to freak Moose out, but this geezer's front did it. We glanced over to the table and both these blokes were giving us the evil eye.

"Fuckin hell," Moose said. "We better get ready here." The bloke knew he'd spooked us and he started laughing, as did his mate and the two birds. He started shouting shit like, "Fuckin Unitedites, I've shit em, fuckin wankers the lot of 'em."

"I'm not putting up with this shit much longer," Moose said.

"Hold on a bit Mull," I said, "just let's see what they do."

Ten minutes later they're still giving us the evils, laughing and muttering comments.

"Come on," Moose said. "I'm going to the bogs, come with me Ron, cos I reckon they're gonna follow us in, if we're not back in a couple of minutes, come in," he said to the others.

We got up and walked towards the bog. The two blokes were up straight away and followed us in. The big fucker started gobbing off, but before he'd finished talking Moose decked him with one punch. I dropped the other one and as they lay on the bog floor we went crazy, screaming, dancing and stomping on their heads.

"You fuckin Wednesday bastards, fuck about with us and see what you fuckin get, we'll fuckin kill ya," I got quite emotional.

"All right, all right we've had enough," one of them shouted.

"Like fuck," Moose shouted and carried on stomping. Hiram came through the door and joined in. The one who I'd dropped lifted his body to try and get up; his hair slipped to one side and fell on the floor. Fuck me it's a fucking wig.

"Fuckin hell," Moose laughed. "It's a dead rat." Moose picked up the guinea pig and threw it in the piss trough. He slopped it around a bit until it was nice and wet and neatly arranged it like a hairdresser on the bloke's bald head. By this time I could hardly stand up for laughing. Moose stepped back to survey his handiwork.

"Just right," he said, as he slapped the bloke hard on the top of his head to make sure it stuck. "Keep thi fuckin hair on pal," Moose shouted. We were laughing like hyenas; we had to hold each other up.

Both the blokes were in a bad way, blood, shit and hair covered the bog walls and floor. We thought it best to fuck off.

Moose and me were arrested early next morning and dragged off to Dronny cop shop. The landlord or someone in the pub who didn't like us had obviously given the coppers our names.

"Any distinguishing marks or tattoos?" the copper said to me, before he locked us up.

"Well, it just so happens," I said, rolling up my sleeve. They grilled us separately and we denied everything. The coppers gave us the usual spiel, "You're mate's blaming it all on you; he's singing like a bird." But we weren't falling for that shit. There were no witnesses, so we were released without charges. Trenton Wig-on and his mate never came in the Acres again.

Tiffany left the shit hole, and along with the kids, moved into bed-sit up Pitsmoor. Even though he always used to look a bit shifty when I was around, I didn't have the slightest inkling at the time, that the landlord, an old acquaintance from her Arab café days who owned and lived in the house was getting a little bit more than the weekly rent.

Tiff and me had many ups and downs. One of the ups... she introduced me to joys of 'sliced beef curry' sold at Chinese chip shops. Like many other of the Dronny lads, I'd always refused to eat the Chinky stuff. I must have really believed the old myth about the cats, rats and the dogs.

"Just try it," Tiff said to me one night as she walked out of the Chinky on Barnsley Road carrying a tray of the stuff.

"I'm not trying it," I said. "It's horrible, it looks like diarrhoea."

"How do you know it's horrible if you've never tried it?" Tiff said.

I reluctantly tasted it. Fuckin hell, it was the best thing I'd ever tasted in my life. I became hooked on it. I got Moose and the rest of the lads, who were just as unwilling as me to try it and they loved it as well. When the last bus rolled in from town, Arthur's, on Dronny Bottom and Greasy Lill's on Egerton were shunned. We were the Tung Sing boys now.

Tiffany also bought me my first ever pair of undercrackers. They were skimpy, little white 'uns, like women's kegs, with two footballs and the words 'Famous Balls' printed on the front. Luckily for her she didn't have to wesh the fuckers.

Tiff eventually got a council flat at Bernard Buildings on the Bard Street complex. The Bard Street flats were miserable, four storey high tenement blocks, a kind of Cammell's Row in the sky, but without the community spirit. They were run-down, dog-infested and covered in graffiti. Bin chutes, often overflowing or jammed up, were situated half way along the open balcony walkways. The flats were squashed between the high-rise Park Hill and the Hyde Park districts. You needed to be a bit nifty walking through the Hyde Park flats, anything from shit filled nappies to TV sets could be launched from the balconies. I'd promised Tiff if she ever got a proper flat I'd move in with her. I had no excuses now, but I kept putting it off.

After a spell of labouring work on the new Gosforth Valley housing estate at Dronfield Woodhouse and paying emergency tax, I received a large tax rebate. I thought I'd treat Mum to a couple of luxuries we'd never been able to afford.

First I splashed out £20 deposit on a colour telly. Now

View from Dixon Lane, Sheffield City Centre, to the Bard Street Flats with the Hyde Park Flats Behind

I've got this figure in my head, what with the finance interest and shit, the TV cost £600, which surely can't be right can it? That was more than a fuckin house cost. Anyway the deposit was the first and last payment. Mum loved the new telly and was genuinely amazed at the colour picture.

One of Mum's favourite programmes was the Wednesday night wrestling, with Kent Walton commentating. Sometimes I'd arrive home from the pub when the show was on. Just like the audience, Mum cheered the goodies (Les Kellet, who was at least twenty years older than her) and booed the baddies (Mick McManus, who was about her age). She knew all the holds, like step-over-leg-locks, forearm smashes, Boston crabs and body-slams. She counted along with the referee, "One-arr-two-arr-three-arr," on the knockouts and the falls.

She'd crease me up, shouting stuff like: "Gerroff him, leave him alone ya big bleedin bully."

"It's a bleedin wrestling match Mother, he's hardly gonna leave him alone is he?" I'd tell her.

"I don't care, I don't like him. He's always cheating the rotten bleedin sod."

"Anyway I've told ya a hundred times Mam, it's all fixed."

"It's not bleeding fixed," she'd say. "You're always same when you've had a drink. I'm bloody fed up on ya, why don't you piss off to bed."

Good old Mam, God love her.

After about six months or so the telly started to go wrong, it was still colour, but only one colour... green. It would stay green for a few days and after a few thumps on the side, revert back to full colour for a week or so, before it went green again. I'd never had much fuckin luck with televisions.

Even though the telly was guaranteed for a year I couldn't get it fixed because I'd not paid any money since the first payment. It took well over a year for the finance company to repossess it. The box, now immune to any amount of booting and thumping was going through one of its green periods when they finally carried out of our house.

Then Moose's mother, who'd just bought a brand-new fridge, flogged me their old one for a fiver. We never had much snap in it, but at least the milk stayed fresh for a few days.

Around this time, but I can't remember exactly when, we acquired another luxury: our first washing machine, a Hotpoint twin-tub. I've no idea where it came from, my sister Joan probably bought it. Up until then, Mum used the old galvanised Peggy tub and a copper 'poncher' that knocked muck and fuck out of the garments. The clothes were all but dry when they emerged from the back end of the old mangle (one of the few items we brought from Cammell's Row when we moved in 1960). Strangely enough we can't have been the only family on the estate at the time who didn't own a washer, as many of the neighbours often called round to put their bed sheets or their son's jeans through our mangle. Spin driers! I've shit-em.

A buzz of expectancy surrounded the last home game of the season. In their best campaign for years and with two games left to play the Blades were in with a good chance of qualifying for Europe. Nearly 29,000 saw us stuff Leicester City 4-0, but I was more interested in the couple of thousand Leicester fans massed on the Lane end. Now I don't know when or how it started, but tradition dictated that at the final home game, a mass pitch invasion took place. Despite me barking out orders to stay together and get ready for it going off outside, ten minutes before the final whistle, most of the Blades mob moved from the back of the Kop.

Hundreds hung on the white railings at the front, ready for the invasion. If it hadn't been the last home game we would have been outside the Cricketers waiting for the Leicester fans to come out. Looking towards the Lane end I saw the Leicester mob rush to the exit gate on the corner of Bramall Lane/John Street. They gesticulated, bounced, waved their arms and urged each other on, and, by the way they moved, I knew they were heading for the Kop. Only a handful of Blades were still stood at the back.

The coppers who always hung around keeping their eyes on us, had all disappeared and were stood around the pitch perimeter ready to try and stop the invasion.

"Them fuckers are coming round," I said to Stocksy. "Get down to the front and tell the lads to get back up here," I shouted to one of the lads. Stocksy and me went out and stood at the top of the steps looking out through the open exit gate on to John Street.

The Leicester mob appeared, and at first stood a little apprehensively at the gate. Seeing no coppers or Blades waiting to face them they stormed in and started bouncing up the steps towards us.

"Fuckin hell," I said to Bob. "Them stupid bastards are poncing about on the pitch, I told every fucker to stick together but the thick cunts don't listen." Another couple of Blades appeared and again I shouted, "Go and tell the lads and be fuckin quick." I glanced behind me and waved my arm forward at our imaginary mob behind us shouting, "Come on lads, they're here." Stocksy and me looked at each other and without a word ran down the steps screaming "Fuckin come on then."

The sight of a couple of nutters must have freaked the Leicester front line as they stopped dead in their tracks. We waded in swinging and booting. In a split second we heard the roar behind us as the rest of the lads arrived. Chaos followed as Leicester turned and ran. We smacked backs of heads and kicked calves and arses as they scrambled though the gate.

Out on John Street the fighting continued as Leicester tried to regroup. As we forced them towards Shoreham Street I heard a voice shout, "You bastard, you promised you were moving in with me and I've not seen you in weeks. I knew I'd find you here." I glanced to my left to see Tiffany, with a little toddler in each hand stood outside the beer-off.

"Oh fuck off," I shouted. "What the fuck are you doing here, are ya trying to show me up or summat? You can see I'm fuckin busy." The fighting continued all around us as we stood arguing on the corner of Shoreham Street. Both the kids were screaming and crying.

Dressed in exactly the same clobber: brown baggies, tank top and Charlie Chaplin shirt, the Leicester fan who six months earlier tried to strangle me with my own scarf came into view.

"I'll come and see you tonight, promise." I shouted to Tiff as I sprinted towards Charlie Chaplin.

"You can fuck off," she shouted back. "I never want to see you again." Charlie turned and ran, and I just missed booting his trailing leg in an effort to trip him up.

A win at Birmingham three days later and we're in Europe. The *Sheffield Star* reckoned some twenty thousand Blades would travel to St Andrews to cheer on the team. Like fuck I thought, we'll need twenty thousand if we're going to do owt there. I'd been to Birmingham a couple of times before and they weren't to be fucked with at home. Not only that, thirty or so of us kicked the shit out of a dozen Brummies outside St Mary's church before the game at the Lane six months earlier, they won't have forgot about that.

I set off around four o'clock in Beetroot's car. We hit heavy traffic just south of Chesterfield. Scores of cars with scarves hanging from the windows were stuck in huge jams all the way to Derby. We reached the other side of Derby just after six o'clock.

The car started to chug and splutter; it gave off a loud metallic sounding clang before grinding to a halt. We lifted the bonnet and poked at wires, sparkplugs and strange carburettor-type things, not knowing the fuck what we were doing.

"I think it's fucked, Ron," Beetroot said.

"Sorry about this Beetie," I said, "but I'm gonna hitch it, I'm not missing this fucker."

"I'll have to stay here with the car," Beetroot said. "You get off."

A car full of Blades pulled up straight away. The female front seat passenger wound down the window and said, "We can squeeze you in, but you'll have to sit on my knee."

"Sound," I said. "But it'd be better if you sat on my knee."

Meanwhile, Wafe and Dinky who'd travelled by train, arrived at Birmingham New Street and entered what Dink described as: 'The roughest fuckin boozer I've ever set foot in.' Both had flags tied around their shoulders. The wording on Wafe's flag read 'Currie's Crusaders March into Europe' The whole pub fell silent as they walked in and they heard the door creak shut behind them. Half a dozen huge monsters propped up the bar. They only had one ear between them and that was sat on the counter, packed in ice in a crisp bag waiting to be sown back on.

"Fuckin hell,' somebody shouted, "It's Batman and Robin." The whole pub erupted into laughter. The Caped Crusaders swivelled on their heels and shot straight back out.

We reached the ground about ten minutes before kickoff and I headed to the first turnstile I saw. I found myself in a seated area behind the goal packed with Blades. To my right, on a large covered terrace a group of around a thousand Blades under constant attack from hundreds of crazed Brummies were squashed together in the top corner. The coppers had their work cut out trying to hold the Birmingham fans back. Blades were dotted in groups all around the ground, the majority in the seats. Twenty thousand? Like fuck, maybe five-six thousand at the most.

The game kicked off, but my eyes were focused on the fighting on the side terrace. The Brummies were now at the front as well as the side and they were fighting the police to try and get through to the Blades whose numbers were shrinking by the second. Along with a few more lads I made my way over to the bottom corner where a fence prevented access to the terrace, not that I had any intention of scaling it to lend a hand. The Brummies broke through behind the Blades forcing them down to the bottom corner. Many of Blades were normals and young kids, but there were a few of the lads amongst them. I saw Gibby and shouted over to him, "What's up wi ya, Gibby? Get thi sen in."

"Fuckin hell, Ron," he shouted back. "It's fuckin bad on here."

"Yeah, I can see it is," I answered.

The game finished in a 0-0 draw, I don't remember the Blades having one fuckin shot on goal. My European dream was now in tatters, but fuck it, I thought, I'd never have managed to thumb down a ferry anyway.

Thirty years later I'm stood in the Railway on Bramall Lane after a game chatting to Stan Lake's son.

"Oh, by the way Ron," he said. "Me Mam sez, tell Sharpy if you see him, he's got a bony arse."

"Bony arse?" I said. "What ya on about?"

"Me Mam said you once sat on her knee all the way to Birmingham and your arse was right bony," he said.

"Fuckin hell, your mother, eh?" I said. "Tell her it's not bony these days."

I'd been watching bands at the Black Swan since the late 60s. Some spot on, local acts played the joint, including Frank White, who took me backstage one night and taught me the intro to Chuck Berry's *Johnny B Goode* on his twin-necked Gibson SG. Good on ya Frank.

Other local acts who gigged there were Shape of the Rain, a great band who I think came from Chesterfield, Lazy Jake (I still own a Hiwatt 100-watt cab with the band's name stencilled on the back.) Mickey's Monkeys and Rock 'n' Roll pianist Chuck Fowler, the Killamarsh Killer, who knocked out brilliant versions of Jerry Lee Lewis and Little Richard numbers. Brewers Droop and their giant stang, appeared there a few months after I'd seen them at the Bardney festival. Hackensack might not have originated from New Jersey (as their name suggests) but every time they played they brought the house down.

At the height of the pub rock scene, the London based bands travelled up north and played (usually on Sunday nights) at the Swan. The bands I saw there included, Kilburn and the High Roads – who later became Ian Dury and The Blockheads, Brinsley Schwartz, Ducks Deluxe and Patto. Smokie (of *Living Next Door to Alice* fame) did a surprisingly brilliant set one night. and our own Joe Cocker would have been proud of their version of *With a Little Help from my Friends*.

I can't quite remember if I'd heard of Dr Feelgood, or if I just happened to walk in on them one Sunday night at the Mucky Duck. What I do remember is they totally blew me away. This was Rhythm 'n' Blues in its purest form. I drifted back to my early teens, back to the glory days, back to the time of the Stones, the Pretty Things and Them.

The Feelgoods belted out a mixture of standard R&B tracks and their own songs performed in the traditional Rhythm 'n' Blues style. Their stage presence and their sheer power sent the Swan crowd wild. Wilko Johnson's dead-pan, spaced-out expression and head jerks gave the impression he'd escaped from a nuthouse. I was convinced he had when he set off on his crazy runs across the stage, pointing his black Telecaster like a machine gun, pretending to mow down the audience. Wilko's choppy, staccato, guitar technique, strummed with the fingers of his right hand was quite unique. I couldn't get my head around how he produced such marvellous licks without using a plectrum. Lee Brilleaux dressed in a grubby, crumpled suit, looked like a passing tramp who'd stumbled on to the stage; his feet planted firmly, one each side of the mike stand in the classic bluesman stance. His left leg shook Elvis style as he sucked long, wailing notes out of the harmonica. The back line of Sparks on bass and the Big Figure on drums kept it all flowing along effortlessly. I had no idea at the time of course, who the band members were.

Johnny Hall, me and Kev Pearson in the Dronny Contact Club 1978

I left the pub feeling I'd witnessed something really special and I knew I had to see them again. The chance came a few months later when the band played Sheffield City Hall. I went to the gig with Johnny Hall and Lou. The Feelgoods were on fire. Tracks from the show made up their live album *Stupidity*. On the last song, Bo Diddley's *I'm A Man*, it was yours truly who got the crowd going by standing up and starting off the hand claps after the first four bars.

In the summer of 75 I broke my old mum's heart by reluctantly moving in to live 'over the brush' with Tiffany. Tiff was on benefits, so I kept my mum's address in Dronny for signing-on purposes. I added to the graffiti on the flats by painting, S.U.F.C. and BLADES in large white letters on the block where we lived. The only good thing I can say about living on the Bard Street flats was the five-minute walk into town. I did exactly the same things I'd always done: boozing, nightclubbing, womanising and brawling at the football. I had no intention of settling down, choosing curtains and being a family man, even though the kids (on Tiff's insistence) had called me 'Dad' for the past couple of years.

I did do some of the dad-stuff though. I took the kids swimming, took them to the Lane a few times when there was no chance of any shenanigans, taught them a few footie skills and took them to the pictures. I always treated the lads right and the one and only time I ever smacked their arses was after they got up in the middle of the night, pulled all the valves out of the telly and decorated the front room walls with flour, eggs and sugar.

I had the misguided view though, that Tiffany owed me an internal debt of gratitude for taking on her and the two kids. Who knows? Maybe if I'd been castrated and if Tiff had kept her knickers on a bit more often, especially when she was in the company of Arabs, we could have lived happily ever after.

All this might sound as if we had some kind of open relationship… far from it. It always broke me up when I found out she'd been fucking about. She should be at home, looking after the kids and doing the housework while I'm out gallivanting, that's how it works isn't it?

Problem fans, 1977

Chapter 7

The judge in the courtroom pounded his gavel

Man Utd's the first away game of the 75-76 season. It's not a trip for faint of heart. Twelve of us meet up in the Penny Black at opening time. There's Stocksy, Bent Nose, Brid, Schitz, Lefty, Ray Williams, Tommy Ridley, Chris Midgley, a couple of others and me. A van's supposed to be picking us up at half twelve.

Bernard Statford's 'fatha' is driving the van. Now Bernard's fatha, wasn't really Bernard's fatha, he's a mate of Bernard's who's in his thirties, but that's so fuckin old, he's known as Bernard's fatha. I'm not holding my breath; vans and Bernard's fatha's van in particular have a tendency not to show up. There's no plan of action, a dozen or so lads just getting into Manchester and back out again in one piece will be an achievement in itself.

Most of us are wearing red and white scarves, it's not a sign of our allegiance to the Blades though, more a kind of blending in procedure. At 12.30 there's no sign of the van.

"Let's fuck off and catch the special," somebody suggests.

"No give em a bit longer," someone else says. So we all sink another couple of pints of courage.

At one bell we amble down to the station to find the special's been cancelled due to lack of bodies brave enough to travel to Old Trafford.

"Service train" somebody reckons. We check the train times and find out the next train won't get us there until way after three.

"Who's Rotherham playing?" somebody asked.

"Hereford at home."

"That's it then, let's fuck off to Rotherham and stand with the Hereford mob."

"Hereford haven't got a fuckin mob," someone else says.

"Fuck it, we'll go anyway. Everybody agreed, yeah? We'll just have to take the Tivoli instead of the Stretford, eh!" Everybody laughs.

So it's off on the ten-minute journey to Rotherham. We do one or two boozers in the town centre and reach the ground just before kickoff. The Dirty Dozen enter at the Tivoli turnstiles. We snake our way through and plant ourselves slap-bang in the middle of the Rotherham mob, who's stood directly behind the goal at the back of the stand.

A few of the Rotherham lads are a little unsure of the strangers in their midst, but we're all wearing red and white (Rotherham's colours) so most of them take no notice. We ready ourselves and the chant goes up.

"Shef-fi-eld U-ni-ted." The Rotherham mob's still not sure what's going on. The chant goes up again: "Shef-fi-eld U-ni-ted." "Come on, we're fuckin Blades." A gap caused by youngsters and lads not fancying it forms around us. The Rotherham fighters move down from the back and from the right. We're straight into them, punching and booting. A Rotherham lad squeals in agony as

257

Lefty jibs him with the sharp end of a steel comb. We're attacked from all angles, but we're holding our own as the coppers arrive.

"There're Sheffield bastards, they've got knives," a Rotherham fan shouts to the coppers. The coppers can't work out what's going on as the fighting continues. More lads pile into us and force us towards the front, it's coming on top. Coppers from the pitch perimeter scale the fence and surround us. One of our lads says to the coppers, "We're from Sheffield mate; we've just come here to watch a game, cos we couldn't get to Manchester in time to see United and we got attacked." The Rotherham fans are remonstrating to the coppers, "Search the cunts; they've got fuckin knives."

"Come on," one of the coppers says. "We'll take you round to the Railway end." Some of us voluntarily scale the fence on to the perimeter; others are forced over by the coppers. I didn't realise what was about to happen and neither did any of the others. Lefty however did, he moved over to one side, grabbed a bird and started snogging her; the slag responded by ramming her tongue down Lefty's throat. More coppers arrived until there was at least twenty stood around us.

A copper, who seemed to be in charge of the operation shouted at us like we had learning difficulties, "Is everybody here? Are you all here? Right come on we'll take you round. Everybody keep together now, are we all together? Right; on we go."

Eleven lads ready themselves for the swagger around the pitch to the Railway end. I'd been in this situation before, infiltrating home ends, getting sussed and then being marched around the pitch, taking abuse from the home fans and accolades from the Blades on the away end – it was the ultimate pose. We've only moved a couple of yards before twenty-two arms are grabbed and slammed behind backs.

"You're nicked." The crafty bastards; some of the lad's put on a show for the crowd. They wriggle and try to escape, no fuckin chance. We're ferried off to Rotherham nick, searched and thrown in the cells.

At five o'clock a copper sticks his head through the hatch in the cell door, laughs and shouts: "Man U's beat ya 5-1."

"Fuck off," we shout back. Half an hour later we're charged with threatening behaviour and released. We plot up in a boozer near the cop station. One of the lad's nips out and returns with the *Green 'Un*.

"Fuckin hell," he says. "We've made the papers." In the Rotherham match report it read: 'Just after kickoff fighting erupted on the Tivoli end, the police moved in and the troublemakers were removed and ejected from the ground.'

One of the lads takes up the story: "Lefty however, escaped and at this very moment he's probably having his cock sucked by a Rotherham slut."

The case came up weeks later at Rotherham Magistrates' Court. Most of us met up in town on the Monday morning and caught the 69 bus into Rotherham. Dinky came along with us for the crack. I'd travelled from Dronny, as Tiffany had kicked me out a few days earlier for being A.W.O.L. for a week.

"You'll miss me when I'm in the fuckin nick," I'd told her.

"Like fuck I will," she said.

Brid, who'd been released from the North Sea Camp detention centre three days earlier, was missing when we assembled in the courthouse corridor at ten o'clock. Brid turned up ten minutes later and told us he'd overlain, so he'd nicked a car and drove to court.

"Where's the car, Brid?" one of the lads asks him.

"It's in the court car park," Brid answered. "I'm going home in the fucker if I don't get sent back down." Just before we were called into the courtroom, Brid cocked his leg up and rattled off a long, loud fart. We were in bits as we entered the dock. We all pleaded guilty and stood grinning and smirking waiting to be sentenced.

The judge told us our behaviour in court hadn't helped our case and fined us all ninety quid; ninety quid I thought, that's a lot of giros; why not make it a round fuckin hundred?

The judge asked us in turn, how the fines would be paid. When he came to me I answered, "Well sir, I can't work because I have to look after my invalid mother. I do all the shopping the cooking and the housework. It'll be a struggle, but I can pay the fine at 50p a week?"

"Yes," the judge answered. "That's acceptable." Sound I thought, I'll have paid the fucker off in about four years. Stocksy's the next in line.

"Six pounds a week," Bob sez.

"You'll pay twelve," the judge answered. I could hear Stocksy mumbling, "Ya fuckin bastard," under his breath. Whatever the rest of the lads offered to pay, the judge doubled it. We left the courtroom and Stocksy shouted, "Fuckin Sharpy, ya jammy cunt. Fifty fuckin pence a week and I've got to pay twelve fuckin quid."

"Down there for football, Robert," I said, pointing to my feet.

We went back to Sheffield and Dinky came with me up to Bard Street to collect my stuff from Tiffany's. When we reached the flats I said, "Right Dink, I'll hide round the corner. You go to the door, tell her I've got three months and you've come to collect my stuff. She'll get all emotional if she thinks I'm inside and welcome me back with open arms, either that or she'll drag you in and fuck ya."

Dink put on his best Uriah Heap voice and said, ever so humble like, "Gi-owa Ron, I wouldn't do owt like that, honest."

"Tha fuckin would Dink," I said

Dink knocked on the door and I heard him say, "I've come for Ron's stuff; I've just been to court with him and he's got sent down."

"Oh he's not got sent down has he?" I heard her say.

"Yeah, three month," Dinky said.

I bounded into view and shouted, "No I've not got sent down love, I'm here."

Tiffany went crazy; she ran inside, grabbed my carrier bags and threw them at me, there were socks, shirts, and Dylan and Stones records strewn around the balcony.

"That's it," she screamed. "I've done with you, for good this time, and you

259

can fuck off as well Dawson, you lying bastard." It took many weeks of crawling and a proposal of marriage to get back in her good books.

I duly paid the 50p for the first few weeks, but it became a bit of a bind sending off postal orders to Rotherham. I had the fine transferred to Chesterfield where I could nip in and pay a bit every now and again when I signed on. I'd missed quite a few payments and was summoned to Chesterfield Magistrates for non-payment. I'd been in court a couple of times before for non-payment of fines; it was no big deal and the magistrates usually just gave me a ticking off or a warning.

I walked into court, cocky as fuck, and gave them my well-rehearsed shit about my mum. The magistrate glared at me for a good ten seconds. I don't like the look of this cunt, summat's not right here I thought. I looked down at my feet.

"Ronald Sharpe, you'll go to prison for twenty-one days, take him down," he said.

Fuckin hell, I nearly shit my pants. An officer grabbed my arm and began to lead me from the dock. Twenty-one days, that's three weeks, nigh-on a month of screws and snout and noshes and nonces and wings and things. I'll go stir crazy. Lifer Sharpe's on his way to death row.

The magistrate must have noticed the colour draining from my cheeks.

"Wait a minute," he said. "You look shocked, Mr Sharpe. Are you shocked?"

"Yes sir," I answered.

"Well, I'm glad you are. I'm going to suspend the sentence. You'll pay the fine at £3 a week, and if you miss one payment, you'll go straight to prison, do you understand?"

"Yes sir," I said.

Oooo fuckin hell, another lucky escape. I scuttled out of the courtroom rather sharpish, before the fucker had chance to change his mind.

Buster Pask lived in the ground floor flat below us on Bard Street. Born and bred down 'The Cliffe' (Attercliffe), Buster, a real old-skool Sheffield character, wore his Brylcreemed hair slicked straight back and he couldn't see further than a couple of inches without his milk-bottle-bottomed specs. Buster was in his mid-thirties, but his small stature and shabby appearance made him look a lot older. I got to know Buster

A young Robert Stocks mid-70s

when I stepped in and stopped a bunch of teenage lads who were pushing him around outside his flat. Buster and his family came in for a lot of stick from the young 'uns on the flats. His wife was fat and filthy, and his tribe of kids were always dressed in rags. The teenagers painted: 'A cunt lives here' in large white letters on the wall outside his front door.

Buster was a scrap/rag and bone man who knew all the tricks of the trade. One day he asked me if I wanted to come on his round with him. I'd got nothing better to do so I agreed to join him. We set off bright and early (8 o'clock) the next morning, walked into town and caught the bus to Buster's patch – Attercliffe. Still a bit puzzled about how we'd collect the scrap without a vehicle, I asked Buster.

"Oh," he told me, "I leave mi wheels at the scrap yard." Buster's wheels turned out to be a wheelbarrow. Not a normal wheelbarrow, oh no, this was a fuckin giant twin-wheeled wheelbarrow, as big as six wheelbarrows joined together and made from plate steel.

We grabbed a handle each and trundled out of Bradwell's scrap yard. I found it surprisingly easy to push, but then again it was empty. We hadn't gone fifty yards down Attercliffe Common, when Buster spotted two blokes carrying stuff out of a derelict building and chucking it in the back of a box van.

"What ya doing with that lot?" Buster shouted.

"We're dumping it," the bloke said.

"Can I have a look inside?" Buster said. Buster nipped in, came back out after a couple of minutes and said to the bloke, "I'll give you £2 for everything."

"You're on," the bloke answered. Buster gave him two quid notes.

"Come on, Ron. We've struck fuckin gold here," Buster said. We went in and it all looked like junk to me. Buster sifted through draws and wooden crates filled with bits of old machinery. He emptied a box and began filling it with brass cogs and washers.

"A bit of fuckin cream here, Ron lad." Buster laughed. Fuckin cream, I thought, what's he on about? It took us about six journeys to empty the building. The weigh-in amounted to sixteen quid. Buster took back his two quid lay-out, leaving us with seven quid each. Fuckin brilliant for a couple of hour's work.

"Look Ron," Buster said. "You're a good lad and you helped me out. I'll tell you how it works. I come down here five days a week, Monday to Friday, I work until dinnertime and then I'm in the boozer. I spend most of what I earn. It's the way I've always done it and you're welcome to come with me anytime. We'll split the earnings straight down the middle."

"That's sound, Buster," I said. So armed with the scrap man's most important tool – a magnet – I became an apprentice rag and bone-cum-scrap man, roaming and tatting around the streets of Attercliffe and Darnall. I learnt all about the non-ferrous stuff: copper, brass, ally, lead, stainless steel and gunmetal. "If the magnet dunt stick, it's fuckin good tackle," Buster told me. Like Buster said we only grafted until around twelve bells when the pubs opened. We'd usually earned around a tenner between us by opening time. Sometimes we'd have a good day and pick up a tenner each, other times only a couple of quid each, but we never went a day without earning a few bob.

Buster knew everybody down the Cliffe, and everybody knew Buster. Blokes would stop us in the street and tell us where they'd seen a bit of scrap.

Small steel factories, shops and warehouses saved bits of scrap for us. Like all good scrap men, Buster knew all the spiel and had the gift of the gab.

Buster told me some crazy stuff. "Have you ever heard of Ferrous O'Flanagan? Irish bloke, he is, Ron. One of the richest scrap men in Sheffield," Buster once asked me.

"Yeah. Bust. The name sounds familiar," I answered, trying to make him think I was in the know.

"He's not as rich as his brother though, Non-Ferrous O'Flanagan," Buster laughed.

Sometimes we went tatting around the terraced streets collecting rags.

"Tha's got to shout fuckin loud, Ron," Buster told me. "All women are in back kitchen so go down the gennels and shout in backyard." I felt a bit of a fool at first, but I soon got into it. I used the old Fat Freddy Ashmoor (the Cammell's Row rag man) tatting holler: "Raaaa-aaaaaag's, old iron."

Back at Bradwell's the rags were separated into different bundles. Woollens fetched more money than the cottons and linen. Buster sorted through the rags and saved some of the stuff to clothe himself, his wife and his tribe.

When we hit the pubs Buster bought all the drinks, he flatly refused to let me buy a round.

"I'll buy the beer and when this fuckin lot's gone, Ron, we'll earn some more tomorrow," he'd say. It didn't seem right for Buster to buy all the beer, so I used to get a round in when he went to the bogs. He really didn't mind, though. Buster just lived for the day. I went tatting at least three days a week and sometimes every day. We'd arrive back at the flats about four o'clock, after the pubs shut, usually pissed as farts, but unlike Buster I'd still got most of the cash I'd earned to be used as a sweetener.

I'd always wanted a sheepskin coat for the matches, especially in the winter when I froze half to death stood on the Kop. Sheepskins were part of a football hooligan's attire, but I'd never been able to afford one. One day Buster called round wearing an imitation sheepskin he'd picked up from the rags. It was bit tatty but not in bad nick.

"I'll give ya a quid for the sheepy, Bust," I said

"Don't want a quid, Ron. It's yours mate," Buster said. I wore the coat at the matches for a good couple of years. On long coach trips it was a god-send. I snuggled up under the fucker and was out for the count until we reached home. I had to sling it when, in a pissed-up state I'd lobbed it on the bedroom floor. I woke up in the middle of the night to yelps and squeals and found our dog, Lassie, laid on the inside of the coat licking blood off six puppies.

We boozed in most of the many pubs on Attercliffe Common; Buster knew all the regulars and the characters of the area. We were sat in the Cocked Hat one day when this bloke asked Buster, "Have ye seen owt of Scotch Mary?"

"Not seen her for a couple of months," Buster replied.

"I think she drinks in the Britannia now," somebody else said.

"Who's Scotch Mary?" I asked Buster.

"She's this Scottish prostitute I know," Buster said. "She doesn't charge me, though, she always gives me a freebie. You can fuck her if you want the next time we see her."

"Shall we go and have a pint in the Britannia then?" I said.

Over the next week on my insistence we called in the Brit every day. There was no sign of Scotch Mary, though. I thought it must be some kind of wind-up, until we walked in the pub one Friday afternoon and Buster pointed over to this woman sat alone at a table.

"There she is, Ron," Buster said, "Scotch Mary." I'd been imagining over the last week what Scotch Mary would look like but having seen the state of Buster's wife I hadn't built my hopes up. Buster bought her a drink and we joined her at the table. Scotch Mary wasn't too bad, she wasn't too good either. She looked to be in her mid-thirties and well-worn around the edges, but I'd fucked worse.

"This is my mate, Ron;" Buster said. "Is he all right for a fuck?"

"Yeah, course he is," Mary answered in a broad Scottish accent. I got an instant iron-bar stonker and had to adjust my stang under the table. I got chatting to Mary and found out she came from Kilmarnock. Mary was well in to me. She told me she was going back up to Scotland 'working' for a few weeks on the following Monday. She'd be staying at her sisters and I was welcome to join her. She said she would pay my train fare and pay for everything while we were up there. My stonker got bigger and harder. Fuck me I thought, I'm gonna be a pimp. When the pub shut at three she took me in a derelict house near the Cocked Hat. I'd had the horn on for about two hours and every time I'd gone for a piss in the boozer I'd had to force it down to stop it hitting the ceiling. We lay down on an old carpet and did the business.

When I'd finished I got off and started to piss like a racehorse in the corner, it was the first proper slash I'd had in hours. Suddenly a thought hit me, she's a fuckin prostitute, I can do whatever I want to her. I shot a jet of piss straight into her face.

"What the fuck are you doing you dirty bastard?" Mary shouted, shielding her face. I was a bit shocked; I thought she'd enjoy it.

"I'm fuckin pissing on you, ya dirty fuckin whore," I shouted.

"Well, fuckin don't," Mary said. She's gonna fuck off now I thought, but no.

"Look, I don't like that. You can do anything you want, and I still want you to come up to Scotland with me, but I'm not having that." She said she'd meet me at the train station at five o'clock on Monday evening.

All weekend I pondered over the trip to Scotland. One minute I'd be going for certain, the next I wasn't so sure. All sorts of shit went through my mind. Would an English bloke be all right in Kilmarnock? Would I get beat up in the boozers? Was Mary's sister younger than her? Would Mary let me fuck her sister? Yeah, course she would. Would Mary come home with a full slice every night and would I get fed up of fucking her? Probably, but would it be an exciting, unforgettable experience? It certainly fuckin would.

After another fallout with Tiffany, we'd only recently got back together. I might be able to get away with a day or two, but a couple of weeks, no chance. Right up to Monday teatime I was still in two minds.

There's two things I've regretted all my life, one: never riding a giant wave on a surf-board, the other… not going up to Kilmarnock with Scotch Mary.

Fast forward about fifteen years to the test centre at Manor Top. I'm sat in the waiting room ten minutes before my driving test. A young girl aged about eighteen sits on a row of seats opposite me. To say I'm nervous is an understatement; the girl's in a far worse state than me, she's visibly shaking.

The door swings open and in walks a character who'd turn anybody's head. He's dressed in a check jacket with a giant collar that would have been the height of fashion in 1976, but this is 1992. His shirt collar is frayed at the neck, but he's made the effort and he's slipped on the loudest tie ever seen. His half-mast, grey flannels are threadbare around the bollock area, his hair is greased and slicked straight back, his black rimmed specs have lenses two inches thick… fuck me; it's Buster. Buster doesn't even notice me; he looks at the girl and shouts, "Is there a bog in here darling? I'm bustin for a shite."

The girl looked like passing out.

"Narthen, Bust. How ya going?" I shout. Buster leans his neck forward, screws up his nose and squints at me.

"Fuckin hell, Ron. I've not seen you in years," Buster says. "I'll speak to ya in a minute; I'm nearly fuckin shittin mesen." Buster comes back out of the bog wafting his hand in front of his nose.

He reaches in the inside pocket of his jacket and pulls out a foot-long screwdriver. "Look at this fucker Ron," he shouts. "It's mi fuckin ignition key, come and have a look at mi wheels." We nip outside to check out Busters wheels. "What about that fucker?" Buster says, pointing at the wreck.

Now I've never been a 'reg' kinda guy, so I've no idea of the make or year of the car. All I can say is, it wasn't much of a step-up from Buster's tatting barrow. Fluffy dice hung from inside mirror and a trio of nodding dogs sat in the back window. Stickers from Ingoldmells market saying shit like: 'My other car is a Porsche' and 'The cunt in front is a cunt' covered the windows. Buster jumped in and slammed the screwdriver into the ignition slot, he gave it a twist and it fired up.

"First fuckin time, every fuckin time," Buster said.

Back in the waiting room the test examiners, armed with clipboards, enter and shout out our names. I set off and the test bloke instructs me to turn left onto City Road. A couple of hundred yards further down he tells me to take the next left turn. As I go to flick the indicator, I notice it's still flashing from the first left turn. I'd forgot to switch it off. That's me fucked I thought, and I was. The test ended, and Buster came back in a minute or two after me.

"How'd ya do Ron?" Buster shouted.

"Failed Buster," I said

"Me anall," Buster said. "I don't think the cunt liked my ignition key, but fuck 'em, I've been driving fuckin years. I don't need that cunt to tell me if I can drive or not."

I've not seen Buster since, I hope he's still around somewhere, still tatting and still pulling fast 'uns.

Moose's younger brother, Phil, and a few of his mates, kept the Dronny Dockers' bikers tradition and name alive. The colours on their Levi cut-offs, worn over leather jackets, were professionally made and really looked the bollocks. The top patch read 'DRONNY' and underneath the 'Death's Head' insignia the word 'DOCKERS. What they didn't know, is that rules and regulations apply in the Hell's Angels cult. To form a new chapter and to wear the colours, the bikers needed permission from the American Angels, who'd started the original movement.

On a weekend bike run the Dronny lads were approached by a Sheffield Hell's Angels chapter called the 'Blue Angels.' These were an off-shoot of a Glasgow gang who went by the same name. Phil and his mates were threatened and their colours, along with their cut-offs were taken by the Blue Angels... a bad move.

The following Thursday, around twenty tooled-up Dronny lads, plus Bent Nose, Wafer and a few other Blades lads met in Sheffield city centre. After a pint in the Penny Black we marched up to the Minerva Tavern – the Blue Angels headquarters. The Angels reputation went before them, but we were a bunch of footie lads and reputations meant fuck all to us. We were at it every Saturday, not once a year chucking deck chairs at Skeggy sea-front on Easter bank holiday Monday.

We'd found out the president of the Blue Angels went by the name of 'Skull', 'Bones', 'Death' or some intimidating tag, intended to scare the shit out of the establishment. We reached the boozer and as planned, split in to two groups, one guarding the front door, the other the back. Moose and Phil walked in. I'd had enough waiting and along with the rest of the back-door guard, entered the pub. Around a dozen Angels and a few of their mammas hung around the pool table.

"Which one of you cunts is Bones?" Moose asked. A small, scruffy, skinny lad stepped forward. "I'm Bones," the skinny cunt said. "Who wants to know?" The other lads entered from the front. Bones and the rest of Angels looked a tad worried when they saw twenty-plus lads tapping iron bars and hammers on to their hands.

"Well," Moose said. "You've got a few choices here, you bring back our young 'uns jacket, come outside and fight me one on one, or we kick fuck out of the lot of ya."

"Go on, Bones. Fight him," one of the mammas shouted. Bone's face dropped.

"Come on then: outside, just me and you. None of these'll join in," Moose said.

"I don't want any trouble," Bones said. The mammas were going crazy, screaming at their leader to fight. The rest of the Angels stared at the floor, like the Rogues on Coney Island beach when the Riffs surrounded them.

The only way we'll get a scrap tonight I thought, is with the slags, maybe we could fuck 'em all, after? Bones and his posse agreed to meet Phil and the rest of the Dronny lads at a neutral venue and return the colours. They chose the Big Tree pub at Woodseats for the hand-over.

On the following Sunday both groups of bikers rode to the boozer and the colours were handed back. We heard rumours the Glasgow Angels would be travelling down for revenge. We're still waiting.

A few months later a bus hit Phil's 750 Norton Commando as he rode through the Batemoor estate. Phil didn't come out of the coma and I was at the hospital with the rest of his brothers when he died from his injuries a couple of days later. He was nineteen years old.

R.I.P. Nupper – the name I'd always called him from being a toddler on Cammell's Row.

At the Tottenham game in early December, Moose, Wafe and me, all well-oiled from a long dinnertime session, entered the Lane end as the game kicked off. Wafe, like me was probably thinking, we'd suss out the situation, see if any more Blades were on, check out the size and quality of the Spurs mob before attempting anything rash, but Moose was having none of that shit. Moose had always been crazy, but since the death of his brother he'd got even worse.

"Come on," Moose said, and we had to follow as he pushed his way into the mass of 500-600 Spurs fans gathered behind the goal. The Tottenham fans had no idea who we were until Moose shouted, "Come on, ya Cockney bastards. I'll have any of ya fuckers."

Oh fuckin shit I thought, here we go again. We should have been wiped out, but a gap formed around us, until a Spurs fan with all his front teeth missing moved down towards us.

"I'll fackin av ya," he shouted at Moose.

"Come on then," Moose said. "Let's go to the bogs where there's no coppers, just me and you, one on one."

"Let's fackin do it here," the Spurs lad said. By this time the Tottenham mob realised there were only three of us and moved towards us from all sides. My heart started thumping and I braced myself for the ragging. Then this big Spurs lad dressed in a long sheepskin appeared by our side. He steamed into his own lads shouting, "You fackin wankers, what's wrong with ya? There's only three of em."

Now fuck knows who this lad was, but I saw genuine panic in some of the Spurs mob's eyes as they backed off.

"They're fackin useless," he said to us. "They only wanna fight when they've got the numbers."

Seeing the commotion, the coppers moved in, and as we were ushered out, the Spur's lad shouted, "Well done, lads. You've got some fackin bottle you av."

Coventry, in early January 1976. After hitching all morning Moose and me walk into a city centre boozer around dinnertime. The pub's packed with a coach load of lads and other Blades. We receive a loud cheer as we walk in. Fists raised, Higgy, one of the Manor Blades comes bouncing through the crowd.

"Come on then ya fuckin bastards, I'll have ya," he shouts. Everyone knows it's just a joke, but as I move towards him a gap forms as we jig around sparring up to each other. I throw a right-hander aiming to just miss his head, but he

266

moves slightly to one side. There's a loud crack as my fist connects with his nose and I know I've done some damage as the blood squirts out.

"Fuckin hell, Higg. Sorry pal, but you moved," I say. Somebody passes him a bar towel to mop up the blood.

"Don't worry about it, Ron. I know you didn't mean it," Higgy says. I felt really guilty about breaking Higgy's nose, but it was an accident. Higgy never held a grudge, and that's what Blades are all about. I still see him now and again and when we meet; we hold up our fists and have a bounce around; no punches are thrown though, not even in jest.

Educated, Dedicated, Supporters, or EDS for short. That's the name Sheffield United F.C. gave to the under sixteen Blades who stood in the fenced-off kids' pen in the bottom corner of the Kop. These young fuckers were supposed to be the future of our great football club. Educated and dedicated, a kind of nursery supporters' club, schooled in the principles of fair play and sportsmanship. An antidote maybe against the rising tide of football hooliganism, now escalating out of control.

It's late January 1976, Moose and me stand freezing to death on the slip road at Trowell Services just north of Nottingham. We're dressed in donkey jackets and steel-capped boots, issued free from R.D. Nichol and sons where we worked at the time. Nichol's – known locally in Dronny as 'the Fat Works' manufactured motor oils, anti-freeze and all different types of vehicle fluids, lubricants and engine greases. (Now the donkey jackets, or 'donks' as we called them, weren't really a fashion statement, they just kept us warm. A year or so later though, loads of football lads from every part of the country wore them as part of the hooligan attire. So fuck all the shit about Londoners starting off all the football fashion trends, the southern monkeys were a good year behind us.) We're on our way to Notts County for a friendly. We must be fuckin mad, the Blades have only won one game all season. A coach approaches; we see the sign in the front window, EDS Sheffield United F.C. The coach pulls up at the side of us. We must have been wearing scarves, which was usual on hitching expeditions – any passing Blades would usually pick us up if they had room. The door opens, a bloke leans out and shouts, "Going to County lads? Yeah? Jump aboard." There's just two empty seats at the front of the bus on the opposite side to the driver, the rest of coach is packed with mostly ten to fourteen-year-olds and a couple of middle-aged blokes who seem be in charge of the embryos. We plonk ourselves down, glad to be out of the cold.

Pointing to a cardboard box in the aisle, one of the blokes in charge says, "There's pop and crisps there lads, if you want some." Moose grabs a bag of crisps, rips it open and starts ramming the contents down his throat.

"No, no you've got to pay for them," the bloke shouts.

"Don't fuckin want 'em then," Moose says and lobs them back in the box.

Our arrival has caused a bit of excitement amongst the whipper-snappers. They've come down from the back and are squeezed in the aisle trying to check us out and get as close as they can to the two old hooligans.

"Eye-eye-eye-eye," one of the young 'uns shouts out, it's followed by the entire coach, including the blokes in charge singing: "Shoreham Republican Army, wherever we go we'll fight the foe cos we are the S.R.A." Slightly wrong but hey, who cares?

"We'll never be mastered by no Wednesday bastards," and the full repertoire of Blade battle hymns follow. Ten minutes later the coach is rocking as we hit the city centre. The fired-up EDS posse bang on the windows and hurl abuse at passing County fans.

A lone infant voice squeals out, "You're gonna get you're fuckin heads kicked in." As the clapping follows one of the blokes in charge shouts, "That's enough, you're going a bit too far now," but the baby Blades are having none of it.

"They're not usually like this," one of the blokes tells us.

We spot a boozer and the driver pulls up and drops us outside. As we leave the coach one of the blokes shouts, "If you want a lift back lads, the coach'll be parked outside the ground after the game."

"It's all right pal, we'll make our own way back, but thanks anyway," I say to the bloke. All the EDS have moved to one side of the bus and are squashed up against the windows waving to us. We wave back and double up laughing as the coach pulls off.

A week later Bernard Stratford's fatha's van made a rare appearance for the trip to Arsenal. The bus, with Bernard sat in the passenger seat next to his dad arrived in Pond Street about 8 a.m. I met up with Dinky, Grizz and three Hackenthorpe lads: Erik Foster, Alan Inckles and Butts. Sam and Ess, two inseparable, terrible young rogues, also from Hackenthorpe, had booked on the bus, but only Sam turned up. Three or four other lads arrived, and we set off. We drove up to Ess's house to try and drag him along, but Ess had been a naughty boy during the week and his mother wouldn't let him come out.

The fun started as soon as we hit the M1. Dinky shouted to his fellow Wybournite, Grizz, "Nah then Grizz, were there any Dracula films on telly last night?" Grizz, who stood well over six foot and weighed in at around eighteen stone said, " Just fuck off, Dawson."

"Look at the fuckin size of him," Dinky said to us all. "Every time there's a Dracula film on box, Grizz takes a big wooden cross to bed and puts it under his pillow."

"I'm fuckin telling ya now, Dawson, shut the fuck up," Grizz said.

"Every fucker on Wybourn knows you take a cross to bed when Drac's on," Dinky said.

"I was only about eight when that happened," Grizz said. "And why don't ya fuck off and have a fuckin wash, ya dirty bastard."

"Fuckin eight," Dinky said, holding his arms in the shape of a cross. "I heard it was only a couple of weeks ago. Please help me, Dracula gonna get me."

By this time we were falling about laughing. Grizz was quite capable of ripping Dinky's head off, but he knew the score and just about managed to keep his cool during the wind-up.

We hit London about one o'clock and did the session at a pub near the ground. We entered Highbury on the Clock End just before kickoff. A few Arsenal lads dressed in sheepskins were stood behind the goal, but although they sussed us, none of them bothered us. Maybe they thought a dozen or so lads weren't worth it, or maybe Grizz's size put them off.

A group of about forty Blade singers were stood on the side terrace to our left so we went over and stood next to them. The game kicked off in front of a massive fourteen and a half thousand. Having won only one game all season, the Blades weren't exactly a big draw.

We stood freezing to death and watched the Blades fuck up again, losing 1-0.

Our bus was parked on a back street with one other van and two coaches. The back of our bus faced the back seat of one of the buses. Two young girls aged about fifteen were waving through the window at us. Dinky and me, whipped our stangs out and waggled them at the girls.

The girls started giggling, until a few blokes appeared on the back seat. The next minute a group of blokes, led by one of the girls' dads surrounded our bus.

"Somebody on here's fuckin flashing in front of my daughter. I'll fuckin kill 'em," he shouted.

"Get the fuck out of here," we shouted to Bernard's fatha and the bus skidded off down the street.

After a good session around Soho, we had an hour or so left before the bus left at midnight. The pubs had shut, so half of us decided to hit a strip club.

"We're leaving at bang on midnight," Bernard's fatha told us. "And if you're not back, we're going without you."

"Fuck off you old cunt," we told Bernard's fatha.

We entered the strip-joint and stood in line at the pay-in desk. I can't remember the exact entrance fee; it could have been two quid maybe, but in the split-second the bloke on the counter looked up towards the next customer, I'd lifted my two quid, along with another couple of notes from the open cash tin on the desk. I'd visited a dive of a strip club in Soho back in the 60's, but this was a more up-market joint that had the look of a small night club. The stage, with proper velvet curtains stood on the same level as the hundred or so seats in front of it. To the left of the main area, a separate, smaller room with comfy seats, sold weak, flat, southern beer at extortionate prices.

We took our seats about halfway from the front and settled down for the show. The lights dimmed, and the first dipper walked on stage and sat on a chair in the middle. We learnt from one of the punters, that the girls, because of new licensing laws were no longer allowed to dance. The girl, still sat in the chair, slowly clothed off.

After a couple of minutes, she's down to just her pants. After a swift two second flash of her slice, the curtains drew. A few minutes later the curtains opened again, and a different girl's perched on the chair. After three or four more dippers, once more the curtains opened, and a familiar face and body came into view.

"Fuckin hell," I said to the lads. "I know her, she's from Page Hall. I pulled her at the Penthouse a few months ago."

269

"Yeah sure ya did," one of the lads said.

"I'm telling ya, her name's – I can't remember her name now, but I could then.

"Fuck off, Ron, ya lying cunt," Dinky said.

"Right ya cunts, I'll show ya."

I stood up and shouted the girl's name. She looked up straight away, saw me and shouted back, "Hey-up Ronnie, what are you doing here?" I sat back down beaming like a loon.

"Ya jammy bastard," Dinky said.

During the break in the show the girl came from the dressing room and we had a chat. She told me she worked the club, along with another Sheffield bird most weekends. The night at the Penthouse had been a one off. I'd been chatting her up every Thursday night for weeks and one night I'd finally managed to get back to her flat. She didn't mention owt about being a dipper though; if she had, I would probably have proposed marriage.

Before the next show started, Dinky performed the original version of the Full Monty. (Those with nervous dispositions and weak stomachs, look away now.) Dink walked onto the stage, dropped his pants to his ankles, turned around, bent forward and pulled open the cheeks of his arse. The area around his starfish was a sickly yellow colour, decorated with bits of pink bog-roll and funklenuts. The audience were in bits. The manager, all dinner-suited and dickey-bowed up, rushed to the stage and said to Dink, "That's the funniest thing I've seen in years, the drinks are on me." So Dinky copped for a couple of free pints.

It must have been well past one o'clock when we left the club, the only reason being we'd all spent up. Not for one second did we think Bernard's fatha would dare to leave us, but when we got back, the van had gone. We couldn't really blame him for fucking off. So there we were, six of us, stuck in London with hardly a penny between us.

We must have walked to St Pancras because we ended up there, dossed out on the benches. We woke up feeling like shite and discussed ways and means of getting home. The Page Hall dipper and her mate, both carrying overnight bags and no doubt on their way back to Sheffield walked through the station and gave us a wave. I thought I could maybe scrounge the train fare off the girls, but that would have been pushing it. We decided to thumb it back and jumped the tube up to Hendon. After walking to the start of the M1 we split up into twos and tossed one of the few coins we had between us to see who got the position to get the first lift. Dinky and Grizz won, Sam and me were second in line, the other two third. So Dinky and Grizz are at the nearest end to London, Sam and me, fifty yards further up, the others fifty yards further up than us.

We'd only been stood there for ten minutes or so when we saw a car indicate and slow down. The car stopped about ten yards in front of Dinky and Grizz and they ran towards it. As they reached it, the wheels screeched and smoked like a getaway car on an armed blag.

As it neared, the indicator came back on and it pulled up at the side of us. The door opened and before the driver even spoke, Sam and me knew exactly what had happened.

Now imagine you're a driver, maybe on your way home after a night in the capital, or maybe just out for a leisurely Sunday morning spin. You see two people hitching on the end of the M1, you're a good-natured kinda chap and think, well, I'll give 'em a lift. From fifty yards away they look like two ordinary people, but as you get closer you notice one is an eighteen-stone dishevelled giant and the other one looks like Charlie Manson fresh from a weekend slaughter orgy.

"I didn't like the look of those two," the bloke said. "I'm only going up to the next services, but you're welcome to a lift."

"Yeah that's sound," we said, and jumped in. We turned to see Dinky and Grizz running towards the car screaming threats. We gave them a smile and a wave as the car set off.

The driver looked to be in his late thirties/early forties, slightly built, with a raggy, black moustache. The weird looking little cunt had a touch of the shakes. I have to say at this point, neither Sam nor me had any idea the bloke had ulterior motives. We chatted away, as you do when you manage to hitch a ride, it's the code of the road; it's the polite thing to do. Ya know, useless shit like where we were going, where we'd been, anything to avoid a long embarrassing silence.

In the area behind the back seat of the estate, we noticed a crumpled blanket that looked like it could be covering something around the size of say... a body. Red coloured stains that could well have been... blood covered the cloth. Sam nudged me and whispered, "Look at that fucker Ron; ya don't think it could be a body, do ya?"

"No, it can't be," I answered. We reached the services and the bloke offered to buy us a cup of tea in the café area before he left, we must have told him we had no money. Food never smells so good as when you're starving and you're skint. In the queue he asked if wanted anything to eat. We didn't want to push it and asked him if we could have a slice of toast each.

"You can have anything you want," the bloke answered. "Do you want a full breakfast?"

"Yeah, if It's okay," we said.

"Just get what you want. It's on me," the bloke said. So, it's bacon, egg, sausage, tomatoes, fried bread, toast: the lot. As we wolfed down the mashings the bloke nipped off to buy a paper.

"Fuckin hell, we're all right here, Sam, aren't we?" I said.

"What about the blanket in the back," Sam said. "I'm sure there's a body under it. I bet the cunt's a serial killer."

"Is he, fuck," I said. "It'll be a decorating sheet with a bit of paint on it or summat, anyway there's two of us. If he tries owt we'll kick his head in." The bloke came back with a pile of Sunday rags and handed us one each. We were straight into the back pages for the footie results and the league tables. The Blades were still rock bottom, 62 points from safety.

"I'll tell you what, lads," he said. "I'm not doing anything today, so I'll take you up to the next services, it'll get you a bit closer home."

"Yeah, that's great," we said. He pulled two cunt books from the bottom of the pile of newspapers and handed us one each.

"Have a look at them," he said. Ah-ah, so that's his game, the old cunt book sketch. I don't think Sam twigged on at first, but I'd been the victim of a groomer who'd pulled the exact same stunt ten years earlier on the way back from London on a train.

As we walked back to the car I whispered to Sam, "Just play along with the cunt, he's a bummer, keep him sweet and we'll get him to take us all the way home." As we reached the car he said, "One of you can sit in the front with me if you want."

"Yeah okay," I said. "I'll sit in the front."

"You look tired," he said to Sam. "Get your head down for an hour." He started with the shit as soon as we set off.

"Do you like naked girls? Are you getting worked up?"

"Oh yeah, they're lovely," I answered. Sam had his head down in the back pretending to be asleep. The shit carried on until we approached the next services.

"I'll pull in here and drop you off," he said.

"Right, okay," I said.

We parked up and the bloke said, "I don't like leaving you stranded, I'll take you up to the next services if you want, are you still hungry? We can get something to eat while we're here." We went into the café area and ordered some more snap.

Back in the car the shit carried on. We were about ten miles from Leicester Forest Services as twelve o'clock approached.

"Do you fancy going to the pub for a drink?" the bloke asked.

"Yeah why not," I said. Sam's still dossed out in the back.

We took the next exit and pulled up at a little country type pub. Sam's still blowing Zs with the dead body.

The bloke didn't seem too bothered; this was his chance to get one of us on our own. I knew that, but he didn't know I knew that. Even at this early hour the pub was pretty full.

"What do you want to drink?" he asked me.

"I'll have a double brandy and a pint of bitter please," I answered. He bought the drinks and we found a table. I downed the brandy in one and he went to bar and bought me another.

I don't know if it was his first time out on a cruising mission, but he seemed really on edge. Although he'd hinted all through the journey, he'd never actually mentioned his intentions. I swigged another pint and brandy and said we'd better get off. As we were leaving the pub he asked, for obvious reasons, if I wanted to use the toilet.

"No, I'm all right," I told him, and we went out to the car. We drove up to the services, pulled in and got out of the car.

"Look lads," he said. "I can't take you much further. Well, I can, but you must know what I want, don't you?"

"What the fuck do you mean?" I said

"You know what I want," he answered.

Sam and me looked at each other, registering false shock. I grabbed the

272

bloke's neck.

"What are you saying, ya dirty basted," I shouted. He started to whimper.

"I'm sorry, I'm sorry, please don't hit me, I thought you knew. Here, have some money." He pulled out about a fiver in notes and change and handed them to me.

"Right ya cunt," I said. "Fuck off, and think yourself lucky we haven't kicked ya fuckin head in." He jumped in the car and sped off. Sam and me, felt not even a twinge of remorse as we shared out the money. We walked down to the slip road and stuck out our thumbs. We hadn't been there long when a car with two Pakistani blokes inside pulled up. They were from Sheffield and said they would drop us off at the end of the Parkway, fuckin great stuff. It took the driver a few hundred yards to pick up speed. We hit 80 M.P.H. then 90 and then 100. We flew up the outside lane, shooting past everything in sight. One of the downsides to hitch-hiking is you have no say about how fast, or how slow the driver chooses to travel. Memories of my two previous crashes came flooding back. I pictured myself in terrible pain, slowly dying, trapped in a mangled wreck. Slow down ya bastard, I'm thinking. I didn't think the car could go any faster, but it did. My thoughts got quite racist, slow fucking down, ya dirty, stinking, fuckin Paki bastard, ya gonna kill us. At this moment I would rather have been bent over the back seat getting rogered… slain even, by the serial-killing cruiser. We reached Sheffield in about half an hour; the longest fuckin half hour of my life.

At the Everton home game in early February there's a good two hundred lads in the Whetstone. I took the lead, somebody had to, two days later Wednesday are back at the Lane for a County Cup game. Wednesday now plied their trade in Division Three. Their numbers had been steadily growing since the early 70s and now a combination of easy pickings, lack of opposition and the bullying of small town, lower league teams with hardly any lads saw their numbers increase even more.

After five years of defending the Shoreham against the First Division's best mobs, hundreds of arrests had started to take its toll on the Blades mob.

With Wednesday successfully defending their Kop against the likes of Aldershot, Rochdale and Crewe, it had been the in-thing in Sheffield for the last couple of years to be a 'Pig.' It weren't the in-thing though when Man Utd turned up in 74. Most of the in-crowd suffered a brief memory lapse and forgot their way to Hillsborough that day

Success on the terraces was far more important to the lads of the time, than success on the pitch. Not only were our numbers shrinking, but some Blades were even defecting to Wednesday. We were getting down to the bare bones. It's a case of which do you prefer? Taking thousands to places like Chester, Bury and Oldham to hound and bully the locals, or stood in the crowd at West Ham, Tottenham or Chelsea, hoping no one would ask you the time. There are other issues to consider though and it could be something to do with success on the pitch.

273

Wednesday reached the Cup final in 1966 and every football fan dreamed of a Wembley appearance. It's been diluted in these modern times, but throughout the 60s, 70s, and even the 80s and 90s the FA Cup final was the highlight of the season. Young kids of an impressionable age, let's say ten to fifteen years old seem to jump on bandwagons.

A personal experience (and he's gonna hate me for this) came, when Wednesday got to Wembley in 66. We were playing football on the Crick-Crock on the Friday teatime, the day before the Cup final when half a dozen or so Wednesday mates walked across the playing field carrying a large Owls banner. All these lads were a bit younger than me, making them twelve-thirteen years old. Butch, a diehard Blade held one of the banner poles; he nearly shit his pants when he saw us.

"Fuckin hell, Butch," I shouted. "What the fuck are ya doing?" Butch didn't answer. He'd been caught up in the euphoria and it must have warped his young mind.

A few weeks later, after all the fuss died down, Butch realised the errors of his ways and returned to the fold. I never let him forget it, and to this day I still give him some stick about it.

What I'm getting at here, is how many more young kids around that age did Wednesday's Cup final appearance influence? And more importantly, eight to ten years later, did a lot of these kids come of age and were they now Wednesday's boys? The same could be said of the Blades short period of success, promotion in 71 and the fantastic start to the 71-72 season.

Ten years later in the comfort zone of the 3rd and 4th Divisions, some of the young Blades who'd hung on the white railings marvelling at the skills of Tony Currie and the rest, went on to form the Blades Business Crew.

When it came to the question of organisation and leaders, there simply weren't any. At twenty-four years old, I was one of, if not the oldest in our group. Herman, Wafe, and Dinky were all eighteen months younger. Moose and Dick Dung were twenty-one. Stocksy, Johnno, Horton, Knockers, Bent Nose, Gibby, Chris Midge, Tommy Ridley, Brid, Sully, Black Lol, the Cromford Street boys, some of the Darnall lads, and quite a few of the others were only eighteen-nineteen. Younger still at fifteen-sixteen were Sam, Ess, Blacks, Clarky, Sparky and Chesterfield Charlie, the same age as Pie-Eye, Keith Bullet and Mark Woodhead from Pitsmoor, and Dreads, a happy-go-lucky, fresh-faced, young skinheaded rascal from Darnall, who along with a few more whipper-snappers had started to emerge through the ranks.

Even though I could rally the troops, get them out of the pub when it kicked off, or get them to turn left or right onto certain streets, I didn't feel confident enough or hard enough to take on the responsibility. Some of the lads did look to me for leadership though. Moose would have been the natural leader, because no one would ever have dared to say to him, "Who the fuck are you, telling us what to do?" But Moose just wanted to fight.

Now it wasn't like I stood on a soapbox or anything, issuing orders, I just said to anybody who'd listen, "We've got to get sorted for them bastards on

Monday or we're gonna get fucked again." The word spread, and everybody said they were up for it.

"Everybody wear your colours," I said. "Lets show the cunts who we are."

We arranged the meet for half six-seven in the Royal Standard. I can't remember why we chose the Standard, but we did meet there now and again, as the away coaches parked across the road from the pub.

I walked in the boozer, scarfed up, at about quarter to seven and found Stocksy and about ten others inside. Only Stocksy wore colours. By seven there's about twenty in, by seven-fifteen, there's around forty lads altogether, only a dozen or so wore their colours.

"I can't believe this," I said. "The fuckin wankers have shit it again." We all agreed that no matter how many Wednesdayites were on the Kop, we'd steam straight into them. We left the pub just before kickoff and walked up Shoreham Street to the ground. The first lads through the turnstiles waited inside until we were all together. We walked up the steps trying to psych each other up, shouting, "Fuckin come on. No messing about. Straight into the cunts."

It was a different kind of buzz and a different kind of fear against Wednesday. Not a fear of getting hurt, it's the dread of humiliation. The shame of getting run, or even worse, losing face to some fucker you could bump into while shopping on the Moor, or out boozing in a nightclub. But we needed to show the bastards there was still a few of us who'd fight for the Blades.

A few Wednesdayites at the concourse at the back of the Kop scattered as they saw us approach. More Wednesdayites stood in the entrance to middle of the Kop moved back as we ran in screaming "United." We had no idea how many would be on the Kop and by now we were so fired up, we didn't care. The Wednesdayites moved back and we ran through the gap they'd left, punching and booting anything in front of us. Only when they realized our numbers did they respond. We were surrounded by hundreds of Wednesdayites, and were attacked from all sides. After thirty seconds or so on the defensive, we were rescued – that's the only word to describe it by a squad of coppers. Another minute in there and we would have been wiped-out. The coppers surrounded us and ushered on to the concourse.

"Keep together lads," one of our lot shouted, as the coppers herded us along the back of the Kop towards the Cherry Street side.

"Where the fuck are you taking us?" one of the lads said to a copper.

"Shut the fuck up and keep moving," the copper replied. We reached the exit gate and we were pushed out of our own ground onto the Cherry/Shoreham Street corner.

"Now fuck off," a copper shouted. "If you try and get back in, we'll arrest the lot of you." Some of the lads wanted to go back in, but we reasoned if we did, Wednesday would be ready for us, and if not we'd all be nicked.

We retreated back to the Standard to plan our next move. A couple of lads had been nicked and we'd lost one or two in the melee, so there's about thirty-five of us left. I wasn't too downhearted, at least we'd shown some bottle, I knew forty Wednesday wouldn't even have the arse to run into forty Blades, let alone hundreds.

But the night was still young. We stayed in the Standard until the game nearly ended. We left the pub carrying glasses and bottles. Stones and lumps of wood were picked up before we gathered on the corner of St Mary's Road. Again we urged each other on and psyched each other up. The game ended and the first batch of Wednesdayites walking down Shoreham Street filled the road. We ran towards them, which stopped them in their tracks. They backed off as a hail of bottles and bricks landed around them. We advanced twenty yards or so, until Wednesday, boosted by more of their own leaving the ground, ran towards us. Vast numbers saw us retreat and scamper back down Shoreham Street.

One or two of the lads stopped and picked up the bricks we'd thrown before shooting off again. The coppers were now back on the scene. They ushered the Wednesdayites towards town and a few police stopped and turned back after chasing us towards the Standard. Somebody noticed we'd lost Chris Midgley in the melee. We'd been run for a second time, but again we'd shown some bottle.

"There's too many of the bastards," was the general opinion. Someone suggested we give it ten minutes to let their numbers dwindle a bit before venturing into Pond Street for another pop. We armed ourselves with anything at hand and headed towards the bus station, again we had no idea how many would be hanging around Pond Street. We entered the main terminal and on seeing us approach a few Wednesdayites stood in the bus queues removed their colours, none of these were lads though and they were left alone. We reached the escalators leading up to the gallery and found Chris Midgley, unconscious and covered in blood lain out at the bottom. We helped Chris to his feet, and he came round a bit. He told us he'd been jumped by a group of Wednesdayites. Chris weren't in any fit state to carry on, "I've had enough, I'm fuckin off home," he told us.

Reaching the threepenny bit kiosk, we spotted a group of about fifteen Wednesdayites outside the Friary chippy on the gallery. A few of us turned back and ran up the escalator to cut off one escape route. The rest turned right and ran up to where the gallery merged with Flat Street. The Wednesdayites dropped their chips and scattered towards Fitzalan Square. We chased them up to the Square, but they ran in different directions and escaped.

That was it for the night; we retired to the Penny Black and mulled over the night's events. The main topic of the conversation centred on the Blades who'd failed to show. We decided from now on we'd do our own thing.

The following Saturday before the home game against Aston Villa, most of the lads who attended the Wednesday game were sat together in the Whetstone. The atmosphere was different from any pre-match Blade gathering I'd ever seen. Absentees, some who I'd known for years, were shunned when they tried to speak to us. One or two, who mumbled excuses like "Fuckin hell, it weren't even a proper game" "Who's bothered about the County Cup?" "If it had been a League match everybody would have been there," were shot down in flames.

I said, "Fuck the County Cup; do you think any of us are bothered about the fuckin County Cup? What did we say last week? Everybody out for the

Wednesday game and all you cunts shit it; what the fuck's up with ya?" The mob was split, but around two o'clock something happened that could and probably should have united us. A lad ran in the pub and shouted, "Villa's here; loads of 'em on Arundel Gate." The pub came alive and the shout went up, "Come on, Villa's here." Everybody ran towards the door – everybody except us.

"Fuck em," I said. "Let them cunts go and do something for once, I'm not going." Everyone agreed. Lads running to the door who tried to urge us on were told to: "Fuck off."

A few minutes later they came back in, all full of it. They'd run Villa, who were no mugs. Only a year earlier, Villa fucked Wednesday all over Hillsborough, but for some ridiculous reason these Blades wouldn't turn out for Wednesday! I couldn't get my head round it. Our boys left the pub and ended up in the Lansdowne on London Road.

At the game, we abandoned the middle of the Kop where the mob stood, and moved to the right-hand side toward the John Street terrace, roughly opposite the corner flag. Anybody who tried to join us, who wasn't at the Wednesday game were fucked off. Stocksy just wanted to move over to the middle of the Kop and in his words 'batter the bastards.'

Over the next few weeks we continued to go it alone. We met up before the game, stood together, left the ground together and drank in town together. Stories circulated from the Wednesday game and we heard tales of Blade kids who'd been slapped and had their colours taken. I hated the Wednesday bastards more than ever; they were arrogant, smug cunts, but who could blame them? They'd proved they were number one on the terraces in Sheffield, so they took this self-assurance into the pubs and onto the streets of the city centre. They looked down on Blades and bullying was rife, but football battles weren't just fought on the terraces and maybe that's why they came unstuck when they bumped into lads who stood up to them.

The Dronny lads, along with a few Sheffield mates had dozens and dozens of confrontations with Wednesday throughout the mid-70s. We fought in pubs, nightclubs and on the streets. Not once, and I mean not once, did Wednesday want to know, unless the numbers were in their favour.

These fights were almost entirely down to Moose, who'd grown from a skinny teenager into a strapping twenty-one-year-old scrapping machine. We'd be in town on Thursday, Friday and Saturday nights, every week, and no matter where we were and no matter how many we faced, Moose would announce we were Blades and ready for anything. Moose's front could unnerve any fucker and it rubbed off on the rest of us. But it wasn't just front, Moose looked and fought like a Viking, he was as hard as a turnip, fearless and lethal with both his fists and his nut. Wednesday lads who'd had their noses splattered or their teeth removed by Moose's forehead didn't seem so cocky any more.

What was it with the fuckin Geordies? 'Why-eye-like bonny lad' 'Gannin doon the fooking Blaydon races' and shit. There's no denying Newcastle had a huge mob, took thousands away and had some big, mean, hard fuckers amongst their ranks, but what made anybody want suck up to them?

Sinny and Podge switched allegiance a couple of years earlier and now Bent Nose and his mate Brush got friendly with some Newcastle fans they'd met somewhere on their travels. Arse-licking Blades were making our already dilapidated mob look even worse.

March the 6th 1976, Newcastle's playing at Derby which means they'd probably be stopping off in Sheffield either before or after the game. The Blades were away at Man City. I nipped in the Penny Black at opening time wearing my trusty sheepy and a red and white scarf with the black horizontal stripes I'd nicked off a Man Utd fan.

No meet up or arrangements had been made, but I thought there might be a few Blades knocking about who'd be making the trip. Nobody came in, so after a couple of pints I decided to go up to the Lane to see if I could get on one of the supporter's club coaches as I didn't fancy going on the train on my jacks. There was just one bus from the headquarters' branch of the supporters' club parked outside the players' entrance on John Street.

The headquarters' branch were, or thought they were, the elite Unitedites. These were the proper fans, the real supporters, the life-blood of the club who travelled to every game, home and away. The trouble with this lot though, the majority didn't have a clue what supporting the Blades was all about. Although not quite the tartan-blanketed, politely applauding, multi-badge wearing, stereotypical football 'fan', they weren't exactly fanatical in their support for United. They'd never swayed or got crushed on the Shoreham, fought to defend their end, sung until their throats were hoarse or ran a gauntlet of house bricks and bottles. They had no idea how to celebrate a goal, no idea how to hug and kiss a fellow Blade in a moment of euphoria.

Yeah, the headquarters' branch, a bunch of miserable fuckers, loners who mixed with other loners, forming groups of loners, who were married to the Blades and knew fuck all about anything except the Blades.

There were one or two lads aboard who would have loved to have been 'lads' but they couldn't quite bring themselves to take the plunge. I reckon every football club in the land had a headquarters' branch, or its equivalent.

The supporters' club buses sometimes bore the brunt of the shit us lot caused at home games, so I got plenty of uneasy stares from the normals aboard. They'd no doubt seen me rampaging around the Lane and I could tell they were thinking, what's this trouble-causing cunt doing on here? This is a respectable bus don't you know. But I thought: fuck you lot.

I learned on the journey the bus was booked in as guests of their Man City counterparts. We arrived at Maine Road about 2 o'clock and filed off the bus. The maze of back-to-back terraced streets, narrow alleyways and snickets surrounding Maine Road made it one of the most shit-ya-pants grounds in the country.

We entered the City supporters' club bar at the side of the ground. Only a hand full of Blades wore colours and everyone removed them before they left the coach. Fuck-em, I thought, and I left my scarf on, again this caused a bit of concern. In the safety of the club, a few pints loosened up the dedicated followers and Blade songs rang around the room. kickoff approached and as we left the club I found out every single one of the Blades had tickets for the seats. There was no segregation or areas for away fans at Maine Road, but it was against my principles to sit in the stand, and, after removing my scarf, I joined a large queue for the Kippax terrace, the only standing area in the ground. City's mob occupied the middle section of the terrace, so I stood over to the right-hand side, on a line with the corner flag.

City won the League Cup a week earlier and just before kickoff the players paraded the trophy around the pitch.

I'd had a good few ales, but I wasn't drunk or stupid enough to put my scarf on or start showing off. The City fans around me were all flat-capped old blokes and after a few minutes I thought I'd test the water by shouting – not very loud: "Come on United get in to 'em." Nobody took any notice. I got a bit braver and shouted a little bit louder, but kept my support nice and polite, making sure I made no insulting remarks about City.

Into the second half I got even braver; I arranged my scarf so about an inch of the colours were visible under my sheepskin collar. A bad move. A group of half a dozen twelve-year-olds moved up from the front and one of them noticed my scarf. They stood a couple of yards behind me. I could see spit flying past my head and feel it hitting and dangling from my hair. This went on a few minutes and with the Blades losing 4-0 and the game nearing the end I decided to fuck off. I felt the back of my head, soaked in gozz, I took off my sheepy to check it out, it looked like the contents of a spittoon had been emptied on it.

I asked a copper outside the ground where the coaches were parked, and he pointed me in the right direction. When the buses (a fleet of two) came into view, I checked no City fans were around, whipped out my scarf and put it on to make everybody think I'd worn it all through the game. Most of the Blades were already aboard. I cleaned myself up the best I could by wiping off the spit with the pages of a newspaper.

The coach dropped me off in Fitzalan Square and I walked down to the Penny Black. Bent Nose and Brush, both wearing black and white Newcastle scarves were stood outside the pub with a group of Geordies.

"Well fuck me," I said to them. "Look at you two cunts, all cosy with the fuckin Geordies."

Bent Nose just laughed.

"We've had a right fuckin day in Derby," he said.

"Yeah, I've had a right fuckin day in Manchester. Stood on the Kippax on my own, getting flobbed on by a bunch of fuckin chabbies."

Mitch guffawed and shouted to his Geordie mates, "Sharpy's been to Man City and got flobbed on by some young 'uns."

I couldn't stay mad at him for long though. Baskin Shark made everything in to a joke and he rarely lost his rag. He could defuse any tricky situation with a laugh, but he was capable of ripping any fucker's head off who'd got on the wrong side of him.

The only music scene in the mid-70s that remotely united the football lads was 'Northern Soul' (I don't know if there was a Southern equivalent as I wasn't into it, but there probably was). I knew a few Blades who were into the scene. They hung out at Samantha's (formally the Heartbeat) on Queens Road, a nightclub we used on Saturdays at the time. Northern Soul nights were held there every so often and lads and lasses from all over the North of England travelled to Sheffield for the all-nighters. My Blade mates knew quite a few football lads from places like Nottingham, Stoke, Manchester and Wigan, the home of the famous 'Casino.'

One Saturday in Samantha's, one of the Blade lads told me about an all-nighter starting at 2 a.m. when the club closed, and finishing at eight in the morning. He had something to do with organising the event and he asked me if I wanted to come in (free of charge of course). I thought yeah why not.

We had to leave the club at 2 o'clock for some reason, probably so the DJs could set things up. The queue of Soulies stretched all the way down the stairs past the entrance to the skating rink. Every one of them carried holdalls. I asked my mate why? He told me the bags contained a change of clothes and towels. I was still a bit puzzled.

When the doors opened we went straight to the front of queue, got a nod from the bloke on the pay-in counter and walked in. I walked to the bar and ordered a pint.

"Sorry we don't serve alcohol only soft drinks," the barman said.

"Fuckin hell," I said to my mate. "You didn't tell me they didn't serve ale, I can't go all night without a drink."

"You'll be all right," he told me. "Wait till it gets going, you'll love it."

The club filled up and after half an hour the dance floor literally bounced; I could see it moving. I wasn't really into the music, but the dancers amazed me, some of them were incredible. I'd not heard any of the songs before, but the music had a sort of early-mid 60s, up-tempo, soul, Tamla Motown feel. Most of the lads were dressed in high waist Oxford bags, with sleeveless star jumpers or vests. Some of them sprinkled talcum powder on to the floor to assist their spins and twists. When the dancers came off the dance floor dripping in sweat I realised what the towels were for. I couldn't take my eyes off the dancers and a lot of them were looking at me, being the only one in the club not dancing.

It sempt like some of the songs were just run-of-the-mill and some were classics. Every now and again as the intro to a song came on, or the DJ announced the title, a huge roar went up and everyone ran to the dance floor. I stayed in the club for a couple of hours and I would have probably stayed all night if there'd been some ale on. I really enjoyed the experience, and so I salute you, my young, soul-rebel brothers and sisters. 'Keep the fuckin faith.'

Gibby started running a coach for the lads. As always, the organizer travelled for nowt and made a few quid profit which everybody knew and accepted. We were a tight-knit little bunch of around forty-fifty, who stuck together and looked out for each other. We drank together in town after the home games and if we came straight back from away matches we stuck together in town for the rest of the night. Wednesdayites wouldn't come anywhere near us.

After the win against Villa (only their second of a disastrous season), the

Blades failed to win any of their next seven games and after a 5-0 defeat at Tottenham they were relegated at the end of March.

Four Blades: one brave, one foolhardy, one Kung-Fu expert and a lone drunkard travelled to Tottenham. A week later on the 3rd of April, thousands of Blades converged on Norwich. Fuckin strange breed us U-bleedin-nitedites.

As if to reward our loyalty the Blades stuffed Norwich 3-1, their first win for two months. Fuckin strange team, that U-bleedin-nited.

Gibby's coach dropped us in Norwich at dinnertime before moving on to Great Yarmouth where it would pick us up at midnight. We caught the train to Yarmouth after the game, planning to drink the resort dry.

We plot up in a massive sea-front boozer called the Ship or some other nautical name. Another coach load of Blades, plus lads who'd travelled in cars and vans arrive and the festivities begin. Dinky starts the evening's insanity by announcing – for a whip round – he'll do a streak around the boozer, wearing only a black top hat he's borrowed from me (bought from a jumble sale, where else.) Dinky cloths off as a pint pot is passed around the boozer.

"Put some silver in, ya tight bastards," he shouts. "Or I'm not doing it."

Dinky sets off on his run, lifting his legs high, so his stang and bollocks bounce up and down. This cracks everybody up. Dink comes back to collect his money and I say, "No Dink, you've got to go outside and run around the pub before you get the money."

"Fuckin hell, all right," Dinky says as he runs to the door and out on to the street. Everybody's up at the windows watching and cheering. I grab Dinky's clothes and the pint pot full of money, nip in the bogs and hide them in a shit cubicle. Dinky shoots back inside covering his meat and two veg with the top hat and runs over to where he's left his clothes, shouting, "Quick where's mi clothes? There's a cop car parked up the road and I think they've seen me."

"Gimme half of the money, Dink, and you can have ya clothes back," I say.

"Alright," Dinky says. "But fuckin hurry up."

We fly into the bog and Dink nips in the shithouse and whips on his togs. He scoops out a hand full of brown soap from the pint pot and hands it me, the rest is secreted, alongside a one-gram block of Lebanese Red inside his sock-'emergency money,' Dinky calls it.

The coppers enter the pub and check us all out for bareness. They're jeered, abused and insulted. The coppers fuck off and leave us to it. Half a dozen young Dronny lads, Dicky, Chip Scothern, Browny, Dec Smith, Tyke, Benny and Black Launty (Eight Ball Launt was dark-skinned but not of African heritage) are sat at the far end of the pub.

"Watch this," Moose shouts as he grabs a dart from the dart board. Moose launches the tungsten tip a good twenty yards. It sails through the air towards the Dronny lads and lands slap bang in between Benny's eyes. We run over and see the dart embedded up to the hilt in Benny's head.

"Fuckin hell, Ben," Moose says. "Sorry about that, I only meant to scare ya."

Benny grimaces as he grabs the dart; he pulls and twists until the dart plops free from his head. A trickle of blood runs down his nose and drops off the end.

We all crack up, even Benny has to laugh.

"Good arra, Mulligan."

Then we're out on the street, its early spring, the weather's fine, we're Blades at the seaside and we're buzzing. We march along the sea front singing battle hymns, putting on a show, scaring the locals and the holidaymakers.

'Sheff United's back in town again.'

As we approach the next pub, a suited-up, middle-aged Scottish geezer beckons us towards the boozer.

"Get in here lads, I work here," he says. "It's half price drinks up to 10 o'clock and there's a night club in the basement." We pile in and get stuck into the cheap beer. As 10 o'clock draws near, Blade songs bounce around the boozer. The words from the old-time music hall ditty, 'I do like to be beside the seaside' are changed to: "I do like to be beside the steelworks, oh I do like to be beside the steel, with a bucket and a spade and a fuckin hand grenade beside the steelworks beside the steel."

Lads dance on the tables and women are fondled and mauled. The Jock bloke, who'd been hovering around us all night, shouts: "The nightclub opens in a bit lads. It's only 50p to get in. It's through them doors and down the steps." One hundred bodies pile through the doors and mass on the stairs leading to the nightclub. The Scottish bloke's trying to calm us down shouting: "There's no need to push lads everybody'll get in."

We sway and surge forwards down the steps; it's like we're stood on the terraces. Lads fall and stumble, everybody's laughing. A cigarette machine is ripped off a wall and crashes to the floor. Its prised open and the contents are rifled.

The Scottish bloke starts to panic. "Fuck's sake lads there no need for this." He's engulfed as we charge forward. We swarm past the pay-in counter and into the club. We're the only punters inside.

A DJ spins records from a booth to our left and a long bar directly in front is manned by a couple of bar-staff. A look of terror comes to their faces as we flock towards the bar. Lads vault over the counter and head for the top shelf. The bar staff flee towards the exit and the DJ joins them.

A couple of lads take over the DJs booth; 12-inch singles and LPs frisbee through the air and disintegrate as they collide with the wall. I'm behind the counter pressing till buttons, but the bastard won't open. I try to lift the till to smash it open on the floor, but the fucker won't budge. Tops are smashed off wine bottles, optics are ripped from their mountings and the furniture is reduced to kindling. Pint pots sail through the air, smashing against walls and landing on the dance floor. Everybody's gone mental, we're out of control, it's a teenage rampage.

Black Laurence becomes a victim of friendly fire as a chunky-handled pint pot smashes into his face. That's it; we've gone too far. Lol's in a bad way, blood's gushing from the wounds and he's laid out on a pool table. A couple of lads stay to try and help Lol, while the rest rush up the stairs, through the boozer and out into the night. The whole riot has lasted less than five minutes.

So what makes us behave like pillaging Vikings, just stopping short of rape and murder? Simple really, it's because we can, just like a dog can lick its own bollocks. Who the fuck's gonna stop us? CCTV cameras only existed in the pages of Jud Orwell's novel. We can't blame the parents. Our mums and dads might have had a scuffle in the local Palais, but they never demolished the place. I blame the sea air.

Police sirens wail into earshot and it's every man for himself. We scatter in all directions as cars, vans and coppers on foot arrive on the scene. Moose and me run down a side street, still buzzing from the destruction and emerge in a built-up area a couple of hundred yards from the sea-front. We spy a bowling alley and nip inside, planning to hide there for ten minutes until the heat's died down.

We notice two young birds aged sixteen, seventeen maybe, sat in the bar area. Both are wearing green and yellow Norwich City scarves, and both are smiling at us. Moose is wearing the black top hat that's been passed from lad to lad all night. We walk over to the girls and saddle up at the side of them. In a lovely bumpkin accent one of the girls says, "Are you Sheffield?"

"Yeah," we both answer.

"Well," she says, "my name's (whatever her name was) and I fuck. This is (whatever the others name was), and she doesn't." Well ya can't beat a bird who comes straight to the point, eh!

"You're with me tonight darling," I say, as I slip my arm around her shoulder.

"Like fuck," Moose says. "You're with me," as he parks himself next to her.

"Fuck off Mulligan, I saw her first." Both the girls fidget and giggle as we vie for the fuck-girl's attention.

A few more Blades run in looking flustered, they notice us and walk over. "Fuckin coppers everywhere," one of them says.

"Fuck off then," I say. "We're with these; if the coppers come in and see us all together we're fucked." Moose and me agree on a compromise: a 'two's up' seems the logical solution.

We leave the alley with the two girls and walk back towards the sea front. A police van pulls up at the side of us and four coppers jump out. We're grabbed and forced towards the back doors. As we struggle, the girls protest to the police, "They've not done anything; they've been with us all night," the fuck-girl says.

The coppers are having none of it and we're whisked off to the nick. Not only have we missed a certain fuck, we're fucked.

The cells at Great Yarmouth Police Headquarters are bursting at the seams, but after searching us and taking our names and our stuff, they manage to squeeze us in. Blade songs and foul and abusive language ring out from every dungeon. After half an hour or so the coppers start taking out lads in groups of four. It's close to midnight when Moose, me and two others are taken out. We're taken into a room where a copper sat at a desk calls us cunts and bastards. No charges are pressed, and we're told we're free to leave. Moose notices a big flip in the ashtray in front of the copper on the desk.

"Can I have that dock?" Moose says. "I'm gagging for a fag."

"Yeah, go on then," the copper says.

As Moose leans forward to pick up the flip, a plain clothed copper enters the room and says to Moose, "You're the ringleader, you're not going anywhere."

"I'll have that flip, then," I say, and I fish it out of the ashtray. Moose is taken away, the rest of us collect our shit and walk out to two coaches parked outside the nick.

A couple of minutes later Moose walks out. Moose said they tried to pin the ringleader tag on him because of the top hat. Moose told the coppers at least another dozen lads wore the top hat during the evening and they let him go.

Black Lol's refused to stay in the hospital, he's laid out on the back seat, his head resting on a sheepskin coat, thirty-two stitches are holding his face together.

The season drew to a close with a Thursday night County Cup game at Rotherham. Hundreds of Blades swamped Rotherham town centre and packed out the pubs at opening time. Wednesday played Southend at Hillsborough on the same night, needing a win to save them from the humiliation of relegation to Division Four. I hoped and prayed the bastards would slip up. The game at Rotherham meant nothing to us, we only went for a piss-up.

After the match around a hundred of us boozed in the town centre. Four of us: Black Lol, Malc Ali – a mixed race lad from the Bard Street flats, Ginger Spud from Woodseats and me went for a walkabout.

Crossing a bridge on the road back towards the train station, around fifteen Rotherham lads came into view. The Rotherham boys spread out and readied themselves. Spud and me ran into them, Lol and Malc turned and ran. It was too late to turn back as we were already trading punches. We were overwhelmed in seconds and both of us were knocked to the ground. I saw a red flash as a boot connected with the side of my head. One of Spud's shoes came off during the battle and a Rotherham lad picked it up and threw over the side of the bridge, before leaving us for dead and moving off.

Spud and me picked ourselves off the deck.

"Fuckin bad move, Spud," I said

"Fuckin right bad move, Ron, and the bastards have nicked mi shoe, look at the size of your head," Spud said. I could feel my head swelling up and my right eye had nearly closed.

We climbed down the banking at the side of the bridge and spent five minutes looking for Spud's shoe, but we couldn't find it in the pitch darkness. Lol and Malc returned with reinforcements.

"Too fuckin late now," I shouted. "What the fuck did you run for?" I said to Lol and Malc.

"There were too many of 'em," Malc said. "You two daft bastards shouldn't have run in."

"Well, we'd have stood more of a chance with four us, so fuck off ya pair of fuckin wankers," I said. I suppose I could have forgiven Lol, with him still being injured from the glassing a few weeks earlier, but that's the life of football lads, though; win some, lose some – shit happens.

By the time we arrived back in Sheffield the pubs had shut. Wednesday had beaten Southend and we had a brief scuffle with a group of celebrating Owls in the bus station. The coppers were still out in force and soon broke it up. I deliberately stayed back, not wanting to add another head to the two I now carried on my shoulders.

It got rather warm in the spring of 76; summer arrived early and stayed until autumn. Standpipes were erected in the streets, tarmac bubbled, and eggs were fried on the roofs of cars.

In the height of the hottest summer ever known to man it wasn't the best of times to cop for a dose of the dreaded scabies. Whether I'd picked up the disease off some slag or it came from one of Tiff's conquests, I'll never know. The itching started on my wrists and spread all over my body, the same with Tiff. The nights were unbearable and after a few days' scratching until we bled, we could stand it no more. We had no idea what was wrong, so we decided to visit the V.D. clinic on Infirmary Road. When my turn came, a doctor entered the waiting room and asked, "Do you mind if some medical students sit in for the examination?"

"No, I don't mind," I answered. I didn't expect to see about eight young doctors, including a couple of girls, stood around the desk. Fuckin shite! I thought maybe I'd be taken into a cubicle or something to be examined, but no. The doctor told me to stand in front of his desk and to drop my jeans and crackers. I could feel my stang shrinking by the second.

"Pull your foreskin back," the Doc said. Fuck me, that's the only bit that's not itching.

I positioned my stang in my left hand and with the forefinger and thumb of my right, I peeled back the flap. A faint wisp of steam rose into the air and thankfully disappeared. I'm sure I saw one of the bird doctors smirking behind her hand. The doc looked me over and confirmed it was scabies. We were given a large bottle of a lotion that looked like milk. The doc told us to paint the stuff on every inch of our bodies from the neck downwards, including the cracks of our arses. He said if we missed any parts it wouldn't work. We repeated the procedure seven days later and about a week later it finally cleared up.

And still the heat continued, reservoirs dried up and moorlands burst into flames; the government even appointed a drought minister. When it finally rained after about four months, I woke up at five o'clock in the morning and stood on the grass bank outside the flats. Dressed only in my crackers I splashed and danced around in the thunderstorm, dodging lightning bolts and whooping like a Red Indian.

So it's back into the Second Division for the 76-77 season. The season started with a visit from Newcastle in the Anglo Scottish Cup. Mitch's brief flirtation with the Geordies ended, but Brush was still brown-nosing them. Brush had gone the whole hog by having Newcastle United F.C. tattooed on his arm. He thought it would be a good idea to bring a mob of his mates onto the Shoreham. Who the fuck did he think he was? Maybe he thought we were going to buy them a pie or something.

The Geordies took one of the best kickings I've ever seen at the Lane. Brush must have sneaked off with his tail between his legs during the battle.

Our friends the Sunday nationals put us in the spotlight again by filling the back pages with football violence stories. A great photo in the *Sunday People* showed some of the Geordies dangling over the white wall trying to escape the battering.

We'd had some classic battles with the Geordies at the Lane going back to the early 70s. They always brought thousands to Sheffield and took over many of the pubs in the city centre. They came close to taking the Kop in 72, when the young 'uns and the singers did well to hold on until the boozers shut and all the lads arrived. I clearly remember 2,000-3,000 Geordies massed on the right-hand side of the Shoreham belting out a deafening version of Lindisfarne's *Meet Me On the Corner*.

The following Saturday about thirty of us caught an early morning train to Hull for another Anglo Scottish Cup game. It had always been a great day out in Hull and the locals were usually up for a battle. We did the dinnertime session in the city centre and then took the long walk up to Boothferry Park, stopping off at the Silver Cod and arriving at the ground just before kickoff.

After a brief brawl on Hull's Kop, the coppers ushered us onto the side terrace where a couple of hundred Blades were gathered. After the match we walked back down and plotted up in a pub just up the road from the train station. Around fifteen of us decided to stay in Hull for the night and catch a train back on Sunday morning. We had no idea, nor did we really care, where we'd be spending the night. We moved off to a pub in the city centre and it wasn't long before we were at it with a group of locals. The fight spilled out into the street and a cop car containing two officers, one a young WPC pulled up. The coppers jumped from the car and tried to break up the fight. As another police car arrived, Moose grabbed the cop woman's arm and spun her round. She fell into the road grazing her knees and hands. The other coppers dived on Moose and despite our efforts to free him they prized him into the cop car.

The fight stopped, and we stood arguing with the other coppers, giving them the usual shit about minding our own business when we were attacked. The coppers gave us the name of the police station where they were taking Moose. We made our way there and stormed up to front desk demanding Mulligan's release. Thinking of today's climate it seems quite incredible we even got in the police station, but there we were, calling the shots, shouting and swearing at the coppers. A senior figure came out and told us to wait outside and he would try to sort it out. We went outside still issuing threats, and ten minutes later Moose walked out, released without charge. Fuckin amazing.

We spent the rest of the night boozing in the city centre and even got friendly and chatty with some of the locals in a pub called the Manchester. When the pubs closed we tried but were refused entry into a couple of nightclubs. We now had the problem of finding somewhere to kip. We ended up on some waste land at the back of a row of shops near the train station. We went on the forage behind the shops scrounging for sleeping materials. Someone found a large plastic sheet; another lad found a skip full of cardboard which we laid in a line at the side of a wall.

Newspapers and bits of carpet arrived. The best find though was filthy old candlewick bedspread. "Fuckin hell," somebody said. "They must have known we were coming." We tried to settle down for the night. No chance. Even though we'd been on the lash for a full day, we found it impossible to sleep as everyone kept fucking about. It was mid-August and quite mild, but fifteen lads trying to squeeze under a six-foot-wide bedspread caused a bit of disorder.

It was dragged one way and then the other. We shuffled around kicking each other trying to get the best position. A fight broke out disrupting the whole bedding and we had to start all over again. We eventually drifted off to sleep, hugging each other like homos.

I awoke next morning, freezing to death. In the half-light, I sat up stretching and yawning. Moose lay next to me. Knotty, a Woodseats lad with a hair-lip, lay facing Moose, their faces only an inch apart. Moose awoke in shock and sat bolt upright shouting, "Fuckin hell, you foul bastard. If I'd have known you were as ugly as that, you wouldn't have slept next to me all fuckin night." We all cracked up.

Fifteen bedraggled, starving souls tramped into Hull train station as dawn broke, but the weekend still hadn't ended. Brid and Wildy pulled two slags in the station café and managed a quick shag before we boarded the train home.

On the train we met, for the first time, a bunch of up and coming young Blades who'd been to the game and spent the night in Bridlington. Bullet, Spindle, Bri Rawlins, Ronnie-no-neck, Rotten and a few others. These young lads would eventually move up through the ranks and in a year or so become regular front liners.

The first league game's Luton Town away. Moose and me knew Gibby's coach would be leaving Pond Street at eight bells. We didn't fancy paying so we stood at the bottom of the Parkway with our thumbs out. We knew there was no way the coach would pass us. Sure enough the bus pulled up and we jumped aboard for nowt.

In a pitched battle with a well-up-for-it Luton mob in the narrow-terraced streets after the game, Dicky got arrested. The arresting officer told the court that Dicky threw a brick, which ricocheted off the sole of someone's Doc Marten and knocked his helmet off. The copper's bullshit cost Dicky a three-month stretch in Bedford jail.

The Blades had always attracted a good following from the Rotherham area, particularly from the Rawmarsh/Parkgate districts of the town. It was around this time the Parkgate lads started running regular coaches and vans to away games. They must have run the odd coach now and again dating back to the 60s, because I remember spending the night with a busload of Rawmarsh lads in Blackpool after a game at Preston in 1969.

The Rotherham lot were a bunch of good lads who could always be relied on. Sometimes our coaches travelled together, or we would take one coach, half full of Rotherham lads.

The Big Tree boozer at Woodseats started running a coach containing some handy lads.

Mick and Steve, the Holloway twins, usually travelled with the Big Tree crew. Steve, a wild fucker, caused loads of shit and then got out of the way. Mick, quiet and unassuming just went about the business of looking out for his crazy brother.

"I start all the trouble and then our Mick steps in and knocks the fuckers out," Steve once told me. Or it could have been Mick who started all the shit and Steve who knocked them out? Anyway, there were now at least three coaches of up-for-it Blades at most away games, plus regular vanloads from the Manor, Pitsmoor and Darnall. Our little group had kept the flag flying through the hard times and we always thought we were the main lads.

A dozen or so of us boarded a beat-up old Tranny for the trip to Nottingham Forest. Blacks, one of the young Hackenthorpe lads, drove the van. We stopped off for the dinnertime session on the outskirts of the city and after getting lost a couple of times we reached the City Ground half an hour after kickoff. We walked around the ground trying to get in, but all the turnstiles were closed. We spent a good ten minutes throwing bricks over the wall at Forest fans who we could see stood on the open end.

When the game ended (with a narrow 6-1 victory to Forest) we broke up an old pallet, armed ourselves with lumps of wood and stood on a street corner waiting for the Forest fans to come out. We ran into a group of Forest lads, waving the planks in the air. The handle end of umbrella connecting with the side of my head stopped me in my tracks, the bloke wielding it, a seventy-year-old pensioner. The other lads cracked up at my misfortune, before a group of coppers chased us back up the road. My earhole was still ringing as we boarded the van.

"Fuckin hell Ron that was a beauty," one of the lads laughed.

"Fuck off," I said.

We set off and for some reason drove in the opposite direction to home, over Trent Bridge towards the ground. While crossing the bridge we became stuck in traffic. The van stood stationary as Mick Parry, a deaf mate of ours, shot through the crowd pursued by a mob of Forest fans. We jumped from the van armed with bottles, and the Forest fans stopped dead as the bottles landed around them. Coppers were on the scene in seconds and surrounded our group. After informing us we were under arrest, the coppers took the van keys off Blacks and redirected the traffic, allowing two police vans to get through and escort us to the cop shop. Blacks drove to the station with one police van in front and one behind. We were shoved inside the cop shop and left for ten minutes. The coppers gave us a bollocking but said they couldn't be arsed to charge us and we were free to go. They told us to 'fuck off' out of Nottingham and if they saw us hanging around, we would be locked up for the weekend. We filed out, grateful for a lucky escape, when Tabby Greenwood, fast as lightning whipped a 20 packet of Gold Leaf cigs off the desk sergeant's counter. Tabby didn't even smoke and only did it for the crack. Outside he handed me the cigs and told me he'd nicked them off the sergeant. We were laughing our heads off as we boarded the van, me twenty cigs to the better.

We were just about to set off when a group of coppers, headed by the sergeant shot out and surrounded the van. "Get out, the lot of you," the sergeant shouted. "Now line up in front of the wall. One of you bastards has nicked my fags. I'm going to give you a chance, if the person who took them owns up, the rest of you can go, but if we search you and find the fags, all the lot of you will be locked up for the weekend. It's your choice."

Well, what a fuckin dilemma, what the fuck shall I do? I'm thinking, as we lined up against the wall. I couldn't do anything else but step forward.

"It was me," I said.

"You thieving little bastard," the sergeant said as he grabbed my neck and led me back towards the cop shop. Tabby stepped forward and said, "It wasn't him it was me."

"Right, you get in here as well," the sergeant said. Now this would have been the perfect cue for an: "I'm Spartacus" sketch, but nobody else said owt.

Inside the cop shop I handed the cigs back to the sergeant; Tabby admitted to nicking them and passing them to me. He apologised and said he didn't know what came over him. The sergeant went crazy, screaming at us, he couldn't quite get his head around it, "Nicking fags off a policeman, I can't believe anyone would have the gall to nick fags off a policeman, I've never seen anything like it in my life. Now fuck off and get out of my sight, both of you, before I do something I'll regret," the copper said. We apologised again and shot out, not quite believing we'd got away with it. I have to say what a grand set of chaps them Nottingham coppers are.

We were clued-up enough to have a good idea about the calibre of away support at the Lane. We knew who was likely to turn up and who wouldn't. Now we were back in the Second Division, our rivals were fewer and less fierce.

The conscientious objectors and the sick-note Blades who failed to show against Wednesday, made miraculous recoveries and were suddenly fighting fit again and more of the young lads were starting to come of age. We knew the only possible threat to the Shoreham this season would come from Chelsea. The only real chance of any action inside the ground now, was on the Lane End, so a group of us started meeting up on there. We couldn't go on mobbed up as the coppers would have sussed us, so we entered the turnstiles in ones and twos. Once inside, we grouped up in the open section nearest the John Street terrace.

The easier the opposition, the more Blades sneaked in. Earlier in the season at games against Hereford, Carlisle, Fulham, Notts County and Orient, a couple of hundred or so Blades somehow managed to gain entry – strange.

The Chelsea home game came in early December and for some reason it was switched to a Friday night. We reckoned Chelsea wouldn't travel in great numbers for a night game, so we agreed to meet up on the Lane End. A great turn out from the lads saw six of us massed near the John Street side as the game kicked off. Moose and me came straight from work and we were dressed in the scruff. Making up the numbers, a big fucker who worked as a nightclub bouncer, whose name I can't remember, and three other lads. One of these was a Wednesdayite mate of one of the Blade lads.

Around five hundred Chelsea fans stood directly behind the goal. Moose, only half-jokingly suggested we attack.

"Come on are ya ready? Straight into the cunts," Moose said.

The other lads can't quite believe what there're hearing.

"What ya talking about? There's only fuckin six of us, we'll get killed," one of the Blades says.

I joined in the wind up: "Come on this is what we're here for, let's get into the fuckers."

The Wednesday lad must have wondered what the fuck he'd let himself in for; he looked like passing out. Moose and me burst out laughing and the relief on the lads' faces was a picture. But I knew something they didn't; there's no way Mulligan's gonna stay quiet for long.

Five minutes before half time, Moose and me said we were going to the bar for a bevvy. The other lads decided to stay where they were. The bar on the Lane End was situated in the corner, and actually ran underneath the end bit of the John Street stand. A narrow-tunnelled entrance led in and out.

We strolled to the front of the bar area, where the shutters were still down (they opened when the half time whistle blew). We leaned casually on the counter facing the entrance as the shutters slid up. I ordered the drinks, which were served in cardboard cartons, as dozens of Chelsea fans swarmed into the bar. They squashed up behind us trying to get served and as our drinks arrived I heard Moose shout, "Don't fuckin push me ya Cockney bastards." Oh shit, this is it I thought. I turned; drink in each hand to see fifty faces snarling at us.

The nose of one of the faces was splattered by Moose's elbow. The beer sprayed high into the air in slow motion as we were attacked from all angles. We were both on the deck in seconds, and as I lay face down, I could feel boots stamping all over my body and muffled voices shouting: "Kill the cants."

Instinct told me to crawl towards the exit. I raised myself up onto my hands and knees, but a boot in the ribs had me sprawling again. Never have I been so glad to see the helmets pushing their way through the crowd. As I got to my feet, three or four Chelsea fans were still booting Moose's unconscious body. They moved back when the coppers reached him. Moose was out cold and looked in a bad way. The St John's Ambulance crew arrived and stretchered Moose out through the crowd into the ambulance room on the corner of the John Street terrace. The other three Blades and the Wednesday lad saw Moose being carried out and glad to be off the Lane End and followed us into the first-aid room.

Five minutes later Moose came round, sat up and said, "Where the fuck am I?" It took Mull a few more minutes to get his bearings. He wasn't too badly injured, just a few scuffs, lumps and grazes on his head. The coppers were still there, and they asked Moose if he would be able to identify who attacked him.

Now what happened next probably shouldn't have, but it did. Moose had taken a right kicking and possibly wasn't thinking straight, but the three or four Chelsea lads who carried on booting him while he was unconscious weren't exactly playing by the rules, not that any code of honour existed. Moose said he could pick out the lads, and around a dozen coppers took the six of us back on the Lane end. Moose got his head back together and he said to me, laughing, "I've got no idea who did it, there were too many of the fuckers, I'll just pick one out for a laugh, eh?" The coppers pushed through the crowd and up to back of the Chelsea mob, where their main lads were stood. Some of these boys had obviously been involved and were looking a bit worried.

A small fat, gobby fucker started giving us, and the coppers, some lip; he should have kept his mouth shut.

"That's him," Moose said.

The coppers grabbed the lad and led him down to the front, over the railings and on to the perimeter. Not really knowing what we were doing, we followed and climbed over the fence. I expected us to be attacked on the way down, but nowt happened.

As we walked towards the Cherry Street side the Chelsea lad started to panic. The poor fucker was in tears as he pleaded with the coppers, "I ain't done anyfink, it wasn't me, honest. I ain't fackin done anyfink."

I still had no idea where we were heading or what was going to happen.

We started give the poor fucker some abuse: "We're gonna wait for you outside, ya fat cunt and rip your fuckin head off."

"But I ain't done anyfink. Honest it wasn't me." I felt a bit sorry for the lad, maybe he was one of the lads who booted Moose, maybe not, but if he'd not mouthed off he wouldn't be in the shit. We reached the old cricket pavilion at the back of the South Stand and two coppers took the Chelsea lad inside.

"What are you gonna do with him?" one of the lads asked the coppers.

"We'll keep him until the coaches and trains have left and he can find his own way home," one of the coppers said.

It just goes to show you can never trust a fuckin copper. Without any warning the coppers turned on us. We were grabbed by the scruff of our necks and led towards an exit door.

"You started all this trouble by coming on the Lane end in the first place," one of the coppers said. "If I catch you on here again you'll all be arrested, now fuck off," he shouted as we were thrown out into the street.

Seven days later, after the pubs closed at 10.30 pm, lads started to gather in Pond Street bus station. Gibby's booked a fifty-seater coach for the near 500-mile round trip to Plymouth. The bus is scheduled to leave at midnight. By eleven, more than seventy, mostly pissed-up lads are hung around the threepenny bit kiosk. Gibby arrives and starts taking the fares. His face lights up when he sees the turn out.

He's budgeted for fifty lads at a fiver a man, and he's still making a profit. Another twenty or so extra arses means he's in for a nice little earner. Lads are pushing each other to try to get their money paid, to make sure they get on the bus. I had a quiet word, "Am I on for a freebie, Gibby? You're gonna make a right packet off this lot."

"No freebies tonight. Everybody pays," Gibby said.

Kingy, who works at the Whitbread brewery on Lady's Bridge, arrives with the ale. Moose and me ordered a pack of twenty-four cans of Trophy bitter. I reluctantly pay Gibby the fiver coach fare. Gibby's got money coming out of his earholes, as half a dozen or so of us call into the evil-smelling homo bogs at the far end of the bus station.

As we stand pissing, I notice a bundle of quid notes hanging out of Gibby's back pocket. Some of the notes slip out and fall to the floor. I'm down in a flash and as I pretend to tie my shoe-lace, I scoop up the money and whip it into my pocket, outside I count it up. Six quid, so I've got my coach fare back and made a quid profit.

The coach arrives and Gibby pulls the two drivers straight away to sort out their sweetener. Lads swarm onto the bus and fight for the seats. Moose and me, being well up the pecking order take over the back seats. We allow a few of the young Dronny lads to sit with us. Kingy asks us for the money for the beer and we tell him to, "Fuck off." We leave him hanging and panicking for another ten minutes before we pay up.

As the coach pulls out at midnight, it's three to a seat. Lads are packed in the aisles and some are stretched out on the luggage racks. Its chaos, empty beer cans fly back and forth and mock fights erupt. Blade battle hymns ring around the bus. The comedians keep everyone amused and exaggerated tales of past scuffles and skirmishes are relayed to the young, wide-eyed apprentices. Most of the lads are swigging beer. Brandy Martin, however, is already half way down a pint bottle of his preferred tipple. He bellows out his trademark rendition of Alouette. Martin starts off the song with Alouette's balding head.

"Oh, I love her balding head," and travels down to her two black eyes, broken nose, double chin, bouncing breasts, nautical navel etc. Each verse is followed by the rousing chorus sung by the whole coach: "Alouette gentile Alouette, Alouette je te plumerai"

Kingy's the next act up with his famous party piece. Kingy makes sure he's got everyone's attention, then he stands up on a seat and whips out a full one inch of throbbing manhood. His stang is so tiny it doesn't even hang; he looks like a steroid addict without the muscles.

"Look at that for a fuckin cock," Kingy shouts. Most of us have seen it before, but it still cracks us up. Kingy binds his time, he's set the bait and sure enough one of the young lads takes it.

"Fuckin hell, that's the smallest knob I've ever seen," one of the chabbies shouts.

"How many kids have you got?" Kingy says, as he reels him in.

"I haven't got any," the young 'un says.

"Well this fucker has knocked out four little bastards, so shut the fuck up, ya little cunt. Come back and talk to me when you're a fuckin man," Kingy tells him.

Despite numerous piss stops, vessels of slash are continuously emptied through the skylight windows. Seven mad hours later we pile off the bus in Plymouth city centre. A passing milk float travelling at five miles an hour is chased along a deserted street and rifled. A couple of dozen pints of cold milk are passed around, a bit of a stomach liner for the session ahead. Its eight hours before kickoff. Stocksbridge Pete, a Blade mate who's in the Navy and stationed in the city is meeting us at 10.30 a.m. at a boozer called the Two Tree's on Union Street. It's still three hours or so before the meet. Some of the lads call in a café for a full English, others hang around outside munching bacon butties.

It's mid-December and freezing, so a game of football to warm us up is suggested, everybody chucks in a few pence to buy a football. Wandering Walt, his feet already twitching, volunteers to go and a find a shop. Walt usually travelled with us, but often wandered off on his own to do a spot of decorating. Armed with a thick tipped felt pen, Walt trawled pub and public toilets covering them with Blade graffiti. Some of the lads reckoned he had ulterior motives for visiting the cottages, but we'll never know.

Walt returns ten minutes later wearing a Gorilla mask.

"Weer's fuckin ball, Walt?" somebody asks.

"I saw this mask and couldn't resist it, so I bought the fucker," Walt said.

"Fuckin hell," somebody else said. "We're gonna have to have another whip round." Another lad nips off and returns with a Frido.

We head up to Plymouth Hoe and gaze out over the English Channel. On the very spot where Frank Drake played with his bowls as the Spanish Armada prepared to invade, seventy football hooligans kick lumps out of each other for half an hour.

Stocksbridge Pete's stood outside the Two Trees when we arrive. Hands are shook, backs are patted, and the morning session begins. Most of us have been drinking all night and after a couple of top-up pints we're half pissed again. In another Union Street pub, we bump into a group of Blade beer monsters known as, 'Goodison's Guerrilla's, or was it 'Gorillas'?

The twenty ale-carts, who never miss an away game, have travelled down by train and are staying for the weekend. Derek Goodison (who saved my life at Stockport way back in 66) is the daddy of the Blade guzzlers, his consumption is legendary. He won't even give the time of day to any Blade who can't sink a triple gallon during a dinnertime session. (Mitch and me, walked in the Barrel on London Road one night, and Derek was stood at the bar. "What ya drinking lads? he shouted. "We'll have half please, Derek," I said. Derek looked shocked. "Fuckin half. What ya talkin about? Blademen don't drink halves, you'll have fuckin pints, fuckin halves, never heard nowt like it in mi life.")

As kickoff approaches we walk through a massive park up to the ground. The Plymouth boys must be expecting us, cos as we reach Home Park we see yellow painted graffiti proclaiming, 'SHEFFIELD WILL DIE,' and other threats splashed all over the stadium walls. But where the fuck are the Plymouth lads? We've not seen one all day. We take our place on the open end; it's cold and it's fuckin miserable. Only two other Blades coaches and a couple of vans have made the long trip, so there's around two hundred of us huddled together trying to keep warm. As ever, the support is first class. We might be a bunch of fuckers, but we always give the Blades 100% backing. We treat the bumpkins to an array of songs and chants.

At half time, the announcer tries to whip up the home support. He reckons

Argyle ought to have their own song and because of Plymouth's seafaring tradition he suggests Rod Stewart's Sailing. He plays the track and after a minute or, so we make it our own. At first we just held our scarves above our heads, 'You'll Never Walk Alone' style and sang the proper words, then it changed. Which Blade started it? Came out with words? We'll never know but we were fuckin quick off the mark.

"We are Bladesmen, we are Bladesmen, we are Bladesmen from the Lane, we are Bladesmen, super Bladesmen, we are Bladesmen from the Lane" rang out for the entire second half.

At the end of a boring 0-0 draw we saw the Plymouth boys for the first time. We didn't see them for long though, they scattered across the park as soon as we ran towards them. By five-thirty we were back in the Two Trees sinking the first pints and singing the first songs of the evening. By six-thirty the first brawl of the night erupts. Brid, who's just out of prison on parole, smashes a pint pot over a local's head and the lot goes up.

As midnight approached we'd done most of the Union Street bars. Making our way back to the bus, Wafe and me see a lad, laid unconscious in the road. We try to bring him round, but he's dead to the world. As we reach the coach we mention the knocked-out lad to a group of Blades stood outside the bus.

"Yeah he pulled a knife on us," one of the Blade lads tells us. "So we took it off him and kicked his fuckin head in."

About eight hours later, the bus, minus a few lads who'd been arrested, arrives back in Sheffield. It's been around forty-eight hours since anybody's had a proper kip. Has it all been worth it? Course it fuckin has.

The Shoreham End, looking from the White Wall, late 70s

Chapter 8

The changing of the guard

1977 arrived and booted the music industry straight up the arse. Glam rock had run its course, and a new underground movement that first surfaced in the summer of 76 breathed new life into the Disco and Abba-dominated pop charts. I can't remember exactly when or where I first heard punk, but it was most likely at the Penthouse. A rousing little three-minute number entitled *Stranded* by an Australian band, the Saints, became the first single I'd bought for about four years.

The punk scene in Sheffield didn't really get going until early-mid 77. The Pistols, supported by the Clash – who were playing their first gig outside London, appeared at the Black Swan in July 76. Legend has it, there were just four people in the audience. Over the years I've spoken to at least twenty people who swear to god they were there that night. The truth is though; only me and these three punk birds I was shagging at the time were present at the gig... yeah right.

The first punks started gathering in the down-market, yet up-beat Crazy Daisy basement bar on High Street in the city centre. When the Penthouse introduced a punk night held every Monday, they made the place their headquarters. The 10p admission fee and all drinks at 10p a shot should have made the place an alcoholic's paradise, but surprisingly I never saw the place full or even half-full. A hardcore group of about thirty-forty punks hung around the dance floor. A few more punters who were there for the cheap drinks, and the regulars who just about lived in the place, made up the audience.

Most of the punks were into the look and the scene rather than the music, and who could blame them? It was a new teenage revolution, anti-establishment shit and all young kids, no matter what era they live in, need heads to turn when they walk down the street.

Jonesy, a young Dronny lad and his bird, Patsy, both aged around eighteen-nineteen were part of the punk scene. I used to have a chat with them in the Penthouse, but they always sempt a bit nervous. Jonesy had too much respect to ever blank me, but I could see him keeping one eye on his new buddies, who were maybe thinking, what's Jonesy doing talking to that old cunt dressed like Status Quo? Jonesy became yet another Dronny lad who died in a motorbike crash.

There'd always been a scene based around music and fashion in Sheffield and indeed every other major town and city in the UK. Maybe it wasn't quite a closed shop, but being on the fringe I never felt like I really belonged to any of them.

Going back to my mid-teen years of the Esquire and the Mojo, there was a crowd who thought they were a bit better than all the rest. A sort of an elite band of middle class, avant-garde trendsetters who looked down on anybody who wasn't dressed up to the second.

Perhaps it went back even further to the days of the Teddy boys and the City Hall dances of the 1940s.

Many of the Sheffield punks moved on to the next big thing when the mod revival arrived a year or so later. And after that, the same in-crowd, dressed as 'New Romantics,' pretended to dig Spandau Ballet and Duran Duran.

Tiff and me went to the punk nights every week (it must have been a period of harmony we were going through) and we got well into the music, but not really into the scene. At twenty-six I felt a little bit too old to be a punk, but a little bit too young to lose it. I had my hair cut short for the first time in over ten years, dug out my old leather rocker jacket, and wore it over a red and white striped pyjama top, I donned a pair of tight black jeans and baseball boots, so I was kinda punkish.

The Ramones *Blitzkrieg Bop*, the Clash's *White Riot* and the Sex Pistol's throbbing power chords and riffs gave me a buzz close to the one I'd experienced when I first heard *Gloria* back in 1964. Punk had a kind of 60s feel and that's why I think it appealed to me. The good vibrations returned, we even got up and pogoed like lunatics. Once again Rock 'n' Roll had reinvented itself. One hundred miles an hour, raw, hard-core, in ya fuckin face Rock 'n' Roll that grabbed you by the bollocks. But more importantly the three chord, three-minute songs of verse, chorus, verse, chorus, verse, end, made a comeback. The political side of the movement wasn't lost on me, but I really didn't give a fuck how many people were on the dole as long as I was one of them.

The first game of 1977 in early January saw Newcastle back at the Lane for a third round FA Cup-tie. We knew the Geordies would turn out in force, they always did, plus they had a score to settle for the kicking they took on the Kop at the Anglo Scottish game back in August.

After Meeting up on London Road we entered the ground ten minutes before kickoff. A good five thousand Geordies were packed on the Lane end. Just before kickoff the shout went up, "They're here."

We pushed our way out on to the concourse at the back of the Kop to see around fifty Geordies climbing the steps. One look told me these were the boys. The front lad looked like a Maori warrior with the names of fifty ex-girlfriends crudely tattooed across his face. They reached the top of the steps and after a twenty second stand-off exchanging threats, Copie, a lad who didn't look, or act like a lad, and who'd never had a scrap in his life, walked forward. What the fuck's he going to do, I'm thinking. Copie stopped a couple of yards from the Geordies and calmly announced, "Do you think you're gonna take the Kop then?" Now this wasn't a threat, Copie spoke like he was really interested and like maybe the Geordies wanted to discuss their intentions.

This must have thrown the Geordies, because none of them answered, they just stood looking at Copie and each other for a few seconds. Copie shrugged his shoulders, calmly walked back and stood with us. Sully, a young, fiery, red-haired little fucker who always dressed in the height of fashion broke the deadlock by wading in to the Geordies. They looked almost relieved the action had started.

After a minute of fierce fighting the coppers arrived and got between us. The police didn't have a clue, and what they did now seems quite incredible. They forced us back though the entrance to the Kop and pushed us down the steps leaving a gap at the back. Then they brought in the Geordies and allowed them to stand behind us, fuckin amazing.

More Blades came over from the left and waded in, while we moved up from the front. We now had them on the move, but these were a game set of fuckers who were still trading punches as we forced them over to the top of the back steps that came out behind the white wall. Maybe some of the Geordies remembered dangling over it at the game back in August.

After pooling their fifty brain cells, the coppers finally got their act together. They surrounded the Geordies, pushed them down to the front and over the railing to the pitch perimeter, where they escorted them round to the Lane end. They gave us the rods and the wanker signs, while we gave them, "You'll never take the Shoreham."

After the match another pitched battle took place at the bottom of Charlotte Road and continued down Shoreham Street towards the train station. The game ended in a 0-0 draw, the worst possible result for us lot, because it meant we would have to travel to St James Park for a night match replay.

I've spoken before about the power of the press and what the *Sheffield Star* printed over the next week or so just goes to show how a newspaper article can incite trouble. There'd been dozens of arrests at the game and the *Star*, as usual reported all the violence. It also came out with the biggest load of bullshit I've ever read. The *Star* reporter who wrote the article obviously knew fuck all about the football scene. He suggested thousands of Blades were planning to travel to Newcastle on a revenge mission, and the police force up there had been put on full alert. Whether he got the information from the Newcastle/Sheffield police or just made it up is irrelevant.

I knew, as did every other Blade with an ounce of sense there was no way thousands of Blades would travel to the game. Just getting in and out of Newcastle unscathed would be a major achievement, never mind a revenge mission, but there must have been a few gullible Blades who believed the crap. Newcastle weren't to be fucked with at home; they had hundreds, maybe even a thousand or so lads. I knew exactly who would be travelling, one or two supporters' club coaches, a couple of vans, eight cars and about three on the train and every single one of them would be keeping their heads down and their mouths shut. Not many of the lads (including myself) who'd been involved in the fighting at the Lane would be anywhere near the place. The replay should have taken place on the following Tuesday or Wednesday, but it was cancelled due to bad weather and rearranged for the Monday after. Still the *Star* continued with the bullshit.

After telling Tiffany I was going up to my mother's for the day, I left the flat at dinnertime with three quid in my pocket. I thought I'd nip in the Penny Black, just to have a look if there were any brave souls daft enough to be making the trip. It surprised me to find about fifteen Blades (some of them scarfed up) inside. I knew a few of the lads and they shouted out greetings, just assuming I'd be going to the game. I bought a pint and joined them.

"Hey-up Ron, how ya getting there? We're going on the train." A lad called Stevie, who I'd known from the 60s, asked me.

"I'm not going Steve; skint pal. I've just called in for a pint," I answered.

"Don't worry," Stevie said. "We'll have a whip round to get your train fare, match money and a few pints." So that's it, shit, what could I do? I couldn't lose face, and a freebie's a freebie, no matter who we were playing. I boozed for nowt until the pub shut. The lads sorted out my train fare and collected a few bob to get me in the ground. We boarded the train about half three and found around twenty other Blades (all normals) aboard. Through a combination of the dinnertime sesh, topped up by carry-outs we were lively enough until the train reached the outskirts of the city. We knew the normals would be doing their own thing and they wouldn't want to be within a million miles of us lot. We agreed to split up when we left the train, meet up in the first boozer we came to, when we left the station and take it from there. If the Newcastle boys were waiting for us it would be suicidal for fifteen or so lads to walk out together; circumstances dictated we had no choice in the matter. All the lads wearing colours removed them… all except one. Our carriage fell silent as we slowly rattled into Newcastle station about half past six. The adrenaline and the butterflies kicked in, this is it, we're here, what next?

'Skegness Pat' was ten years behind of the rest of us. Tattooed across his right hand were the words SHEFFIELD UNITED 1899. With a scarf tied around each wrist and others hanging from his belt, Pat staggered off the train. One hand, held the dregs of a bottle of vodka he'd swigged on the way up. None of us were prepared for what happened next. There must have been a good hundred coppers, including a dozen or so dog handlers lining the platform. Skeggy Pat didn't stand a chance, he's dragged to the ground, stamped on, hand cuffed and led away. The rest of us were forced to run the gauntlet. We were thumped, booted and clipped by the coppers and snapped at by the dogs. The coppers were going crazy as we were pushed through the gate on to the concourse.

"Move ya bastards, move, " the coppers shouted. Where are we supposed to fuckin move to? I'm thinking. I managed to escape the chaos and ran out of the station. So what the fuck was that all about? If the Newcastle police had been in touch with the Sheffield coppers, they would have known how many were travelling. Were we set up by both sets of coppers or was it all the shit in the *Star*? I blame the fuckin *Star*. I spotted a pub across the road and went in. The place was packed to the rafters with Geordies. I made my way to the bar and ordered a pint. A lad stood at the side of me said, "From Sheffield mate? How did ya get here?" Fuck I thought, I can't get out of this, so I said, "Yeah, I came on the train."

"Put ya money away I'll get it," the Geordie said.

I stood chatting about football to the lad and his two mates who were great. I kept checking around the pub for any signs of Maori face and his mates. I even imagined Sinny and Podge might walk in and point me out to the rest of the pub. The lads offered me a lift up to St James's and I gladly accepted. We parked up and walked to the ground together. The lads left me and told me to be careful. They suggested I should avoid the Leazes and the Gallowgate ends and to go in the seats. No shit I thought. Big Dave Laycock ambled across the car park, saw me and bellowed, "Nar then Ron ar tha gooing?" Fuckin hell ya big daft bastard I'm thinking, keep ya voice down. Dave told me he'd bought a stand ticket for a quid and pointed out the bloke to me. I paid the bloke a quid and never even looked at the ticket as I sneaked off to try and distance myself from Big Dave who I knew, couldn't keep his gob shut. I looked at the ticket, fuckin bastard shit; it was for the Leazes end.

Kick off time approached, so I took a deep breath and went in. I stood in the bottom right hand corner facing the pitch. I couldn't quite see, but I could hear what sounded like a huge mob of Geordies occupying the middle section of the Leazes, and I could see another big mob swaying and singing on the open Gallowgate end. After ten minutes or so, clapping every Newcastle move, I moved to the front and managed to attract the attention of a copper stood at the side of the pitch.

"Excuse me," I said. "I'm from Sheffield and I've got on this end by mistake, any chance of taking me off?" I thought if he refuses and if anyone's heard me I'm in deep shit.

"Yeah," the copper said. "Climb over I'll put you on the side." Thank fuck I thought. When I got on to the side terrace I could see just how big the Newcastle mob on the Leazes was. The crowd on the side terrace were mostly flat caps, but still I kept my gob shut and my head down. I laughed along with the rest of the crowd when, every time Woody got the ball, a bloke behind me shouted: "Fookin Grecian 2000."

I watched the Leazes mob split into two. Lads from each side ran into the gap booting and punching each bother. I know what's coming here I thought, it's the old mock fight sketch. This was common practice at the time. Lads laid into each other chanting the names of different districts of the city, just to get the coppers into the crowd, to maybe batter a few or just to nick their helmets to throw around. It's strange how the mind works in situations like this. I wore a pair of red, white and black hooped Slade socks, I thought a gust of wind might blow my flares up and reveal to all that I was a Blade. I clapped Newcastle's three goals and when the Blades scored with a penalty I didn't even batter an eyelid. A group of Blades, sat in the safety of the stand next to the Gallowgate end, were the only ones who celebrated when the goal went in.

I left well before the end and went back to the pub I'd been in before the game. Back in the station the lads arrived back in ones and twos. We were all relieved to have made it out alive. I had about a quid left and in a card school on the journey back I won another two quid. The train arrived back in Sheffield well after midnight and I still had the three quid I'd started out with that morning.

At the next home game, I told everybody I'd been on the Leazes end on my own (I left out the bit about moving to the terrace). Stories circulated around the pub that a mob of Parkgate Blades had been on the Leazes. I kept the myth alive by saying, "Yeah I saw some fighting on the Leazes end, but I couldn't really tell who it was."

The blasting of a car hooter and a shout of, "Get thi sen up Ron," woke me in the middle of the night. I pulled back the curtains to see Chip Scothern, Dec Smith and Moose stood outside the flats beckoning me down. I knew why they were there. The bedside clock read 2.30 a.m. I whipped on my togs, sneaked out of the bedroom and skipped down the back steps out onto the street. Tiff woke up and screamed death threats from the bedroom window as the car skidded off.

"Fuckin hell ya bastards," I said. "You'll get me packed."

After stopping in the services near Birmingham for a couple of hours we landed in Hereford, to rain and sleet at around eight o'clock in the morning. We mooched around a while and then went up to check out the ground. A bloke outside told us the game had been postponed due to a waterlogged pitch. Before we left, we called in hardware shop, bought a can of silver spray-paint and decorated the stadium. For no particular reason we chose Worcester for the dinnertime session. Having no football connections none of us had been to the city before.

We walked into a lively city centre boozer just after opening time. There were some dodgy looking fuckers propping up the bar and a few unsavoury characters and tattooed birds dotted round the pub. It had the look and feel of the Cannon, that old den of iniquity on Castle Street in Sheffield. Cut-throats, thieves, loose looking women and vagabonds... fuckin sound, they were our kind of people. Nobody gave us a second glance though, as we found a table and got stuck into the ale. The boozer soon filled up and we'd been in for an hour or so, having a good crack with the locals, when an old bloke who looked to be in his 70s keeled over at the table next to ours. He landed flat on his back and one look at his face told me he'd kippered. He lay perfectly still, with his mouth wide open and his eyes bulging. Everybody jumped up and gathered around him. Somebody started pumping his chest, but the old fucker was a gonna. One of the tattooed birds, who I'd been eyeing up as a possible shag, pushed through the crowd screaming, "Dad, Dad." I thought about copping a crafty sympathetic feel as the bird knelt at the side of her dead papa. Moose picked up the dead bloke's pint from the table and took a long swag.

"Fucking hell Mulligan," Chip said. "You rotten bastard." Moose just smiled and said, "Well it's no fuckin good to him now is it?"

Now all this went off in the space of a minute or so, but a minute is a long time to be dead. Somebody must have called an ambulance and the ambulance men rushed into the pub. They laid the bloke on a stretcher and picked him up. The bird went crazy, screaming and crying.

Then something amazing happened, something fuckin incredible and if I hadn't seen it with my own eyes I wouldn't have believed it. A noise, barely audible at first came from the dead man's mouth. A sort of "Aaaaarrrr." It got louder and longer "Aaaaaaaaaaaaaaarrrrrrrrrrrrrrrrrr." Everybody stepped back. The dead man, with his mouth and eyes still wide open, sat bolt upright on the stretcher. What the fuck shot out his mouth, I'll never know, and I don't want to know. It was about four or five inches long and an inch wide. It looked like a lump of liver fresh from the butcher's slab. Maybe it was his liver. Fuck knows, but like Lazarus, the old fucker had risen from the dead. He came round, and his daughter hugged him as he was taken out to the ambulance and whisked away. The jukebox came back on and the jovial atmosphere from a few minutes earlier returned. If that was a trick, it's the best fuckin party piece I've ever seen.

Back in Sheffield, around five hundred or so Blades who were ready to travel to the match, headed for Mansfield to take in the game between Mansfield and Rotherham at Field Mill. Mansfield must be the only football town in the country with no railway station. The nearest stop is about ten miles away at Alfreton. The coppers must have got wind of the invasion and were waiting as the Blades arrived. Two double-decker buses were laid on to ferry the lads into Mansfield. The first hundred or so lads boarded the buses, but these were wrecked (the buses not the lads, the lads were probably wrecked as well) en route. The bus company refused to send any more, so the other four hundred set off on the long trek, robbing and looting as they went along their merry way.

When they arrived the coppers directed them onto the open away end. This caused a problem because the Rotherham fans turned up and refused to enter the away end. The police moved the Blades onto the side terrace; complicated shit. The Blades lads were neutral in their support and opted to cheer on the officials. Every time the ref blew his whistle, or the linesman flagged for offside they received a cheer from the Blades.

In March 1977 Liverpool played French champions St Etienne in the quarter-final of the European Cup. St Etienne's nickname is 'Les Verts' (the Greens). Allez les verts, roughly translated into English means 'Go the greens'. "Allez les verts, allez les verts, allez" echoed around Anfield that night.

Blades, innovative as ever adopted the chant and changed it to "Allez les rouges" 'Go the reds.' For the rest of season and well into 1978, the song was sung, complemented by the waving of 100s of one-foot square, plastic Union Jacks, both at the Lane and away games.

Moose's wings got clipped a little bit when he married the love his life, Gill.

I didn't own a suit and had to borrow one from a mate for the wedding. During my best man speech, I announced, "I did write a speech, but I've left it in one of my other suits."

Their Steve shouted, "Tha ant got another suit Sharpy, and thaz had to borrow that fucker."

Steve worked part-time as a bouncer and did stints on the doors at most of the city-centre night clubs. We always got freebies and even at some clubs where he didn't work, we could get in for nowt by just dropping his name. He got a job at the Embassy Ballroom at Intake and told me, "Get thissen up to Embassy on Thursday, Ron; it's full of fanny."

I went up with a couple of mates, Steve was on the door and said, "Gaffer's in tonight Ron, so you've got to wear ties, I'll get some from cloakroom, there's always some spare."

He came back with three of the worst ties I'd ever seen.

"Fuck me Steve, we can't wear them. They're fuckin terrible."

"You've got to pal, or I can't let you in."

We put them on and went in. After a couple of minutes, I noticed we were the only blokes in the club wearing ties. The fucker had set us up good style.

UNITED FANS IN TRAIL OF TERROR AT WESTON.

Sheffield United club secretary Keith Walker denounced as 'disgusting' the behaviour of fans who had smashed up a pub and a seafront zoo in Weston-super-Mare on a weekend trip to watch the Blades last match of the season, a 3-1 defeat against Bristol Rovers. Nine people were arrested for offences ranging from assault to burglary. Trouble first flared after Rovers fans invaded the pitch at the end of the game. There was a fight and a stone throwing battle in a car park. Many Blades fans had stayed in Weston on the Friday night before the game and went back to the resort after the match. Fifty fans were detained at one pub, after they smashed windows and glasses, set off fire extinguishers and helped themselves to drinks. At the zoo, fish tanks were smashed, and a monkey was released. The ape, a three-year-old Java Monkey named 'Tinker' walked back to the zoo five hours later.

For the last game of the 76-77 season at Bristol Rovers, I'd decided to don the full *Clockwork Orange* gear. Mi Mam picked up a black bowler hat from a jumble sale, I borrowed a pair of white cricket trousers off a mate and rooted out an old collarless white shirt and braces.

The night before the game I broke into the Dronfield Cricket Club pavilion and robbed a bollock box to use as the old Jelly Mould. The finishing touch would have been the bleeding eye-ball cufflinks, but the outfit was near enough spot on. Gibby as usual ran the coach, all the lads were on board, and along with another half a dozen buses, plus mini-buses and vans, we were to descend on the seaside resort of Weston-Super-Mare after the game.

We stopped somewhere en route for the dinnertime sesh. Maybe we were drinking Colt 45 or perhaps it was just the popular advert of the time, but the tune of the day was, "Any Tom Jack or Walt, Who likes the taste of malt, Will love the malt in a Colt 45." Fuck all to do with football, but the song was belted out every few minutes.

We arrived at Eastville, half two-ish, to a car park full of coppers and were

302

ushered straight to the turnstiles. The game passed without any incident until the final whistle when hundreds of Rovers fans swarmed across the pitch towards us. Pie-Eye, one of the young Pitsmoor Posse, vaulted the fence and ran, arms outstretched towards them. Blades surged to the front, only to be beaten back by the coppers. Pie-Eye glanced over his shoulder looking for reinforcements; undeterred the crazy fucker stood his ground, until the coppers grabbed him and threw him back over the fence.

Out in the coach park things got a bit lively, a mob of Rovers lads arrived launching rocks, lumps of wood and bottles. Blades responded, and this carried on for a few minutes until police dog-handlers arrived and broke it up. As soon as I saw the coppers, I was off. Any other time I would have took my chances, but my outfit would have made me an easy target for the coppers, so fuck that. The scrap carried on for a while until the police managed to force the Blades back on the coaches and we were off to Weston.

We arrived about an hour later and the coaches and vans parked up on the sea front. 300-400 hooligans, plus half a dozen beach balls took to the sands. It didn't take long for the footie game to turn into a mass, mock brawl. Then we hit the Pubs. One boozer, three stories high and surrounded by scaffolding, turned into an adventure playground. Pissed up singing Blades climbed the structure, hanging and swinging off the poles.

It started coming on top with coppers, so fifty of us dodged the law and found a pub away from the sea front. It was OK until about 10 o'clock when this monkey walked in and bounced up to the bar. It stood staring at us for a minute, making everybody feel a bit uneasy. Next thing, the fucker jumped on the bar and started throwing glasses. The bar staff freaked and ran for the exit. Then it's on the optics sampling all the top shelf.

It dragged a fire extinguisher off the wall and sprayed foam at everybody. It snatched a silk scarf from a Blade neck, tied it round its head, grabbed a bottle of whiskey from behind the bar and vanished into the night. Ten seconds later the coppers stormed into pub. We were lined up against the wall and searched.

"Ya not gonna believe this copper," one of the lads said. "It weren't us, it were a fuckin monkey."

"Yeah right, course it was" the copper said. "You're all nicked."

Blades have compiled loads of original songs dating back to early 60s. They don't come any better than the unique and hilarious tribute paid to a player signed from Huddersfield Town for £10,000 at the start of the 77-78 season. Robert McFaul 'Bobby' Campbell was a battling centre forward of the old-fashioned mode. What he lacked in skill he made up for in endeavour. He always gave 100% and soon became one the Blades' favourite sons. Where, or how the chant started, I've no idea. Maybe it began at the pre-season friendly at Torquay where he made his debut? Maybe he did really shoot, hit the post and it should have been a goal, who knows? To the theme tune of the popular 1960s Western series 'Bonanza' the chant started slowly, almost spoken.

"Bob-by Camp-bell-hit-the-post-it-shudda-been-a-goal-Oi!" A little bit of imagination is needed here. Picture, Hoss, Little Joe, Adam and Ben Cartwright

303

riding across the prairie, now get the tune in your head. "Bob-by-Camp-bell-hit-the-post-it-shudda-been-a-goal-Oi!" It's still going slow, but after each rendition it gets a little faster. A couple of thousand Blades are now bouncing and clapping and five minutes later, as the song reaches a crescendo the words are barely recognisable. "Bobbycampbellhitthepostitsuddabeenagoal-Oi!" It's magic moments like this that make me fall to my knees and praise the lord, I took the right path.

Everybody turned out for Blackpool; Blackpool was a must. This season's game meant a double celebration as it just happened to fall on both Herman's and Wafer's birthdays: November the 5th - Bonfire night. We set off early on a ramshackle old fifty-seater hired by Gibby. Like little kids on their first trip to the seaside, everybody got rather giddy when the tower came into view.

"It's there look, the tower. Can ya see it?"

"Course I can see it, daft cunt. It's fuckin nine miles high, fuck me."

We landed late morning and after a stroll along the prom-prom-prom where the brass band played tiddley-om-pom-pom and the dinnertime session, we marched up to Bloomfield Road. We strolled in around kick off time, joining thousands of Blades already massed on the Kop. The Kop end now had a six-foot-high segregation steel fence running from top to bottom. A couple of hundred Blackpool fans stood at the safety of other side of the fence giving us some lip and, being that time of the year, a few bangers exploded in the middle of both mobs.

We had no chance of getting to the Blackpool lads, so we decided to have a bit of fun with the coppers. A mock fight, which must have looked real enough, enticed the police, who were stood pitch-side, into the crowd. You'd have thought by now the coppers would have sussed out the sketch, but no, in they bumbled, truncheoned up like a squad of Keystones. Hundreds of pissed-up Blades attacked from all angles. The coppers copped for a few slaps and one or two helmets got tossed around. Now, I've never liked or had much time for the police, but I couldn't help feeling a bit sorry for this elderly grey-haired copper who took a bit of a battering.

We left the ground after a 1-1 draw with the old warhorse Bobby Campbell netting for the Blades. In the large dirt car park at the back of the Kop we heard the sound of confrontation, the roars and screams of, "Fuckin come on."

We ran forward heading towards the noise, but we were stopped in our tracks by retreating Blades.

"What the fuck's up with ya?" we shouted as the Blades scrambled past us.

The Blackpool mob fronted by a few lads wearing Man Utd scarves and Red Devil patches on their denim jackets came into view. Moose charged forward followed by the rest of us. The Blackpool/Man Utd mob scattered in all directions. We made a beeline for the Man Utd boys. I'd never been one for chasing, because to me, if they ran, it meant the job had been done and, besides, I was fucked after a hundred yards. It could be argued that runners can re-group and reverse the situation, but that rarely happened.

Maybe the kicking I'd took from the Man Utd and Blackpool fans over ten years ago on Blackpool sea front fired me up and that's why I carried on chasing. We must have chased them for half a mile until they all finally escaped, up back alleys and through gardens. Most of the lads on our bus were involved in the chase, and, along with a few more lads, we found a boozer just off the sea-front and began the evening session. After half an hour or so, things got a bit rowdy. Nothing serious, just songs, chants and the odd broken glass or two. The Landlord however decided he wanted us out. He came from behind the bar and after a bit of an argument he tried pushing one or two lads towards the exit. Kingy took a snooker ball off the table and sneaked up behind him. What the fuck's he doing I thought? as Kingy gently opened the landlord's jacket pocket and dropped the snooker ball inside. Kingy walked forward and faced the landlord.

"Look," Kingy said. "We're only having a laugh mate. We're not hooligans. I'm a professional magician. I'll tell you what, I'll not come anywhere near you. I'll hold my hands in the air, like this," Kingy raised his hands above his head. "If can make a snooker ball appear in your pocket will you let us stay? If I can't do it, I promise we'll all leave, okay?"

The landlord pondered for a couple of seconds and said, "So you're gonna make a snooker ball appear in my pocket?"

"That's right," Kingy said, his arms still in the air. "I'll not come anywhere near you."

"All right," the landlord said. Kingy muttered some mumbo-jumbo, "Kalazam-akaba-abracadabara, now feel in your left jacket pocket" The landlord dipped in his pocket and fished out the snooker ball. We erupted into laughter, but the landlord went crazy.

"Get out of my pub. Phone the police," he shouted to one of the bar staff. We piled out, pissing ourselves laughing.

Around fifty of us moved off to the Central pier and somehow managed to enter one of the 'On the pier' type concert hall things. Some washed out artiste from the 60s, like Jimmy Jewell, Clitheroe or Tarbuck headlined the show. We'd arrived during the interval and entered the large concert room holding about 500 punters. Blue-rinse pensioners, their husbands, sons, daughters and grandchildren made up the audience. In a flash of inspiration I nipped down the aisle and jumped onto the stage. I tapped the microphone housed on a stand.

"One two, one two, testing, testing," I shouted into the mic. The mic hummed and whistled a bit, so I moved back a few inches. Now what came into my head, or what made me say what I said, is a mystery, I just kinda came out.

"Good evening ladies and gentlemen, are we all having a good time?" I shouted.

The audience had no idea who I was, but nevertheless a few of them shouted, "Yes we are." The lads were all stood at the back of the room, laughing and wondering what I was going to say next. Now for those who've never seen Bent-Nose-Mitchell, I'll have to tell you, Mitch is a ringer for the boxer Richard Dunn. I shouted into the mic, "Well tonight ladies and gentlemen, we have a special treat. This man recently fought Muhammad Ali for the heavyweight championship of the world. Ladies and gentlemen I want you to put your hands together, show your appreciation and give a rousing Blackpool welcome to the British and Commonwealth heavyweight champion, from Bradford, Yorkshire… Mr Richaaaaaaaaaaaaaard Dunn… come on Richard, get up here and take a bow."

In an unforgettable, magic moment, Bent-Nose, right on queue bounced down the aisle, punching, sparring and shuffling his feet like a true champion. Mitch jumped on the stage and went through a series of mid-air combinations. He danced in a circle, hands clasped together above his head, in the classic winner's pose.

Now the audience must have been thinking, is he Richard Dunn? He certainly looks like Richard Dunn; it must be Richard Dunn. Urged on by me, within seconds, the spattering of applause turned into a standing ovation as the crowd rose to their feet, clapping and cheering.

"Don't anybody ring a bell," I shouted. "He'll think it's round one and knock some fucker out." The lads at the back were in pieces and I couldn't carry on for laughing.

Jenk's Bar stood on the corner of a road directly opposite the Central Pier. The massive, one-roomed bar at street level had large windows and glass doors giving a good view out onto the street. The place was already packed with Blades when we arrived. After half an hour or so of quite civilised drinking and singing we watched a live band do their first set without a hint of trouble. As usual there were shouts of, "Get thi sen on, Ron. Show em how it's done."

I had a good chat to a group of young punks from Leeds who were there for the weekend. Some of the Blades wanted to batter the punks, purely for their Leeds connection, but they weren't football lads, so I stepped in and calmed things down. I could sense trouble a-brewing. The old sea air once again wafted up Blade nostrils, warping their tiny minds; it was only a matter of time.

The band came on for the second set and were halfway through the first song when a pint pot smashed on the wall behind them. They unplugged their instruments and made a swift exit.

"I think ya better get yourselves out," I said to the Leeds punks. The Leeds lads, along with a few holiday-making illumination junkies headed for the door. The demolition process started, but within seconds the first couple of squad cars pulled up outside. Half a dozen coppers charged in and were met by a barrage of pint pots. They retreated and stood outside, looking in through the front doors. A gap of about five yards appeared between the mob of around two hundred Blades and the front doors. More cars and vans with their blue lights flashing and sirens wailing screeched up.

Once again the coppers swarmed through the doors and another volley of glasses, plus the odd table and chair stopped them in their tracks. Blades, thinking they'd got the upper hand, began singing, dancing on the tables and wrecking the furniture. More and more vans and cars arrived until what looked like the entire North-West Constabulary filled the street. I could see the coppers readying themselves for the attack. I thought to myself, we've got no chance of avoiding arrest here and we'll end up in the cells, just like we did at Yarmouth the year before. Fuck solidarity; the night was still young, there was beer to be swigged and hopefully some sluts to be fucked, so I said to Moose, "Right Mull, let's get out before we get nicked. Ready? Put ya hands on the top of your head and follow me." We ran through no-man's-land and pulled open the front doors.

"You've got to help us mate," I said to the coppers. "It's them Sheffield fans, they're like animals. They're gonna kill us, please get us out of here."

"Come on son," one of the coppers said. "We'll get you out, let these lads through," he shouted. The sea of filth parted and with our hands still on our heads we ran through them and across the road.

"Fuck me, Ron." Moose laughed. "Thara cunt, thy are."

Now, whether the lads inside had seen what happened and took a bit of inspiration from us, I don't know, but they must have thought they were fucked if they stayed inside.

A roar filled the air as the Blades released their ammo and charged the doors. They piled out into the street, where some tried to escape, while others fought hand to hand with the coppers. We still hung back as the coppers began to get the upper hand. We heard more shouting as a mob of about fifty Blades arrived on the scene. They ran across the street and laid into the coppers. Moose and me had got away with it, so what did we do? Well, we couldn't resist it could we? Like daft cunts we joined in the attack and within seconds I'm nicked and thrown in the back of a police dog van, lucky for me the dog was out on duty biting Blade arses.

You stupid bastard, I thought to myself. I'd been inside for less than a minute when I heard shouting and banging on the sides and back of the van. The van rocked from side to side and the back doors flew open. I saw Moose and half a dozen other Blades.

"Come on, Ron," Moose shouted. I didn't need telling twice. We joined other Blades scattering amongst the chaos. That was it for the night. The Blades who'd escaped arrest, split into small groups and headed for the back-street boozers. We all met up back at the football ground where the coaches were parked. Quite a few of our lads, plus many more from the other buses, were missing when the coaches pulled out.

As stated earlier, I wasn't really into the drug scene. I'd have the occasional smoke some weekends; certainly not every weekend, and certainly never anything any stronger. I'd been working for a few months at a curtain warehouse on Brown Street, just up from the Howard Hotel in town. I worked with a lad from Manor Park, called George White. George, a part-time Wednesdayite, made up for his misgivings by being a really good mate and an excellent thief.

For some strange reason we spoke to each other in Scouse accents, maybe we thought we were a couple of Scally robbers. As well as stocking ready-made curtains in various colours, shapes and sizes, the warehouse stored hundreds of rolls of material from which the curtains were made.

The security at the factory was pretty tight. The front doors and the large sliding doors in the loading bay at the back of the warehouse were locked at dinner and break times. This prevented any of the workers robbing stuff, while the gaffers were on their dinner hour or their snap break. If any of us wanted to leave the factory at dinnertime, one of the gaffers would open and lock the door behind us and we would have to ring a bell to get back in. Lorries and vans arrived throughout the day, to either deliver new rolls of material or to take away boxes of the ready-made curtains. The half a dozen or so labourers, including George and me, stocked the shelves and loaded or unloaded the vans as they came in. George and me had a pair of curtains away just about every day. They were boxed up in pairs and could be easily carried out, wrapped in a coat or up the back of a jumper with a jacket over the top. Friends and neighbours were informed that brand new, half-price curtains were available.

George however moved in a circle of criminals, thieves and vagabonds. Through his contacts in the underworld he sussed out ways to make plenty of money. The odd pair of curtains every day made me a few extra quid a week and I was happy enough with that. George reckoned we should move on to bigger things and set his sights on the rolls. He sussed out a way to get the rolls out at dinnertime. As I said, all the doors were locked, so the rolls were sneaked into the toilets and squeezed through the bog window. They landed, out of sight at the back of a large oil tank in an alleyway at the side of the warehouse.

When the factory closed at five o'clock, we walked to the end of the road, gave it five minutes to make sure all the staff had left and went back to pick up the roll, or rolls if we managed to get a couple. At first we openly walked down to Pond Street with the rolls over our shoulders. George took them and jumped on the 92 bus up to Manor Park. We only did this a few times and then George got one of his mates to meet us in his van at the end of Brown Street to pick up the rolls. I can't remember exactly how much we got for a roll, but two or three, split between us made us roughly around a week's wages.

I started to get a bit panicky; the bog window sketch became increasingly more difficult as the gaffers would sometimes turn up in the warehouse to check things over. They could walk in at any time. I'm sure some of the other workers knew what we were up to, and paranoia set in. I had a word with George, "I'm packing it in with the rolls, Jud," I told him. "A few pairs a week's good enough for me."

"That's all right, Ron," he said. "But I've got loads of orders, I'll be taking early retirement at this rate."

Excellent thieves need plenty of bottle and George had bottle to spare. During working hours when the loading bay doors were open, but no vans were outside, in the split second the gaffers or the foremen turned their backs, George would grab a roll and sprint out of the door. He'd drop it over the wall a few yards down the street, or his mate would be waiting in the van. George would calmly walk back in, wearing a large grin, and wink at me. If challenged by any of the gaffers, George would say he'd just nipped out to the shops. He'd do this three or four times a day.

If bottle were brains, George would have gone a long way, but no. At snap and dinnertimes when all the labourers and even some of the foremen were sat together eating and chatting, George would announce shit like, "I bought a great suit on Saturday, fuckin beautiful it is, cost me £60." I think the wages we were getting were around £20-25 a week. He started having driving lessons, not one a week but two or three. He bought all his clobber from the Chapel Walk boutiques and his shoes from Ravel. Every Monday morning George would relay his weekend spending sprees to us all.

"Fuckin hell, George," I said to him. "Some of these are gonna start wondering where all your money's coming from; keep it under your hat."

But George didn't give a shit, "Fuck em," he'd say. "I could have won it on the fuckin horses for all they know."

Now, while this is all interesting and riveting shit, I'm sure you'll agree, I hear you asking what the fuck's it got to do with drugs? Well, this next little escapade happened when I worked at the curtain warehouse and I had a bit of money to spare. I'd been in the Crazy Daisy one Thursday night and I'd smoked some bush with a couple of lads I knew from the football. It did absolutely fuck all. Nothing. Not even the slightest buzz. I moved on to the Penthouse and got talking to this bird I knew, who said she'd got some Moroccan Gold resin for sale. I didn't have a clue about Moroccan Gold, but the word 'Gold' sounded good. I could be way out here with the prices because I'd never bought any before, but I think £12 a quarter could have been the going rate. Anyway I bought a lump, which must have been an eighth for £6. I wouldn't have spent a wad like that if I hadn't have been lumped up with some curtain money. We were ready to leave the club, so I thought I'd save the gear for the weekend.

I went to work on Friday wearing the most grotesque shirt that had ever been stitched. Why my Mum bought it from a jumble sale I'll never know, could she have been taking the piss when she said, "It'll be all right for working in." Again, why I'd kept it and taken it from the bottom draw where I kept my working gear at my Mothers, to Tiff's flat is another mystery. The shirt was a royal blue colour, covered with large red strawberries and bright green leaves.

Tiff and me usually went out together on Friday nights, but I'd fallen asleep after tea and didn't wake up until about 8 o'clock, so we decided to have a night in. I couldn't be arsed getting changed, as I didn't really get mucky carrying curtains around all day, so I still had the strawberry shirt on. Months earlier, I'd bought a packet of king-sized Rizlas from Pippy's, a 'Head' shop on Cambridge Street in town. Pippy's sold all kinds of hippy shit like beads, flowered dresses, head bands, pipes and dope-smoking paraphernalia. I've no idea why I'd bought the Rizlas because as I've said I hardly ever smoked the gear. This just goes to show how naive I was at the time. The bush from the night before had done fuck all, so I thought I'll make a good fucker this time. I heated up the chunk of Moroccan, crumbled the whole eighth into a king-size and wrapped up something, loosely resembling a joint.

Tiff smoked less than I did, but she said she'd try a few tokes. We packed the kids off to bed, smoked the joint and settled down on the settee. We had an old black and white telly at the time, and we were watching a cowboy film. After about fifteen minutes or so the giggles started. The film's name escapes me, but every now and again a repetitive song kept playing in the background. A bit like the John Wayne film *Chisum*, when a choir of unseen cowpokes kept bursting in with "Chisum, John Chisum."

Well every time this song came on, Tiff and me doubled up laughing. In one of these bouts we rolled off the settee and landed on the floor. I suddenly got a sexual urge like I'd never had before. We started doing the business, but after only a few minutes Tiff freaked. She pushed me off saying, "I've got to stand up, I've got to walk, what's happening to me? I've got to walk; I've got keep moving." Tiff started to walk in circles around the settee. I followed, like an Alpha-male Macaque in the height of mating season trying to mount her from behind. I managed to get her into the bedroom, but after a ten second plunge, she freaked again.

"I've got to get out, I've got to keep moving," she shouted. Tiff whipped on her shoes and headed for the door. She ran down the back steps and on to the grass bank behind the flats. I followed and tried to calm her down.

"I've got to walk, I've got to keep moving, just let me walk and I'll be okay," Tiff said. We went through the gate and walked around and around the iron railings surrounding the flats. Every now and again Tiff stopped and clung onto the railings. Each time she did, I tried to ravish her from behind. We left the railings and walked past the New Inn boozer onto Duke Street. Tiff's in a real mess now. She started mumbling all kinds of shit and tried to flag down passing cars. Tiff ran to the emergency telephone outside the unmanned police room housed under the Park Hill flats and got through to the coppers. She started muttering shit, saying she'd smoked some cannabis and she was going to die. That's when the fear hit me. I'm in some deep shit now, I thought and panic set in.

"What the fuck did you do that for?" I said. I felt like killing her.

"I've got to get to the hospital, they'll help me," Tiff said.

Duke Street looked about three miles long when the police car, with the blue light flashing first appeared. It got to within a mile of us and as I blinked, it moved back another mile down the hill. Shit, I could see the car coming towards us, but it didn't seem to be getting any closer. Tiff began to wail; she stamped her feet and walked on the spot. Now I'd lost control. I knew when the cop car eventually reached us I'd be in some shit, but I wanted it to get to us anyway. From here on things start to get a bit blurred. Fuck knows what we said to the coppers or what they said to us, but the next thing, we're in casualty. They took Tiff off somewhere and a copper stayed with me in the waiting room.

Now maybe at this point I should have been worrying about the state of Tiff, the small matter of me plying her with drugs, but more importantly, the six and seven-year-old lads, left home alone in the flat. But no, all I could think about was that horrendous shirt. I imagined everybody in the hospital, doctors, nurses and patients alike, had seen it and were now hiding behind corners creased up with laughter. The copper sat with me ran his eyes over the shirt; he knows it's a drug dealer's shirt I thought. My suspicions were confirmed, and my head's fucked even more, when a few minutes later, two Rockers, who turned out to be drug squad officers, arrived and took me away. Bearing in mind my tangled-up state, I'm not too sure if they questioned me in the hospital or took me to the nick. I told them I'd bought the gear in the Penthouse off a long-haired stranger wearing denims; I swore blind neither Tiff nor me had ever smoked it before.

The next thing we're back at the flat and the squad are searching it. One of them picked up the packet of Rizlas, held it in front of my face and said, "Regular smoker are you? I thought you said it's the first time you've smoked it."

"Honest, it is, I just bought the Rizlas for a laugh, months ago." I said. Why didn't they go and arrest the chairman of the fuckin Rizla conglomerate for making giant skins and tempting every fucker. The copper fished the roach out of the ashtray.

"You're in deep trouble," he said. "The Rizlas and the roach are evidence and you could get sent to jail, but we only want the dealers, so I'm going to give you a chance. I want you to meet me next Thursday in the Norfolk Arms on Dixon Lane, we'll go in the Penthouse and I want you to go over to the lad who sold you the gear and put your hand on his shoulder, that's all you have to do."

I agreed to meet the copper and point out the lad, trouble was the lad didn't exist; well, he did – there were hundreds of long-haired, Denim clad lads in the Penthouse.

Tiff came home in an ambulance and although she didn't kick me out, she blanked me for days. It might have been weeks. As always, after we'd fallen out, Tiff covered up the Ron tattoo on her arm with a plaster. This time the plaster stayed on for a good month.

I now faced the dilemma of meeting the copper. I had a word with Herman, and he put me right. He said, if they hadn't found any gear on me, there was fuck all they could do. He said they were just trying to scare me with the roach and the Rizlas. I didn't go to meet the copper and I spent the next few weeks expecting a knock. It didn't come, and I never heard anything about it again.

I left the curtain warehouse on Christmas Eve 77, when they moved to smaller premises in the east end. Staff cuts saw a couple of other lads and me laid off. George kept his job, but he was eventually caught and jailed for robbing the curtains.

The last game of 1977 took us to Hull City on New Year's Eve. We arrived by coach around dinnertime, boozed trouble free in the city centre and marched up to the ground. For some unknown reason I'd attached a three-inch-long yellow feather to my earring (a punk thing maybe?)

About twenty of us managed to sneak onto Hull's Kop. We waited until everyone was through the turnstiles, came in at the side and ran straight into the Hull mob, who were stood at the back of the standing area just in front of the seats. The coppers intervened within seconds, and Herman, me, and about six others were arrested. We were dragged to the detention area behind the stands and stood in line waiting to have our names taken.

"Name?" the sergeant said to me.

"Roger Fanshaw," I answered.

"Address?"

"Flat B, City Road, Sheffield." Fuckin hell I thought, why the fuck did I say flat B?

"Flat B?" The copper said, in a voice that told me he knew I was lying.

311

"Yeah, flat B," I answered. I couldn't change it now.

"Stand over there," the copper said. The coppers took all our names and we gave them the usual shit about getting on the wrong end by mistake and being attacked. We were all released after about ten minutes and put on the side terrace with the rest of the Blades.

Just after half time, a melee with the police saw me dragged out of the crowd and on to the pitch perimeter. They marched me in the opposite direction to the detention room and threw me out though an exit gate. Two minutes later I'd scaled the outside wall and was back in the ground. I squeezed my way into the middle of the mob and thought I'd better keep my head down for the rest of game. Trust fucking United, who were drawing 2-2, to score a late winner and get me all excited. I ran down to the front and leapt the wall to join another dozen or so Blades dancing on the side of the pitch. Next second my arm's up my back and this time I'm marched towards the detention room. Another copper grabbed my other arm on the way. I've got to get this feather out of my ear, in case the sergeant recognizes me, I'm thinking. I managed to wriggle one arm free, but the copper stopped me pulling the feather out. We reached the detention room, the sergeant saw me and said, "Well look who's back, its flat B."

Fuckin shit. I put on my best pleading voice, "I'm sorry, I was getting crushed on the wall when United scored and had jump over on to the pitch or I'd have got squashed to death," I told the copper.

"You're lucky, lad. It's News Year's Eve. I'm feeling in a good mood and I can't be bothered. So just piss off home," the copper said.

Nicked three times at one game and I walked away free. The Angel Gabriel must have been sat on my shoulder that day.

1978 started with a 2-2 home draw against Tottenham Hotspur, and then things started to go a bit wrong. First Arsenal, then Bolton and Sunderland stuck five goals past the Blades in successive games.

A new manager – Happy Harry Haslam was brought in to stop the rot. It didn't quite work; the Blades even lost a battle to pub-team Hastings United in a friendly. Superstars such as Andy Kelley, John Flood and Mike Guy joined the squad, but even talent of such magnitude did nothing to help the cause and home crowds plummeted to around the 12-13,000 mark.

We were singing the standard chants that every mob in the land used after going a goal down. "We'll support you ever more," "we're only warming up," and "we'll see you all outside." Were sung every fuckin week. Shit as the team were, we were still 100% behind them. In March, a couple of thousand Union Jack waving Blades converged on Burnley. It was the height of the 'Allez Les Rouges' period. One of the Nationals (I think it could have been the *Sunday Express*) did a brilliant write up in pidgin French. When Woody (who'd never fouled any fucker in his life) and Kelley got sent off, it told of the Allez-Les-Rouges-singing, flag-waving Blades, fighting running battles with the Burnley gendarmes.

A month a later an equal number of Blades returned to Lancashire. Ten minutes before the end of the game, hundreds ran round and swarmed onto

Blackburn's Kop, scattering all the home fans off their own end. Before the game a mob of us were boozing in Blackburn town centre. One of the lads nipped out to a chippy and on the way back he passed a joke shop. He noticed a plastic face mask in the shop window that was a ringer for Rotten. He walked in the pub wearing the mask and everybody creased up. We all went out a bought a mask. Fifty Rottens shouted to each other, "Hey-up Rotten, how's it going?" "Pleased to meet ya, Rotten. My name's Rotten." One of the lads tried pulling Rotten's face off saying, "Lend us ya mask pal." Rotten wasn't amused.

The last game of a pretty shit season on the pitch brought Cardiff City to the lane. The Taffs arrived early and large groups draped in Welsh flags swanned around town showing off. When Cardiff scored a last-minute winner, hundreds of Blades scaled the fences and swarmed towards the Lane End to confront the Taffies. A large police presence stopped the Blades and forced them back towards the Kop. When the game ended a massive Blade mob rampaged down Shoreham Street on to St Mary's Road and headed for the coaches parked near the Royal Standard/ Truro Tavern pubs.

The Welshies, who lounged around the buses didn't seem quite so keen when a barrage of missiles sailed towards them. They fought and pulled each other back in an effort to scramble aboard. Some were caught, clipped and their flags were ripped up, before the coppers arrived and moved us on.

Blades on the pitch after a last-minute Cardiff winner at the Lane in May 1978

Tiff managed to get a three-bedroom council house on the Wybourn Estate. We didn't want to look out of place, so the first thing we bought for the new pad was an ornamental, pot, shire horse pulling a cart load of beer barrels, which we proudly displayed in the front room window. A framed print of Constable's Haywain, another Wybourn must-have masterpiece, hung above the fireplace. The downside of moving, was the house had a telephone, which meant I had to check in and make up excuses for staying out all night.

I started a new job working as a labourer for the council - the SWD or the Sheffield Works Department – to give it its full title. It must have been all right because I stayed for five years. In fact, for the first three months I didn't have a day off, nor was I late. That must be a world record for any fucker.

I was based at the Arbourthorne depot, working with the plasterers. The lad

I mixed for, Mick Wagstaff, was an old mate off the Manor. I'd known him from the Silver Blades skating rink days back in the 60s. Mick, a dark-haired, handsome fucker was a big hit with the housewives, which meant we always got plenty of brews. He'd worked on the council a good few years and knew all the ropes. We got on really well and always had a good laugh. The first lesson Mick taught me when filling in the bonus sheet was, 'The pen is mightier than the trowel.'

Hundreds of houses on the Arbour had been re-wired and our job was to fill in the chases, holes and cracks left by the sparkies. We were allowed so many minutes for each job. I can't remember the exact times, but when we'd reached the forty hours, making up a week's work, any extra hours were paid as bonus.

It went something like this. Fill in three chases, six holes and eight cracks: two hours. If there weren't six holes, we'd make them, by tapping the walls with a hammer. Walking time to next job: fifteen minutes. Waiting time for materials to arrive: ten minutes, and so on. Plus all the little extra bits Mick had learned over the years. By the middle of the week, or sometimes after the first two days, we'd hit the forty hours, the rest of the week made up our bonus. We didn't abuse the system too much, so there were no comebacks. Our dinner hour, or hours were spent in the Arbourthorne Hotel. or the Vulcan, playing pool.

We had to clock in at 8 in the morning, but we didn't have to clock out, so we finished early most days. On Fridays, with our hours and bonuses already done, we clocked in, walked out of the depot and jumped on the bus home. I was usually back in bed by 9 o'clock every Friday morning, no wonder I loved the job. When I received my first council pay-packet I went on a shopping spree to the swish city centre boutiques of Sexy Rexy and Harringtons to stock up my wardrobe.

Nobody really had any intention of buying owt from Harringtons. The clothes shop, housed in the Sheaf market was manned by a posse of assistants who patrolled the front of the shop. They dragged in anybody who came within twenty yards of the place. The shoppers were forced at gunpoint up a vertical ladder to the changing room in the roof area and no one was allowed to leave unless they'd bought at least two shirts and a pair of jeans.

Living over the brush and working meant I needed to be a bit careful, so in the morning when I left for work and when I arrived back, I used the back door, which led to a field that came out on Cricket Inn Road. I came home one afternoon covered in plaster and as usual I used the back door. I walked through to the front room to see Tiff and a bloke dressed in a suit with a briefcase at his side sat on the settee.

"Hey-up Ron, how's it going?" the bloke said. It turned out that this Social Security fraud officer spent his Saturday afternoons dressed in the height of fashion rampaging around the Shoreham. He said he wasn't supposed to, but he showed us a crudely written, badly spelt letter the social received, saying Tiff was on benefits and she had a bloke living with her. He screwed up the letter, saying, "Right, you'll not hear any more about that. See ya next Saturday, Ron."

It's not what ya know eh!

The new board of directors at the Lane gave Happy Harry a bit of dosh for new players. So in the summer of 78, Hazz nipped over to Argentina (who'd just won the World Cup) to cast his experienced eye over some South American talent. The choice was narrowed down to two players. Alejandro Sabella, a twenty-three-year-old international who played for River Plate would cost £160,000, or a seventeen-year-old, up and coming young lad named... Diego Maradona valued at £160,000 and 50P. In typical United style they chose the cheaper option and signed Sabella, a pity really cos I reckon Maradona could have forged quite a formidable partnership with the prolific Mike Guy, but alas, we'll never know.

Before the 78-79 season started, the Blades went on a three-match, pre-season tour of Switzerland. A mob of the lads, including, Bent Nose, Big Dave Laycock, Rotten, Bullet, Spindle, Cudgy, Gibby and a few more made the trip. The lads told Big Dave the water in Switzerland was undrinkable. On the day of the trip Big Dave arrived at Sheffield Midland station carrying a gallon of bottled water.

S.U.T. Sheffield United Tours. We often travelled on these coaches from the mid 60's to the mid 70's.

Chapter 9

Like ice, like fire

Bent Nose started work as an unofficial bouncer at the Sunday night concerts at the Top Rank. He didn't receive a wage, but the benefits included not having to wear a monkey-suit, free admission, a spot at the side of the stage where he growled at the audience, and access to the after-gig parties in the dressing rooms. Luckily for me he was allowed to take a mate.

Sometimes I stood at the side of Mitch, arms folded in the classic bouncer's stance, but I always felt like a cunt, so I'd give it ten minutes and go for a wander round. We saw some great bands and got to sup plenty of free ale at the backstage parties.

The Jam, the Damned, Buzzcocks, the Specials, Slaughter and the Dogs, Siouxsie and the Banshees, now I wouldn't have minded giving Siouxsie an after gig rub down, the Pretenders – Chrissie Hynde could have had one as well.

After a shit-hot gig we shared a few beers and laughs with the Ramones. Johnny Ramone (or any of the others) didn't come over as 'I'm the rock star' bit; he was quite unassuming and down to earth. I'd loved the Ramones since first hearing *Blitzkreig Bop* at the Penthouse.

I'd always been fascinated with America and particularly New York. I chatted with Johnny about Greenwich Village, the Bowery and CBGB.

Bullet was with us and he'd just recently taken up the bass. Mitch, full of front and spiel as ever, shouted to Dee Dee Ramone, "Oi Dee Dee, this is my mate, Bullet. He plays the bass, have ya got any tips for him?

"You taking the fuckin piss? Dee Dee replied. "I only use one string, so yeah I've got a tip: only use one fuckin string man."

Now the same couldn't be said about Sham69: not the band, but smug cunt Jimmy Pursey. Sham were all right in my eyes, nothing that excited me too much, just unoriginal, but bearable post-punk shit. The band had a quite a good following amongst the Sheffield football lads though, both United and Wednesday. Mitch was on first name terms with Pursey and at the backstage party he pushed through the line of admirers waiting to pay homage to their leader. Pursey, stripped to the waist sat in an armchair signing autographs.

"Jimmy, mi owd mate, ar's it goin pal?" Mitch shouted. Pursey shook Mitch's hand.

"This is my mate, Ron," Mitch said. "He's into Bob Dylan."

Now if Pursey had been taking the piss, well, fair enough, but by the way he spoke I knew he wasn't: "Fackin Dylan, Dylan's finished, what the fack has Dylan done recently?" he said.

"I'll tell ya what he hasn't done," I answered. "Wrote shit like Hurry up fuckin Harry. I bet that took some fuckin thinking about."

Pursey wasn't amused; Mitch tried to lighten the mood by laughing and shouting, "Jimmy and Sharpy's gonna have a scrap." Yeah, I thought, I'll rip the

316

scrawny cunt's neck off.

"What the fuck did ya say that for?" Mitch asked me later.

"Cos he's a fuckin arsehole. You might kiss his fuckin arse, but I'm not," I said.

A mob of us went to see the Boomtown Rats at a Friday night gig at the Rank. We were stood at the back of the dance floor facing the stage when Dinky announced, "Watch this, I'm gonna glass that cunt Geldof." Dinky leaned back and launched a pint pot.

It seemed to glide through the air in slow motion, missing the singer by a couple of feet, before shattering behind him. The band stopped playing and Geldof (who was then, still is, and always will be, a cunt), but I have to take my hat off to the cunt that night, shouted, "Roight who true the fuckin glass? I'll foight him one on one, come on which bastard true the fuckin glass?" Dinky had started running before the glass landed. We saw him sprinting up the stairs and after hiding in the bog for five minutes, Dink's head, with a big grin on his face appeared over the balcony.

The Clash did a great set at the Rank in the summer of 78. Even though they sounded a bit out of tune, their stage presence was incredible. When we tried to get to the backstage do, we were told the party had been cancelled, due to the band members scrapping with each other.

Two weeks earlier Johnny Hall and me boarded a special coach from Pond Street bus station, heading for Earls Court in London. Safely tucked in our back pockets, tickets to see the man himself... Bob Dylan. Dobby, one of the Dronny lads and fellow Dylan fan queued all night for the tickets. The tickets weren't the best in the house, but we wanted good seats and they were the next best. I can't remember how much we paid, but it was a fair old wedge.

After a good Saturday early-evening session in a boozer near the gig, we took our seats in the concert hall and found ourselves in the balcony about three miles from the stage – no matter.

Dylan walked on stage, to a roar to end all roars. There was none of the usual shit like, "Good evening London, I'm Bob Dylan." He never said a word, he just launched straight in to *Love Minus Zero/ No Limit*.

'My love she speaks like silence
Without ideals or violence,
She doesn't have to say she's faithful,
Yet she's true like ice like fire'

The roar when Dylan took the stage paled into insignificance when he blew the first notes on the harmonica. It was like being on the Shoreham after a goal against Wednesday, only ten times louder. The noise was amazing; it bought a tear to my eye and lump to my throat.

During the interval we paid ridiculous money for a couple of beers at the bar. We decided to try and get a bit nearer to the stage and entered the downstairs bit on a level with the stage. There were no spare seats, so we just leaned on the wall near the front and watched the rest of the gig from there nobody challenged us or told us to move. We left the gig buzzing like fuck; I'd finally got to see the man I'd worshipped for over ten years.

At the backstage party after the gig Johnny introduced me to Dylan.

"How's it going Bob?" Johnny said as he shook Dylan's hand.

"I'm good, John, good and who's this fine-looking chap with you?" Dylan said.

"This is my mate Ron; he's a big Sham 69 fan," Johnny said.

"Jimmy Fuckin Pursey," Dylan said. "What's that cunt ever done?"

"I'll tell ya what he hasn't done," I replied. "Wrote Like A Rollin fuckin Stone."

After a 2-2 draw at Preston at the end of August, Sam, Ess, Bullet and me, boarded Fireman Pete's Volkswagen Beetle for a night out in Blackpool. Fireman Pete used to be Stocksbridge Pete, or Cabin Boy Pete, but he'd left the Navy and joined the fire brigade. We were so fuckin inventive with nicknames.

Pete turned the radio to full blast when the opening guitar riff to Jilted John came on. We all joined in when John sang, "But I know he's a moron, Gordon is a moron, Gordon is a moron, Gordon is a moron. Ooooh she's a slag and he's a creep, she is a tart, he's very cheap, she is a slut, he thinks he's tough, she is a bitch, he is a puff, yeah yeah it's not fair. Fuckin marvellous.

The most memorable thing about the Preston game, apart from a brilliant Sabella goal was two Preston lads appearing on our end and fronting a couple of thousand Blades. The lads took a right kicking but received a rousing reception (and no doubt legendary status) from the Preston mob when they were escorted out by the coppers onto the side terrace to join their mates.

With loads of other Blades we did the usual rampaging around Blackpool sketch. Pete didn't want to hang about, what with having to drive and shit, so when the boozers shut we set off back. Nearing the South Pier we pulled onto a side street to grab a bit of snap from a burger stall on the sea front. Three Geordies stood at the stall made some snide comments about Sam and Ess's skinhead attire. We squared up to them, but before anyone threw a punch, they turned and ran, and we chased them down the sea front. We were stopped in our tracks when half a dozen of their mates appeared. So now it's eight/nine Geordies, five of us. We pondered for a split second about taking them on, but discretion got the better of us and we turned and ran. We jogged back up sea front and turned on to the road where the car was parked.

"What the fuck are we doing running from these cunts?" Bullet shouted.

Me: "Are we fuckin stopping or what?"

Glance over shoulder, they're about twenty yards behind.

Sam: "Come on – they're fuck-all these."

Ess: "Let's have the cunts."

"Right get ready. All turn round together, right?"

"Get to the car. There's some tools in the boot," Pete shouted. We reached the car and Pete opened the bonnet which was the boot on the VW. We foraged around and grabbed a spanner and a couple of screwdrivers. Sam couldn't find a weapon, so he picked up a tennis racket.

The Geordies had nearly reached us when we turned to face them. Sam ran forward and then stopped dead in his tracks. He leapt high in the air, his legs – with sixteen-lace-holed Doc Martens hanging on the ends were bent like a frog. Sam let out a scream, "Arrrrrrrrrrrr come on ya fuckin bastards." Sam's action freaked the Geordies and they turned and ran. So the chase, with us now doing the chasing's back on. They turned another corner and ran towards a coach parked about fifty yards up the street. We could see drunken lads stood around the bus and others staggering around trying to board it.

It looked like the coach was about to leave as the engine was running. We slowed to a halt as we saw the group shout to their mates and wave them towards us. The lads that could walk, ran towards us and the coach emptied. Trust us to pick on a stag-night, birthday, jolly-boys-outing, whatever it was.

"Fuckin shit, it's on top." We sprinted off; a damn sight faster than we'd run there. We reached the car and Pete managed to get the key in door lock and open it, but we didn't have time to get in as the mob was nearly on us. We shot off and could only watch the demolition of Pete's wheels from a distance. Like a troop of Longleat safari park baboons the bastards danced on the roof and aimed drop-kicks at bonnet and the boot. They booted in the side panels and ripped off the wing mirrors. Pete didn't have time to lock the door, so they just opened it and set about destroying the interior.

A couple more Geordies arrived and beckoned the lads back to bus which must have been waiting to leave. The mob moved off congratulating each other, whooping, cheering and waving their fists in the air in victory salutes. We gave it a couple of minutes until they were out of sight, before walking back to survey the damage. We looked inside, and the fuckers had ripped the dashboard off and wrapped it around the gear stick. They'd booted the ignition slot in, and we couldn't get the key in to start the car. Luckily the windows were still intact. Pete phoned the AA, but they said they couldn't send anyone until next morning, so we were fucked. Five lads trying to doss in a VW meant a rather uncomfortable night.

The AA arrived next morning and managed to start the car, but they told Pete to keep the engine running, because if it stopped we wouldn't be able to start it again. This meant we couldn't stop for the traditional Sunday dinnertime, journey-home session; Pete wasn't really in the mood for a piss-up anyway.

The day after, a Gary Hamson scorcher was enough to beat Liverpool in a League Cup tie at the Lane. Spindle, Bullet, Keeny and Rotten drove to Liverpool straight after the game and decorated Anfield with Blade graffiti.

Who'd have thought it? Crystal fuckin Palace on the Shoreham. About a hundred or so of us gathered on the Lane End, when just after kickoff we saw the Blade mob moving across the Kop towards the white wall and fighting erupt in the top corner. The coppers were straight in and around fifty Palace lads were taken off and escorted past the John Street Terrace toward the Lane end.

The Palace lads were full of it, jigging around, singing, clapping, posing to the crowd and waving to a group of Palace normals stood behind the Lane end goal.

"Let them all get on here before we wade in." One of the lads said. A good idea, but that was never gonna happen. The bastards had the cheek to go on our end and now they were taking the piss. This fired us up to fuck and when the first dozen or so climbed over the fence onto the Lane end, we ran down and battered them. The rest of the Palace lads, still on the perimeter didn't seem too keen now. After arguing with the coppers for a few minutes they didn't object too much when the police put them on the John Street Terrace.

Big Dave Laycock saw the world through a pair of thick-framed Jim Royle style glasses. Dave wasn't the best dresser in the world, but today he'd made the effort. Clad as usual in an old blokes' gabardine rain mac with Blade badges covering the lapels, cheap Denim jeans, held up by an Elvis belt and an out-of-date shirt, Dave stepped aboard Gibby's coach for the trip to Fulham. Slung around his neck, a dark blue, thick knotted tie.

"Fuckin hell Dave," one of the lads shouted. "What the fuck are ya wearing a tie for?"

"It's fuckin London, innit," Dave shouted back. "You've got to look a bit fuckin smart in London." We all cracked up.

On the journey it was rumoured and speculated on (maybe some of ours had some inside knowledge) that Chelsea, who were playing at Coventry, would be turning out to welcome us. Bullshit I thought.

In the café area at Leicester Forest services, Big Dave took a giant bite out of a bacon and egg buttie. Dave didn't notice the yolk squirt out and land with splat in the middle of his tie, none of us told him.

Around 12 bells, the coach dropped us bang outside our usual meeting up place in the capital: the Cockney Pride in Piccadilly. We swarmed into the large basement bar and began the dinnertime session. We usually took the tube to wherever we were going, but the coach waited and drove us up to Craven Cottage. We arrived ten minutes before kickoff and entered Fulham's Kop. We ran in screaming "UNITED," but the coppers soon rounded us up and marched us round to join another seven-eight hundred or so Blades on the open end.

As the players warmed up and had a kick-about in the goal in front of us, Tabby Greenwood announced, "I'm going on t' pitch to shake hands with Woody." Tabby ran down to the front, vaulted the fence and ran over to Alan Woodward. As he extended his hand, we saw Woody go fuckin mental at Tabby. Tabby turned and ran back. His face was as red as a baboons arse when he re-joined us.

"What did he say to ya Tab?" one of the lads said.

"He said, what do you think you're doing? You stupid little bastard, get off the fuckin pitch. I've fuckin done with the grey-haired cunt from now on," Tabby said.

One of the chabbies, Clarky (another of the lads who died young, R.I.P), and his mates, said they were going to a pub or a club later to see a new band called the Police.

320

"Fuckin Police," one of the lads said. "What sort of fuckin name is that for a band?"

Just before half time, we saw a skirmish erupt on the Kop. We thought it might have been some Blades who'd arrived late, but it turned out to be Chelsea.

The coppers, in their wisdom brought the Chelsea fans (around thirty or so) round and parked them just to the left of us. Some Blades started chatting to them, as though they were best mates. Moose, me and a few others barged through.

"What the fuck are ya talking to these cunts for?" we shouted at the Blades.

Before we even had the chance to wade in, we were grabbed by the coppers and led away. They took us to a detention room at the corner of the away end. As usual we remonstrated with coppers protesting our innocence.

"What ya nicking us for?" I said to one of the coppers "Them Chelsea fans have turned up to start trouble and you put em on our fuckin end." The copper didn't answer. We were locked in a room, but after half an hour or so the police came in, told us we were free to go, and warned us to not to start any more trouble.

"If you hadn't put the Chelsea fans on our end, there wouldn't have been any fuckin trouble," I said.

"You've got a lot of lip lad," a copper said to me. "You're staying for the weekend. The rest of you, on your way."

"Tough shit, Ron," Moose laughed. "See ya later."

Fuckin bastard. My gob had dropped me in it again. After another ten minutes the coppers came back into the room.

"Calmed down yet?" a copper asked me. Time to eat shit I thought.

"Yeah," I said. "I'm really sorry. I apologise. I've had a bit too much to drink today."

"Go on then, on your way and no more trouble, right?"

"Right," I said.

As I left the lock-up the game had nearly ended, and I saw about fifty of our lads, hot on the heels of the Chelsea lads running towards the exit. Having just escaped arrest, what did I do? I joined the chase. We ran past the row of a dozen or so Blade coaches parked on a long straight road a couple of hundred yards past the ground. The Chelsea lads must have done a bit of pre-match planning. They stopped as one, went behind a garden wall and armed themselves with lumps of wood, bricks and milk bottles. The hail of missiles stopped us in our tracks. With their ammo spent, the Chelsea lot turned and ran again, but these fuckers were well organised and, fifty yards further up the road, they stopped again and produced another stash of milk bottles from behind a wall. Again the bottles slowed us, but that was the last of their ammo. The Chelsea mob must have realised we weren't giving up, so they put on a sprint and put some distance between us. Seeing this, most of the Blades gave up the chase. I was fired up to fuck, though, and me, Chip Scothern and a few others carried on. The others gave up, leaving just me and Chip. We stopped after another twenty yards or so and sat gasping for breath on a garden wall.

After a minute's recovery, we set off back towards the coaches. When the coaches came into view in the far distance, none of the other Blades were in sight. As we neared the coaches, a mob of around forty Fulham fans, who, during all the excitement, we'd forgotten about, appeared in between us and the buses. Chip wore his red and white scarf, but I didn't have any colours on. They were now only ten-twenty yards from us and I thought they must have seen Chip's scarf, so the best form of defence would be to attack.

I ran into them, screaming, "Come on ya fucking bastards." After a few haymaking swings I was on the deck. Chip walked straight through the mob and no one touched him. By the time he came back a minute later with reinforcements from our bus, I was laid in a puddle, drenched to the skin, covered in boot marks. The lads helped me onto the coach where Moose came down from the back, laughed and said, "All right, Ron. I thought you were staying for the weekend? Not having a good day are ya?"

As always, none of the lads showed any compassion. It just wasn't the thing to do; we all laughed at each other's misfortunes, it was all part of the game. I wasn't too badly injured, but I was soaked to the skin. One of the lads lent me his leather bomber jacket, which made me feel a bit better.

We were back in the Cockney Pride for six bells, joining another coach load of Blades and a few more lads who'd travelled in vans. A group of Bristol City fans arrived, but after ten minutes of friendly banter and a rousing singsong, the Bristol mob were ran out of the boozer and chased down the street.

Sunderland were the next lot to cop for it and Moose nicked a spot-on red and white striped flat cap off one of them.

We moved off to the familiar stomping ground of Soho and ransacked a couple of sex shops. Kingy robbed a box of fifty 'Horn tablets' and necked the lot in one go. "You'll need more than fifty fuckin pills to do owt with that knob," one of the lads told him.

A mob of forty chanting skinheads danced out of a side street and headed straight towards us. They were clad in flowing saffron robes and tooled-up to fuck with finger cymbals, hand drums, flutes and tambourines. "Hare Krishna, Hare Krishna, Hare Krishna, Hare Rama," they sang as the reached us.

"Harry Roberts, Harry Roberts, Harry Roberts, kills coppers," we chanted back.

Jeff Kev cut our laughter short when he stepped forward and knocked-out a monk with one punch.

"Fuckin hell, Jeff," one of the lads said. "What the fuck did ya do that for, you rotten bastard?"

"I don't fuckin like them Hare Krishnas," Jeff answered. Well, you can't argue with that I suppose, but maybe Jeff should have thought about the Buddhist Karma shit, and he'll only have himself to blame when he's reincarnated as a slug.

Big Dave Laycock, knees a-knocking and with the splat of dried up egg yolk still decorating his tie, ran in the upstairs bar we were plotted up in and shouted, "Fuckin hell, them Sunderland fans are outside and there's a right mob of 'em now." We were on our feet and down the stairs in a flash. Armed with pint pots and bottles, we stormed out and the volley of glass saw the Sunderland fans turn and run.

We arrived back home at around 4-5 o'clock Sunday morning. Kingy and

322

me walked the short distance from Pond Street to the Bard Street flats where we both lived. As we reached Kingy's block, he clutched his chest with both hands and let out a long moaning sound.

"Fuck me Ron," he said. "I've got a right fucking pain in my chest; I think I'm having a heart attack."

"It's them horn pills, ya daft cunt. You shouldn't have taken the full box." Kingy let out another long moan, his eyes rolled, and he collapsed backwards over a wall. He's fucking about, I thought, and besides, I was fucked and needed some kip.

I left him to either sleep it off or die. Four hours later at the casualty department of the Royal Hospital, Kingy was pronounced: "dead on arrival" – only kidding. He slept it off and was back raring to go at the next home match.

Blades up floodlights and collapsed wall Rotherham 1979

Chapter 10

Queen Mary – he's my friend

February 1979 and I sauntered through Pond Street bus station at ten bells on a freezing Wednesday morning to meet up with thirty or so lads for the night match at Wrexham. I'd thrown a sicky from work for the trip. Seeing as we were playing in a foreign country, I'd brought along my old ten foot by six Union Jack. I'd had the flag since the 60s. This fucker was the real deal, with professionally stitched panels, not one of them cheap, shitty, thin cloth things that Yeoman's Army stores flogged.

Because it was so cold I'd also brought with me an original, brown leather Air force flying jacket. I'd found the coat, covered in dust and cobwebs, hanging in the cellar of a school where I was doing a job for the council; it must have been there since 1945. The coat, although falling to bits, had a three-inch-thick sheepskin lining that would keep a polar bear warm: it would make a good doss-bag for the journey home.

After collecting deposits the previous Saturday, Spindle was down Attercliffe, hiring two vans from some dodgy back street dealer.

Lads started arriving in twos, threes and small groups. Fat Terry, head shaved and Crombied-up, arrived with his brother, Fat Steve, and a few more Rotherham lads. Fat Terry left the fold a couple of years later and joined some Outer Mongolian religious cult. He spent a year praying and fasting before graduating to become a full-blooded Utopian hermit monk. He returned a couple of times in the eighties (as Thin Terry) all smiling and serene, telling us he'd found God, but he still had a soft spot for the Blades.

Keeny and Skid – the two gay Blades turned up. At the time though, they were both still firmly in the closet – probably on their knees in the closet at the end of Pond Street most weekends. Keeny proved he had more bottle than the rest of us put together when he came clean a year or so later. A group of around a dozen of us, some with our birds and wives in tow used to do a Friday night pub-crawl around town. One Friday in the starting point of the Howard, Keeny announced-out of the blue, "I've got something to tell ya lads. I've been wanting to say it for ages. I don't really know how to put this, but here goes… I'm gay."

None of us spoke for a few seconds.

"Fuck off, ya having us on," one of the lads said. It took a few minutes for it to sink in.

I know every single one of us must have had the occasional, sly, gross indecency wank, but in the homophobic world of football hooligans, shit stabbing wasn't really considered acceptable behaviour, and now here's Keeny, who'd always been a front-liner, telling us he's a rear-gunner. One of the lads lightened the mood by asking, "Any chance of a quick gobble then John?"

"Well bugger me," somebody else said.

Keeny told me a while after, he'd been dreading telling us – and who could blame him? He said he thought none of us would talk to him again, but it brought home to him what a great set of mates he had for accepting him for what he was.

Skid soon followed suit, but, unlike Keeny, Skid took the fairy route by coming over all camp and limp-wristed. I'd always had my doubts about Skid ever since I fucked him one night at the back of the Wellington boozer at Darnall.

Sparky and Squeaky Alan, two more skinheads arrived (Squeaky Al came off the Hyde Park flats and spoke like Joe Pasquale). Paul Longingmuir, Cudgy, Gibby, Bri Rawlins, Haggis, Kempy, Maz the sandwich man (Maz always turned up for away games with a carrier bag full of sarnies which the tight cunt sold to the lads), Goody, Bent-Nose and few more turned up. We gathered at the entrance of Harmer Lane car park, stamping our feet and waving our arms trying keep warm. I slipped the Biggles coat over my shoulders as we chatted about the weather.

"Fuck me, it's freezing."

"Fuckin hell, cold or what?"

"I'm gonna freeze to death, where's the fuckin vans?"

Half an hour later the vans, a Tranny and a box-van turned up. Spindle drove one, with Rotten and Bullet in the passenger seats. Buggis (Bullet's younger brother) drove the other.

"Fuck me Spindle, where ya got these fuckers from, a fuckin scrap yard?" one of the lads shouted.

"Fuck off, you hire 'em next time cunt, and its six quid a man," Spindle (who had a Jack Nicolson, à la 'One flew over the cuckoo's nest' look about him) shouted back.

"Six fuckin quid," twenty voices shouted. "Tha can fuck off." Now this was all good-natured banter, we always had a bit of a row when it came to paying for away days.

The head count when we left was thirty-five, twenty in the box van and fifteen in the Tranny. I chose the box van as it looked a bit warmer. As always, a couple of skint lads turned up hoping to scrounge their way through the day, a trick many of us had done at one time or another.

We picked Cockney up on the road to Buxton. He'd purposely made his way there, knowing we'd be taking that route and knowing he'd get a freebie by pleading poverty. Cockney travelled up from St Albans for most of the Blade games, both home and away. Cockney's Dad, an exiled Sheffielder made sure 'Gargoyle' took the right path.

Us lot in the back of the box van, kept braving the cold and opening the back flap for a few minutes to see where we were. As we hit the main road into Buxton we noticed signs saying: 'Slow-loose chippings – Max Speed 20 mph.' The van slowed to a halt and the driver and front seat passengers came round to the back.

"Fuckin windscreen's gone through," one of them said. "A lorry on the other side of the road came past at 100 fuckin miles an hour, shot some chippings up and put it through."

"Fuck me, what we gonna do?" we said.

"Fuck knows," the driver said.

The Tranny, minus its windscreen pulled up behind us, Spindle got out, and shouted, "Fuckin windscreens gone through, a mad cunt in a lorry shot past and it's gone through." So some bastard in a lorry fucked up two vans with a couple of pieces of gravel. So, what to do?

"Right, it's nearly opening time, let's get into Buxton, find a boozer and take it from there," somebody suggested. We drove off and ten minutes later pulled up at a pub in Buxton. We decided to have a quick pint and carry on to somewhere nearer to Wales for the dinnertime session, then on to the game. Fuck the windscreens. The pub was deserted, apart from the landlord and a suited-up bloke who looked to be in his thirties sat at the end of the bar. We ordered drinks and the landlord, who'd probably never seen as many customers at this early hour, was friendly and chatty. He asked us where we were from and where we were heading as he struggled to pull thirty-odd pints. We told him we were going to Wrexham to watch the Blades and about the windscreens getting smashed.

The bloke sat at the end of the bar, looked us over like some kind of disease had just walked in his local. We found seats, and suitie was still looking us over and giving us the evils. Suitie pulled a small walkie-talkie from his inside coat pocket. He shielded his mouth and stared whispering into it. What the fuck's this cunt doing? I'm thinking.

One of the lads went to the bar and asked the landlord, "What's his fuckin game?"

"Take no notice of him, he's not all there, he thinks he's a copper," the landlord answered. We all laughed and one or two of the lads went over, gave him a bit of grief and ragged him around in a friendly kinda way.

"Are gonna arrest us then Constable?"

He pulled the walkie-talkie back out, turned away from us and said something into it.

"Saddle up Blades," one of the lads shouted. So we downed our drinks, shouted, "See ya" to the landlord and swarmed out. The suitie stood in the doorway and watched us cross the car park towards the vans. Three cop cars skidded into the car park and half a dozen of Buxton's finest jumped out and headed towards us.

"Stand still, don't move, stay where you are," one of the coppers shouted at us. Walkie-talkie joined them.

"Fuck off," we shouted back. The sergeant of the police posse spoke in a fuckin horrible, sarcastic, patronising voice, "So we're from Sheffield are we? Going to Wrexham are we? And we think it's clever to push and threaten police officers do we? Well you're not going anywhere; those vans are unsafe to drive."

"Well what the fuck are we gonna do, leave em here and walk back to fuckin Sheffield? Daft cunt," one of the lads said.

We could see the coppers losing it and they were still shouting, "Stay where you are, stand still," as we boarded the vans. We gave them a round of "Fuck offs" and shot off. The coppers jumped in their cars and followed us for a while, but as soon as we reached the outskirts of the town they stopped, maybe they just wanted us off their patch.

So what was the shit with the walkie-talkie copper? Was he a copper? He must have been a copper, so why did the landlord tell us he was a nutter? Strange shit always sempt to happen, out on the road with the Blades.

We did the dinnertime session in some small town en route and when the pubs shut at three we drove off towards Wales. With a belly full of ale, things got a bit rowdy and mock fights erupted in the back of our van. Keeny, the intellectual homosexual calmed things down and grabbed everyone's attention with a lecture on the fundamental principles of classical physics. He attempted to educate a bunch of cavemen – by explaining the theory of inertia.

"Right," he said. "There's a lorry travelling down the motorway and it's filled with thousands of budgies all sat on their perches. At the exact moment all the budgies start to fly... so now, with all the birds off their perches the lorry weighs less, right, but they're still inside, so would the lorry travel faster? We'll do an experiment, on the count of three everybody jump in the air and we'll see if the van travels faster." Now this was a bit stupid as we couldn't see the Speedo in the front. We all did it anyway, landed in a heap and started hitting each other again.

The good-natured banter on long away trips could sometimes (depending on how drunk or how bored we all were) turn quite ruthless. Any physical defect, from being fat, thin, bald, short, lanky, ugly, bad teeth, bad breath and bad hair would be seized on immediately. Bad clothes, bad shoes, bad socks and any other imperfections also came in for plenty of stick.

The lower down the pecking-order you were, the more shit you took. On rare occasions it could get too much for some of the lads and only a real fist fight would end it. Even worse were accusations of 'bottle loss.' That could get really nasty.

"I saw ya, stood at the back, tying ya fuckin shoe-lace when Newcastle turned up on London Road."

"What about you then cunt? I thought I was running fast when them Tottenham fans chased us, but you were twenty yards in front of me."

"Narthen driver, pull up, fuckin get out of the van ya cunt. I'll show you who's a fuckin runner."

We hit Wrexham about five and with both vans stuck in traffic we lifted the back flap, swarmed out and attacked the Tranny.

"Box-van aggro, box-van aggro, aggro, aggro." One of the wing-mirrors got ripped off in the assault. Bad fuckers we were.

We found a pub close to the ground and parked up in the pub car park. After a pint, Bent Nose suggested him and me go up to the ground, wait for the team coach to arrive and try and scrounge some tickets off the players. We hung around outside the players' entrance awhile and the bus turned up. As the players got off, Mitch greeted them as if they were lifelong buddies.

"Narthen Tony," to Tony Kenworthy, "How's it goin pal?" Then under his breath: "Who's shaggin ya wife tonight?" Followed by a loud guffaw. Mick

327

Speight's the next player off. "Hey-up Micky, got any tickets, mate?" Speight looked a bit worried, but he reached in his inside coat pocket and pulled out two tickets.

When Harry Haslam left the bus, Mitch shouted, "Gizz a few tickets, Harry. There's about thirty of us and we've come all this way with no fuckin windscreens in the vans. It were fuckin freezin."

Harry pulled out a wad of tickets and handed them to Mitch.

"Here you are, that's all I've got," Harry said as he ushered his boys towards the players' entrance.

We counted the wad – fourteen tickets, plus the two Speighty gave us, making sixteen. The tickets were for the main stand seats. We discussed the distribution.

"There's not enough for all of us, and we don't want to go in the seats, what ya reckon?" I said to Mitch.

"Sell the fuckers," Mitch said.

"Couldn't agree more," I answered.

Ten minutes later we were eight quid a-piece richer, the tickets flew out at a quid each. Back in the pub we bought half a bitter for the skint lads, all heart we were, Bent Nose and me.

Ten minutes before kickoff we made our way up to the ground and gathered outside Wrexham's Kop as heavy snow started to fall. We didn't know too much about Wrexham's mob because we'd never played there before, but as far as we were concerned they weren't even on the radar. Once through the turnstiles we grouped together and entered in the bottom corner of the half-covered Kop. We snaked through the crowd, heading for the mob who stood behind the goal at the back of the stand. We couldn't have timed it better. As we neared them a chant went up, "Where are the Sheffield fans?"

We're fuckin here. We readied ourselves. This is the buzz. This is it, this minute of madness is the best part of the day.

"United, United," rang out as we ran in. The Wrexham mob (mostly young 'uns I have to admit) scattered. We stood in the gap they'd left and unfurled the Union Jack. The coppers were straight in and we were pushed down to the front and over the railings.

We'd done the business and with the Union Jack aloft, we were marched around the pitch and cheered onto the away end by about five hundred Blades. Quite a few of the Blades stood in their stocking feet. They told us the coppers checked everybody's footwear at the turnstiles and those who wore boots were made to remove them.

The Blades dipped 4-0 in the snowstorm. Footballers back then took snowstorms, blizzards, even cross-fire-hurricanes in their stride.

Back at the boozer we found the vans' front seats covered in snowdrifts. After a couple of pints in the pub we cleared the snow out of the vehicles and set off back. We stopped at a chippie in Chester to get some snap and to allow the drivers and the front seat passengers to thaw out and warm up a bit. An argument with two gobby squaddies inside the chippie, ended with the squaddies unconscious and us lot under arrest. Dozens of coppers arrived within seconds.

They made us board the vans and escorted us to the cop shop. An eagle-eyed young constable, who was surely destined for detective work, noticed the missing windscreens and suggested the vans were unfit to drive. We were crammed into a small room and taken out one at a time to be interrogated. Nobody admitted to the assault. My turn came after about an hour and the lovely Chester coppers informed me they were confiscating my Union Jack. Fuckin bastards, I'd had the Jack since 66.

"What the fuck as the Union Jack got to do with owt? I asked them, but they were having none of it.

An hour or so later we were all released – all except Mitch and Gibby who'd been identified as the assailants by the squaddies. The coppers told us they were keeping Mitch and Gibby and we were free to go. Back at the vans, arguments followed about waiting for the lads or fucking off. Goody, the box van driver, wanted to fuck off, Buggis wanted to stay and wait for Gibby and Mitch. We didn't know, but Buggis did, that Goody once knocked over and killed an old woman. It had been an unfortunate accident, but Goody had to serve a three-year driving ban.

"What the fuck do you know about driving?" Buggis shouted at Goody. "You killed that fuckin old woman." Goody and Buggis squared up for a scrap.

"Pack it in, daft twats," somebody shouted as lads got in between and broke it up. The commotion brought the coppers back out.

"Look," a copper said. "There's no point in hanging around here, they're not going to be released, they'll be straight in court in the morning, so you might as well go."

We set off in a raging blizzard and every few miles we stopped to change drivers and allow the front seat passengers to warm up in the back. The lads in the front seats wiped snow from the driver's eyes. We reached Manchester about 5.a.m. and took the Woodhead Pass route to Sheffield. We'd travelled a few miles to find the Woodhead closed, forcing us to turn round and go back to Manchester. We headed for the Snake, but that fucker was closed as well.

I wrapped myself up in the Biggles coat and managed to get a bit of kip. Fuck knows the route we eventually took to get home, but we arrived back in Pond Street about 10 a.m.

What Cockney said as he climbed out of the front seat of the box van will live with me forever. With tears in his eyes and in a lovely St Albans, squeaky drawl, he murmured, "I was so fackin cold, I thought I was going to die."

We left Spindle and whoever drove the other van, to take the vehicles back and take the rap for all the damage.

I caught the number 56 Wybourn bus that stopped directly outside our house, planning to jump into bed and to stay there all week. I'd only been in the house a few minutes when Bent Nose turned up. They'd been released and bailed to appear in court at a later date. They'd thumbed it back and made it home at the same time as us. After the 24 hours we'd just been through, you wouldn't have thought anything else could have happened, but oh no, back at Chester nick, the drama had continued.

There were no cells at the cop station, so the coppers gave Mitch and Gibby a couple of blankets and locked them in a room. Mitch fell asleep, only to be shook awake by a copper standing over him with a mop and bucket, there was no sign of Gibby.

"Get up you dirty bastard," the copper shouted at Mitch. He didn't have a clue what was going on.

Gibby, who had been busting for a shit, had banged on the door for the coppers to let him out. Nobody came, Gibby couldn't hold it, so he shit in the corner, took his T-shirt off to wipe his arse and covered the turd up with the T-shirt. A while later Gibby heard voices outside the door and this time when he banged on it, a copper opened the door.

"Can you let me out please," Gibby said to the copper. "My mate's shit in the corner and the stink's killing me." The copper put Gibby in another room, woke Mitch and despite his protests made him clean Gibby's shit up.

Two weeks later I'm stood at the back of the segregated Longside terrace for a night match at Burnley when a lad walks up, laughs and says, "Narthen Sharpy, I was on my way here and I saw your mate Bent Nose stood at the end of Halifax Road holding up a piece of cardboard with Bunley written on it. I'd have given him a lift, but I've got no idea where the fuck Bunley is."

Notts County at Meadow Lane on a Tuesday night wasn't a fixture to set the pulse racing. The only chance of any action would be if the Forest fans turned out, which they usually did when the Blades were in town.

I set off thumbing around half past four from the bottom of the Parkway. A van pulled up after a few minutes and dropped me at the Woodhall services just a few miles down the M1. In the cafe area I noticed a Blade, who I didn't really know too well, but I'd seen him around with the lads at a few games. I went over, said hello and told him I was hitching to the match. He recognised me and said I'd be sound for a lift and he'd also take me back after the game. He'd come straight from work and borrowed his boss's car for the trip. By the way he was dressed he must have done some kind of office work.

The lad came from Rotherham and said he was meeting his mate Steady at the game and giving him a lift back to Rotherham. Steady, one of the Parkgate lads, was well known and well respected amongst the Blade ranks for his party piece, the 'Solo.' Solos entered home ends alone and in a kinda suicide mission, waded into the opposing mob. A dangerous stunt you might think, and it took plenty of bottle, but it was usually over in seconds. The police nearly always stepped in and dragged out the soloist before too much damage could be done. The solos were rarely arrested because they could easily convince the coppers they'd entered the home end by mistake. Only a mad man would wade in to hundreds of lads on his own, so the coppers would just throw them out, or march them round the pitch to the cheers and accolades of the fans on the away end. Maybe that's what turned them on? It was the ultimate pose.

We left the cafe and jumped into the brand spanking new set of wheels. He must have been well in at work for his gaffer to lend him a motor like that. We arrived in Nottingham around six and parked up in a pub car park close to the train station. Rotherham (I'll call him that because I can't remember his name) said he didn't want to park near the ground for fear of damage to his boss's motor. The pub was a bit of a dump, but I love dumps. Two loose looking birds sat opposite us and after a few minutes eye contact we moved in. Now these lasses weren't the best-looking girls in the world, but a fuck's a fuck. One of them had a cold sore on her top lip the size of a fifty pence piece. She'd made the effort though by trowelling a thick layer of make-up onto the scab. We had a couple of drinks and arranged to meet the girls back at the pub after the game.

We met up with Steady at the match (no Forest turned up) and when the game finished the three of us went back to the pub to find the birds still there. I moved into the marginally better one and we ended up in the back yard for a ten-minute knee-tremble. Back in the boozer, Rotherham drooled all over Scablip and she invited us back to her pad for a coffee. The girls told us they lived on an estate about five miles to the south of Nottingham. Having just got my rocks off, I wasn't too fussed about going to the girl's house, but Rotherham was adamant. Steady wasn't bothered either way. I needed a lift back though, so that was it.

Scablip sat in the front with Rotherham; Steady, the other bird and me in the back. For some reason (probably because I wanted to get back home) I got into an argument with Scablip. It got rather heated, "You ugly bastard," I shouted. "Look at the fuckin state of your lip. Kick the cunt out and let's fuck off home," I said to Rotherham. Now Rotherham obviously wanted his end away so he tried to calm things down.

Still rowing, we arrived on the estate and pulled up outside a semi. Graffiti covered the walls of the house, an old fridge and the insides of a washing machine lay embedded in the surrounding privet and a mattress with protruding springs sat in the front garden – it was a kinda upmarket version of the Manor estate back home. The girls left the car and told us to wait a few minutes, fuck knows why. Music blared out from the open front room window and we could hear voices and see silhouettes moving past the curtains.

Five minutes later I said, "I don't like the look of this fucker, they'll not come back out, they just wanted a lift home. There's a party going on and it's probably full of lads, lets fuck off." Steady agreed, but Rotherham was having none of it.

"Come on," he said. "Let's go to the door."

"Are you fuckin mad?" I said, but Rotherham's already on his way to the front door. Steady and me reluctantly joined him. We knocked on the front door a couple of times, but no one answered. We moved down the side of the house and I picked up a couple of empty milk bottles stacked outside the back-door step.

"Get some bottles and get read,." I said to the others. Steady picked up two bottles.

"Put them down," Rotherham said. "We don't want any trouble."

"Well its odds on we're gonna get some fuckin trouble," I said.

Instinct told me to fuck off, but where to? I'm on the other side of Nottingham on a strange estate. After arguing the pros and cons of brandishing

331

milk bottles for a minute or two, we put them down and banged on the door. The door opened and a monster with a thick Indian-ink cross decorating his forehead filled the door frame. Oh shit, I thought. We could and should, shame or no shame, have done a runner at that very fucking moment, but no: "The girls invited us back for a coffee," Rotherham Mumbled. In a thick Geordie accent the monster snarled, "O yoose come back forra coffee like have ya?"

The Geordie wore a fuckin horrible Starsky and Hutch style knitted cardigan with a large collar and a matching woollen belt tied at the waist. He stepped outside and as he turned to push Rotherham through the door, I noticed a big fuck-off eagle embroidered on the back of his jumper. "Come forra coffee have ya? Come in, come in, like," he said as he dragged Steady and me into the kitchen.

I've often looked back and wondered how the fuck I could have let it happen? How the fuck I lost it? But it happened so quick, maybe I was in some kind of shock. It's on top here I thought and if I'd had the milk bottle, I'd have smashed the cunt in the head, and we could have got away.

My heart started to pound, and I couldn't think straight as the Geordie locked the door and shoved the key in his back pocket. Fuckin hell we're in some deep shit now I thought, how the fuck are we gonna get out? There's no escape. We're trapped. Filthy pots and pans and half-eaten plates of dried up snap littered the kitchen sink and sides.

"Come forra fookin coffee have ya? I'll give ya fookin coffee," he said.

I don't think this cunt's got any intention of putting the kettle on I thought. The side door opened, and half a dozen lads heads popped round it. As the Geordie removed the horrendous cardigan, revealing a vest and a Rambo type body covered in death's heads and dripping-blood sword tattoos, the two birds walked in.

"Which one was it?" he said to the birds. Both pointed their fingers at me. Now I don't know what they'd told him and if he meant, which one fucked you, or which one insulted you, but I was guilty on both counts. Had I fucked Geordie's bird or had I slagged her off? And which was worse? There's only one way to find out.

The punch he threw didn't quite connect; it glanced off the top of my head. Fuck this I thought, I'm playing dead and sank to the floor. Within seconds Rotherham and Steady, who when you think about it, were both innocent parties, joined me on the deck. Plates, dishes, pots, pans, as well as boots and punches rained down on us. Out of the corner of my eye I saw Geordie smashing Rotherham on the head with a disgusting frying pan. What Rotherham said next will stick with me forever.

"Stop it, stop it, please. We're not from round here." Well fuck me, I thought, that's gonna make a lot of fuckin difference. Oh, you're not from round here? Okay, I do apologise. Off you go, sorry for the inconvenience.

Geordie went mental, screaming, "I'll fuckin kill ya bastards." I half expected a kitchen knife to plunge in between my shoulder blades. The lads in the doorway must have realised the mad fucker had murder on his mind.

"That's enough, you'll fuckin kill 'em," one of them said to the Geordie.

They jumped in and managed to drag him off. It took four of them to hold h‌
back as the others ushered him down the hallway.

"Fuck off now ya bastards and don't come back," one shouted as th‌
pushed us through the front door. We ran up the path and picking up hal‌
house brick I said to Rotherham,

"Get the car started and get ready to fuck off, I'm gonna put the wind‌
through."

"No, no," Rotherham said. "Just let's get out of here, it's not my car an‌
don't want it smashing up." Steady started freaking out, in Incredible Hulk st‌
he clenched his fists and let out a load roar. He pulled off his tee-shirt anc‌
thought, fuck me, he's stripping for action, it's fuckin solo time. This revved ‌
up and I thought we could maybe save a bit of face, so I shouted, "Come on, ‌
some bricks, let's have the bastards." Steady undid his belt and dropped his je‌
down to his knees. What the fuck's he doing?

Steady took the tee-shirt and scooped out a lump of shite from his crack‌
Now this wasn't a follow-through fart kinda shit, it was a massive, steaming tw‌
pound dollop. Another equally large scoop followed and landed with a splat ‌
the pavement, the stench nearly knocked me out. Rotherham and me just sta‌
in amazement; I didn't know whether to laugh or cry. We jumped in the ‌
picked off bits of rotting pease pudding from our clothes, wound down all ‌
windows and screeched off.

I laid into Rotherham. "What the fuck did I say? If we'd kept hold of th‌
fuckin bottles we could have done the cunt, but no, 'put them down, we dc‌
want any trouble' (I said in a girlie voice), fuck me, ya stupid bastar‌
Rotherham didn't answer.

We reached the M1 and even though we were freezing, we had to keep ‌
windows open, the stink was so bad. Rotherham kept moaning about the sn‌
and what his boss was gonna say. Steady, surprisingly never said a word u‌
they dropped me at the bottom of the Parkway,

"For fuck's sake Sharpy, don't ever tell anybody about tonight."

"It's all right, pal. Your secret's safe with me," I answered.

At the next home game, four days later, when all the lads were assemble‌
the Lansdowne, I shouted: "Gather round lads and listen to this, you're ‌
gonna fuckin believe what happened at Notts County the other night."

Stox & Co.

coal shute

Chapter 11

Slow train coming

After clearing Blackburn's Kop the previous season, a couple of hundred of us tried the same sketch. The Blackburn mob, armed with bricks and lumps of wood, were ready for us this time. They gathered at the top of the steps and when we were half way up, the barrage stopped us in our tracks. We fought a running battle from Ewood Park, down to the train station and around twenty of us missed the connecting train to Manchester.

The main mob of around 200 Blades, who we'd travelled with, were aboard. We waited for another train to Manchester where we hoped to meet up with the rest of the lads.

We arrived at Manchester Victoria about half past six/seven and checked out a couple of pubs near the station to see if the lads were still around. We didn't find anyone, they must have either moved on, or gone back to Sheffield. Somebody did a head count: 19 lads – Tiger, Zal and Gilly from Parkgate, Sparky, Bullet, Cudgy and Bri Rawlins, Razz and Presty from Dronny, Paul Longingmuir, Gibby, Big Dave Laycock, Wandering Walt and a few more. We decided to stay in Manchester for the night, booze our way back to Piccadilly station and catch the last train back to Sheffield. As we left the pub we noticed two lads stood across the road eyeing us up. Two lads posed no threat, but they could have been spotters. Footie lads were well clued-up, they knew which fans would pass through their towns and cities en route to away games. These lads could have been City or United or just a couple of street lads. None of us wore colours, just Blade lapel badges, but football lads instantly know who other football lads are, colours or not. They'd clocked us, and they knew we'd clocked them. We were in a strange city; we didn't know the lay of the land and we needed to keep our wits about us. We called in the next pub and stayed for half an hour or so. We left to see the two lads who'd followed had now grown into six. In the next pub, a few hundred yards from Piccadilly, one of the lads nipped out and reported a dozen or so Mancs, some tooled up with sticks and bottles were gathered across from the boozer. We reasoned they must be City fans as City had played at home and we now knew for certain it's game on.

"Come on," one of ours said. "These cunts want it, let's go and fuckin give 'em it."

"Fuck 'em," somebody else said. "They'll probably run as soon as we go out."

A bit of leadership was needed here, so I said, "Come on, lets fuckin do it."

Out on the street, more Mancs arrived and it was now more or less even numbers. There was no charge, no screaming or shouting. Bullet and me calmly crossed the road with the others a couple of yards behind us. The Mancs readied themselves and a punk, carrying a four-foot length of 3x2 moved to the front. He swung it a couple of times to let us know his intentions, then he made a stance with the log hung over his shoulder. Neither Bullet nor me slowed. In situations like these you only have seconds, split seconds even, to think. I know exactly what he's going to do, I thought. He's gonna wait till I get near, and then swing the timber, aiming for the head. I'll wait till the last second, duck under, come up, grab his lapels with both hands and nut his fuckin face off. I had it all worked out.

It was all going to plan until I got to within three yards of him. He swung the wood all right and his timing was perfect. It flashed through the air and smacked me on the forehead. I felt my knees buckle and I sank to them. Fuckin shite. Bullet picked up the lump of wood and ran screaming at the Mancs. They backed off giving me a bit of breathing space to get myself together. Bullet launched the wood, but it sailed straight over their heads and one of them chased it up the street and recovered it. The rest of our lads finally came to life, about fuckin time I thought. We dodged bottles and sticks but held firm until a few more tooled up Mancs arrived. A hail of milk bottles backed us off a few yards. A few more Manc lads ran out of a boozer and joined in. We were backed off to the bottom of the slope leading up to Piccadilly Station. Again we held firm, and a milk crate, thrown by the Mancs was returned putting one of them on his arse.

The brawl had been going on for at least five minutes before the coppers finally arrived. We were ushered into the station and the Mancs were chased off. A few minutes later Gibby walked in the station. Nobody noticed he'd been missing during the brawl. The last time I'd remembered seeing him was a good half an hour and two boozers ago.

"Where the fuck have you been?" somebody asked him.

"I've been for a shit," Gibby answered.

"That must be the longest fuckin shit in history," somebody else said.

"Right," one of the lads said. "I think that's it for the night. Let's get the train, stop off somewhere and have a few quiet pints." Everybody agreed.

We chose New Mills, a small town about half way between Manchester and Sheffield for the few 'quiet pints.' We boarded the train and twenty minutes later, jumped off in New Mills. One of the lads checked the train times. We had about an hour boozing time before the last train home. We left the station and climbed a steepish hill with hardly any street lighting up towards the town. We spotted a pub and most of us went in. Zal and the other Parkgate lads said they were going to find a pub that looked a bit livelier.

Inside the pub a few local lads and lasses stood at the bar eyeing us up. We could hear the sounds of a disco coming from an upstairs room, so a couple of our lads went up to check it out. They came back and said it was pretty full and there were plenty of birds up there. A few minutes later a group of birds came downstairs to check out the fresh meat. We sat around two or three tables under a window facing the bar, the front door and the entrance to the disco room From this position we knew nobody could get behind us.

Two of the lads stood at the bar, drank up and walked out. I know where them fuckers are going I thought. A couple of the other lads, who looked like football lads and who obviously knew we were football lads, came over for chat. They must have noticed our badges because one of them said, "Sheff Ut are you? We're Man City, most of the lads in New Mills support City."

"We've just had it with some of your boys in Manchester," I said, fingering the hen's egg on my forehead. We carried on chatting a while and the lads were friendly enough at first, until another group of locals walked in.

"We've got some Sheffield here," the lad shouted to his mates.

"Fucking Sheffield," one shouted back. "Who the fuck are Sheffield?" The lad moved off and stood with his mates. Our group looked at each other and smiled. Here we go again. The front door opened and Zal and the others, followed by a dozen or so locals walked in. Zal nodded his head backwards. His gesture told us what to expect from the lads behind him.

So here's the situation, there's sixteen lads sat facing the bar. Zal, Tiger and Gilly stood at the bar surrounded by twenty-five/thirty, full-of-it locals. We didn't have to tell each other what was about to happen.

A group of the locals pushed over towards the Parkgate lads. One of them, his arms stretched out and his fists clenched stood in front of Zal, their faces about a foot apart. The lad leant his body back in slow motion. The attempted head butt, in even slower motion, had got to be the worst effort I've ever seen. Zal moved to one side and smiled as the lad's head went past his shoulder.

"What the fuck was that?" Zal said.

We were all on our feet by now. The Parkgate lads walked over and stood with us, facing the locals.

"Come on, fuckin outside," one of our lads shouted.

We grabbed bottles and glasses from the tables as we moved out through the door. We fanned out in front of the pub as the first wave of locals moved through the doorway. A shower of bottles and glasses stopped them in their tracks. The lads inside the pub pushed the lads in the doorway outside. We ran into them punching and booting.

I heard a roar coming from the left and glanced to see another group of locals and a shower of rocks coming towards us. This allowed the lads in the pub to exit and we now faced an attack from two sides. We were forced to retreat and sprinted down the hill towards the station. Rocks and lumps of wood bounced all around us.

On reaching the station it dawned on us all, the only escape would be to run up the train lines. This called for some serious bottle, but we really had no choice. We turned to face the New Mills mob, psyching each other up as you do in desperate situations. We ran into them picking up and returning the rocks scattered around the road. This forced them back and they turned and ran back up the hill. We followed and as they scrambled back inside the pub we laid siege and most of the pub windows were shattered.

We'd turned what looked like a certain battering into victory until another group of locals appeared. A stripped to the waist, tattooed skinhead led this group. This fucker really looked the business as he leapt up and down aiming mid-air Kung-Fu kicks and screaming death threats in ancient Cantonese. Fuck me, how many lads lived in this fuckin one-horse town? On seeing reinforcements arrive, the pub emptied again, and we were forced to retreat back down the now familiar hill. As more rocks whistled past our heads, I passed the

336

lumbering twenty stone frame of big Dave Laycock, and, tapping him on the back, I shouted, "Come on, Dave. Keep up, lad."

"Fook me, Ron. I'm fooked," Dave bellowed back.

As we reached the station, the most beautiful sight I've ever seen came into view. The lights from the last Manchester to Sheffield train could be seen, one hundred yards away slowly grinding into the station. Come on ya bastard, fuckin hurry up, I thought. With the mob nearly on us we ran up the platform and wrenched open the train doors before it came to a halt. We all managed to scramble aboard, but the New Mills boys were out for blood and despite us trying to hold them back they fought their way onto the train. We again retreated down the corridors, stopping every few seconds to trade punches. A few pissed-up, scarved-up, half-asleep Blades, already aboard, copped for the wrath of the New Mills mob. They must have wondered what the fuck was happening.

We retreated to the back of the train and with nowhere else to go, battled in the confined space of the train corridor. After what sempt like an eternity the coppers finally arrived. Some of the New Mills mob escaped through the doors and out of broken windows. Others, especially the fuckin crazy Kung-Fu skinhead carried on the battle. The police eventually overpowered the mad man and dragged him from the train. Within minutes the train, that now looked like it had been in a head-on collision, filled with helmets.

Two hours later, after every single passenger aboard had been questioned and had their names and addresses taken, we pulled out of New Mills. We gave the coppers the 'stopping off for a quiet pint minding out own business story' and none of our lot were charged.

We were back in Wales two weeks later. We travelled to Cardiff in two vans containing roughly forty lads. Most of the lads who'd travelled to Wrexham were on board.

We arrived late, about ten minutes after kickoff and had a brief scuffle with about thirty Cardiff lads outside the turnstiles. The coppers were straight in to break it up. We entered the side terrace, with the seated area behind the goal to our left. I'm not quite sure if this was the away section, but a mob of Cardiff was on there, trying their best to get into the three to four hundred blades already inside. The Blades were glad of reinforcements, but we didn't really make much difference. The Cardiff mob, some who'd maybe been clipped at the Lane were after blood and if it wasn't for the large police presence we would have probably been fucked.

After another 4-0 defeat we were kept inside for ten minutes while the coppers dispersed the Cardiff mob and then escorted us back to the coaches and vans. We stopped off in Worcester on the way back and had a couple of pints in the 'Boozer of Death' we'd visited after the postponed Hereford game.

The usual end of night brawl with the locals saw Cooperman and the Beadle brothers (two gangsters off the Manor) arrested. All the drivers got pissed, so we decided to sleep in the vans and wait for the arrested lads to be released.

Early Sunday morning we went to the cop-shop to see if we could pick up the lads.

"Have you got Kevin Cooper and Giles and Jeremy Beadle from Sheffield in here?" one of the lads asked the desk sergeant. The copper looked on his list.

"We've got three lads from Sheffield, the Beadle brothers and Eric Burnit, there's no Kevin Cooper. They've not been charged, and they'll be released at nine o'clock," the copper told us. We hung around outside and at nine bells, Cooperman and the Beadles walked out.

"Didn't think you were in here Coops," somebody said to Cooperman.

Cooperman laughed and said, "Told 'em I'm a fireman and my name's Eric Burnit."

Squeak O'Brian walked in the Claypit after a home game and joined us in the seats under the window. I'd known him and their Pete since the mid-60s. They were both part of the original Sheffield skinhead movement. The skins hung out at the time in Merrie England bar, housed under the Black Swan. Small, thick-set and as hairy as a Barbary ape, Squeak was a real character and comedian; just looking at him made me smile.

"Narthen Ron," Squeak said to me. "I pulled this bird the other week, Mucky Liz they call her. She's off Norfolk Park and she's a right fuckin goer. I've got her phone number if you fancy a fuck?" Not being one to turn down a piece of fresh bag I said, "Yeah, I'll give her a bell." I went to the phone and rang the number.

Mucky Liz answered, and I said, "You don't know me, my name's Ronnie. I got your number off Squeak."

"Fuckin Squeak, he's a fuckin animal, and what the fuck do you want?" Liz said.

"Nowt," I said. "I just thought I'd give you a call, and maybe pop up later for a coffee?"

"Yeah," Liz said. "You can come up for a coffee, but don't think you're fuckin me, cos you're fuckin not."

"No, I've got no intention of fuckin you," I said. "Just a coffee and a chat; I'll come up after the pub's shut: half ten-eleven, okay?"

"Yeah, okay, but you're not fuckin me," Liz said before she gave me the address.

I went back to the table and Squeak said, "Are ya sorted? She's a right fuckin belt, Mucky Liz. She's up for owt."

When the boozers shut I jumped on the bus up to Norfolk Park. Mucky Liz lived in one of the high-rise tower blocks. I took the lift up to the tenth floor and knocked on the door. The door opened, and a twenty-stone bird filled the door frame. You bastard, Squeak, I thought.

"Are you Ronnie?" the fat bird said. "Liz's through here, come in." Pheeeew, I walked in and half expected to see an even fatter bird, but no. Mucky Liz, lounged on the settee, looked quite tasty. The fat bird and her skinny boyfriend left after a couple of minutes.

"I'm tired," Liz said. "I think I'll go to bed; you can come with me if ya want, but don't think you're fuckin me. I'm not like that."

"No, I don't want to fuck you. I'm tired myself. We'll just have a kip, eh?"

We went in the bedroom and both clothed off bare naked. Liz had straddled me within half a second. We spent the next couple of hours trying every position in the book and then the phone rang. Liz got up and went in the hallway to answer it, I heard her say, "No you're not fuckin coming up. My new boyfriend's here and he'll kick your fuckin head in, so fuck off and leave me alone." New fuckin boyfriend I thought! Liz carried on arguing for a couple of minutes, before shouting: "Fuck off" and slamming down the phone. She came back in the bedroom and said, "That was my ex-husband. He said he's on his way up and his mates will probably be with him, but they're wankers, all the fuckin lot of 'em."

Fuck me; what have I got myself into? I thought about doing one, but then thought fuck it and we carried on where we left off.

Next morning Liz mashed me a brew and said, "You can move in any time you want."

This fucker doesn't hang about and it's moving a little bit too fast I thought. Three toddlers ran in the bedroom and started bouncing around on the bed, time to get out I thought. Before I left, Liz asked me a couple of times when I wanted to move in. I told her I'd have to think about it, but I'd come up and see her next week. I went back about half a dozen times over the next couple of months before it petered out.

I always took Tiff on the Friday night pub crawls around town and I usually bumped into Squeak somewhere on the route. Every time he saw me, the fucker would shout, "How's Mucky Liz going on, Ron? Have ya seen her lately?"

"Who's this Mucky Liz?" Tiff asked me. "Every time we see Squeak he always says it."

"Oh, it's some bird we knew back in the 60s. I've not seen her in years. I don't know why he keeps saying it."

I got my revenge a few years later, after my relationship with Tiff had ended. Squeak was now all loved up and going steady and whenever I saw him out with his new bird, I'd shout, "How's Mucky Liz going on, Squeak. Have ya seen her lately?"

When I saw Squeak on his own at the games, he'd say, "For fuck's sake, Ron. Don't keep shouting about Mucky fuckin Liz when I'm out with the bird."

"You fuckin started it," I'd tell him.

Squeak passed on in 1992. R.I.P. you crazy fucker.

Chapter 12

It's just the old American way

Shit as the team were, none of us really expected relegation to the Third Division. It couldn't happen, and it just didn't bear thinking about. With three games to go the Blades still had a chance to avoid the drop. First, a ten-man Blackburn team, who'd already been relegated, beat us at the Lane and on the last Saturday of the season we faced Cambridge United away. That meant an after-match trip to one of our favourite seaside towns... Great Yarmouth.

After a Friday dinnertime session in town, a coach load of lads (wearing Millwall style surgical masks) arrived in Cambridge around teatime. We'd started to travel to some of the away games in Les Well's works van. Boring Les worked for a company call Lazorlight, and the name was emblazoned on both sides of the van. 'Lazorlight tours' we called it. About eight lads could squeeze into the Lazorlight: six in the back and two, including Les in the front seats.

Les's speciality was boring folk to death. He could natter for hours about absolutely nothing.

"For fuck's sake Les, shut the fuck up," we'd say to him. This didn't faze Les.

"I'm not boring you am I?" he'd say, and just carry on with his ramblings. Sometimes we had to physically attack him to shut the fucker up.

The Lazorlight, containing Les, Paul Longingmuir, Bent Nose, Keeny, a couple of others and me arrived in Cambridge about six o'clock. We parked up in a multi-story car park in the city centre, found the lads and started the evening session. In the first boozer, a bird walked over to our table and said in a lovely American drawl, "Hi, my names Mary-Lou, I'm from Toledo Ohio in the U-S of A, can I join you guys?"

"Course tha can love," I said patting the seat at the side of me. "Park thi arse next to mine." Mary-Lou took the seat.

Mitch shouted to Mary-Lou in an American accent, "Hi, I'm Bent Nose Mitchell from Pitsmoor, Sheffield, England and I'm a godam motherfucker." We all cracked up. Mary-Lou looked slightly confused, but she said, "Can I buy you guys a drink?"

"Ya certainly fuckin can, love," I said. "I'll come to the bar and help ya carry 'em."

Mary-Lou paid for the round and we sat back down. For the next few minutes Mitch had us in stitches. He kept shouting out American shit.

"What did ya have for lunch, honey? Pastrami on rye, heavy on the anchovies, eggs over easy maybe? I'm from New York City, Arizona, but I was raised in Saskatchewan; hold the fuckin mayonnaise I wanna take a shit."

Mary-Lou probably didn't know what the fuck we were on about, but she joined in the laughter. She couldn't get her head around what a bunch of footie lads were doing in Cambridge. Mitch carried on, "Do ya wanna French fry,

340

baby? Well suck my dick and kiss my ass, yeee-ar."

A bird with a nice pair of knockers walked past our table.

"Gee that chick's got really swell tits," Mary-Lou said. Fuck me she's one of us I thought.

All the lads (except Keeny) wanted to get into Mary-Lou, but I moved in first. We got chatting and I found out she'd come over on holiday for a month and was staying with relatives in London. She'd made the trip to Cambridge for the day to check out the university city and would be returning to London on the nine o'clock train. She also told me she was three months' pregnant, but there was no noticeable bulge.

About eight o'clock I left the lads to walk Mary-Lou to the train station. We stopped off behind a building near the station and I treated her to a stand-up full English, before putting her on the train to London. By the time I'd got back things started to liven up. More lads who'd travelled in cars and vans arrived and Blades roamed all over the city centre. The first battle started after the pubs shut. When we were refused entrance into a nightclub, the bouncers got bashed and one of the lads picked up a push-bike and launched it through the front window.

Most of the Lazorlight crew and few others managed to get in another club. Mitch left early saying he was fucked. He got the van keys off Les and went back to get some kip. Keeny left before the rest of us, and when we got back to the van Keeny said, "I opened the back door and saw Mitch sprawled out, snoring like fuck. He looked like a big fuckin Basking Shark." From that day Mitch was known as Basking Shark. Nobody could get in the back of the van; Basking Shark had taken up all the room. We'd bought doss-bags, so we climbed in and slept at the side of the Lazorlight.

Every one of the coach crew spent the night in the cells. They'd been rampaging around town all night and the Cambridge coppers simply waited for them all to return to the bus, surrounded it and arrested the lot in one fell swoop. The police kept them until half an hour before kickoff, took the coach under heavy escort up to the stadium and dropped them outside the turnstiles a couple of minutes before the game started.

After spending a delightful night on a concrete mattress, we were back out boozing when the pubs opened at eleven. By twelve bells hundreds of Blades packed out the city centre bars. Dinky and few more lads arrived, and we ended up in a pub, which probably wasn't, but should have been called the Cricketers. Cricket memorabilia covered every wall. There were photos of old cricket teams, caps, bails and stumps in display cabinets and dozens of autographed cricket bats. Dinky slipped a miniature bat, around a foot long under his jacket. The bat had been autographed by the England cricket team.

We made it up to the ground around kick off time. The coppers, doing random searches at the turnstiles pulled Dinky; they found the cricket bat, carted Dink away and charged him with carrying an offensive weapon. He had to return to Cambridge a few weeks later. He managed to persuade the magistrates he had no intention of using the bat for violence, but they hit him with a £100 fine for theft.

Blades at Cambridge 1979

In true Blade style the team fucked up once again, dipping 1-0 to a fuckin pub side. At the end of the game Harry Haslam, Danny Bergara and the excuse for a fuckin football team came over to applaud the Blade fans. They got to within twenty yards of us, when a barrage of missiles sailed towards them.

Blades busted up the terracing and launched lumps of concrete at the useless cunts. I climbed up to the top of the fence and shouted, "Fuck off Haslam, fuckin come near me ya bastard and I'll fuckin kill ya." I jumped back down and threw a few more rocks. Some of the Blades wanted none of this shit. They applauded Harry and the rest and started arguing with us. A Blade shouted at me: "Stop throwing, what's wrong with ya? It's our players you're throwing at."

I didn't answer; I just ran at the Blade and chased him out of the ground.

Blades wandered around the wasteland at the back of the ground like Zombies. Nobody could quite believe it; every fucker was in shock.

On the road to Yarmouth the Lazorlight fell silent; we'd gone a few miles before anybody spoke. I can't remember who said, "I think I've got summat in my eye," as a tear rolled down his cheek. We all started sobbing. No shit, the corners of our mouths dropped, and we started fuckin sobbing.

"Come on, for fuck's sake, what the fuck are we doing?" one of us said. The sobs turned into laughter. Not that we were happy; we were laughing at ourselves for crying. Set of fuckin puffs.

Such was the sombre mood, that Great Yarmouth, for the first time ever after a Blade visit was spared a Blitzkrieg. Still all was not lost; mathematically we still had a chance. In the last game of the season (Leicester at the Lane on the following Tuesday) the Blades needed to win 37-0.

15,000 optimistic blades turned out for the match. 300-400 lads gathered on the West terrace keeping their eyes on a few hundred brave Leicester fans stood behind the goal on the Lane end. Five minutes into the game a group of Blades, who'd managed to get on the Lane end steamed into the Leicester fans. The terrace mob scaled the fence to try and join in. Loads made it onto the perimeter but were held back by the coppers. The police restored order on the Lane end by removing the Blades and putting them in with us on the terrace.

Leicester scored, meaning we now needed 38. A Blade, who maybe thought United could do with a helping hand, jumped out of the South Stand and started booting and punching one of the Leicester players. The Blades equalised giving

342

us fresh hope, but the game ended 2-2 and down we went.

By the summer of 79 the mod revival was in full swing as Quadrophenia hit the silver screen. A new generation of Skinheads had returned to the terraces a year earlier. Harringtons in the Sheaf market who's speciality was – Harringtons, no longer needed to drag its customers in.

The 3rd generation Ska sound of Madness and the Specials, plus the crop of new wave bands – Ian Dury and the Blockheads, Elvis Costello, Joe Jackson, XTC, Devo and Squeeze meant there was a few decent tunes around. Imagine the dizzy heights Squeeze could have reached if Tilbrook and Difford had invested in a rhyming dictionary, but I suppose anyone who tries to make 'happen' rhyme with 'Clapham' deserves a pat on the back for effort.

Where music was concerned I was set in my ways. I wasn't bothered about any of the new bands. I still listened to Dylan, the Stones, etc. I was pushing thirty: pensioner age; the music of the time didn't really excite me any more, and I had no intention of joining any movements.

It didn't matter which division we were in, because the football buzz never stops. We'd all forgiven the Blades and couldn't wait for new season to start. There'd be new grounds to visit and new towns and cities to terrorise. A pre-season Anglo Scottish Cup game, took us back to fuckin Cambridge of all places. In true Blade style the bastards won 1-0 nil, if they'd done that three months earlier, they wouldn't have been in this shit.

We travelled in the Lazorlight and hit Yarmouth after the match. We did the pubs and a nightclub and spent another night dossed in and around the van. During the leisurely Sunday morning, sobering-up stroll along the sea front, we stopped outside a stall, when we saw a baboon chained by its leg to a perch. We all creased up when Kempy shouted to the stallholder, "Narthen, missus. What's up with that monkey's ring?"

"What do you mean?" the woman answered.

" What's wrong with its ring? It's as red as fuck," Kempy said, pointing at the ape.

"Oh it's in season," the woman answered.

"Fuck me," Kempy said to the woman. "That's the reddest fuckin ring I've ever seen."

We did the dinnertime session and arrived back Sunday tea-time. Mitch's missus Karen had stayed at our house for the weekend. Mitch and me walked in and Tiff said, "I've got your tea ready; it's in the kitchen." We walked in to see two plates on the table, each with half a dried-up tomato, a leaf of shrivelled lettuce and a small plastic football on them.

"Seeing as you two like football so much," Tiff said, "that's all you're getting."

Ten days later after a 3-1 defeat at Doncaster Rovers in the League Cup, about 300 Blades caught the last train back to Sheffield. After a few rowdy miles a group of Blades grabbed a couple of guards, slapped them around a bit and dangled the poor fuckers out of the door.

We reached Conisbrough station to find about a hundred coppers waiting on the platform. The coppers swarmed aboard and forced every single Blade off the train. We were herded out of the station and told we would have to walk back to Sheffield. Ah well I thought, it's only twenty fuckin miles. We strode off towards home flanked on both sides by police on foot and others in cars. Blade songs were belted out, and, along with the barking cop dogs, the noise brought people out of their houses to check out the commotion. After a couple of miles, Spindle said, "Fuck this, I'm not going any further," and sat down in the middle of the road.

The coppers tried to make him get up, but Spindle wouldn't budge.

"If you don't move I'm arresting you," a copper said.

"Fuckin arrest me then," Spindle said. The coppers dragged him off, bundled him in a car and drove him to the cells.

A couple of hours later when we reached the outskirts of Rotherham, four of us flagged down a taxi and made it home at around three in the morning. The Conisbrough walk made front page headlines in the *Star*.

At the beginning of September, eight lads boarded the Lazorlight for the trip to Hull. The weather was still warm enough for an after-match Bridlington seaside session. After the game Bullet, Buggis and me hung around the van waiting for others to return. Cockney arrived and told us Mitch had been arrested. He said Mitch had decked a Hull fan bang in front of the coppers. Les and Paul were still missing when we saw about fifteen Hull lads crossing a grass roundabout and heading straight towards us. They'd seen us, and their pace quickened. Time for quick thinking. I pulled a flick-knife out of my back pocket, flicked it open and waved it in the air. Trouble was, it wasn't really a flick-knife, it was shaped like a flick-knife, but the blade was a plastic comb. I gestured to Cockney and shouted, "Get the others." Bullet, Buggis and me moved towards the Hull fans, as Cockney ran the other way, waving his arms and shouting, "Come on they're here" to nonexistent reinforcements. The Hull fans looked a bit hesitant and slowed, maybe they thought there were more of us, because three lads moving towards fifteen didn't seem quite right.

As usual, Buggis the nutter was first out of the blocks, two or three yards in front of Bullet and me. Our bluff seemed to be working until a brick sailed through the air and smashed Buggis straight between the eyes. Buggis sank to his knees holding his face. Seeing his little brother out of it, Bullet ran screaming at the Hull fans forcing them to back off a bit. They must have realised no one else was coming and as we helped Buggis to his feet they moved towards us.

Les and Paul arrived with a few more Blades who must have been parked near us, but before they had a chance to help, the coppers turned up. The police got in between us, and we shouted abuse at each other. The Hull bastards must have grassed us up, because a copper near them came over and shouted, "One of these has got a flick-knife." The coppers lined us up against a wall and searched us.

I'd still got the knife/ comb in my back pocket. A copper frisked me, but somehow managed to miss the knife. Finding nothing the police told us to get on our way and we boarded the van. I took the knife/comb out and balanced it on a ledge that ran all the way around the top of the inside of the van. We were just about to set off when a copper opened the back door and said, "Get out, we're searching the van." Shit I thought, I should have kept the knife in my pocket. Two coppers climbed in the back and one in front. After a few minutes they got out and told us we were free to go. They weren't very good at the old searching malarkey, them Hull coppers; maybe they should have used a fine toothcomb?

We cleaned Buggis up a bit and went to the cop station to see what was happening with Mitch. We were told they were keeping him until his court appearance on Monday, so we drove off to Brid. The highlight of the Bridlington session came when we stumbled into a sea-front bar to see a poster announcing the appearance tonight, of go-go dancer extraordinaire 'Mighty Melvin.' We watched Mel (now carrying a bit more timber and a bit less hair) act out his shit and had a chat to him after the gig. He told us he now lived in Brid and still performed every weekend.

As we left Mel shouted in a lovely camp drawl, "Don't forget to tell everybody in Sheffield, Mighty Melvin is alive and well and living in Bridlington."

On every Lazorlight trip, we'd always chucked in a few bob for a couple of cans of spray-paint to leave our mark: BLADES 79. When the pubs shut we went back to the van for the paint and decorated Bridlington sea front.

"Gimme that can," Buggis shouted. Buggis sprayed a two-foot-high letter F on a wall. BLADES 79's coming I thought, but no. Buggis carried on and we all creased up when he wrote, BUGGIS IS A PSYCO.

It must have been near midnight when, returning to the van to set off back we saw a large figure approaching in the distance.

"It's fuckin Bent-Nose," somebody said. The figure got nearer and, yes, it's the Basking Shark. Mitch told us he'd talked the coppers round to giving him bail and he'd caught the train to Brid to try and find us. He'd been lucky to bump into us: a couple of minutes later we'd have gone, and he'd have been stuck in Brid.

The day after, Mitch came up Dronny for Sunday dinner at my mum's and the Sunday night session with the Dronny lads.

"What do you reckon about court tomorrow, Ron?" Mitch asked.

"Put a shirt, tie and a suit on, plead guilty and they'll probably go easy on you," I said.

"I'll do that then," Mitch said.

A few days later a letter arrived from Strangeways, the first line read: 'Put a suit on and plead guilty? You bastard.' Mitch went on to tell me what happened in court. He said loads of Blades were in the dock and Spindle was the first one up. Spindle had been kept over the weekend and still had the same gear on: Doc Martens, half-mast jeans, short sleeved Fred Perry and braces, all covered in blood. Spindle copped for a £200 fine. Another dozen or so Blades all received fines, and then Mitch, dressed up all nice and smart took the stand, pleaded guilty and copped for three month. Squeak O'Brian also got three month, so at least Mitch had a cell-mate.

Years later Dreads told a story about doing a stretch in Strangeways. He said he'd been in a while and he'd got a cushy job delivering books or something along the landings. Mitch had just arrived, and Dreads saw the name Gary Mitchell on the cell door. He looked through the peephole and saw Mitch sat on his bunk. Dreads shouted through the hole, "Mitchell, stand up." Mitch jumped to his feet. "Stand up straight Mitchell, you piece of shit." Mitch mumbled something, Dreads said, "Don't answer me back and when you speak to me you call me, sir. Right?"

"Yes, sir," Mitch said.

"What are you in here for, Mitchell?"

"Football hooliganism, sir," Mitch said.

"Oh, you're a football hooligan are you? Now touch your toes ten times. I'll get you in shape Mitchell." Dreads couldn't carry on for laughing. He shouted through the door, "It's me Mitch: Martin, Martin Kartiwick."

"You fuckin bastard," Mitch said.

Basking Shark used to have us all in pieces. We were walking from town on the way to the match one Saturday, when Bullet said he was calling in Wilson Peck's to buy a new set of strings for his Bass guitar.

"How much is it for a set of strings?" Mitch asked Bullet.

"They're about eight quid," Bullet said.

"Eight fuckin quid, for a set of strings," Mitch said. "Why don't ya just put some fuckin normal string on it?"

Another time we'd walked up the Moor towards town and at least twenty people had said hello to Mitch as they passed.

"Fuckin hell, Mitch. You know a lot of people," one of the lads said.

"I know everybody in Sheffield, and everybody knows me," Mitch said.

We'd reached Fargate and Mitch said, "I'll bet anybody 50p, I'll walk down here and at least ten people'll say hello before we get to the bottom." One of the lads took the bet.

Fargate's about one hundred yards from top to bottom.

A couple of yards from the bottom Mitch slowed down. Nine people had acknowledged him on the short walk. Mitch looked from side in panic trying to spot the final familiar face.

"I'm sure I know him," Mitch said as a studenty-looking lad approached.

"Narthen, what's-tha-call-thi-name, how ya going on? Mitch said. The kid completely blanked Mitch and walked past.

We fell about, as Mitch tried to get out of paying up. He shouted after the student, "Oi ya fuckin ignorant cunt, I'm fuckin talking to you. I do know him though, I do, honest."

Two van loads of lads travelled to Scotland for the Anglo-Scottish Cup match at St Mirren. After a brawl with the Jocks inside the ground Spindle and John O'Leary were arrested. They were kept overnight and appeared in court next morning. The lads in the vans stayed to wait for them and were assembled in the public gallery as Spindle and John were called to the stand.

"Call John O'Leary." John took the stand.

"Call Paul Bradshaw."

The lads in the gallery were in bits as Spindle took the stand. John O'Lear and Paul Bradshaw were fined £50 each. Paul Bradshaw played for Sheffield Wednesday at the time: I wonder if he paid it?

The landlord of the Brown Bear pub in Sheffield city centre sported a foot long Jimmy Edwards-style, waxed handlebar moustache. In his modesty he'd proudly displayed a life-sized photo of his head just above the till. A good mob of seventy to eighty Blades assembled in the pub after a home game. For no reason whatsoever things started to get a bit rowdy. A few glasses got smashed and a couple of chairs and tables were turned over. The landlord ran from behind the bar going crazy.

"Get out. You're barred," he shouted at the lads responsible. This made things worse and a few more glasses got smashed. Turning from one lad to another he shouted, "You're barred. Get out. You're barred, and you're barred." Every time he said it somebody else dropped a pint pot. The landlord was now in a real state, as glasses smashed all around the boozer.

Wandering Walt decided Jimmy needed a helping hand, so he nipped behind the counter and grabbed the photo. Walt held it in front of his face and stood at the landlord's side, pointing and shouting, "Get out, you're barred, you're barred and you're barred."

"Can you dig it? Caaaan yooooou diiiiig iiiiiit?"

By now every football lad in the land imagined himself to be a 'Warrior' as they hopped and bopped around the tube trains on the London Underground trying to make it home.

Travelling back from away games, when the coach hit the Sheffield Parkway and passed the slaughterhouse on Cricket Inn Road, I'd say to Dinky,

"Here we are Dink, back on Coney Wybourn, when we see the Abattoir we figure we're home, figure we're safe."

The last away game of the 1970s fell on Boxing Day and just happened to be Wednesday at Hillsborough. The Blades were riding high and heading for promotion, with Wednesday hovering around mid-table. The result as far as we were concerned was a forgone conclusion. On Christmas Day 1979 Great Britain suffered the heaviest snow fall ever recorded since records began. Nothing moved because the whole country lay under a twelve-foot-deep blanket. Every Boxing Day football match in England, Scotland and Wales had to be postponed. Such was the backlog of games, the F.A. ruled the season would be cut from 46 to 45 games. The Pools' Panel (what the fuck did they know) decided to mark the game as a score draw.

Score draw my arse, I reckon the Blades would have whupped Wednesday about 4-0, but alas and alack, we'll never know.

So that was a little bit of my 70s: a roller-coaster ride with plenty of ups and downs, and I wouldn't have wanted it any other way. On the football side, the decade that started off with so much promise, ended with the Blades in deep

347

shit. Things were about to get a lot worse on the pitch, but a lot better off it.

At twenty-eight years old, maybe now was the time for me to call it a day? I had no idea a group of young Blade upstarts, chomping at the bit were waiting in the wings ready to cut their teeth and take over.

So what's it's gonna be then? I asked myself. I'll give it one more season. One more. Swear to god, our kid, swear to god.

Blades on Wednesday's Kop 1970. John Tudor challenging for the ball.

Acknowledgements

For permission to use photographs: Don Hale (Esquire photos), Dronfield History Group (1920s Dronny Lads, View from Cammel's Row, Mason's Arms, Blackpool July 66, Mick Jones (Big Brett Speddings), Maureen Sanderson (Dixon Lane).

Lightning Source UK Ltd.
Milton Keynes UK
UKHW020647280321
381106UK00005B/69

9 781916 362226